EDENS ZERO

14

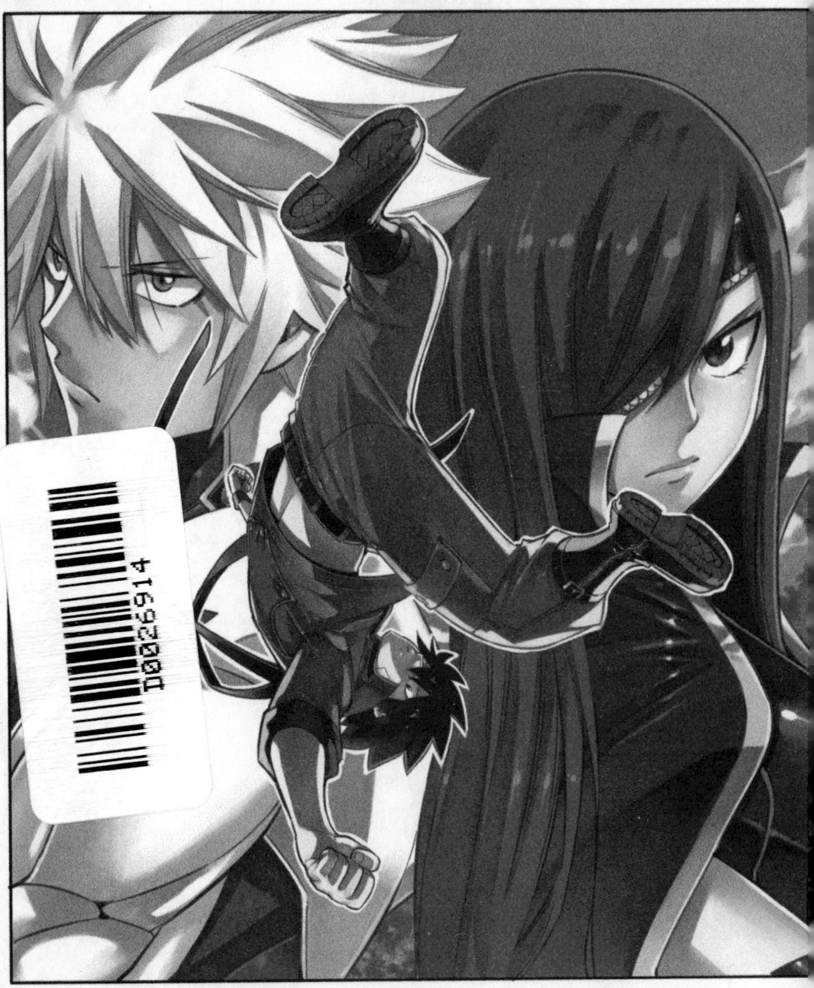

HIRO MASHIMA

EDENS ZERO 14 contents

EDENS ZERO

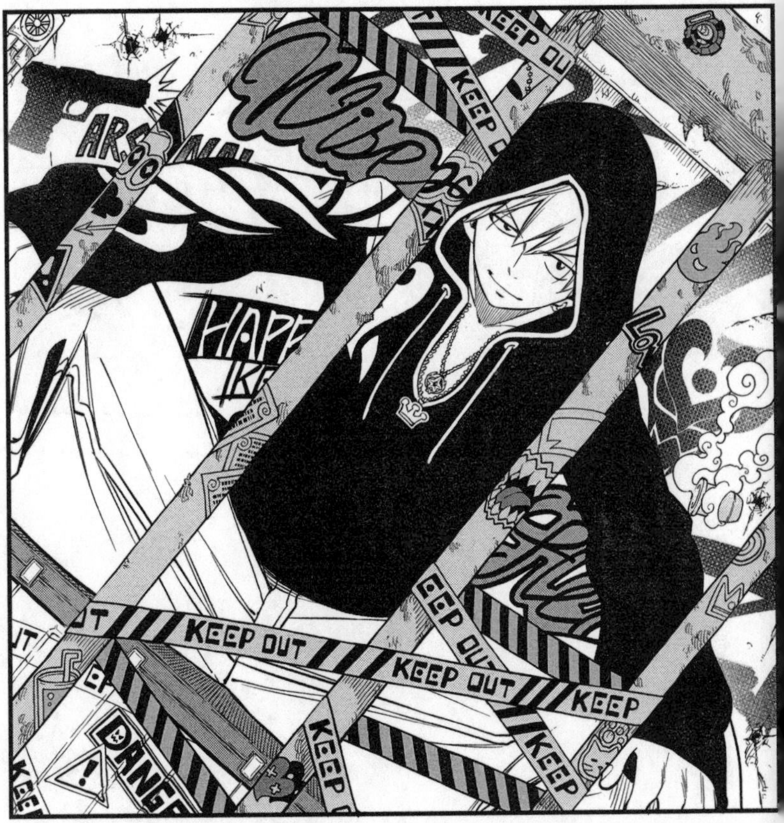
KEEP OUT
KEEP OUT
KEEP OUT
KEEP OUT
KEEP

CHAPTER 114: GLUE

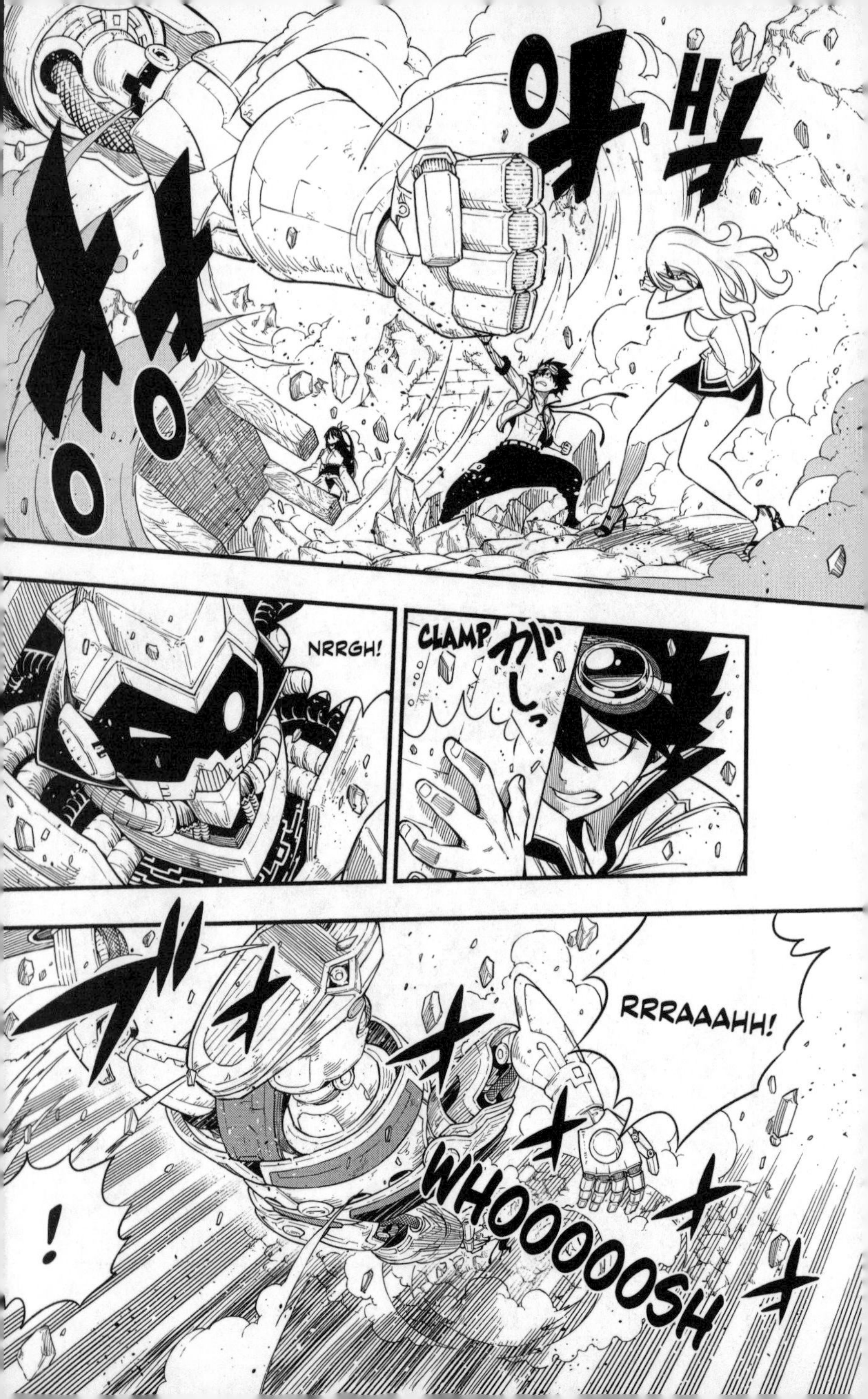
CLAMP
NRRGH!
RRRAAAHH!
WHOOOOOOSH
!

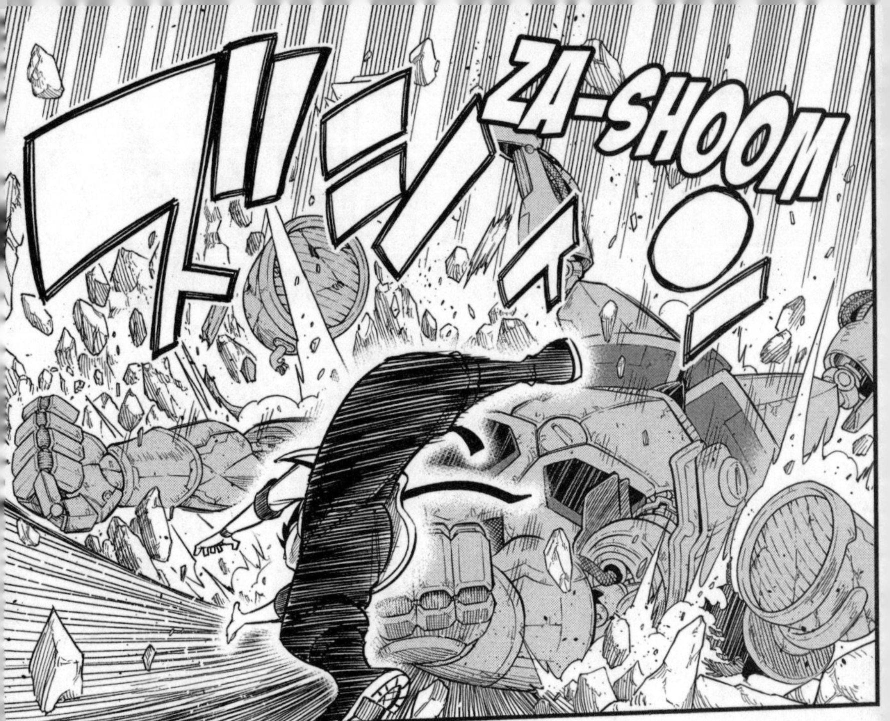
ZA-SHOOM

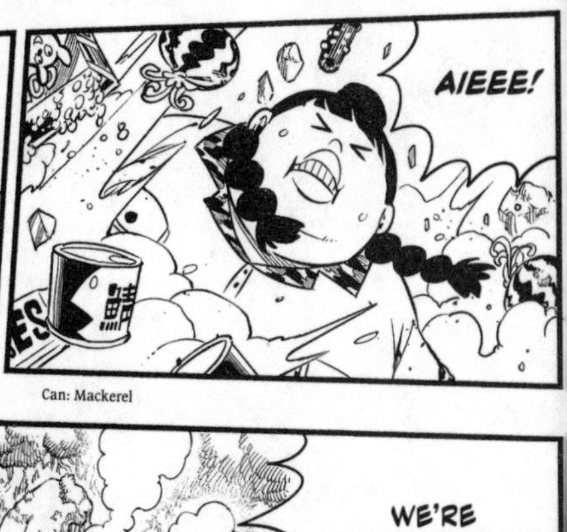
AIEEE!

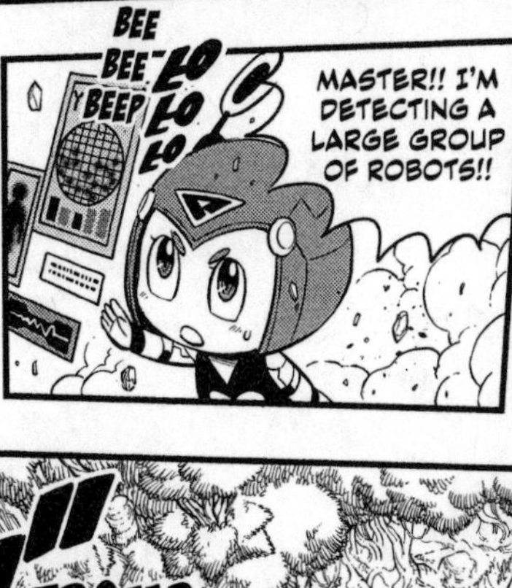
BEE
BEE
BEEP
MASTER!! I'M DETECTING A LARGE GROUP OF ROBOTS!!

Can: Mackerel

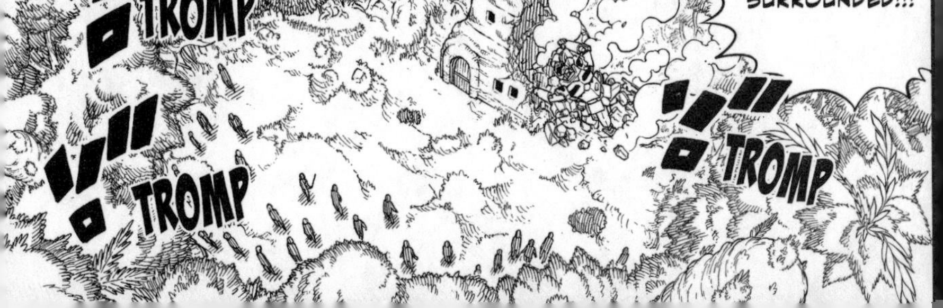
WE'RE SURROUNDED!!!
TROMP
TROMP
TROMP

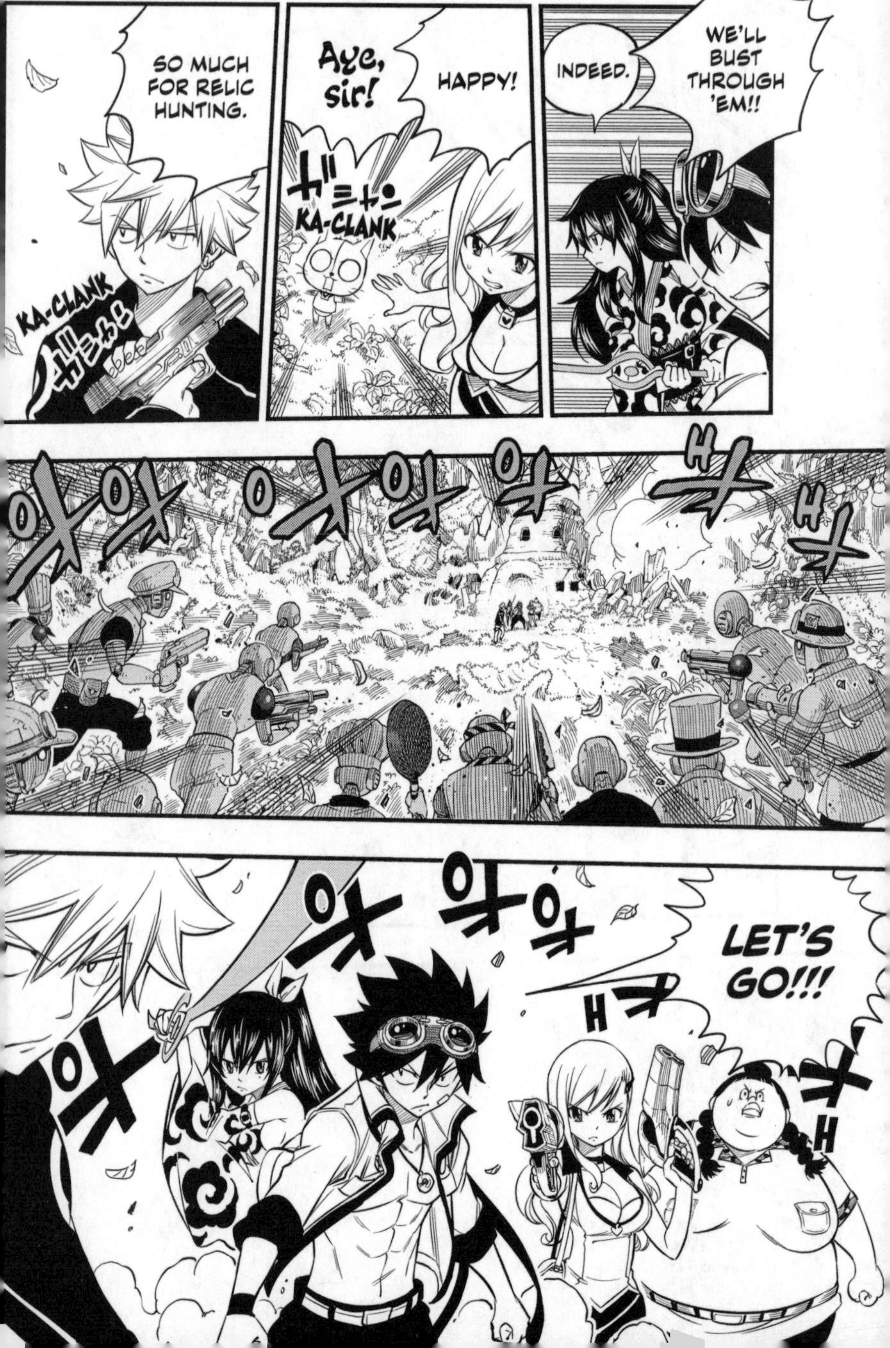
WE'LL BUST THROUGH 'EM!!
INDEED.
HAPPY!
Aye, sir!
ガシャン
KA-CLANK
SO MUCH FOR RELIC HUNTING.
KA-CLANK
ガシャ
LET'S GO!!!

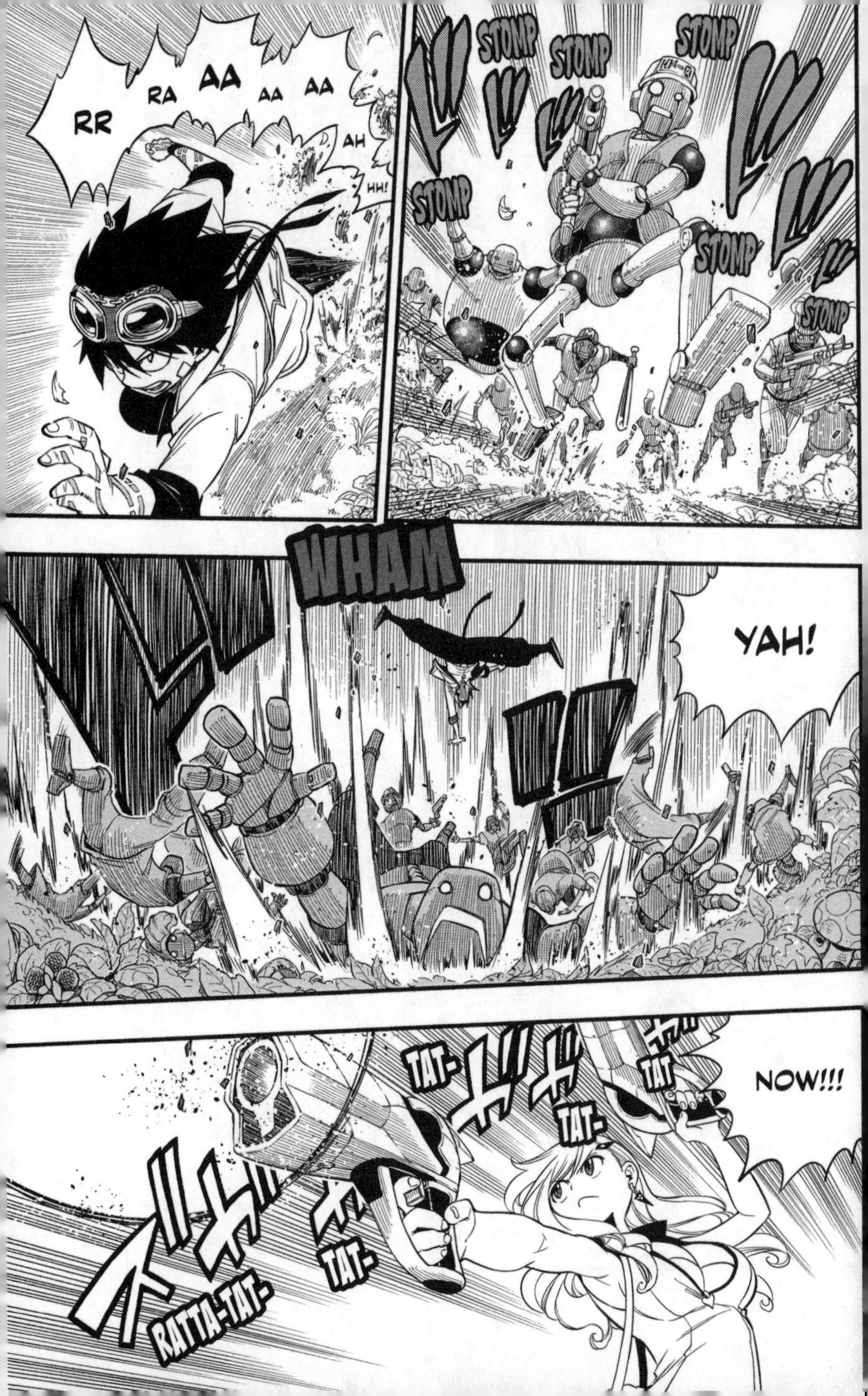
STOMP
STOMP
STOMP
STOMP
STOMP
STOMP
RR RA AA AA AA AH HH!
WHAM
YAH!
NOW!!!
TAT
TAT-
TAT-
TAT-
RATTA-TAT-

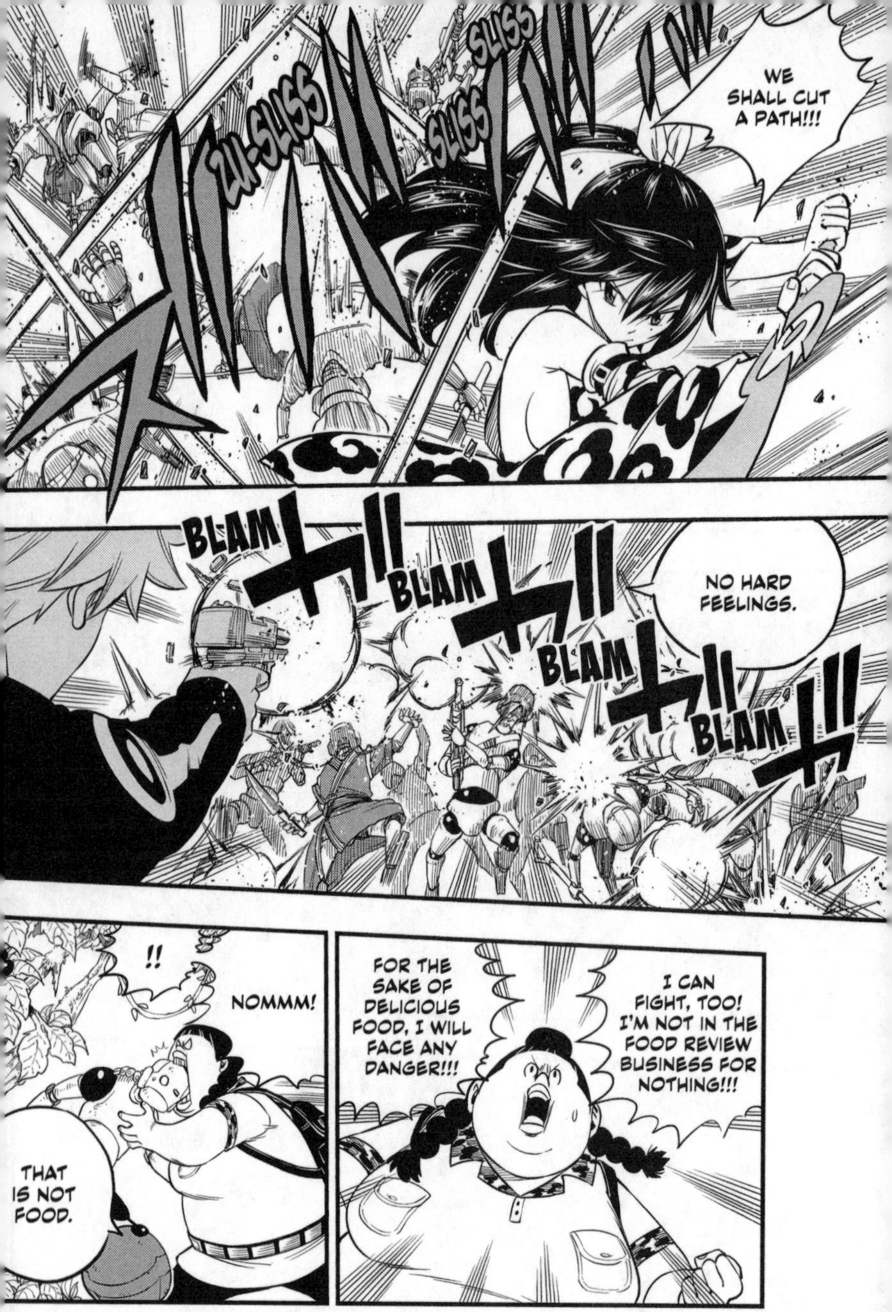
WE SHALL CUT A PATH!!!
SLISS
SLISS
ZU-SLISS
NO HARD FEELINGS.
BLAM
BLAM
BLAM
BLAM
I CAN FIGHT, TOO! I'M NOT IN THE FOOD REVIEW BUSINESS FOR NOTHING!!!
FOR THE SAKE OF DELICIOUS FOOD, I WILL FACE ANY DANGER!!!
!!
NOMMM!
THAT IS NOT FOOD.

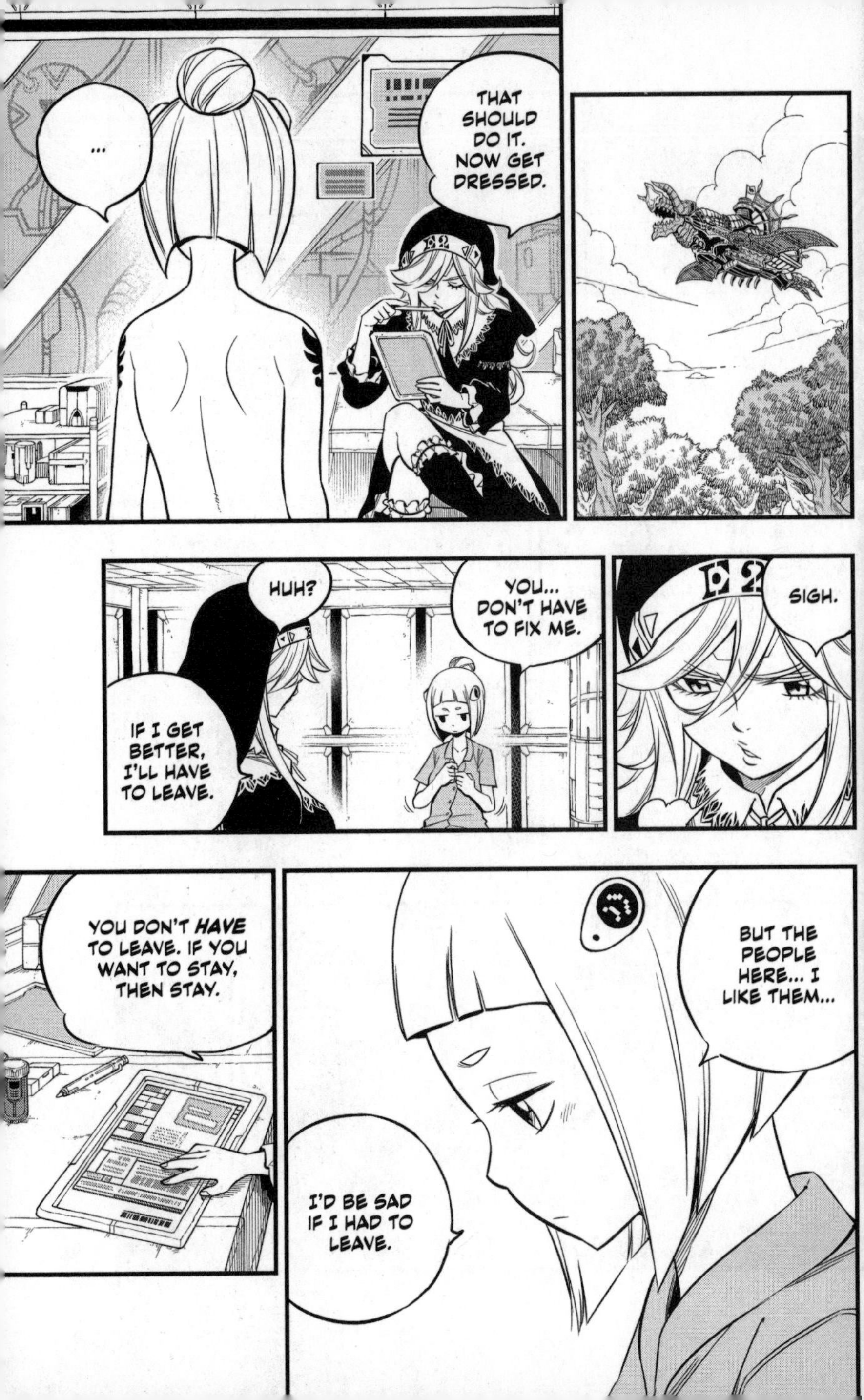
THAT SHOULD DO IT. NOW GET DRESSED.
...
SIGH.
YOU... DON'T HAVE TO FIX ME.
HUH?
IF I GET BETTER, I'LL HAVE TO LEAVE.
BUT THE PEOPLE HERE... I LIKE THEM...
I'D BE SAD IF I HAD TO LEAVE.
YOU DON'T *HAVE* TO LEAVE. IF YOU WANT TO STAY, THEN STAY.

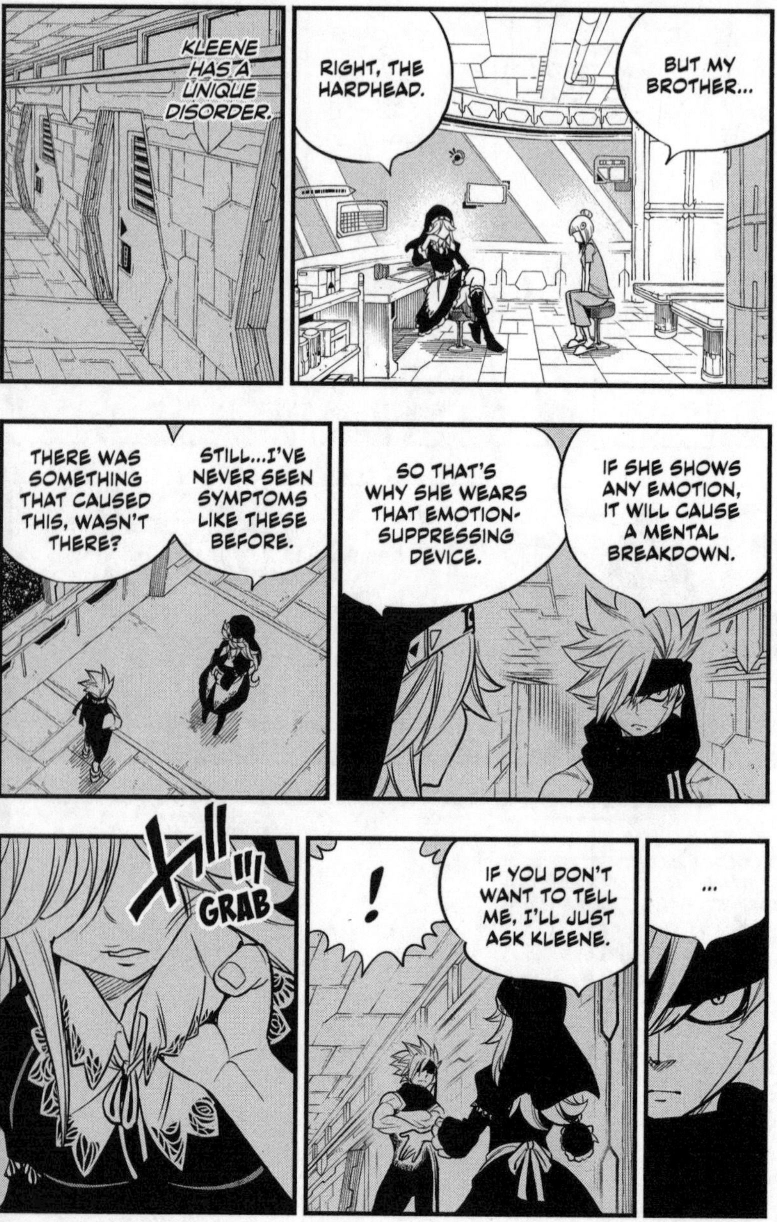
BUT MY BROTHER...
RIGHT, THE HARDHEAD.
KLEENE HAS A UNIQUE DISORDER.
IF SHE SHOWS ANY EMOTION, IT WILL CAUSE A MENTAL BREAKDOWN.
SO THAT'S WHY SHE WEARS THAT EMOTION-SUPPRESSING DEVICE.
STILL...I'VE NEVER SEEN SYMPTOMS LIKE THESE BEFORE.
THERE WAS SOMETHING THAT CAUSED THIS, WASN'T THERE?
...
IF YOU DON'T WANT TO TELL ME, I'LL JUST ASK KLEENE.
!
GRAB

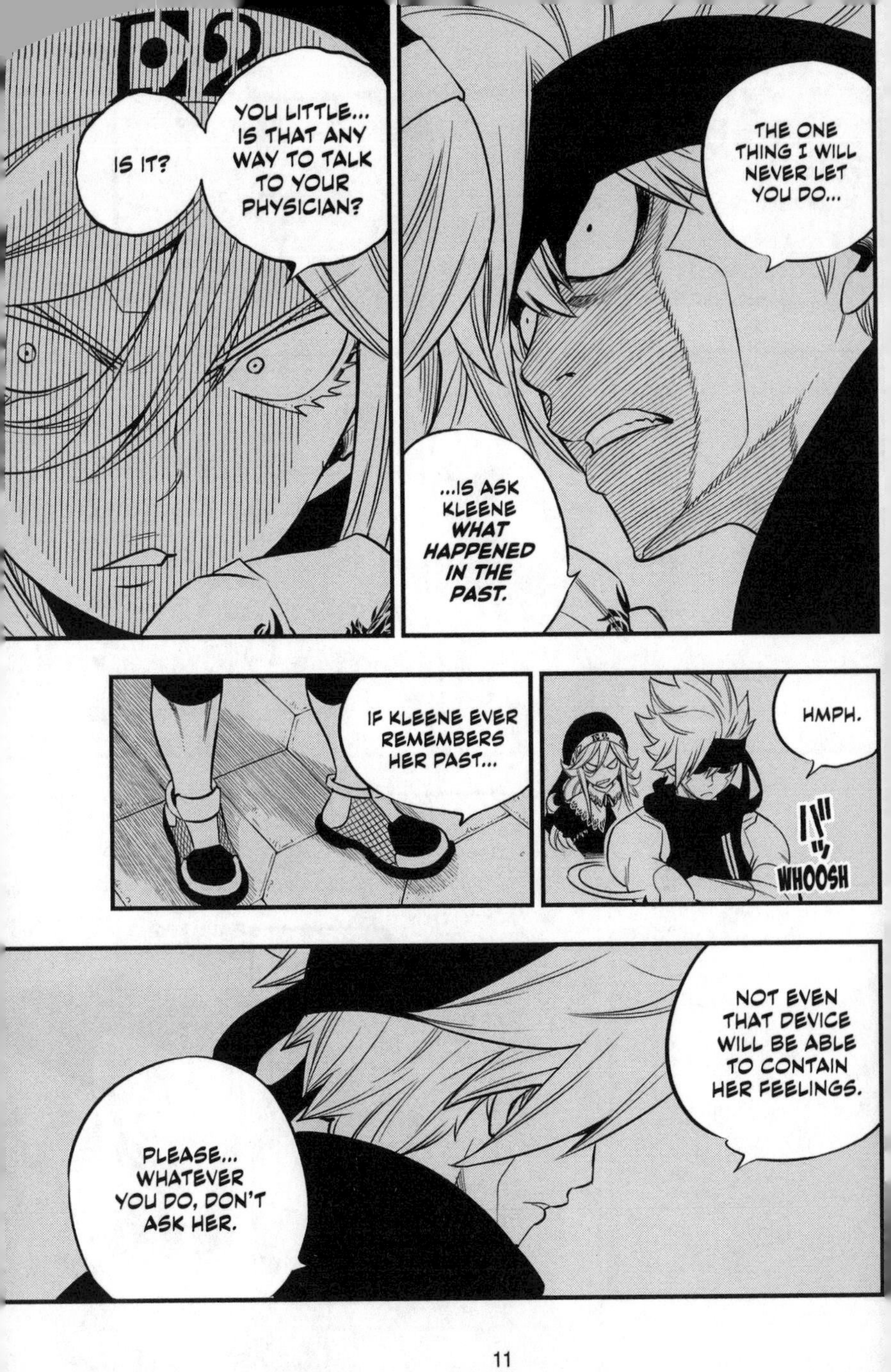
THE ONE THING I WILL NEVER LET YOU DO...
...IS ASK KLEENE *WHAT HAPPENED* IN THE PAST.
YOU LITTLE... IS THAT ANY WAY TO TALK TO YOUR PHYSICIAN?
IS IT?
HMPH.
WHOOSH
IF KLEENE EVER REMEMBERS HER PAST...
NOT EVEN THAT DEVICE WILL BE ABLE TO CONTAIN HER FEELINGS.
PLEASE... WHATEVER YOU DO, DON'T ASK HER.

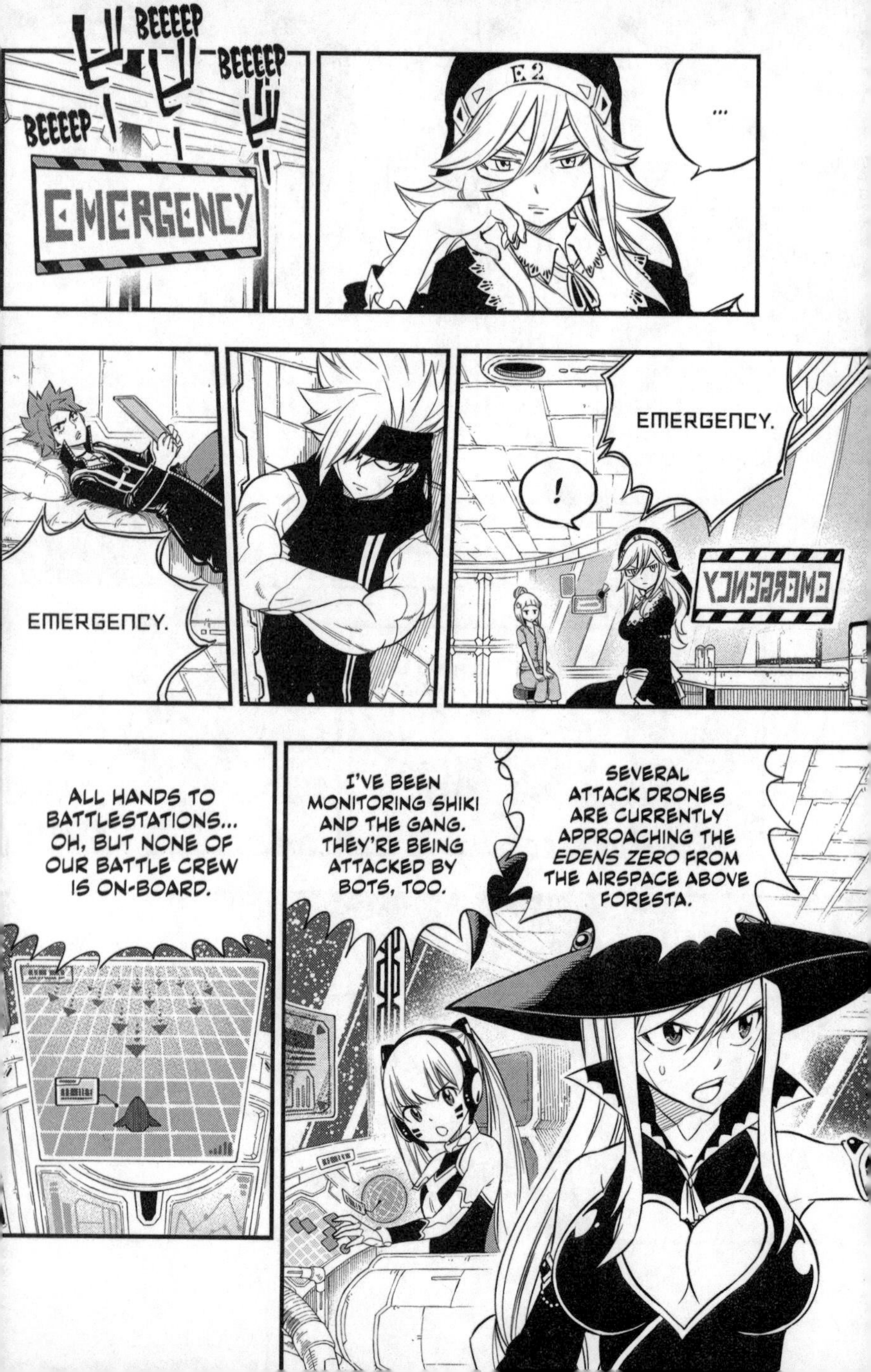
...
BEEEEP
BEEEEP
BEEEEP
EMERGENCY
EMERGENCY.
!
EMERGENCY.
SEVERAL ATTACK DRONES ARE CURRENTLY APPROACHING THE *EDENS ZERO* FROM THE AIRSPACE ABOVE FORESTA.
I'VE BEEN MONITORING SHIKI AND THE GANG. THEY'RE BEING ATTACKED BY BOTS, TOO.
ALL HANDS TO BATTLESTATIONS... OH, BUT NONE OF OUR BATTLE CREW IS ON-BOARD.

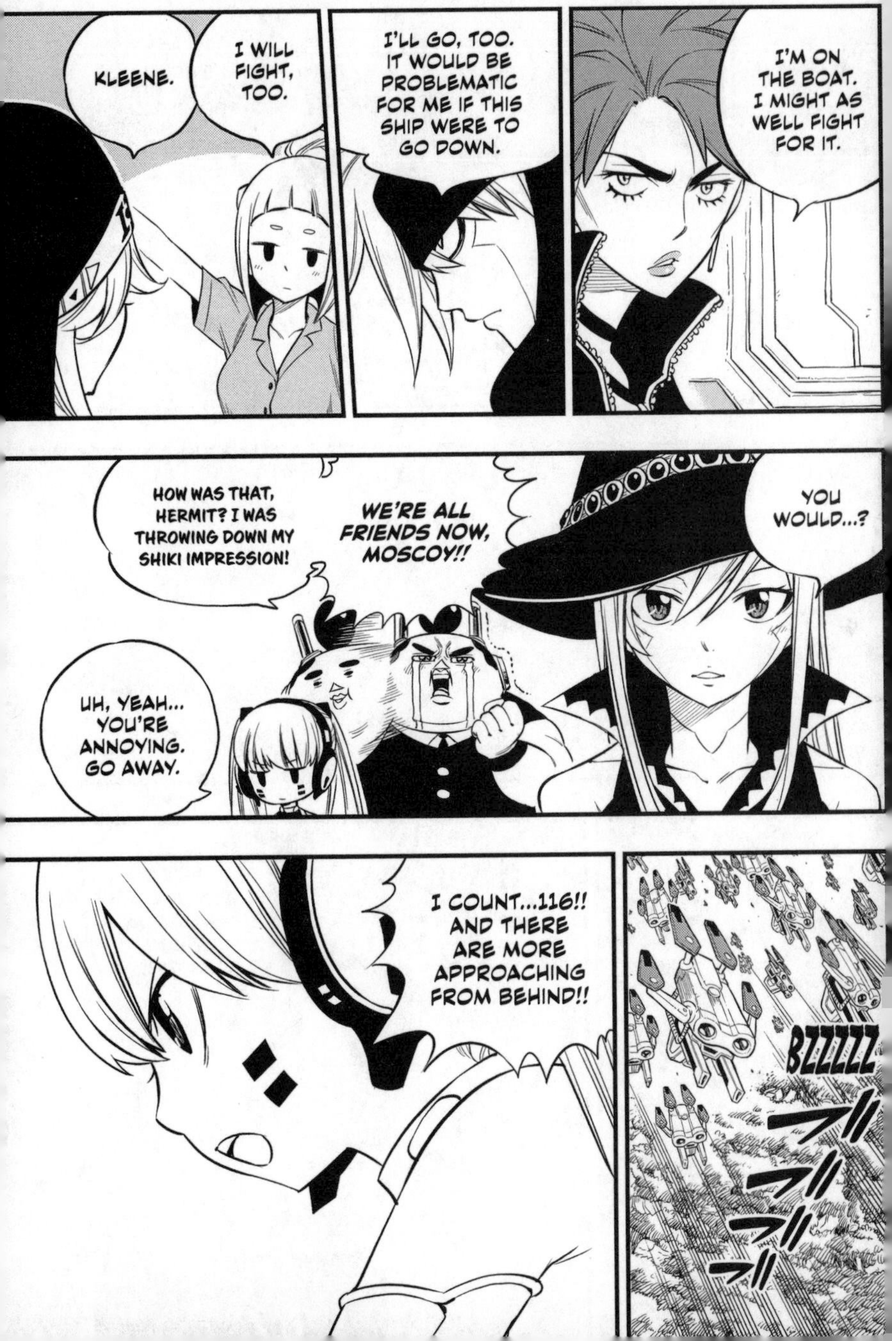
I'M ON THE BOAT. I MIGHT AS WELL FIGHT FOR IT.
I'LL GO, TOO. IT WOULD BE PROBLEMATIC FOR ME IF THIS SHIP WERE TO GO DOWN.
I WILL FIGHT, TOO.
KLEENE.
YOU WOULD...?
WE'RE ALL FRIENDS NOW, MOSCOY!!
HOW WAS THAT, HERMIT? I WAS THROWING DOWN MY SHIKI IMPRESSION!
UH, YEAH... YOU'RE ANNOYING. GO AWAY.
BZZZZZ
I COUNT...116!! AND THERE ARE MORE APPROACHING FROM BEHIND!!

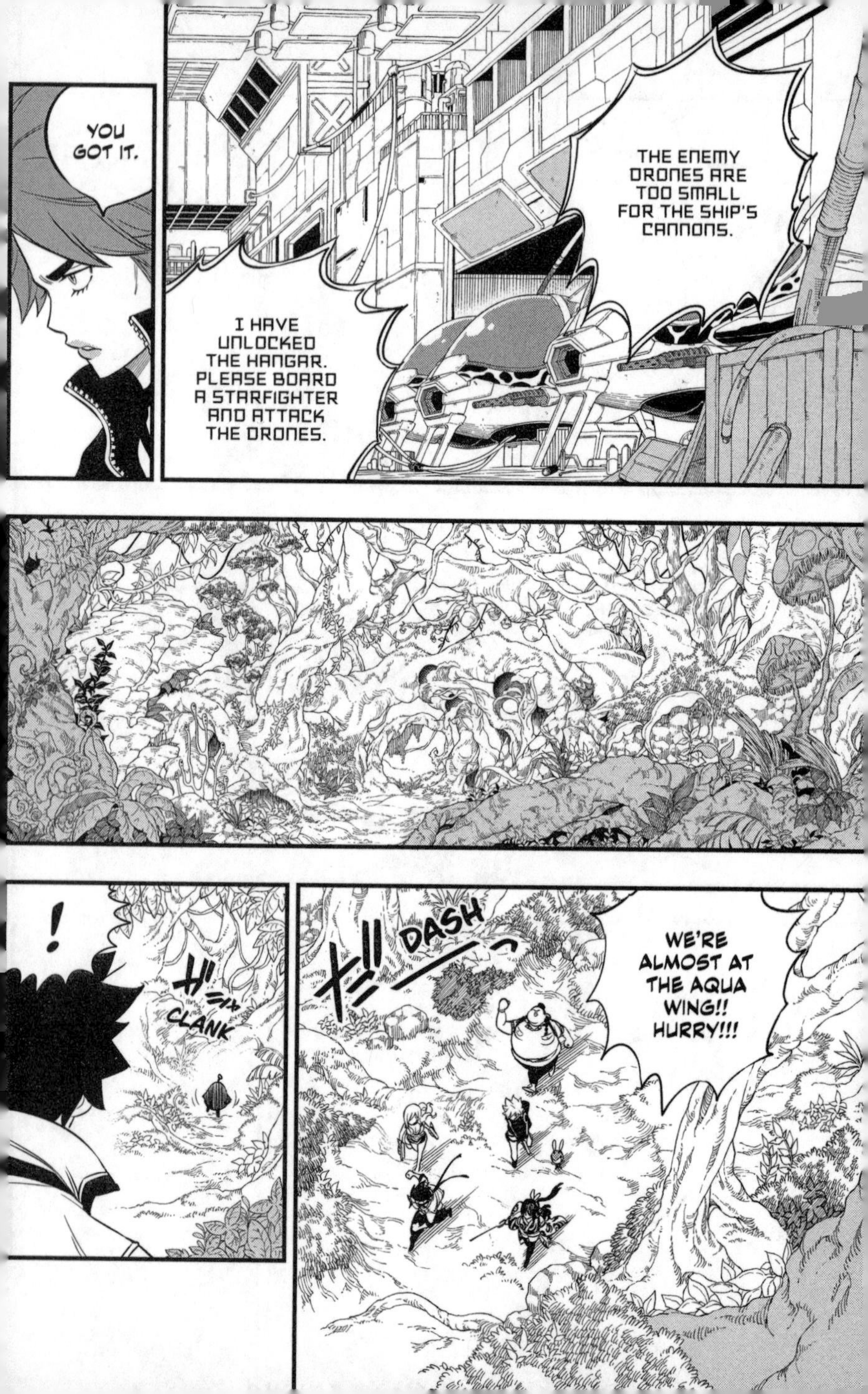
THE ENEMY DRONES ARE TOO SMALL FOR THE SHIP'S CANNONS.
I HAVE UNLOCKED THE HANGAR. PLEASE BOARD A STARFIGHTER AND ATTACK THE DRONES.
YOU GOT IT.
WE'RE ALMOST AT THE AQUA WING!! HURRY!!!
DASH
!
CLANK

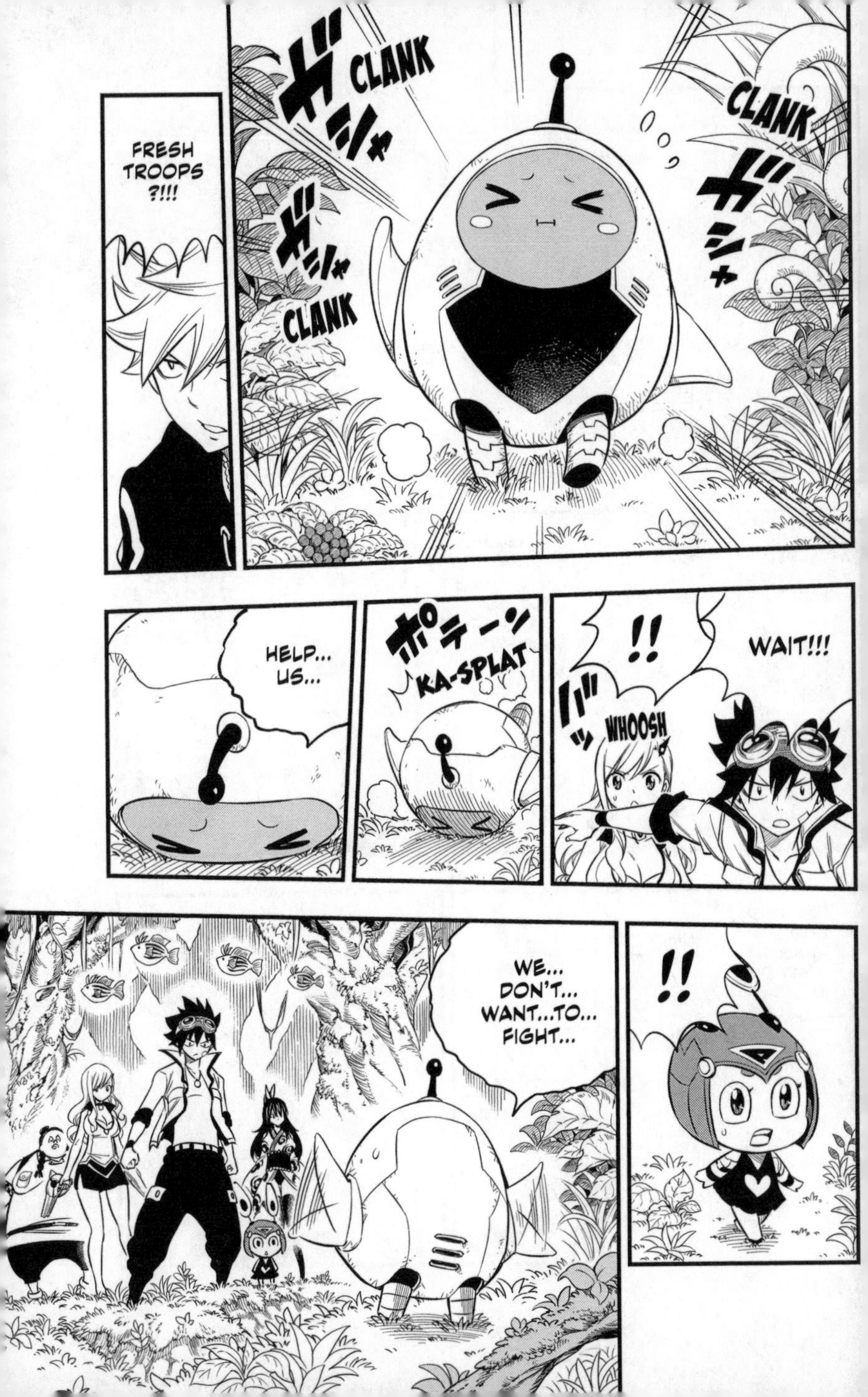
CLANK
ガシャ
CLANK
ガシャ
CLANK
ガシャ
FRESH TROOPS?!!!
WAIT!!!
!!
バッ
WHOOSH
ポテーン
KA-SPLAT
HELP... US...
!!
WE... DON'T... WANT...TO... FIGHT...

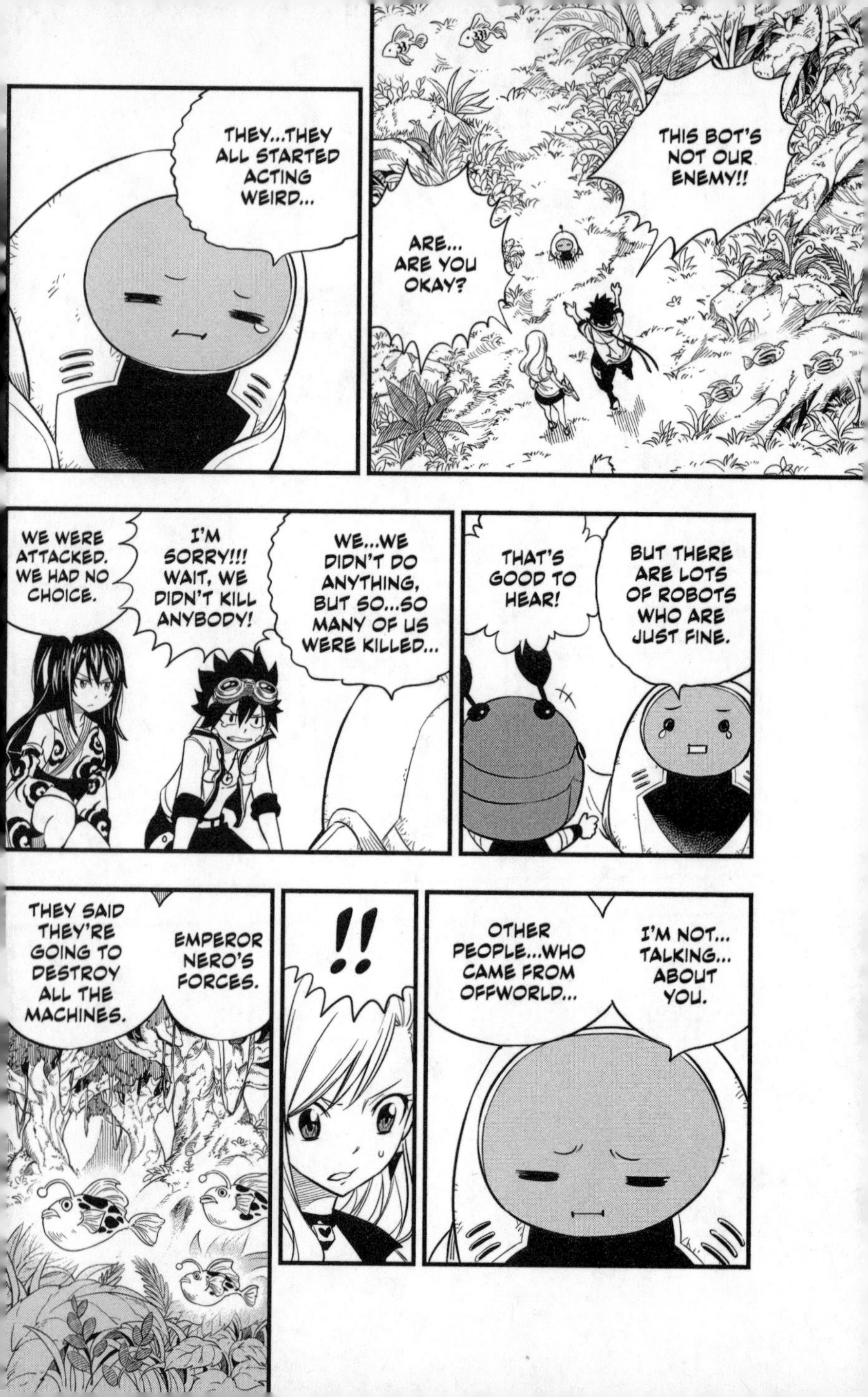
THIS BOT'S NOT OUR ENEMY!!
ARE... ARE YOU OKAY?
THEY...THEY ALL STARTED ACTING WEIRD...
BUT THERE ARE LOTS OF ROBOTS WHO ARE JUST FINE.
THAT'S GOOD TO HEAR!
WE...WE DIDN'T DO ANYTHING, BUT SO...SO MANY OF US WERE KILLED...
I'M SORRY!!! WAIT, WE DIDN'T KILL ANYBODY!
WE WERE ATTACKED. WE HAD NO CHOICE.
I'M NOT... TALKING... ABOUT YOU.
OTHER PEOPLE...WHO CAME FROM OFFWORLD...
!!
EMPEROR NERO'S FORCES.
THEY SAID THEY'RE GOING TO DESTROY ALL THE MACHINES.

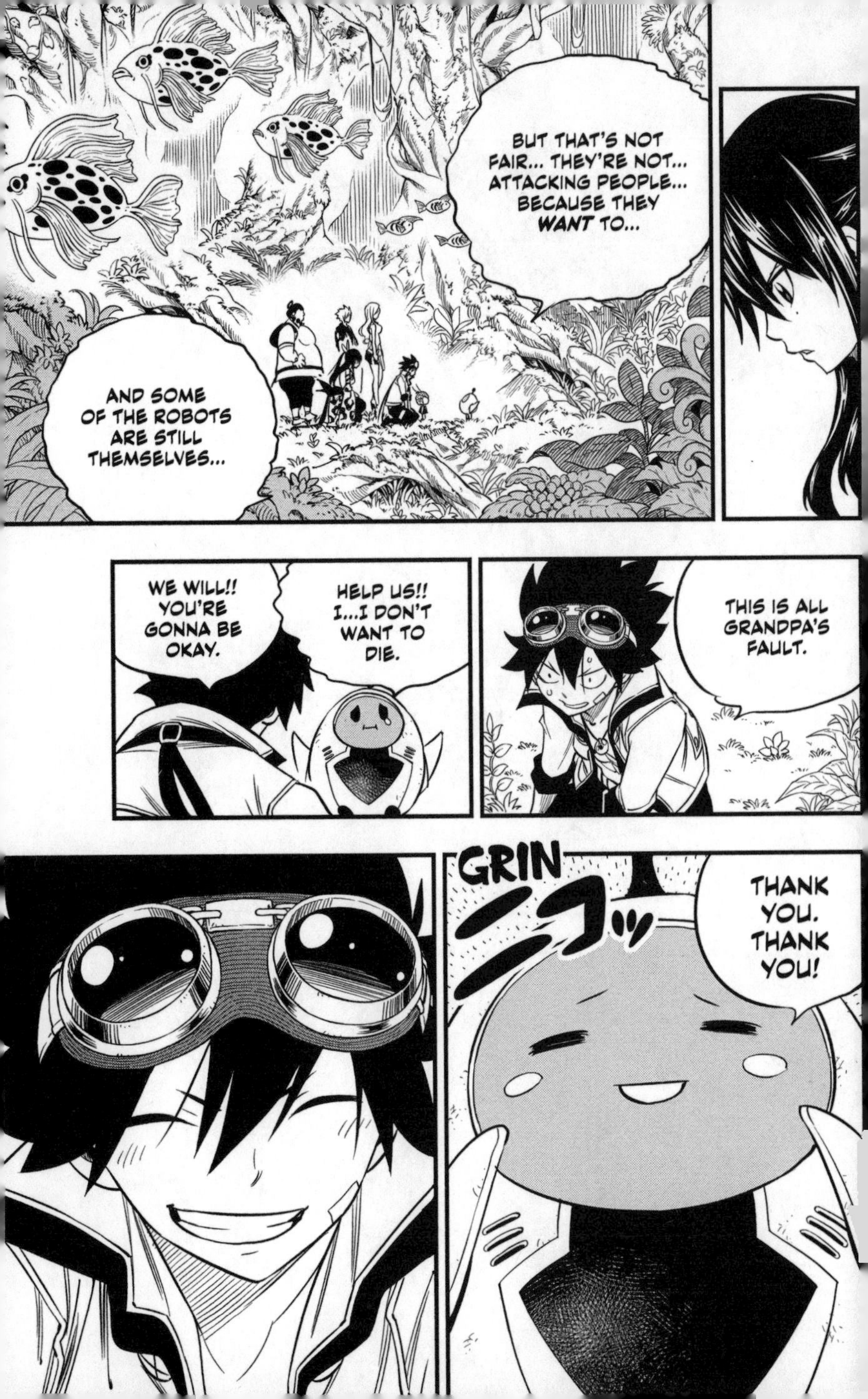
BUT THAT'S NOT FAIR... THEY'RE NOT... ATTACKING PEOPLE... BECAUSE THEY *WANT* TO...
AND SOME OF THE ROBOTS ARE STILL THEMSELVES...
THIS IS ALL GRANDPA'S FAULT.
HELP US!! I...I DON'T WANT TO DIE.
WE WILL!! YOU'RE GONNA BE OKAY.
THANK YOU. THANK YOU!
GRIN

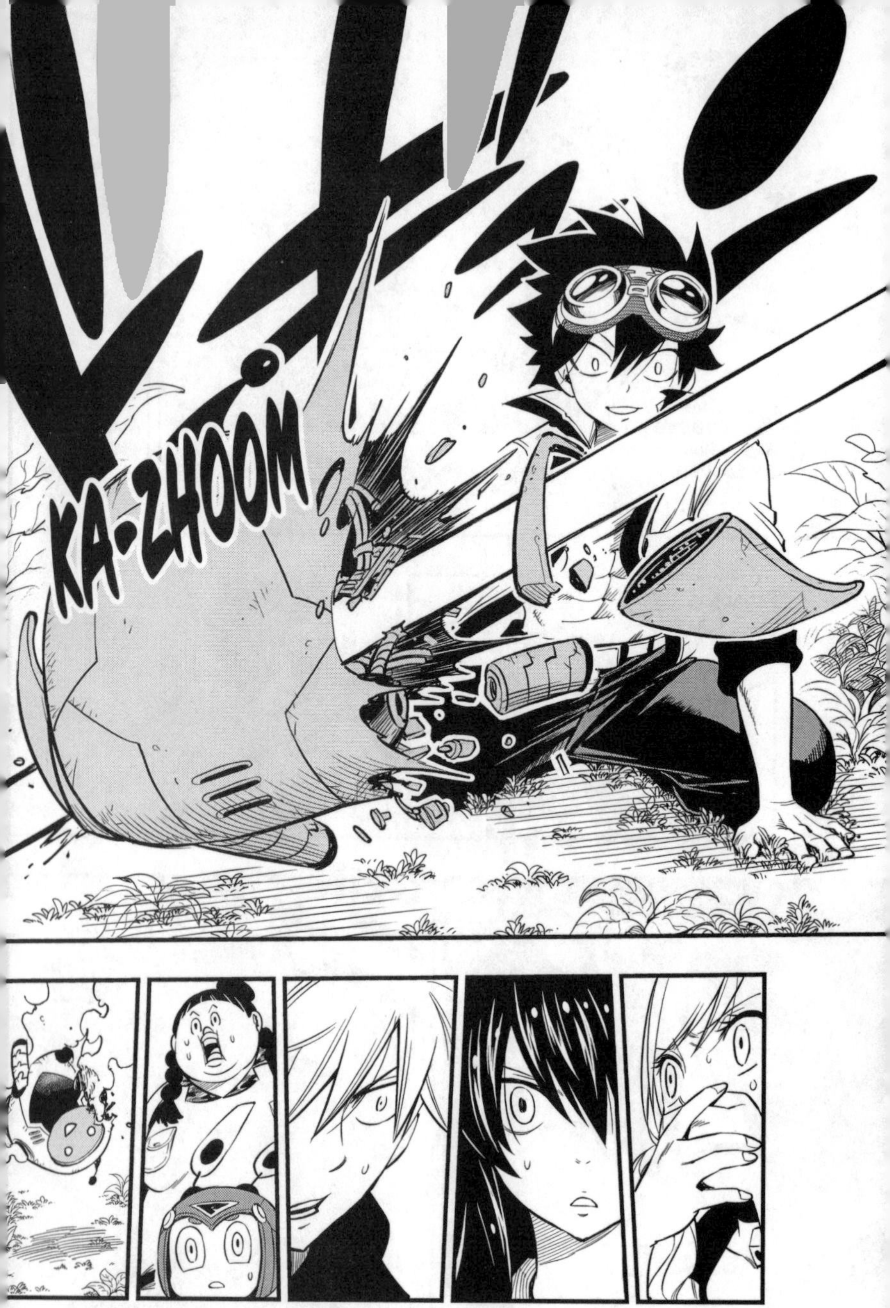
KA-ZHOOM

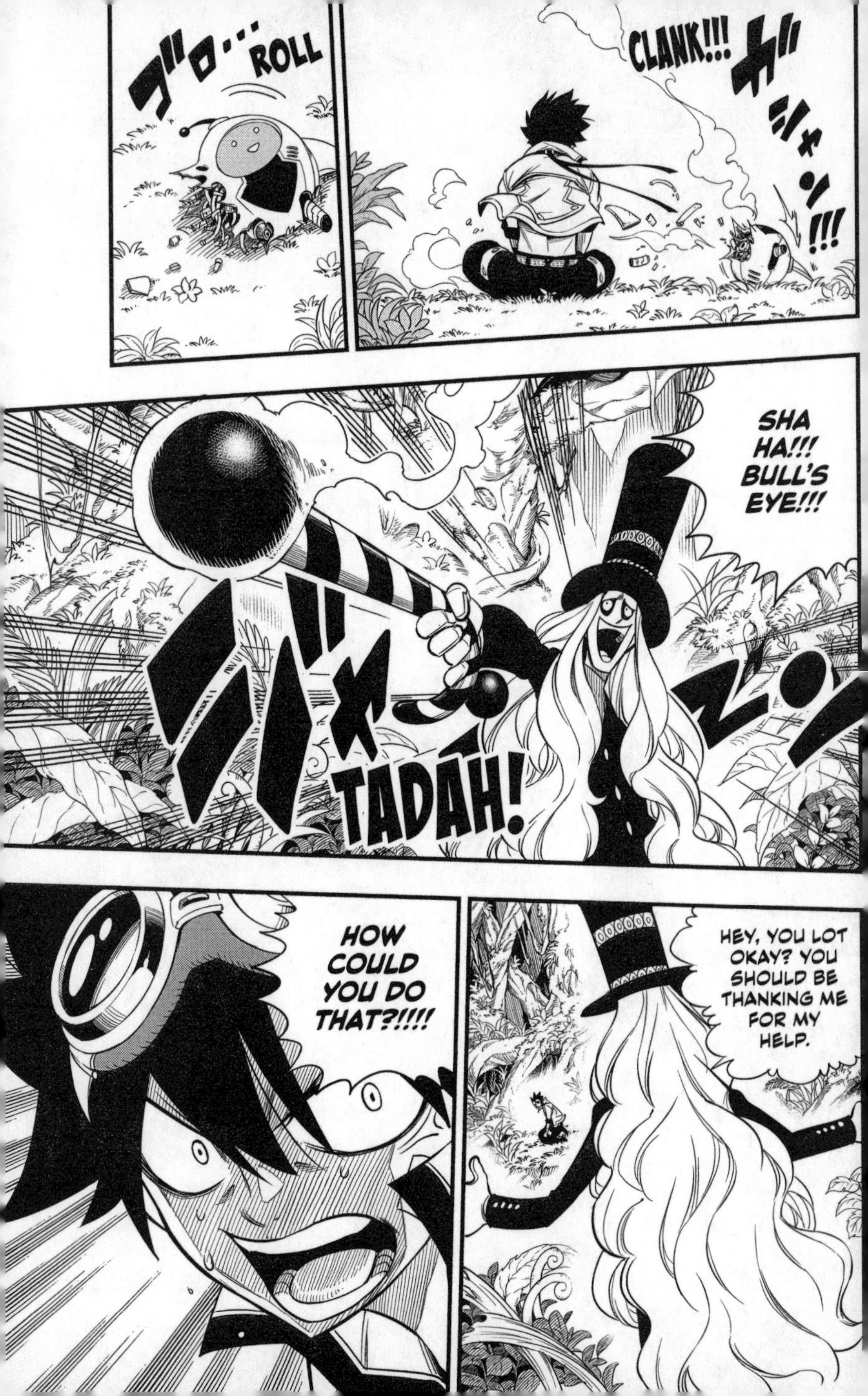
CLANK!!!
ROLL
SHA HA!!! BULL'S EYE!!!
TADAH!
HEY, YOU LOT OKAY? YOU SHOULD BE THANKING ME FOR MY HELP.
HOW COULD YOU DO THAT?!!!!

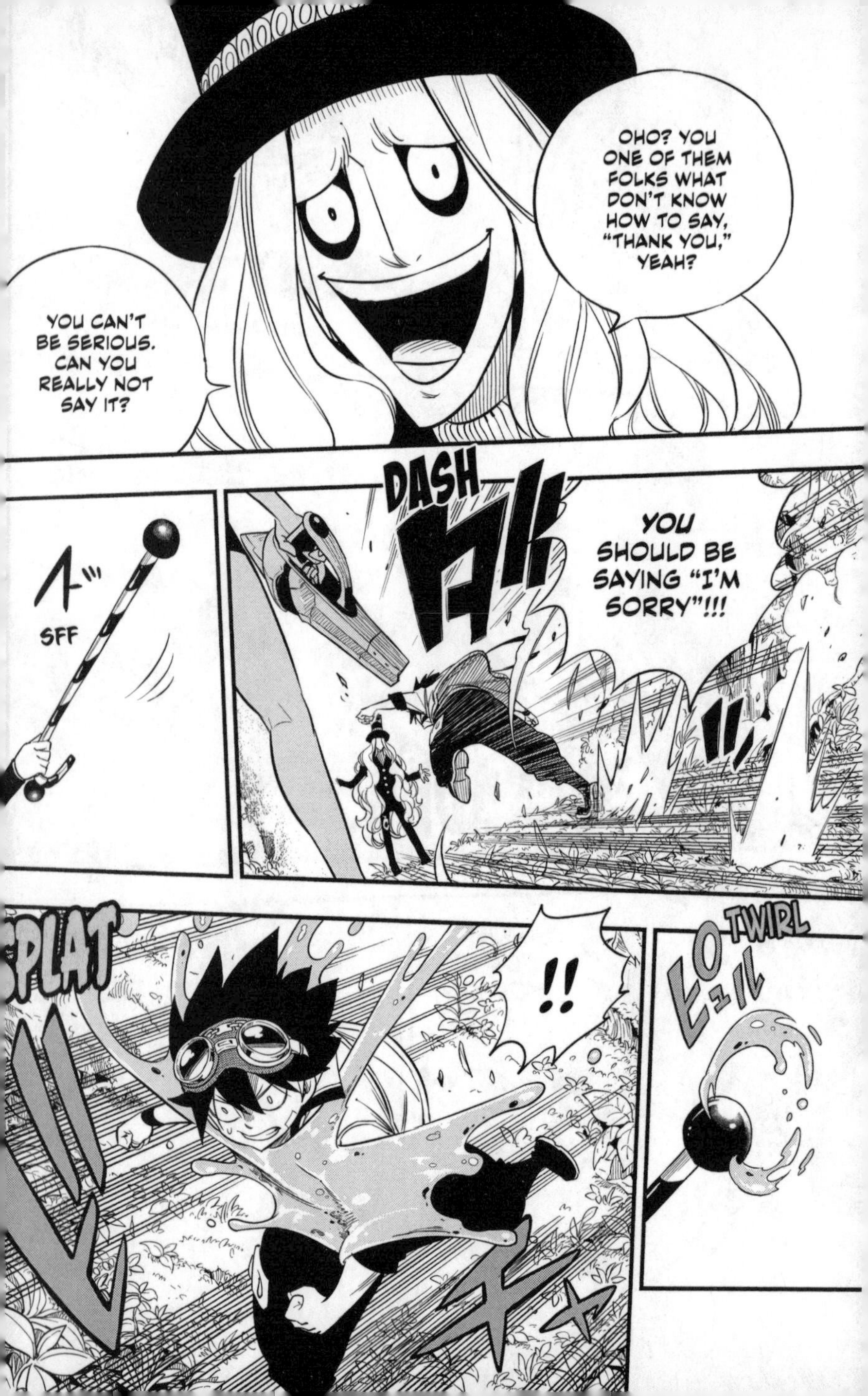
OHO? YOU ONE OF THEM FOLKS WHAT DON'T KNOW HOW TO SAY, "THANK YOU," YEAH?
YOU CAN'T BE SERIOUS. CAN YOU REALLY NOT SAY IT?
DASH
YOU SHOULD BE SAYING "I'M SORRY"!!!
SFF
TWIRL
SPLAT
!!

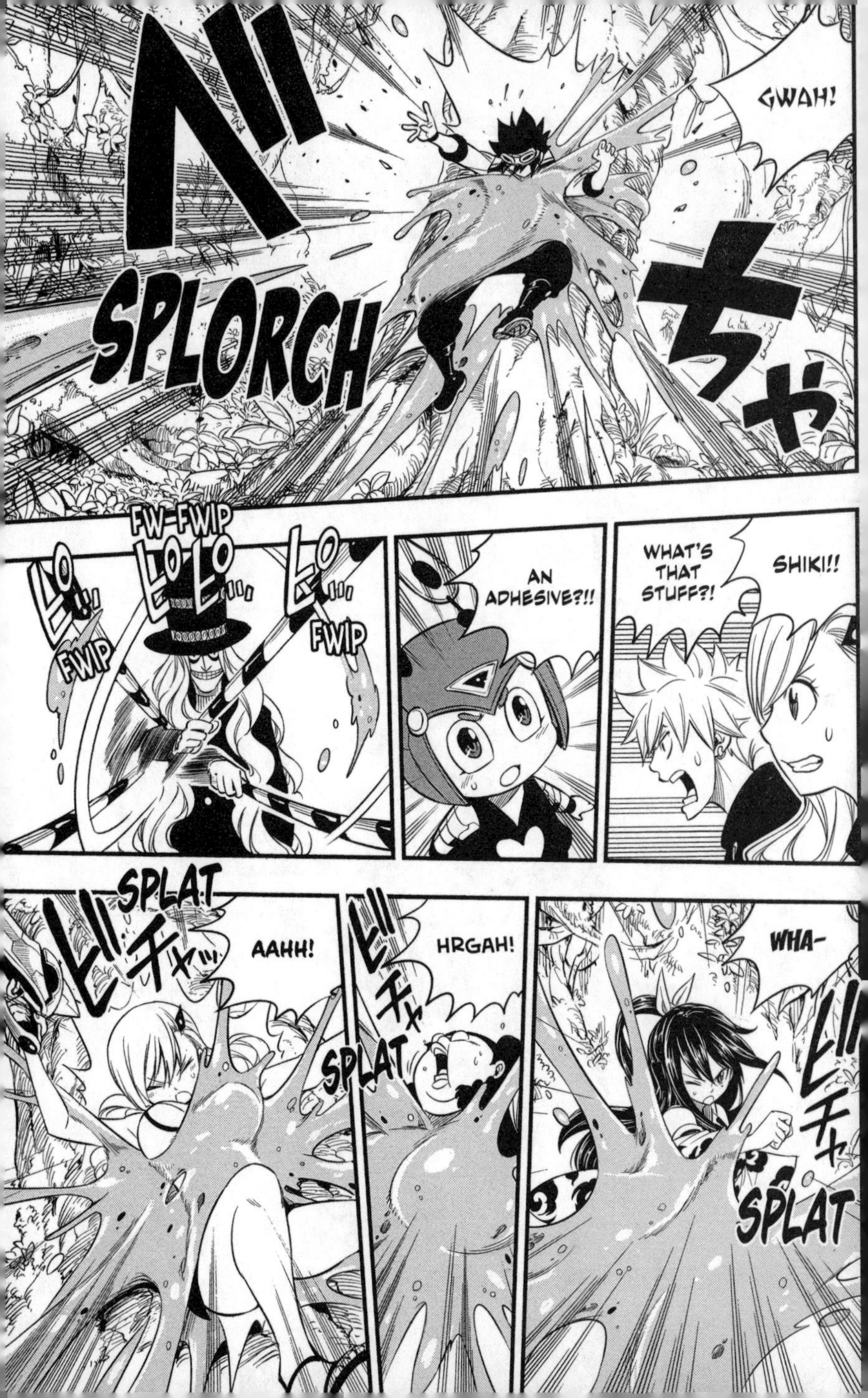
GWAH!
SPLORCH
SHIKI!!
WHAT'S THAT STUFF?!
AN ADHESIVE?!!
FW-FWIP
FWIP
FWIP
WHA-
SPLAT
HRGAH!
SPLAT
AAHH!
SPLAT

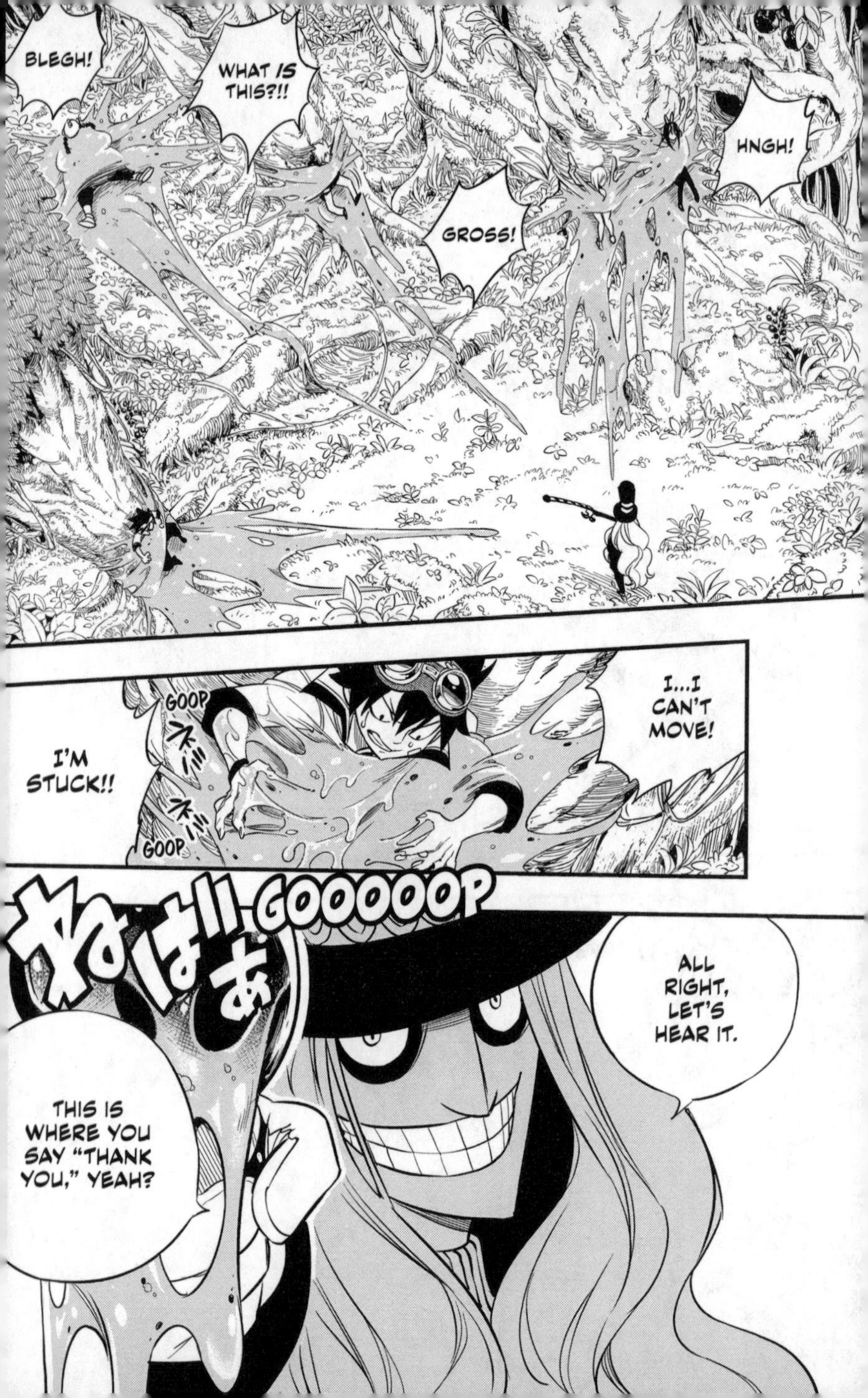
HNGH!
GROSS!
WHAT IS THIS?!!
BLEGH!
I...I CAN'T MOVE!
GOOP
ネバ
ネバ
GOOP
I'M STUCK!!
GOOOOOP
ALL RIGHT, LET'S HEAR IT.
THIS IS WHERE YOU SAY "THANK YOU," YEAH?

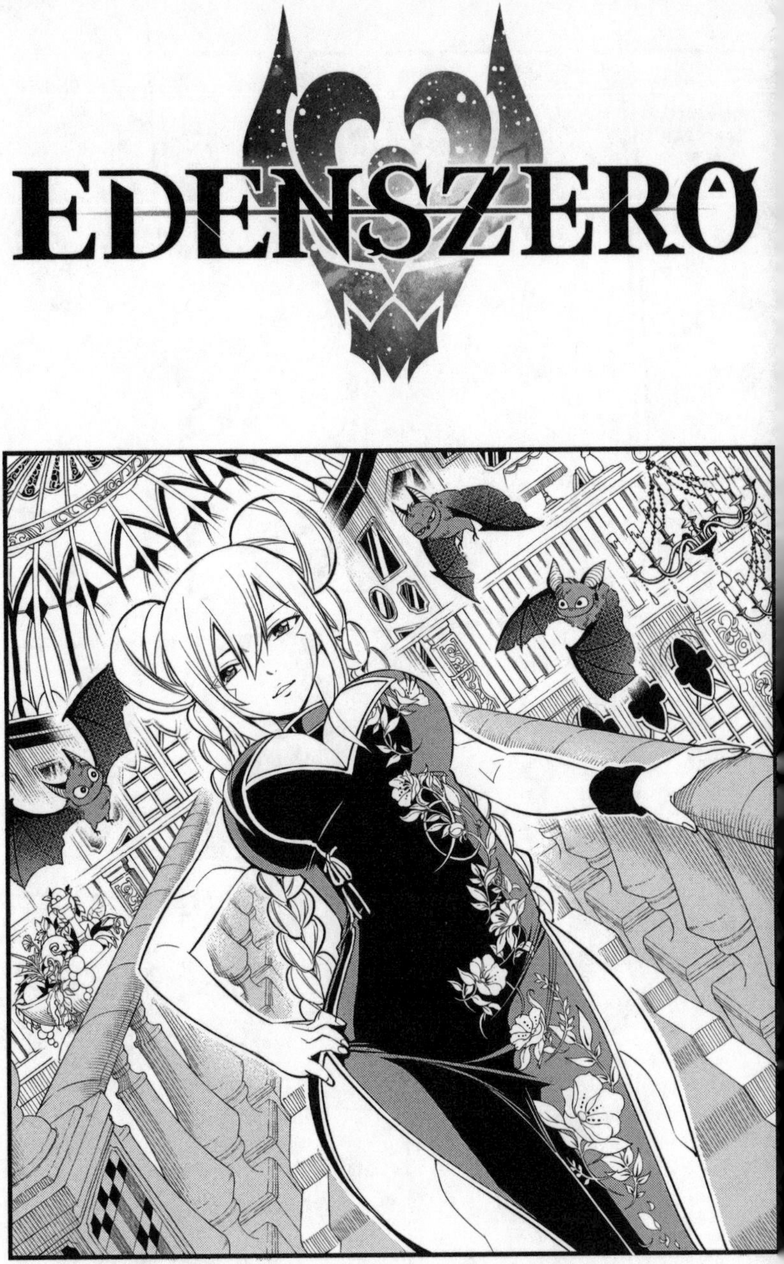

CHAPTER 115: THE BATTLE OF FORESTA

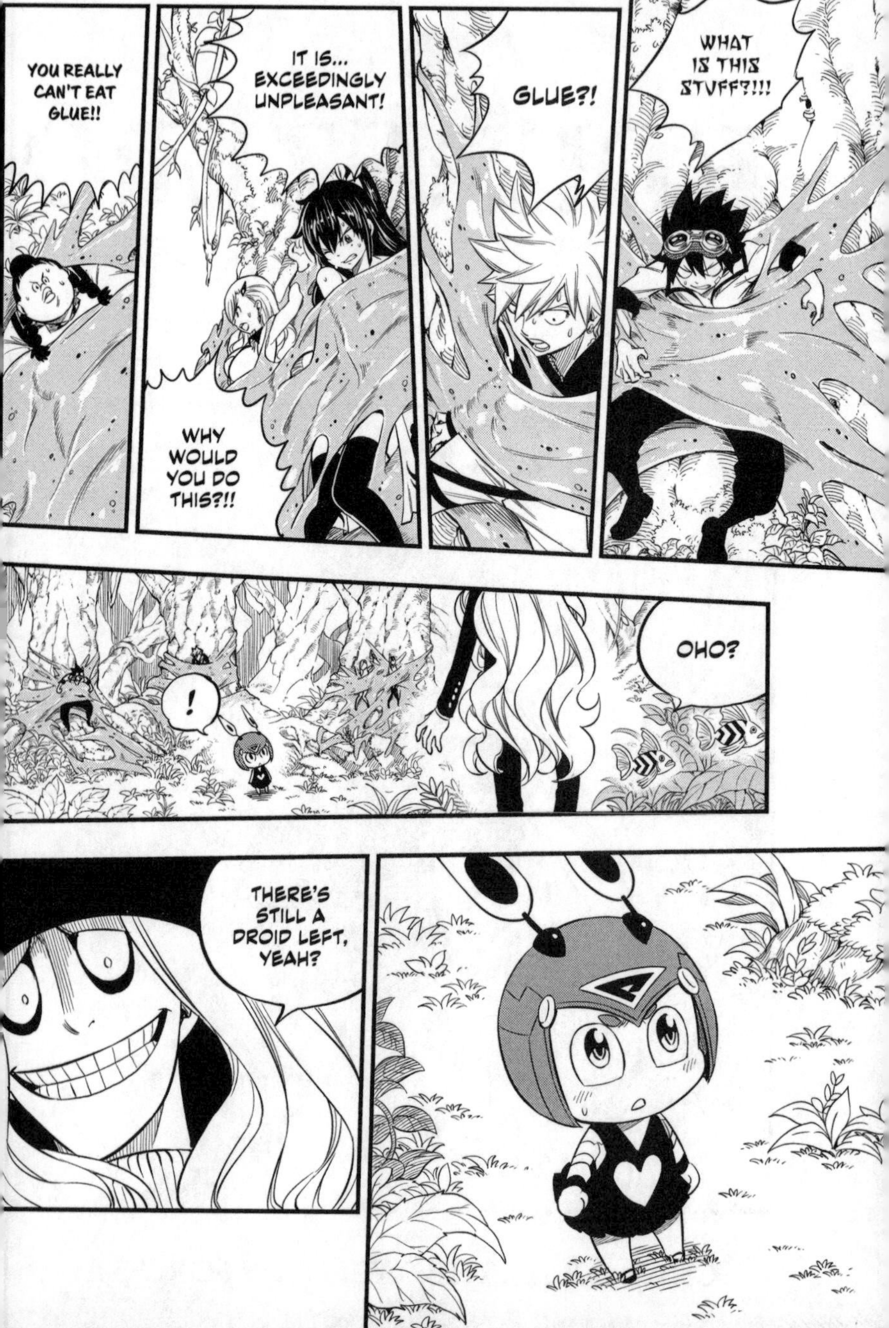
WHAT IS THIS STUFF?!!!
GLUE?!
IT IS... EXCEEDINGLY UNPLEASANT!
WHY WOULD YOU DO THIS?!!
YOU REALLY CAN'T EAT GLUE!!
OHO?
!
THERE'S STILL A DROID LEFT, YEAH?

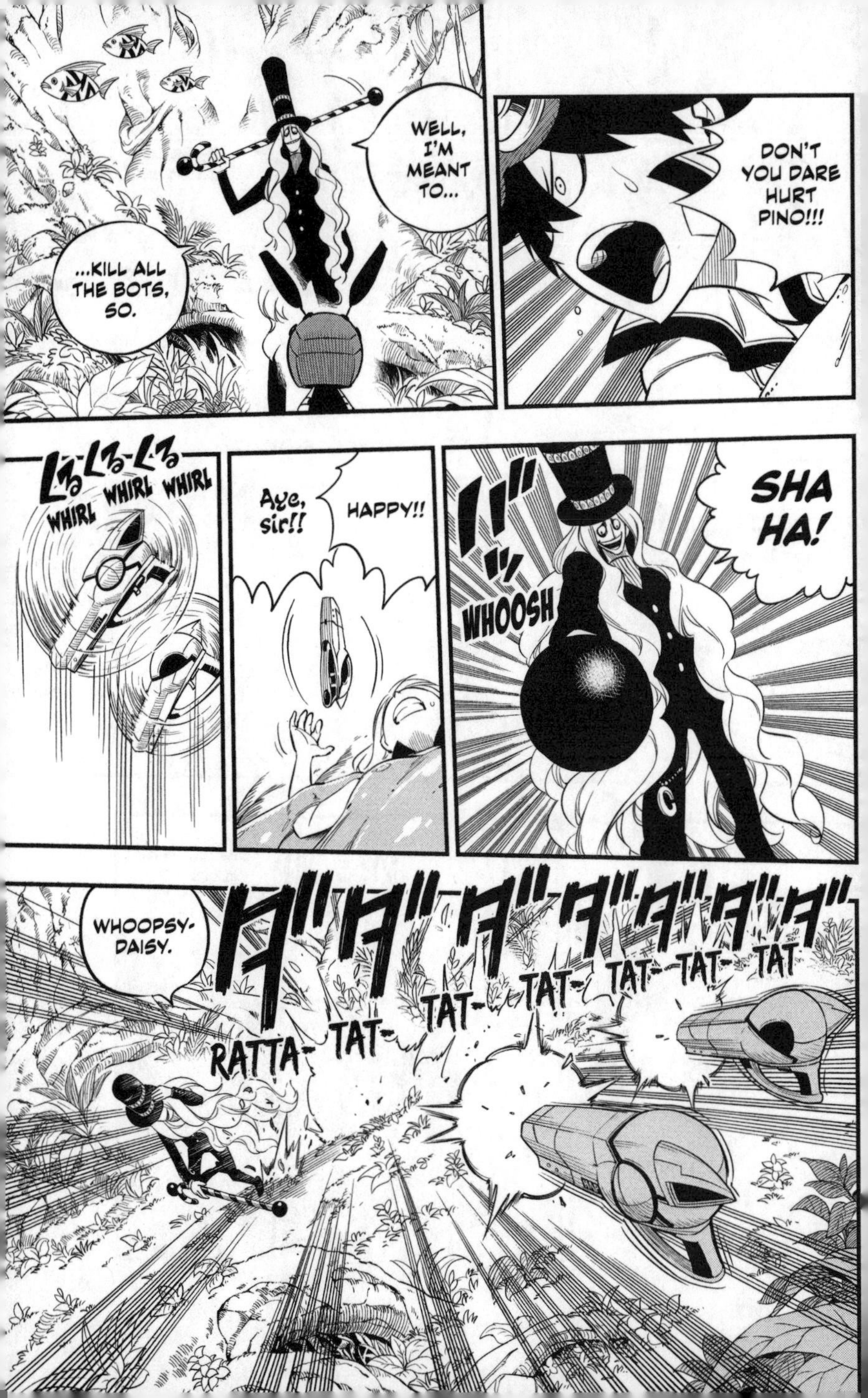
DON'T YOU DARE HURT PINO!!!
WELL, I'M MEANT TO...
...KILL ALL THE BOTS, SO.
SHA HA!
WHOOSH
HAPPY!!
Aye, sir!!
くるくるくる
WHIRL WHIRL WHIRL
WHOOPSY-DAISY.
ダダダダダダダダ
RATTA-TAT-TAT-TAT-TAT-TAT-TAT

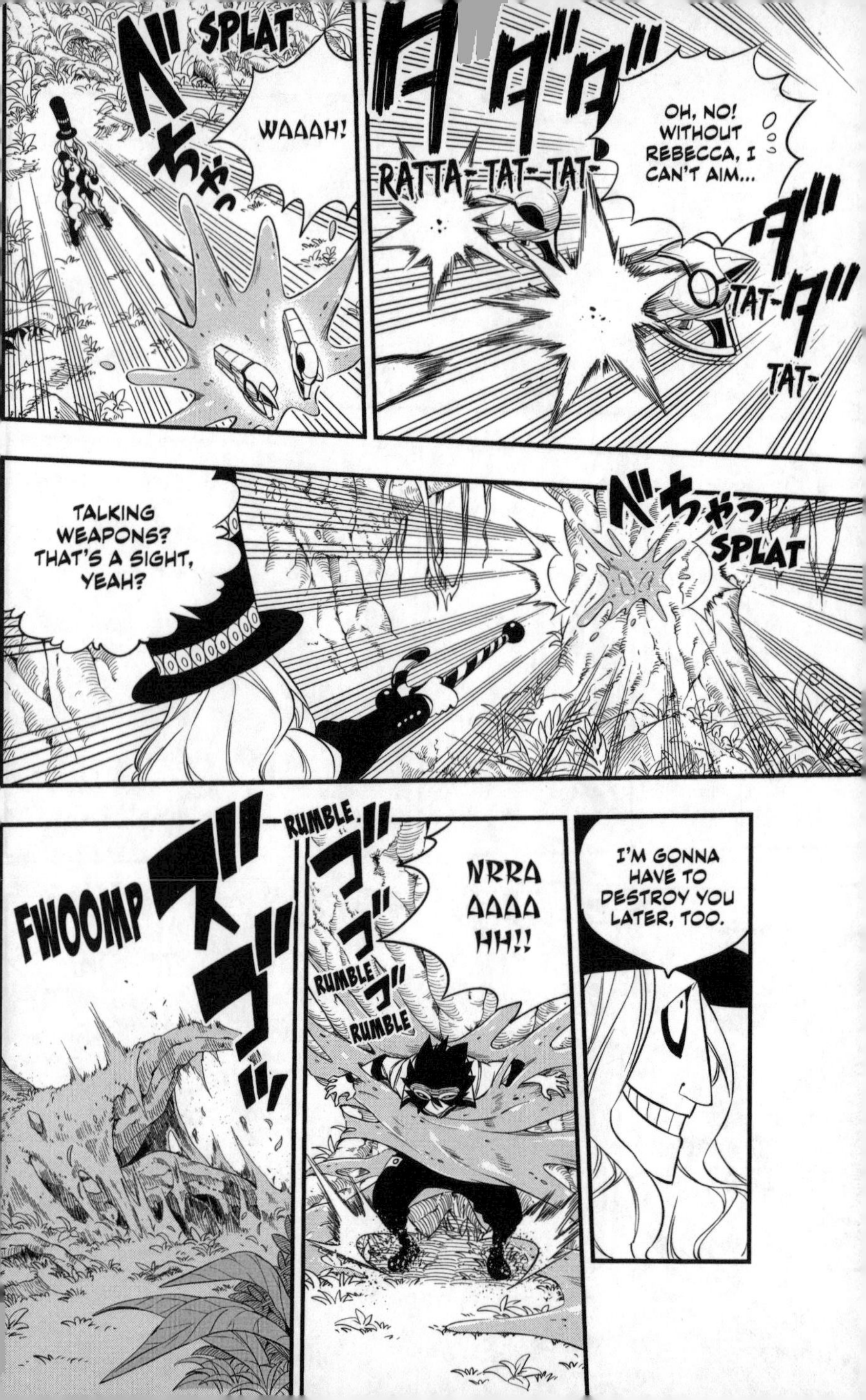

ダダダ
RATTA-TAT-TAT
OH, NO! WITHOUT REBECCA, I CAN'T AIM...
ダ TAT- ダ TAT-
べちゃっ
SPLAT
WAAAH!
べちゃっ
SPLAT
TALKING WEAPONS? THAT'S A SIGHT, YEAH?
I'M GONNA HAVE TO DESTROY YOU LATER, TOO.
NRRA AAAA HH!!
ゴゴゴ
RUMBLE
RUMBLE
RUMBLE
ズゴゴ
FWOOMP

RUMBLE RUMBLE RUMBLE RUMBLE

RUMBLE

AS LONG AS HE CAN MOVE HIS ARMS, IT DOESN'T MATTER IF HE'S TIED UP!	HE IS BOUND, BUT... OF COURSE!!	HOW CAN YOU USE ETHER GEAR WHILE TIED UP?!	HE UPROOTED THE ENTIRE TREE?!	EH?

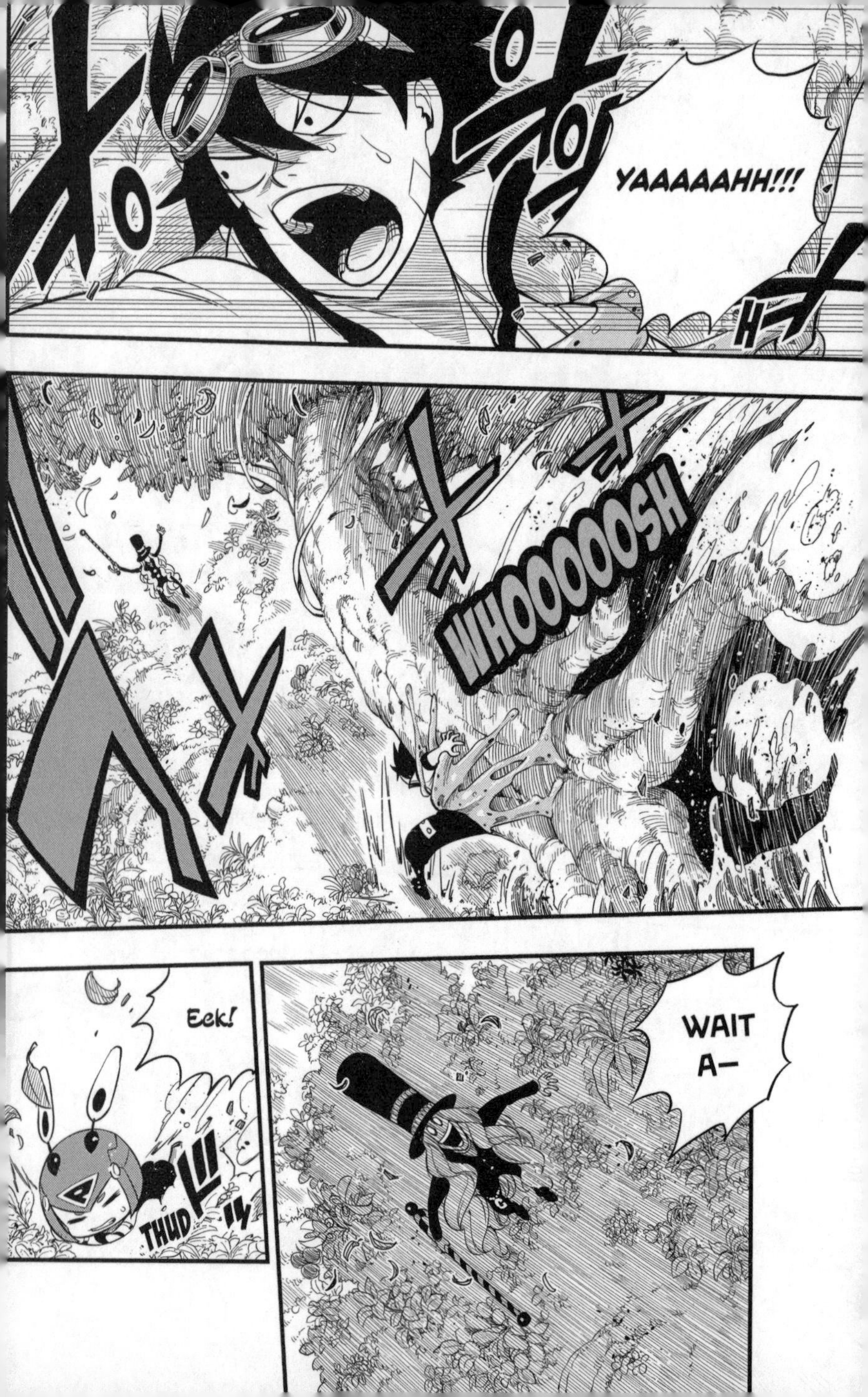
YAAAAAHH!!!
WHOOOOOSH
WAIT A—
Eek!
THUD

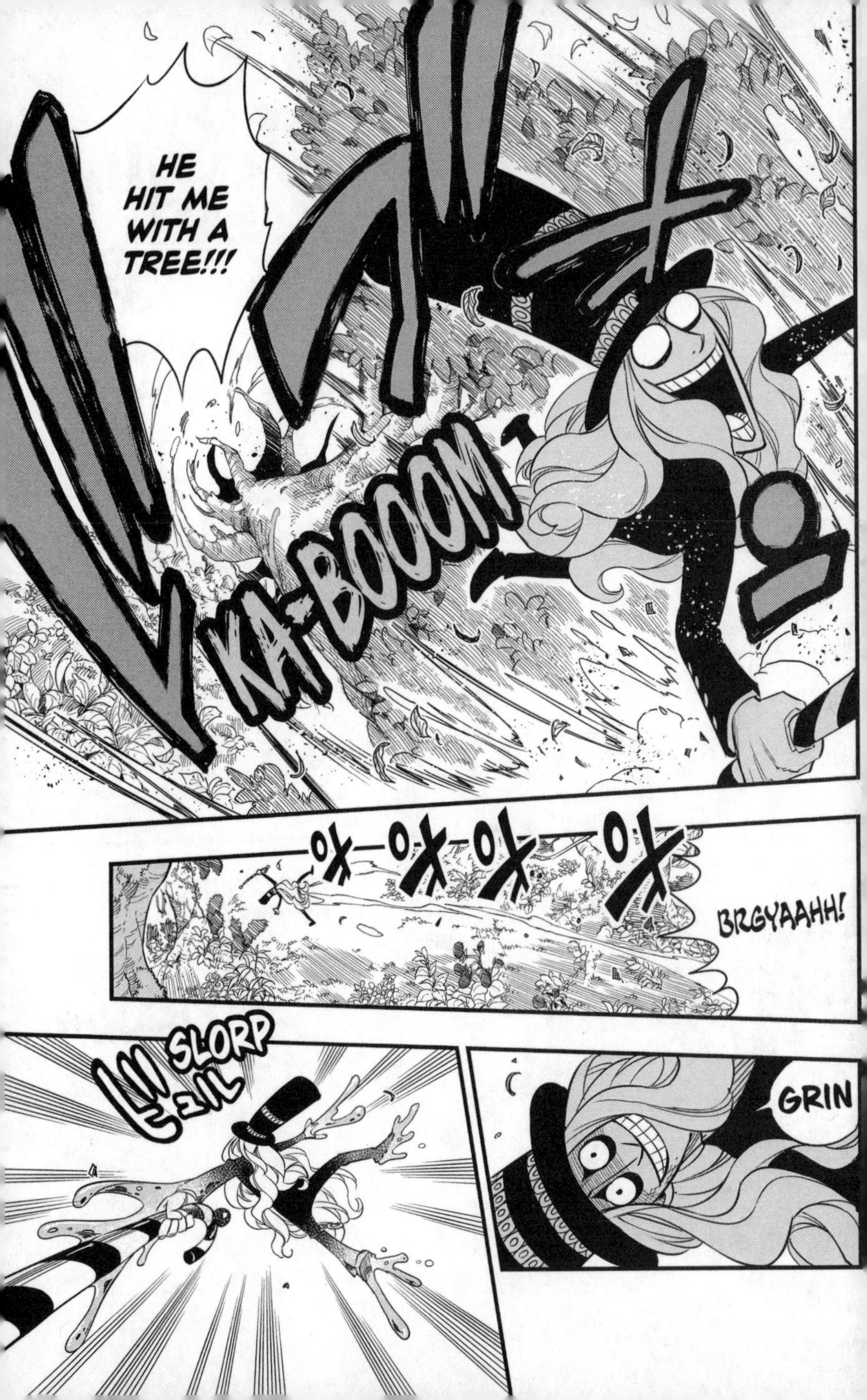
HE HIT ME WITH A TREE!!!
KA-BOOOM
BRGYAAHH!
GRIN
SLORP

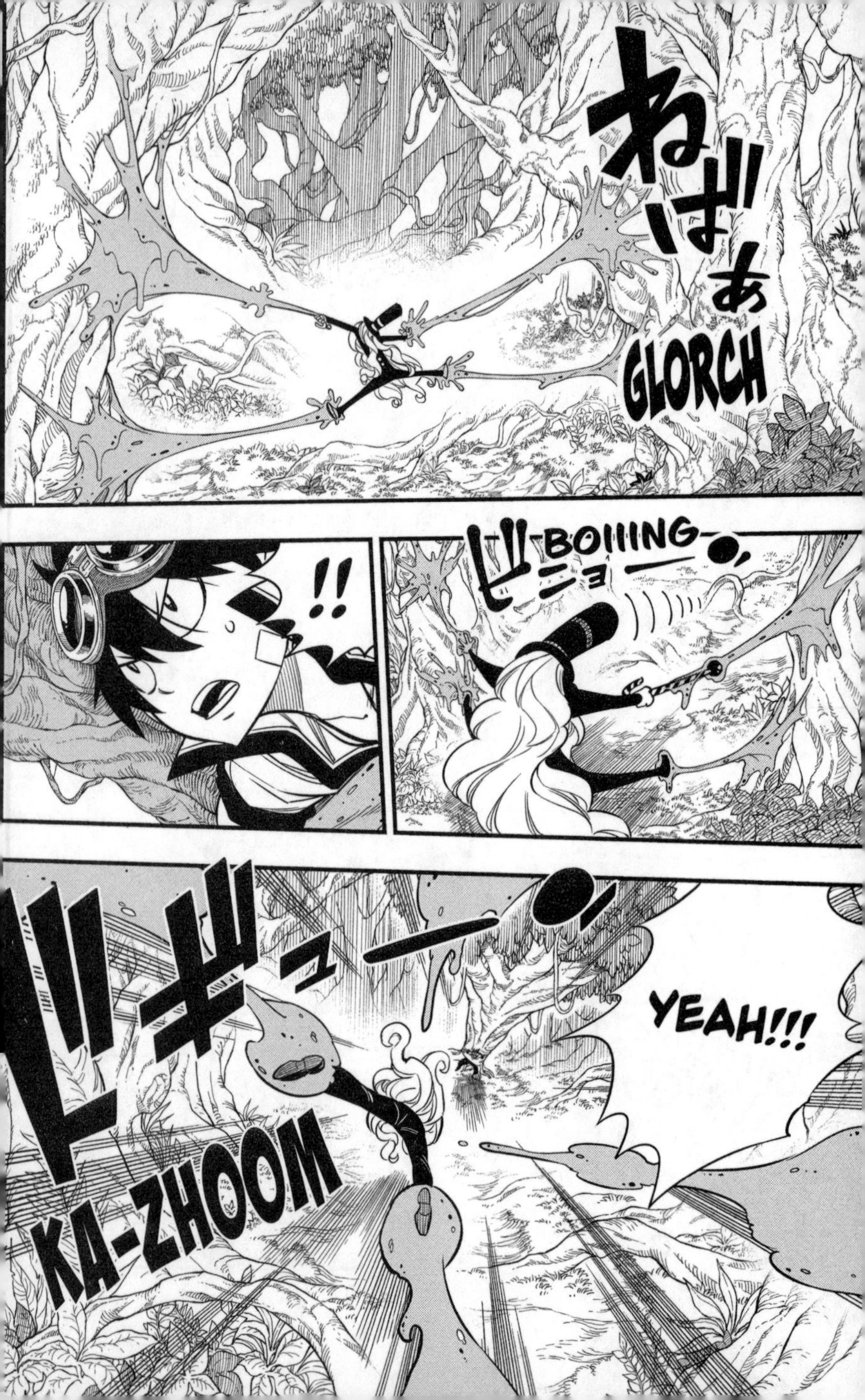

ねばぁ
GLORCH
BOIIING
ビニョー
!!
ドギュー
KA-ZHOOM
YEAH!!!

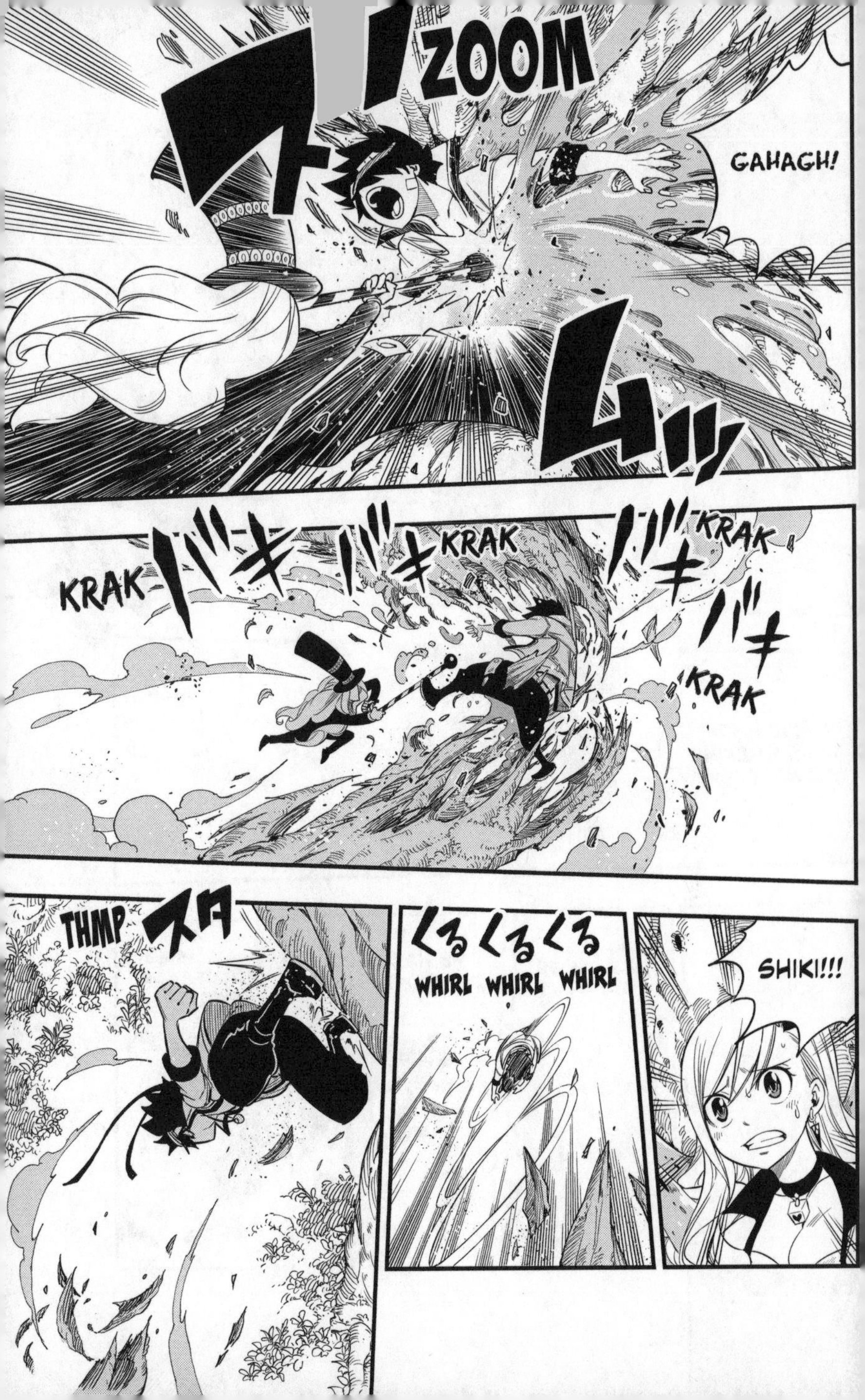
GAHAGH!
ZOOM
バキ
KRAK
バキ
KRAK
バキ
KRAK
バキ
KRAK
SHIKI!!!
くるくるくる
WHIRL WHIRL WHIRL
スタ
THMP

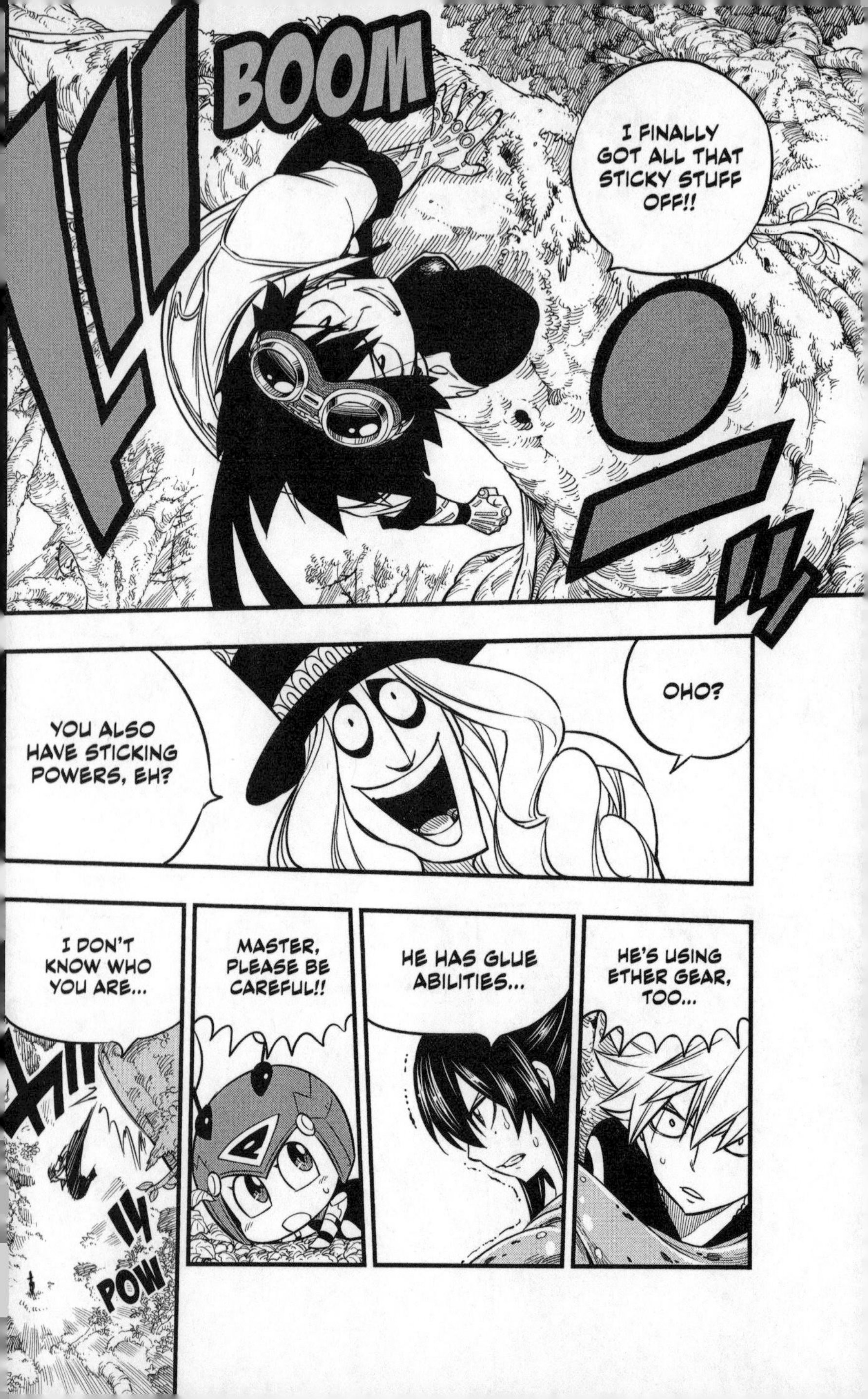
I FINALLY GOT ALL THAT STICKY STUFF OFF!!
BOOM
OHO?
YOU ALSO HAVE STICKING POWERS, EH?
HE'S USING ETHER GEAR, TOO...
HE HAS GLUE ABILITIES...
MASTER, PLEASE BE CAREFUL!!
I DON'T KNOW WHO YOU ARE...
POW

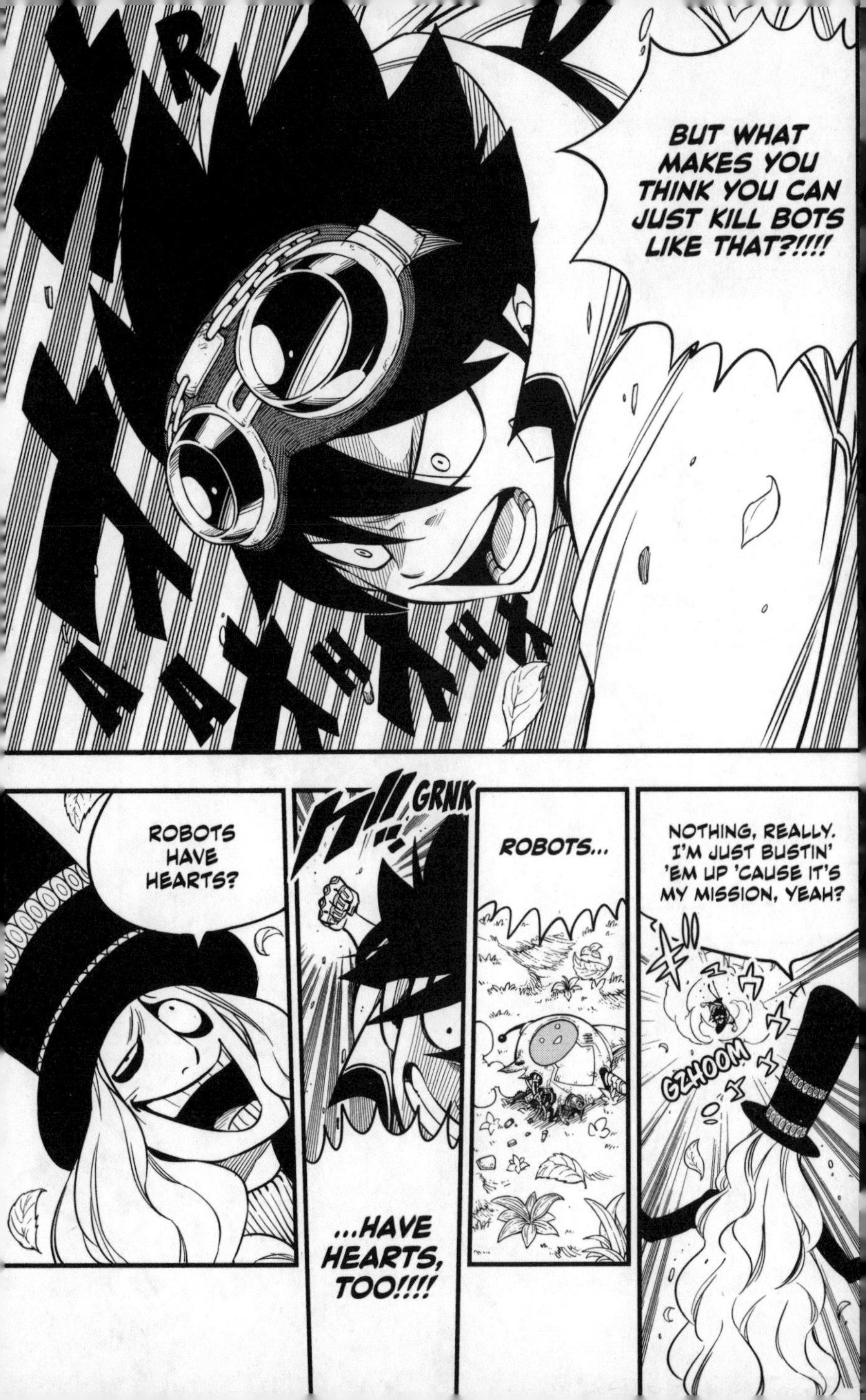
BUT WHAT MAKES YOU THINK YOU CAN JUST KILL BOTS LIKE THAT?!!!!
NOTHING, REALLY. I'M JUST BUSTIN' 'EM UP 'CAUSE IT'S MY MISSION, YEAH?
GZHOOM
ROBOTS...
GRNK
...HAVE HEARTS, TOO!!!!
ROBOTS HAVE HEARTS?

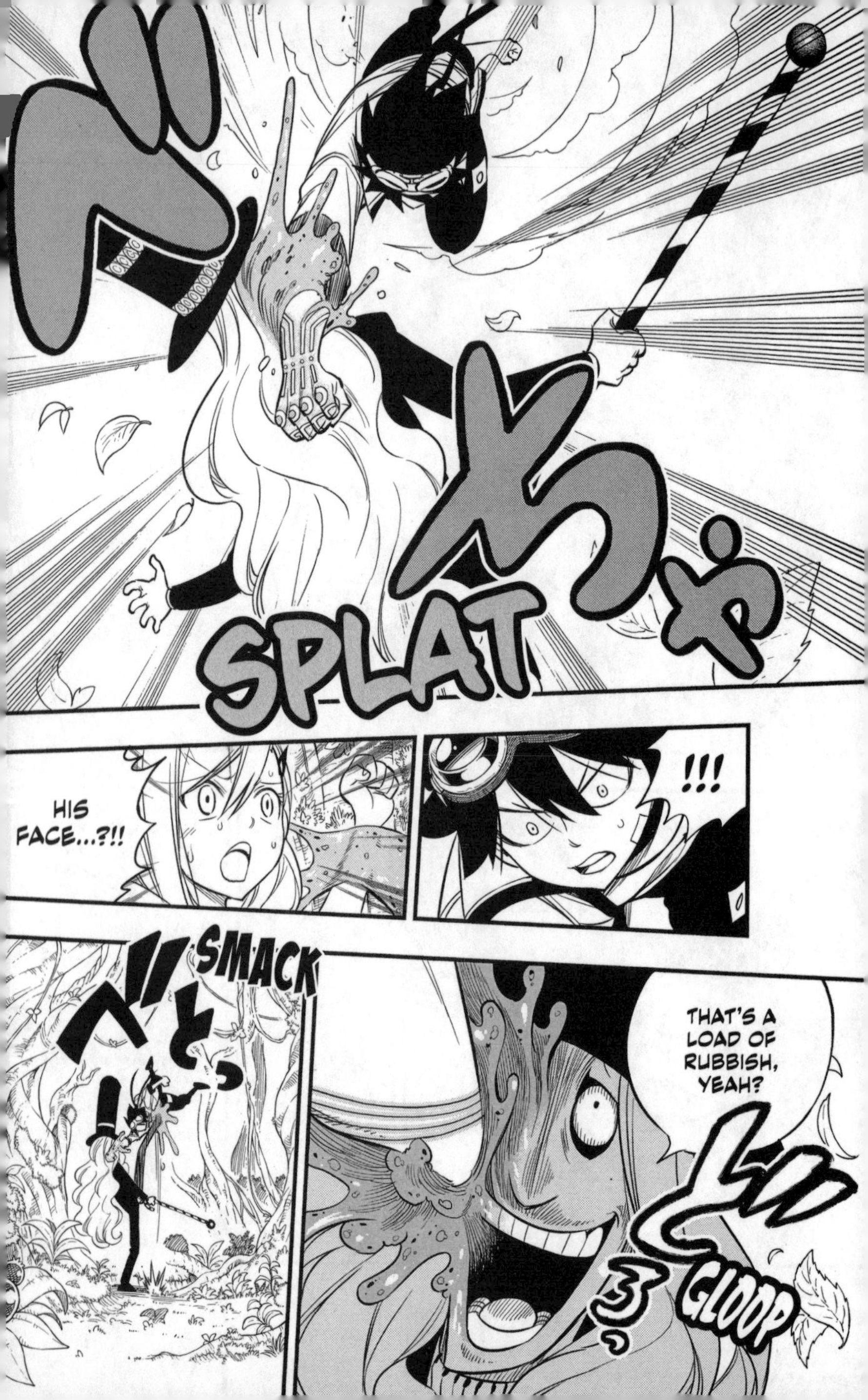
SPLAT
!!!
HIS FACE...?!!
THAT'S A LOAD OF RUBBISH, YEAH?
GLOOP
SMACK

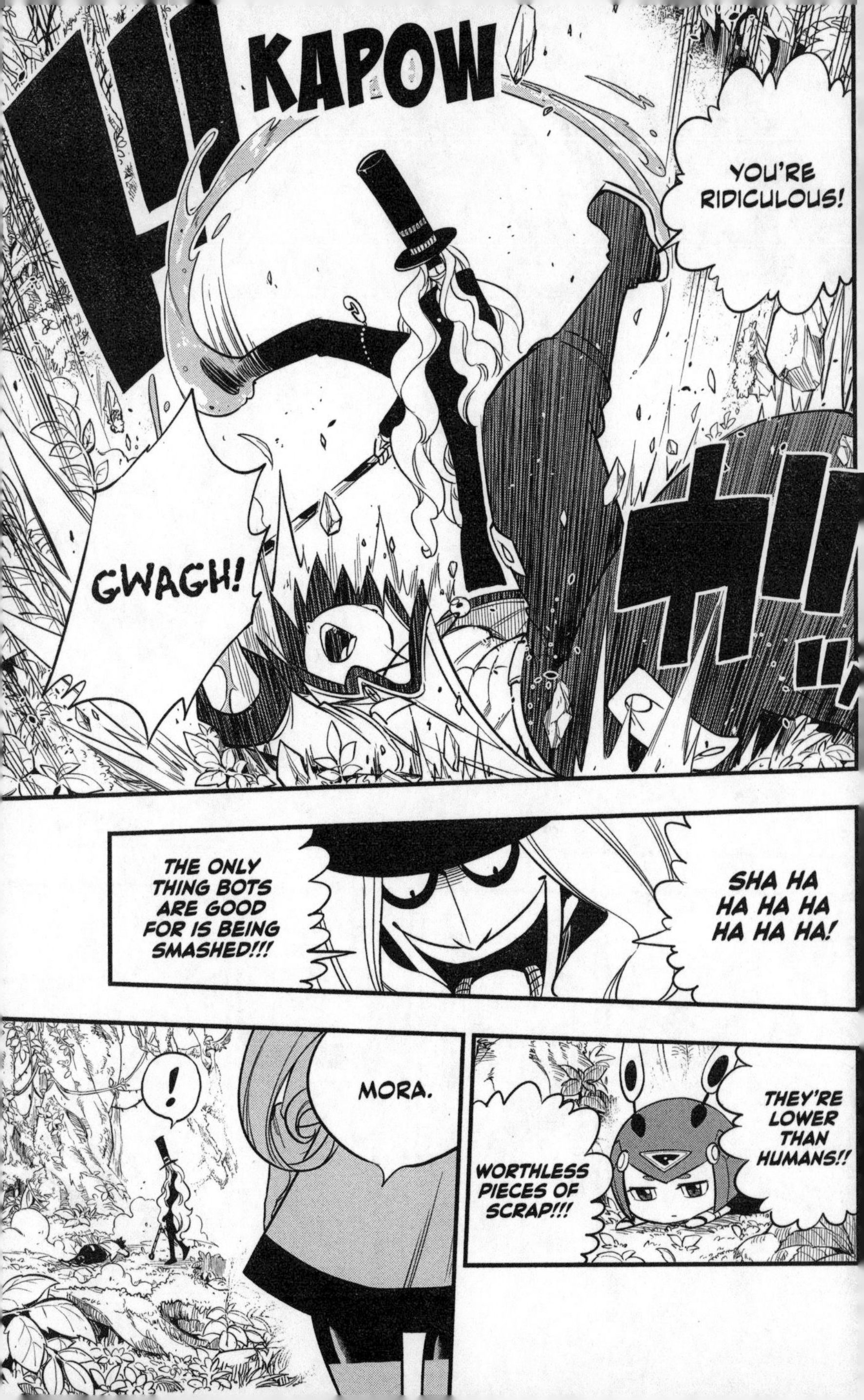
KAPOW
YOU'RE RIDICULOUS!
GWAGH!
SHA HA HA HA HA HA HA HA!
THE ONLY THING BOTS ARE GOOD FOR IS BEING SMASHED!!!
THEY'RE LOWER THAN HUMANS!!
WORTHLESS PIECES OF SCRAP!!!
MORA.
!

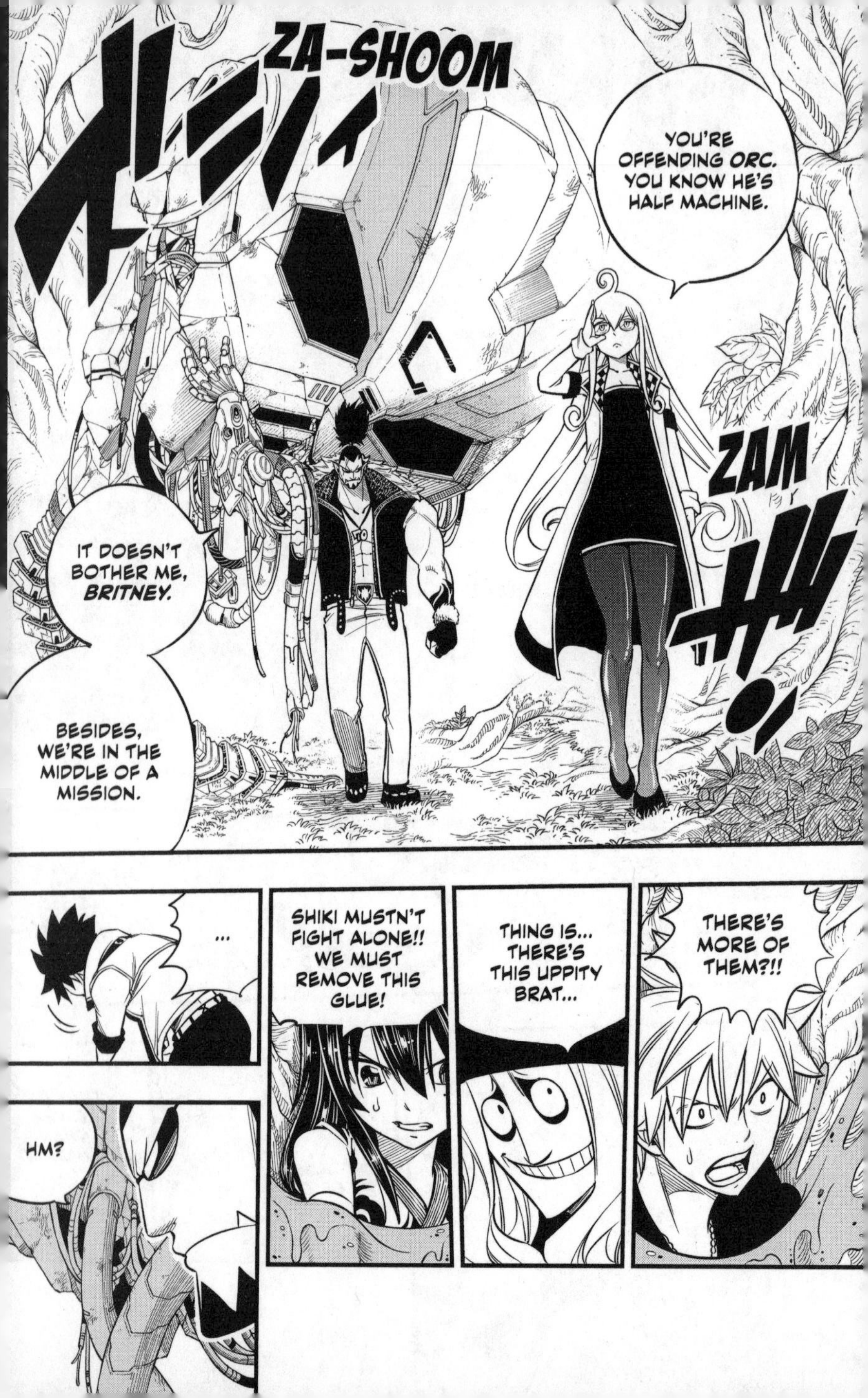

YOU'RE OFFENDING ORC. YOU KNOW HE'S HALF MACHINE.
ZA-SHOOM
ZAM
IT DOESN'T BOTHER ME, BRITNEY.
BESIDES, WE'RE IN THE MIDDLE OF A MISSION.
THERE'S MORE OF THEM?!!
THING IS... THERE'S THIS UPPITY BRAT...
SHIKI MUSTN'T FIGHT ALONE!! WE MUST REMOVE THIS GLUE!
...
HM?

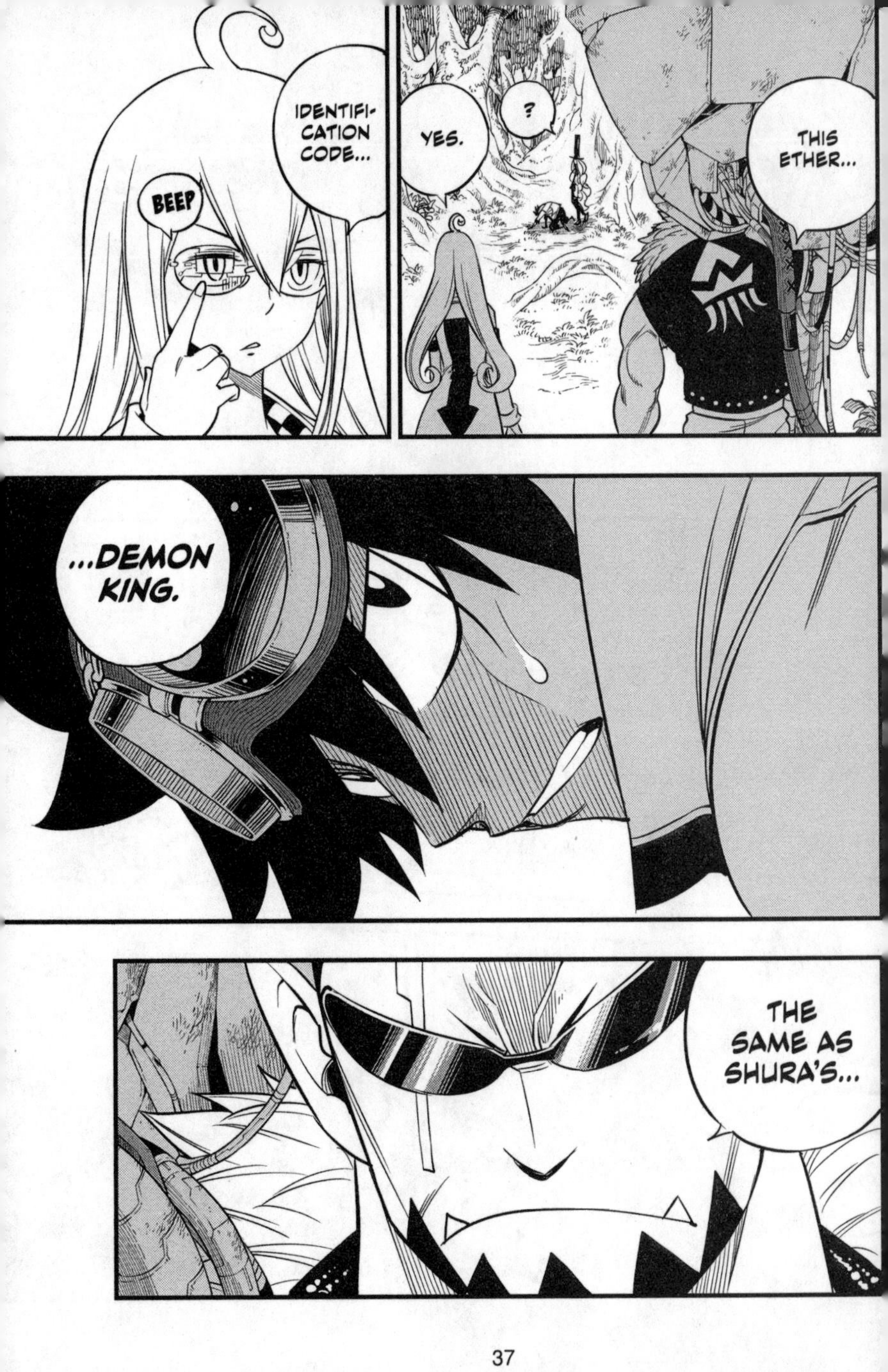
THIS ETHER...
?
YES.
IDENTIFI- CATION CODE...
BEEP
...DEMON KING.
THE SAME AS SHURA'S...

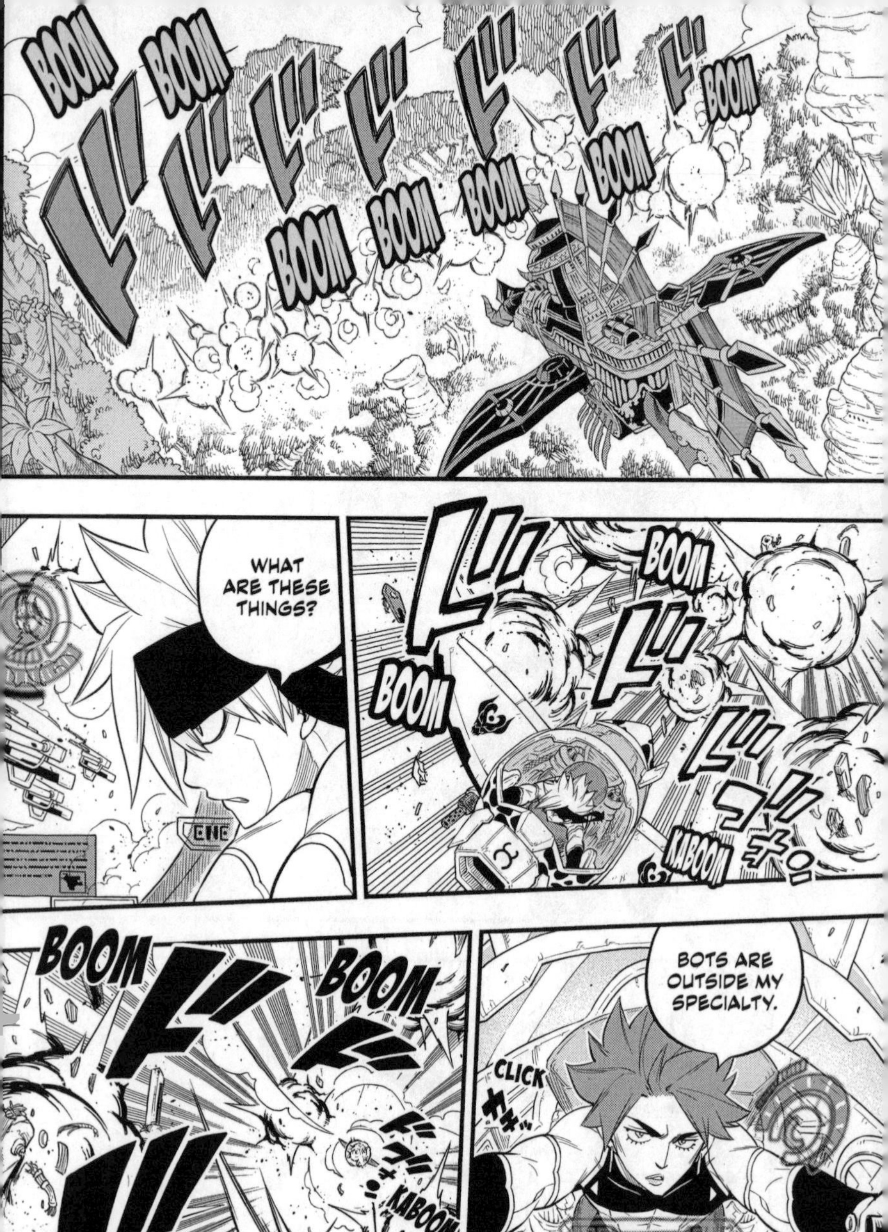
BOOM
BOOM
BOOM
BOOM
BOOM
BOOM
BOOM
BOOM
BOOM
BOOM
KABOOM
WHAT ARE THESE THINGS?
BOTS ARE OUTSIDE MY SPECIALTY.
CLICK
BOOM
BOOM
KABOOM
BOOM

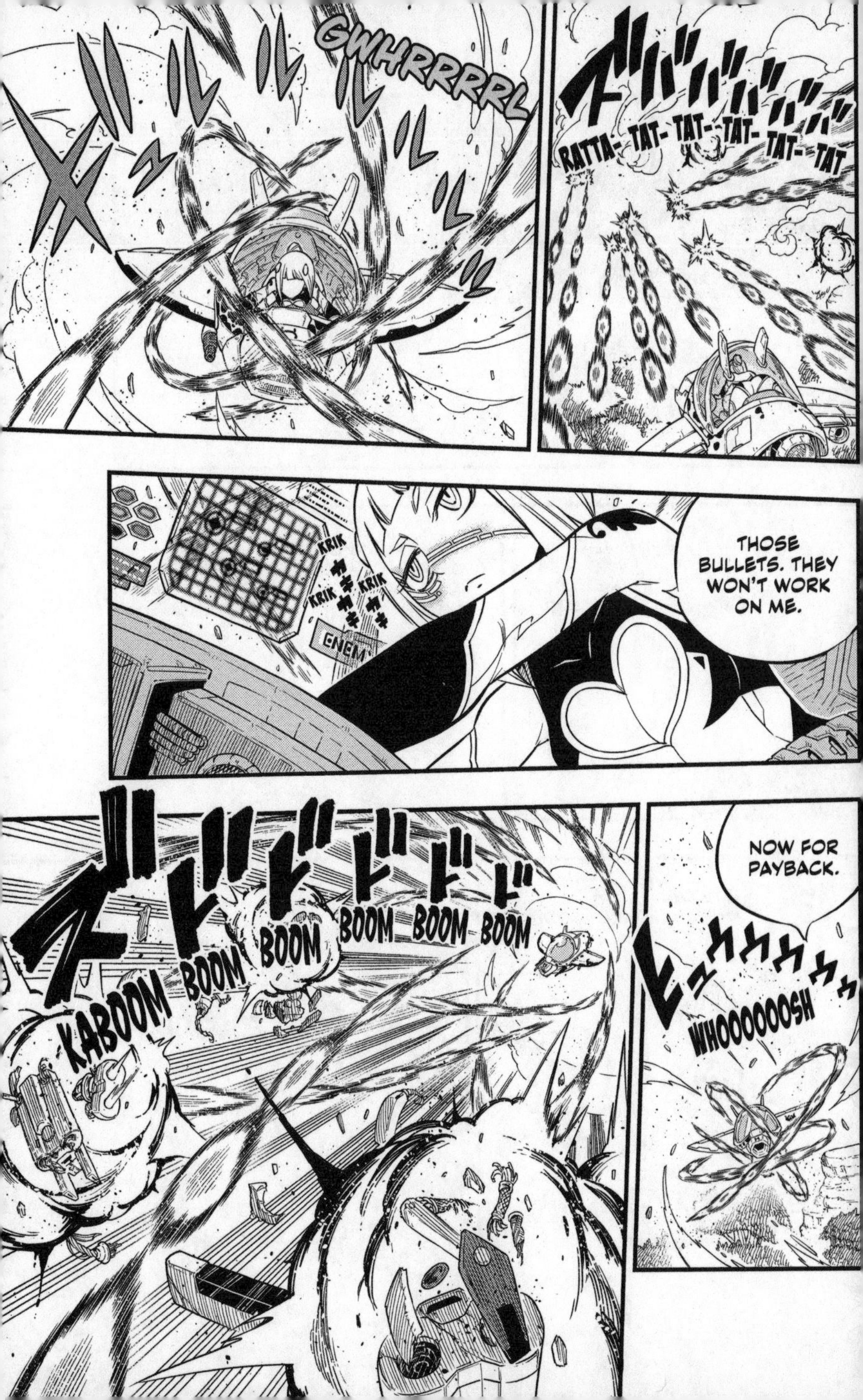
RATTA-TAT-TAT-TAT-TAT-TAT-TAT
GWHRRRRL
THOSE BULLETS. THEY WON'T WORK ON ME.
KRIK KRIK KRIK
ENEM
NOW FOR PAYBACK.
WHOOOOOOSH
BOOM BOOM BOOM BOOM BOOM
KABOOM

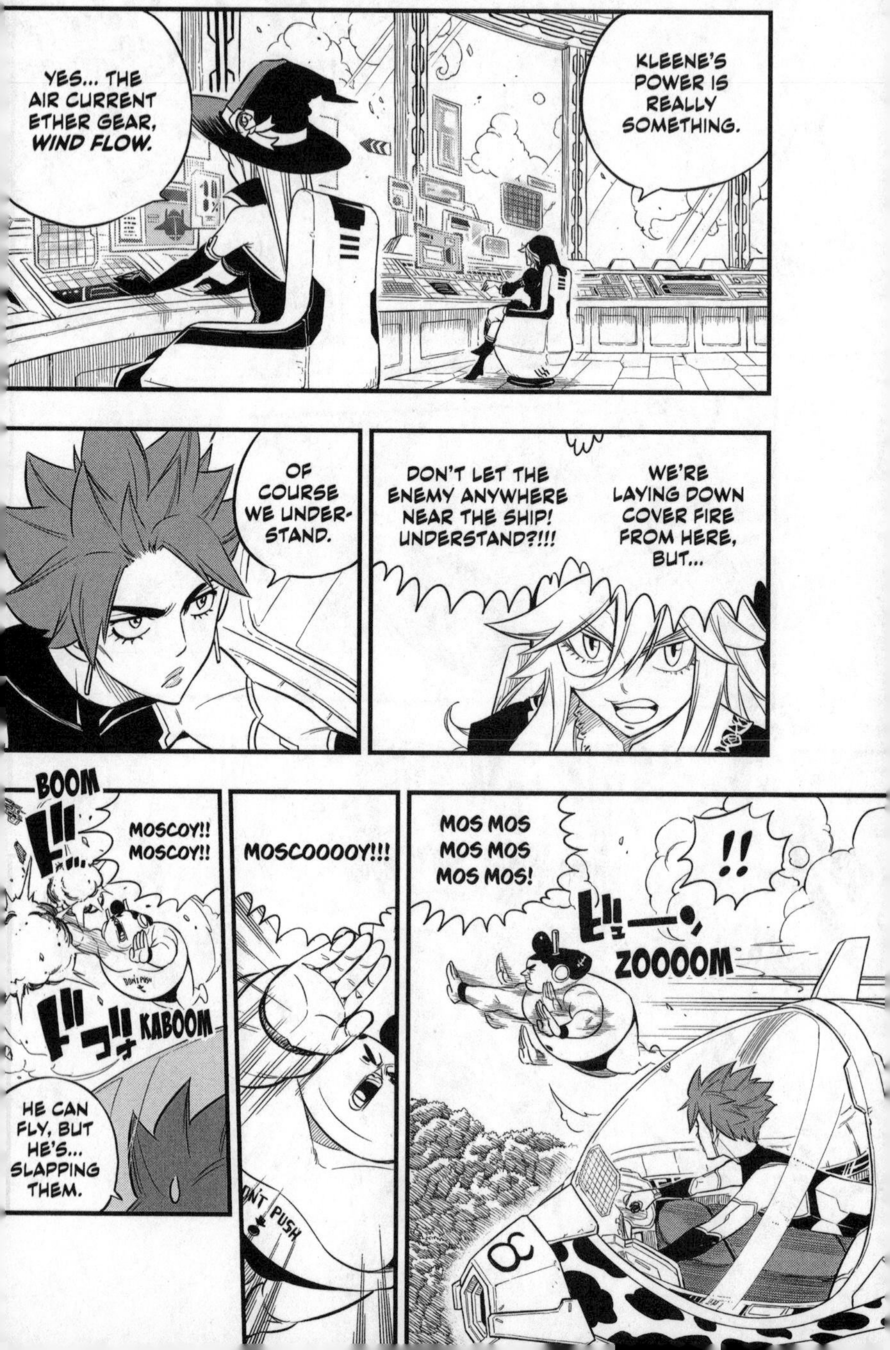
KLEENE'S POWER IS REALLY SOMETHING.
YES... THE AIR CURRENT ETHER GEAR, *WIND FLOW.*
WE'RE LAYING DOWN COVER FIRE FROM HERE, BUT...
DON'T LET THE ENEMY ANYWHERE NEAR THE SHIP! UNDERSTAND?!!!
OF COURSE WE UNDER-STAND.
MOS MOS MOS MOS MOS MOS!
!!
ZOOOOM
MOSCOOOOY!!!
DON'T PUSH
BOOM
MOSCOY!! MOSCOY!!
KABOOM
HE CAN FLY, BUT HE'S... SLAPPING THEM.

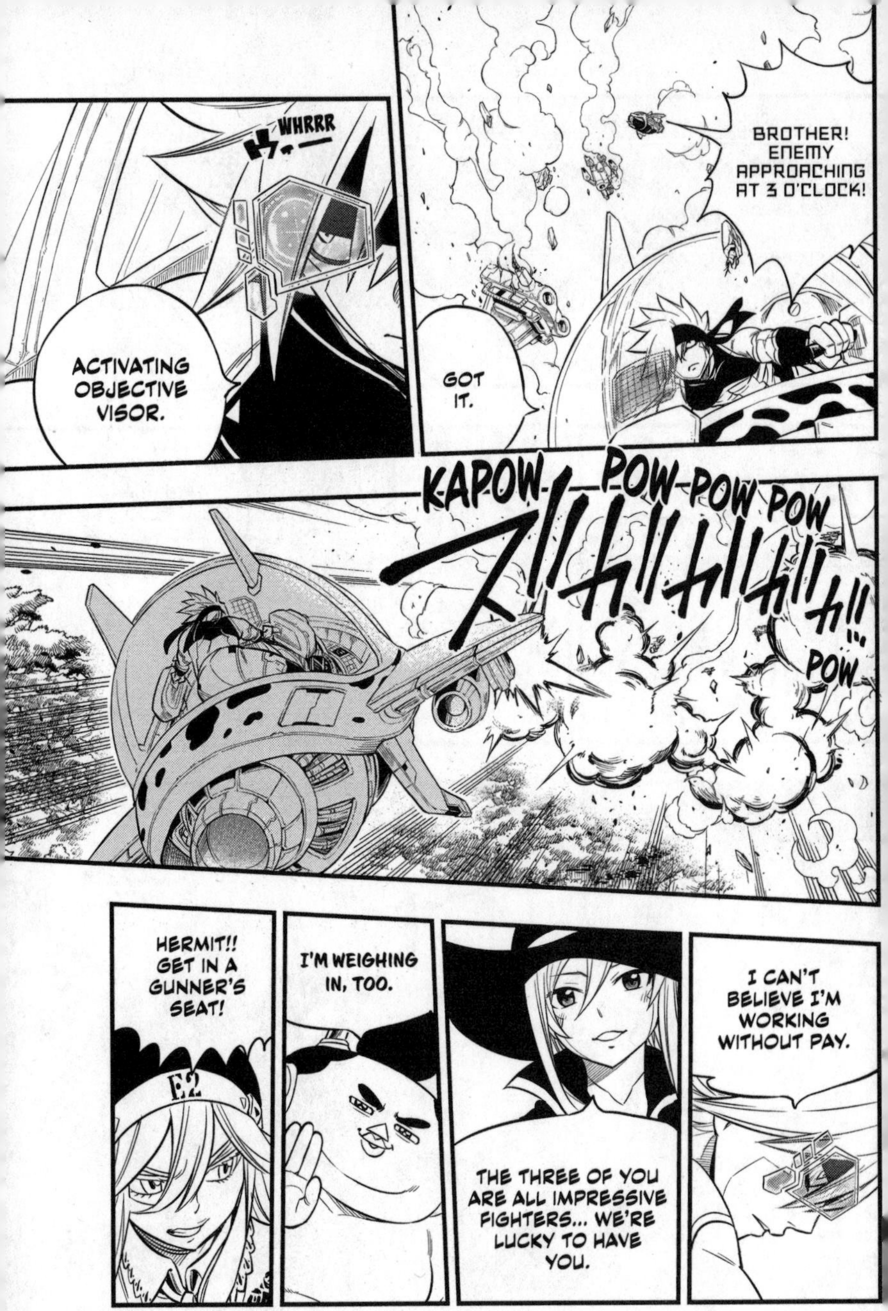
BROTHER! ENEMY APPROACHING AT 3 O'CLOCK!
GOT IT.
WHRRR
ACTIVATING OBJECTIVE VISOR.
KAPOW POW-POW POW
POW
I CAN'T BELIEVE I'M WORKING WITHOUT PAY.
THE THREE OF YOU ARE ALL IMPRESSIVE FIGHTERS... WE'RE LUCKY TO HAVE YOU.
I'M WEIGHING IN, TOO.
HERMIT!! GET IN A GUNNER'S SEAT!
E.2

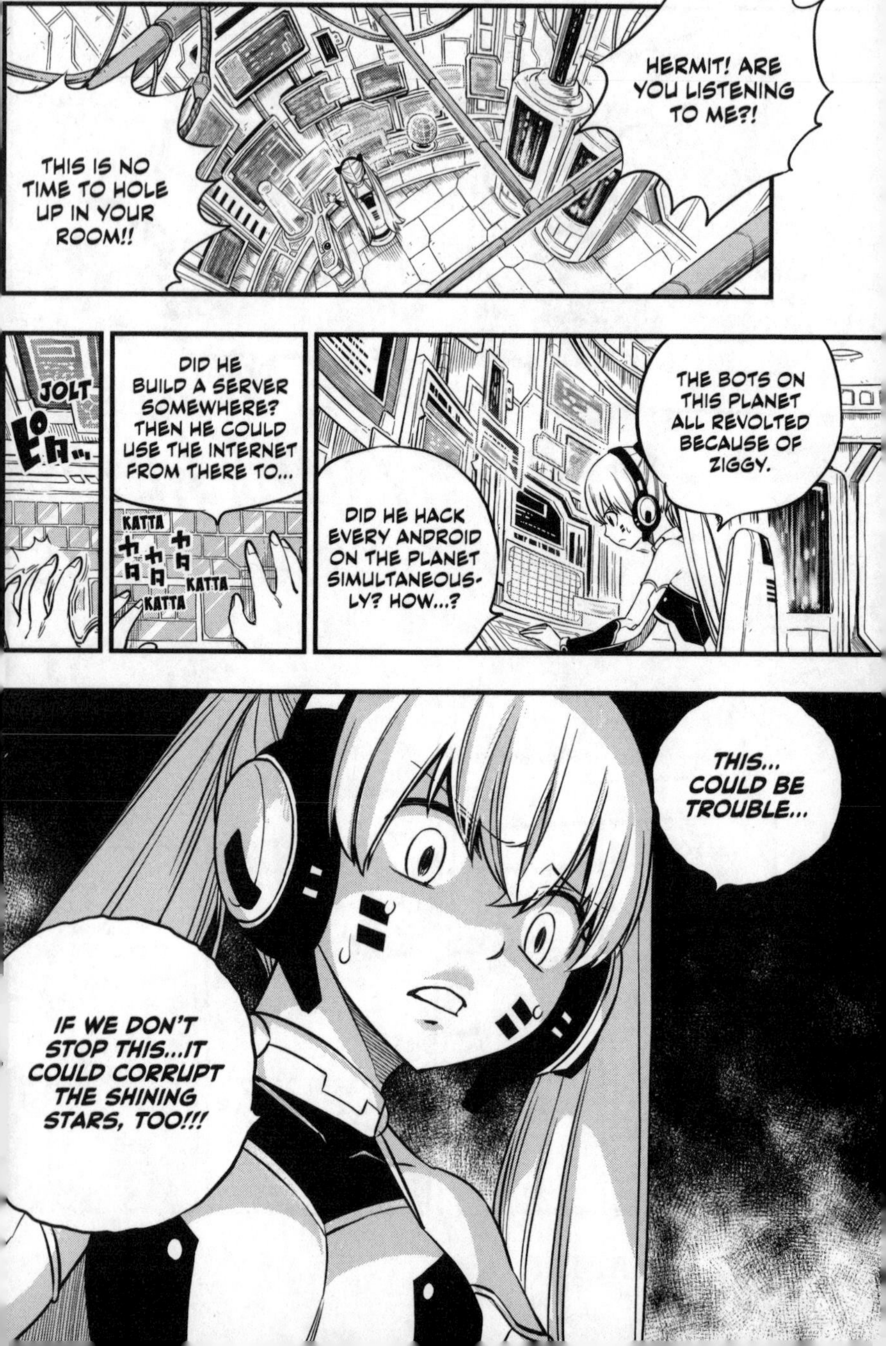
HERMIT! ARE YOU LISTENING TO ME?!
THIS IS NO TIME TO HOLE UP IN YOUR ROOM!!
THE BOTS ON THIS PLANET ALL REVOLTED BECAUSE OF ZIGGY.
DID HE HACK EVERY ANDROID ON THE PLANET SIMULTANEOUS-LY? HOW...?
DID HE BUILD A SERVER SOMEWHERE? THEN HE COULD USE THE INTERNET FROM THERE TO...
KATTA
KATTA
KATTA
JOLT
THIS... COULD BE TROUBLE...
IF WE DON'T STOP THIS...IT COULD CORRUPT THE SHINING STARS, TOO!!!

EDENSZERO

CHAPTER 116: THE SKY SWEEPER

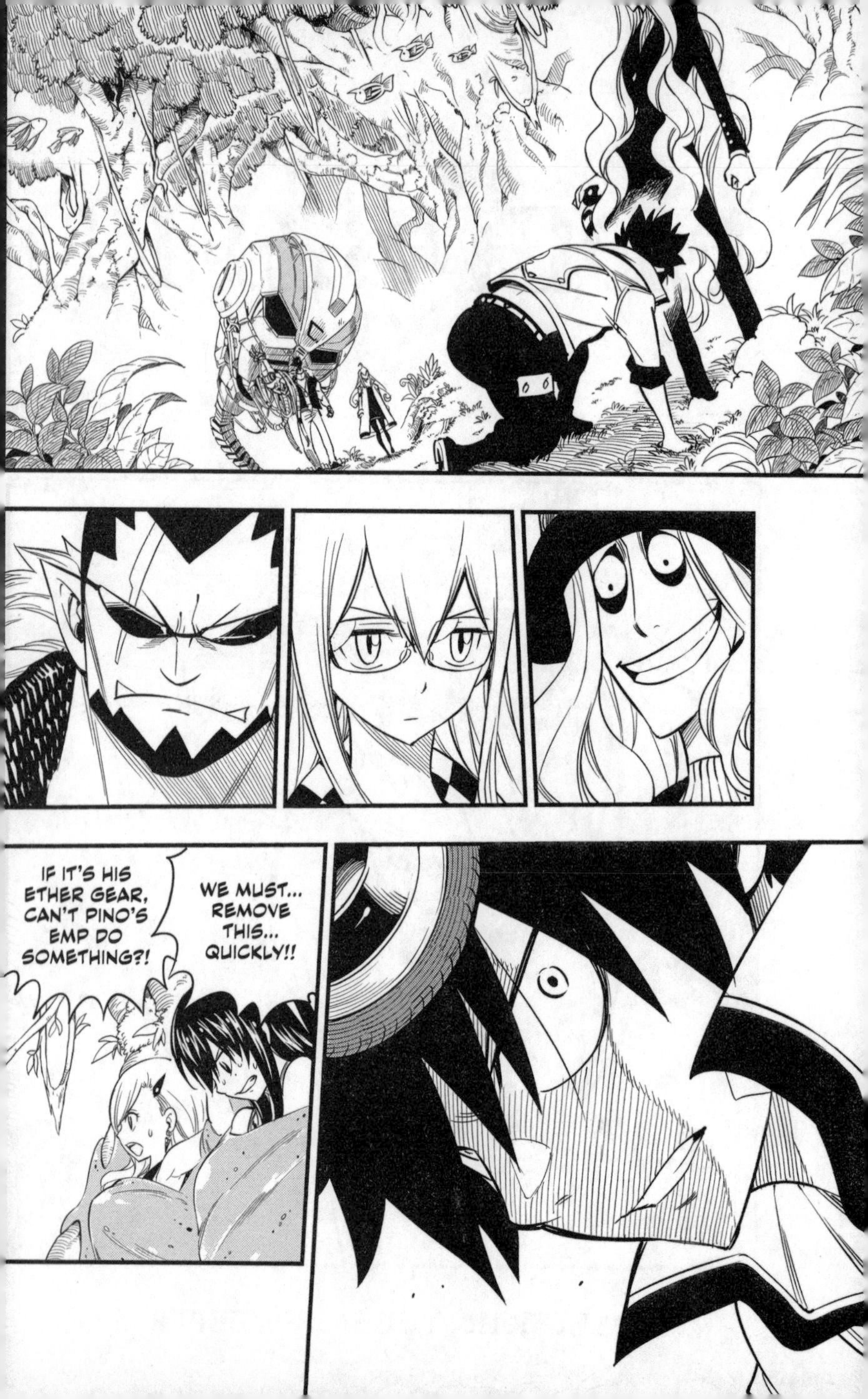
WE MUST... REMOVE THIS... QUICKLY!!
IF IT'S HIS ETHER GEAR, CAN'T PINO'S EMP DO SOMETHING?!

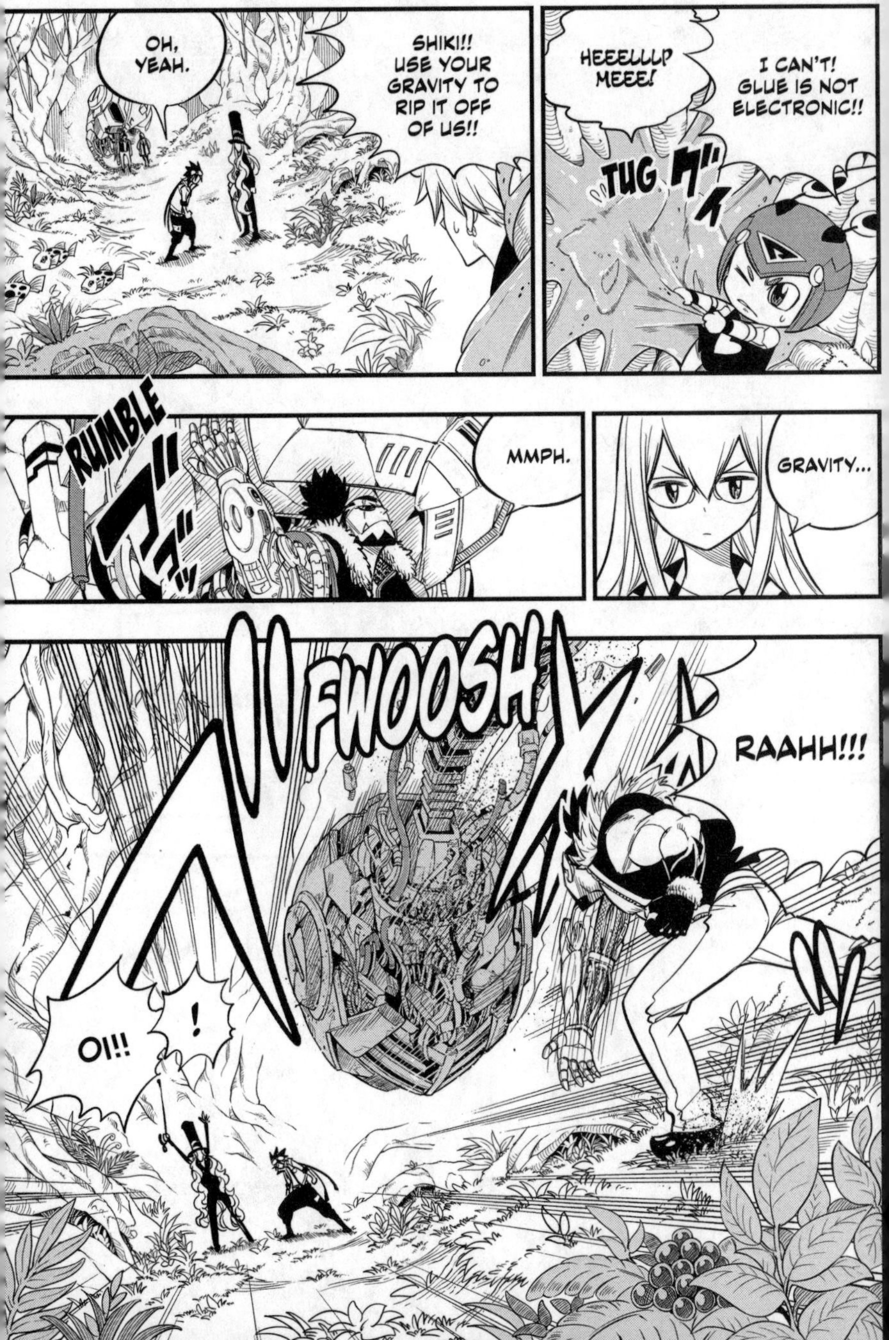
I CAN'T! GLUE IS NOT ELECTRONIC!!
HEEELLLP MEEE!
TUG
SHIKI!! USE YOUR GRAVITY TO RIP IT OFF OF US!!
OH, YEAH.
GRAVITY...
MMPH.
RUMBLE
RAAHH!!!
FWOOSH
!
OI!!

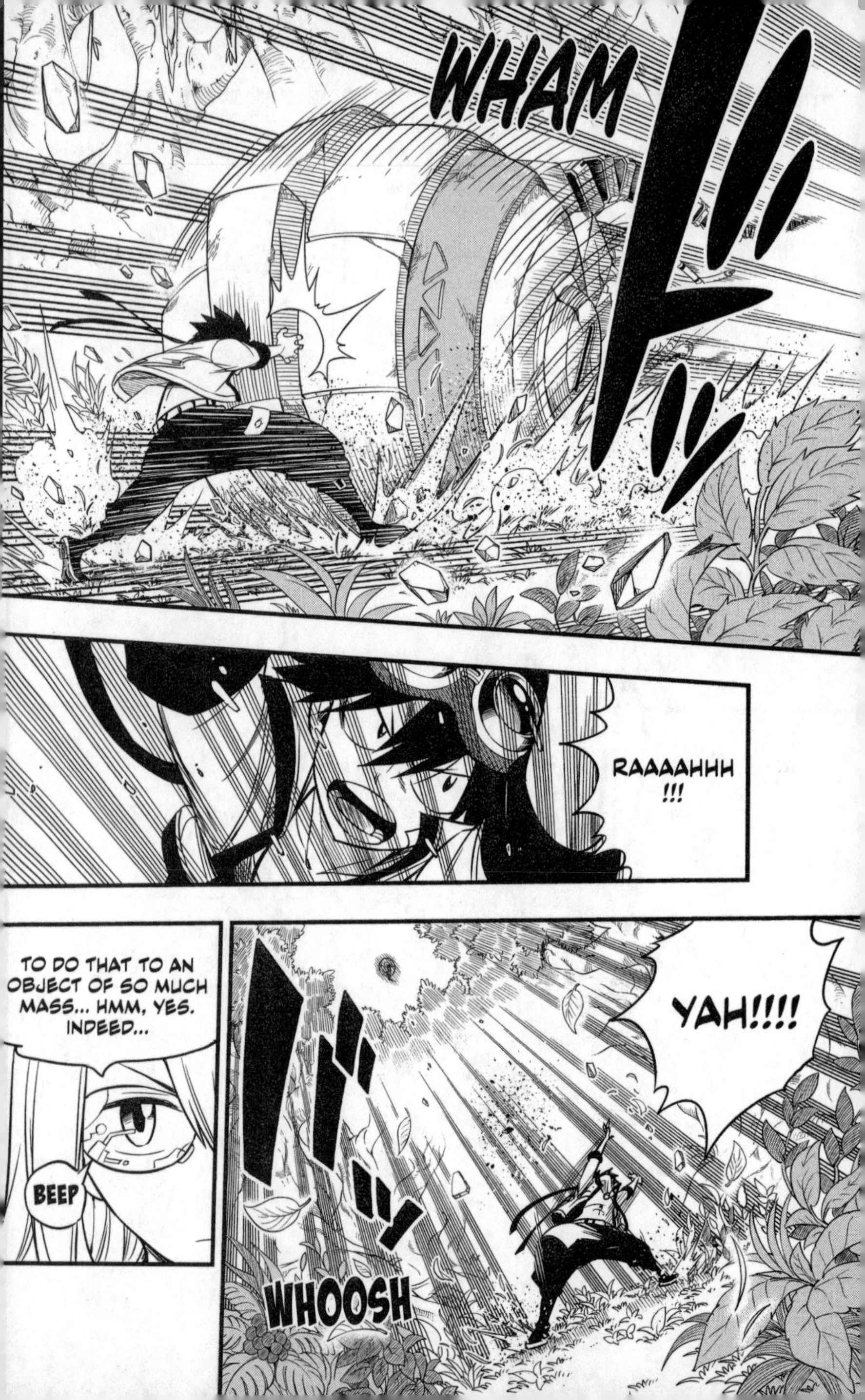
WHAM
RAAAAHHH !!!
YAH!!!!
WHOOSH
TO DO THAT TO AN OBJECT OF SO MUCH MASS... HMM, YES. INDEED...
BEEP

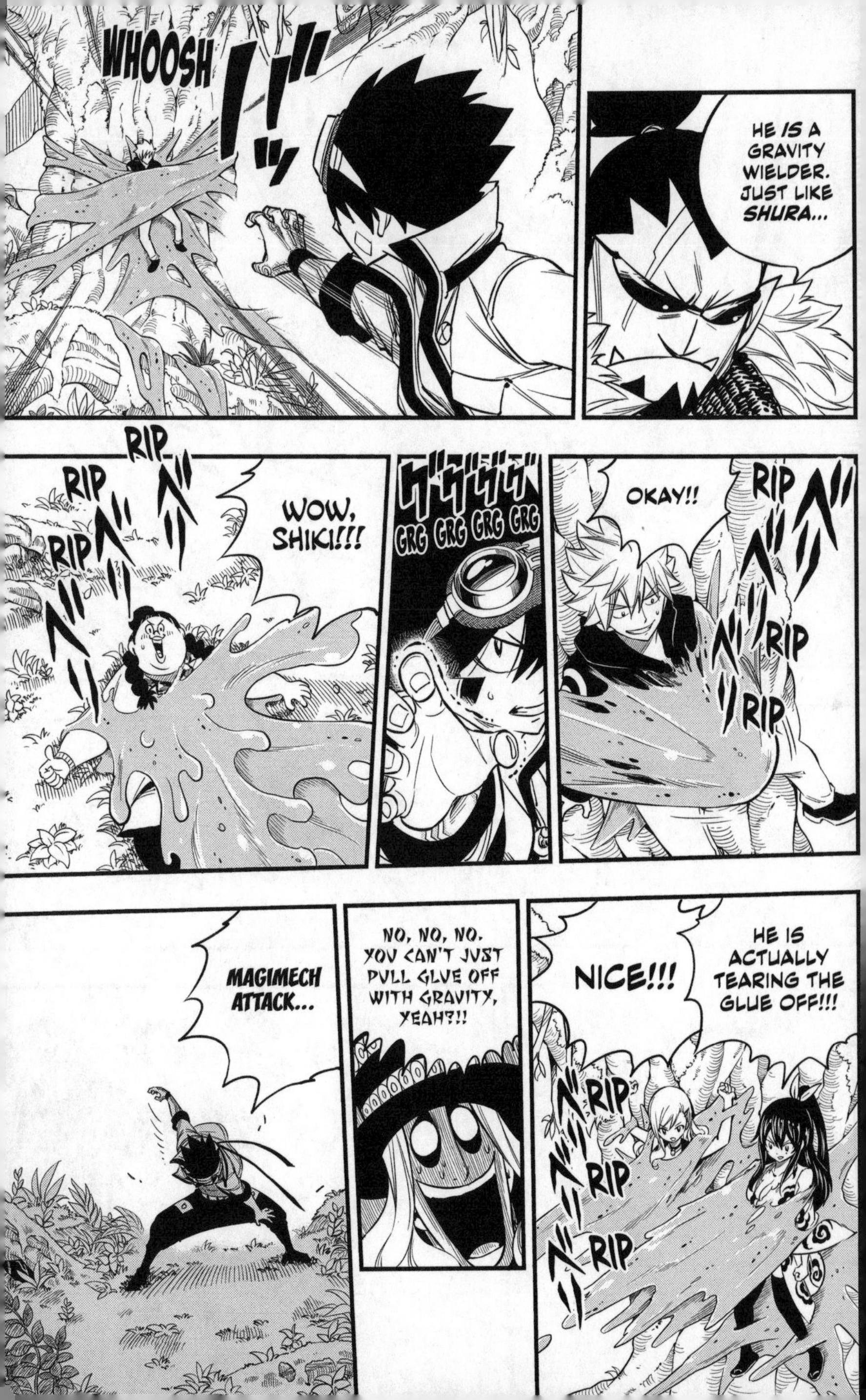
HE IS A GRAVITY WIELDER. JUST LIKE SHURA...
WHOOSH
OKAY!!
RIP
RIP
RIP
GRG GRG GRG GRG
RIP
RIP
RIP
WOW, SHIKI!!!
HE IS ACTUALLY TEARING THE GLUE OFF!!!
NICE!!!
RIP
RIP
RIP
NO, NO, NO. YOU CAN'T JUST PULL GLUE OFF WITH GRAVITY, YEAH?!!
MAGIMECH ATTACK...

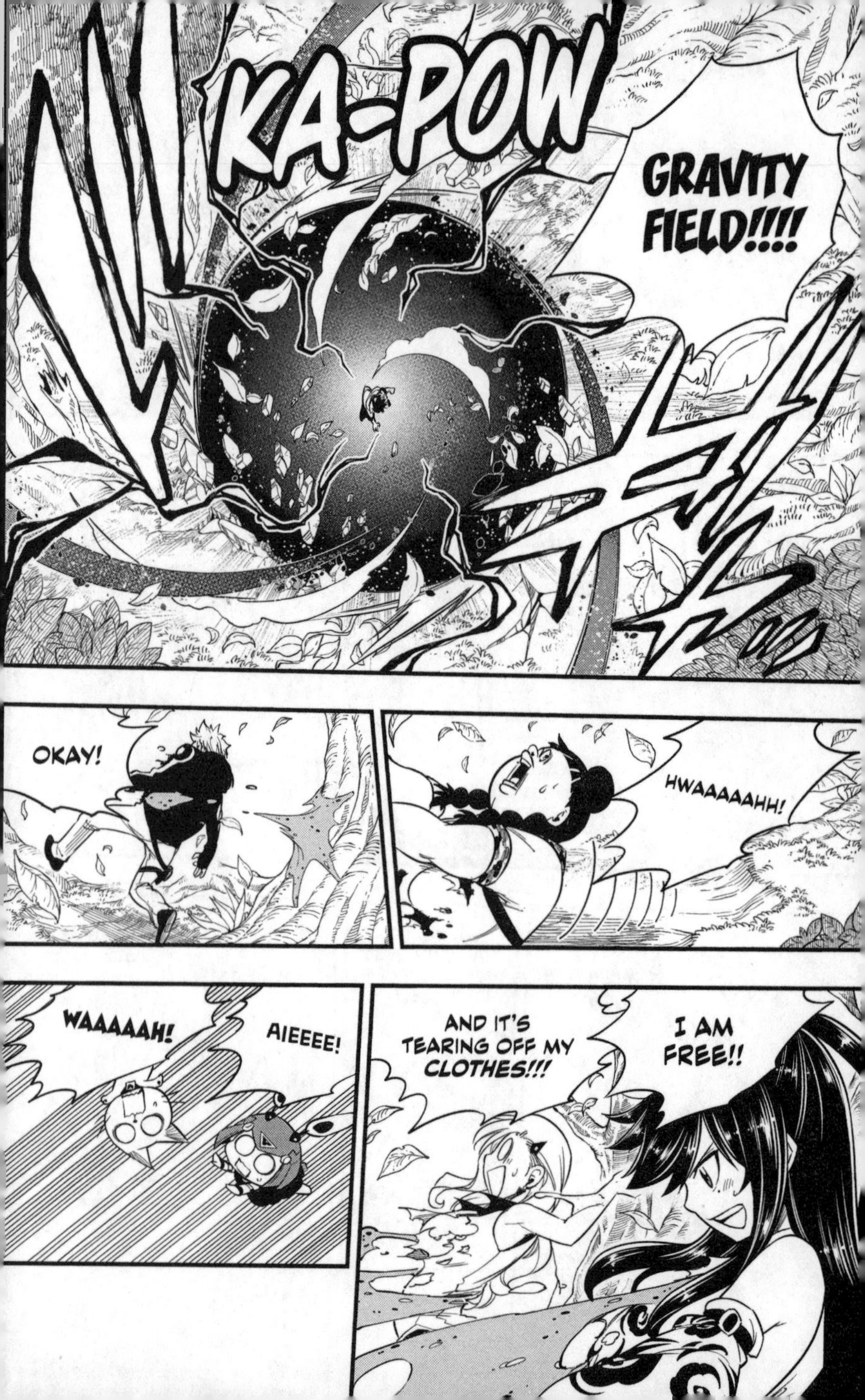
GRAVITY FIELD!!!!
KA-POW
HWAAAAAHH!
OKAY!
I AM FREE!!
AND IT'S TEARING OFF MY CLOTHES!!!
AIEEEE!
WAAAAAH!

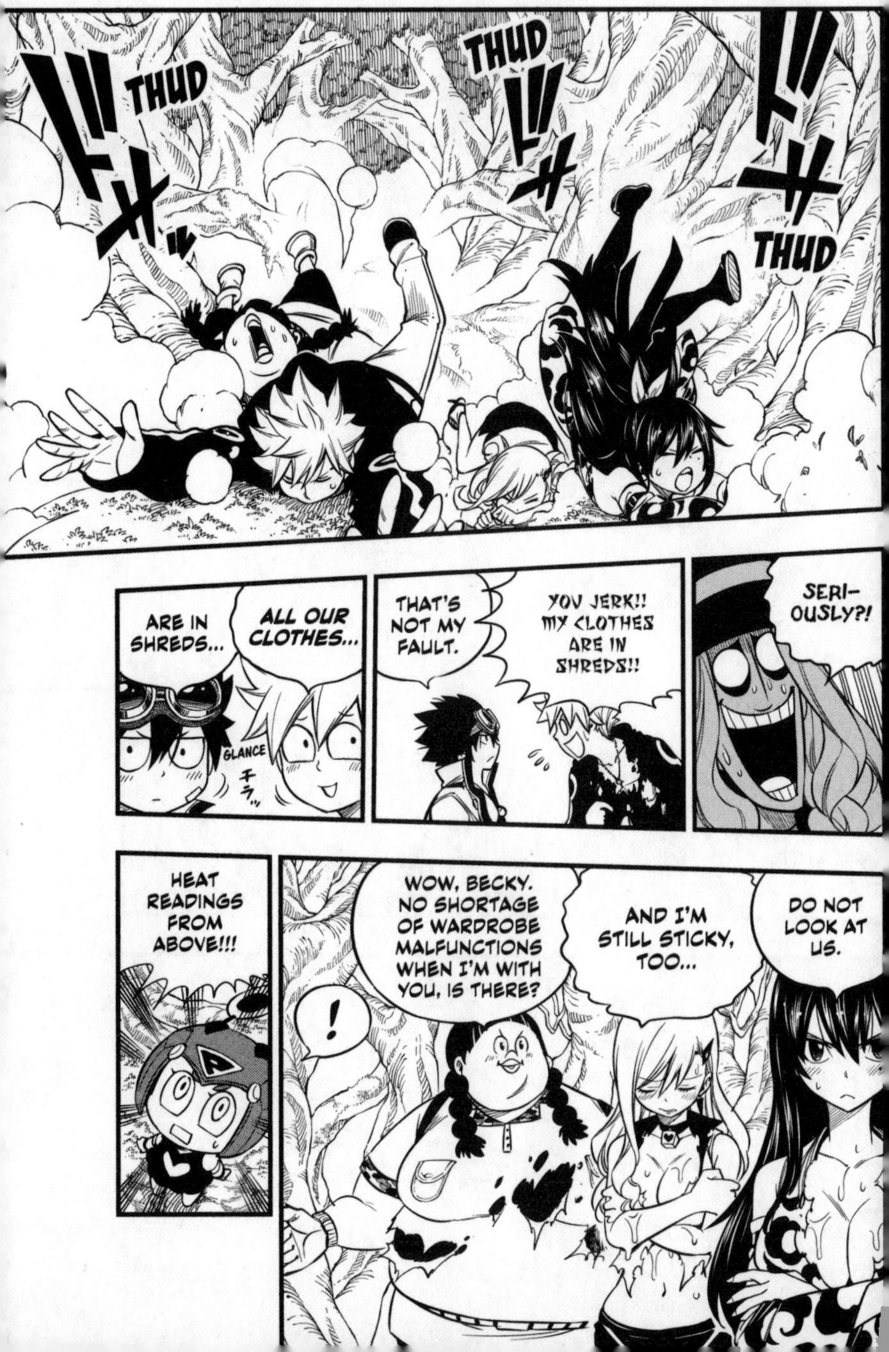
THUD
THUD
THUD
SERI-OUSLY?!
YOU JERK!! MY CLOTHES ARE IN SHREDS!!
THAT'S NOT MY FAULT.
ALL OUR CLOTHES...
ARE IN SHREDS...
GLANCE
DO NOT LOOK AT US.
AND I'M STILL STICKY, TOO...
WOW, BECKY. NO SHORTAGE OF WARDROBE MALFUNCTIONS WHEN I'M WITH YOU, IS THERE?
!
HEAT READINGS FROM ABOVE!!!

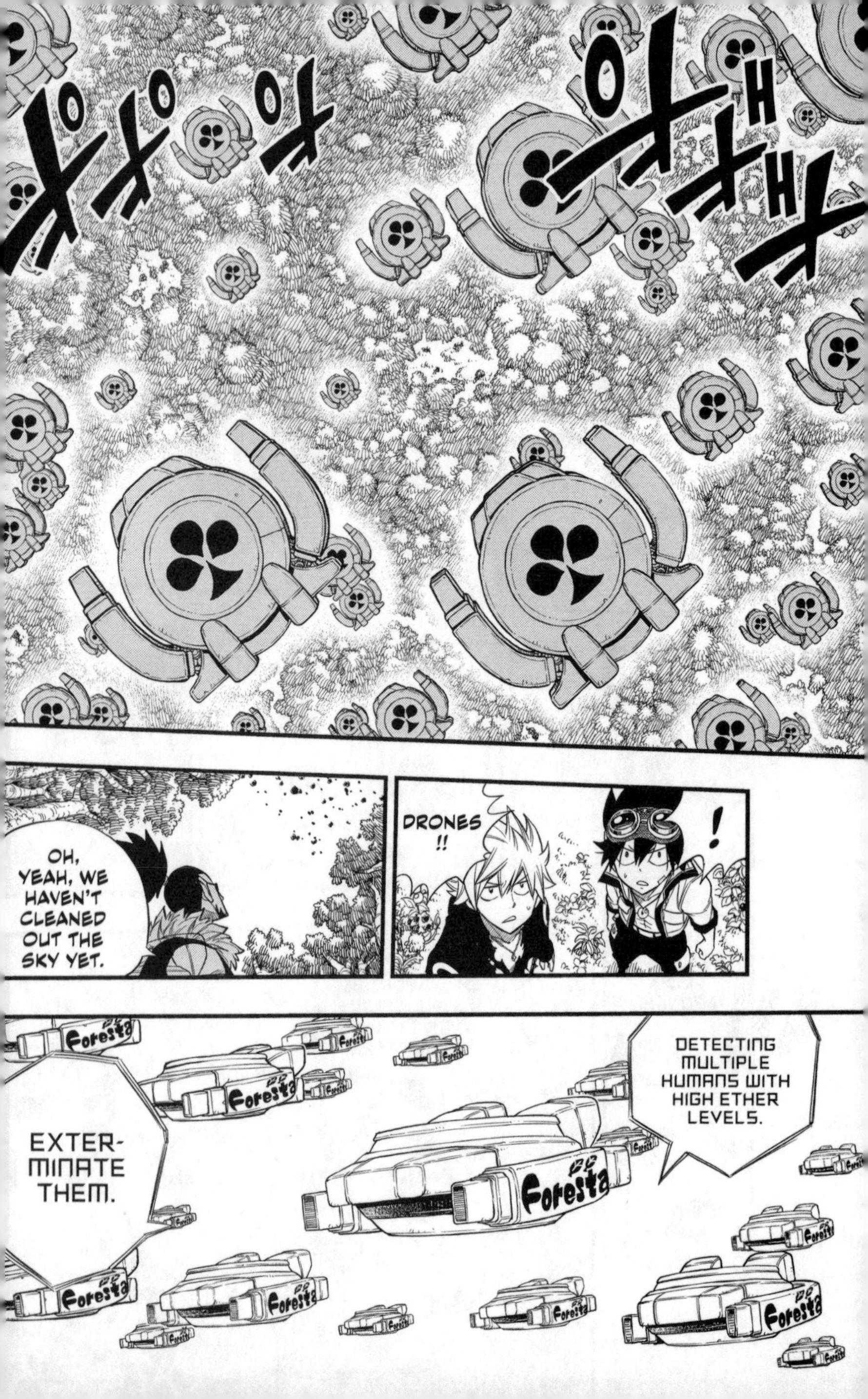
DRONES !!
!
OH, YEAH, WE HAVEN'T CLEANED OUT THE SKY YET.
DETECTING MULTIPLE HUMANS WITH HIGH ETHER LEVELS.
EXTER-MINATE THEM.

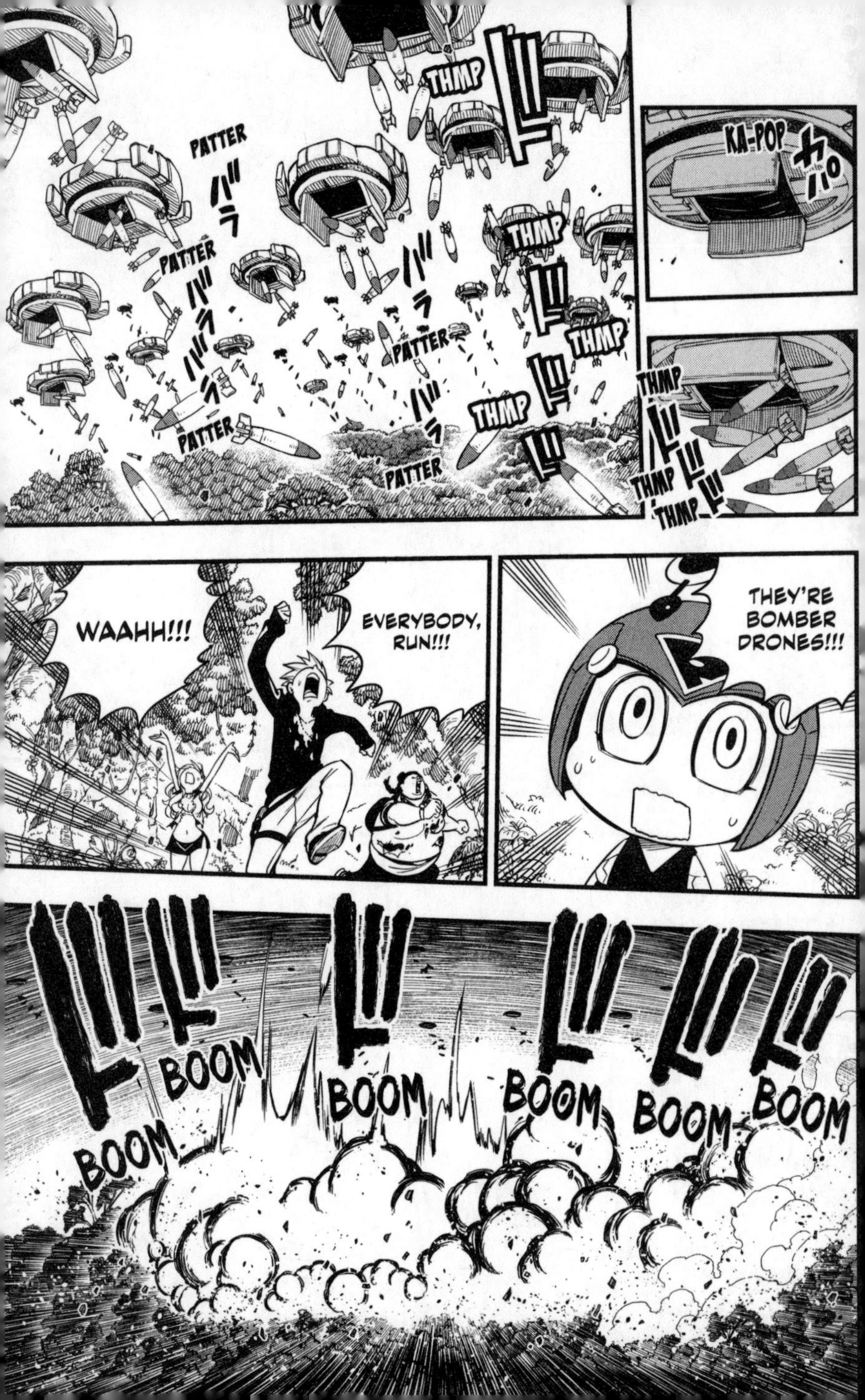
KA-POP
THMP
THMP
THMP
THMP
THMP
THMP
THMP
THMP
PATTER
PATTER
PATTER
PATTER
PATTER
THEY'RE BOMBER DRONES!!!
EVERYBODY, RUN!!!
WAAHH!!!
BOOM
BOOM
BOOM
BOOM
BOOM
BOOM

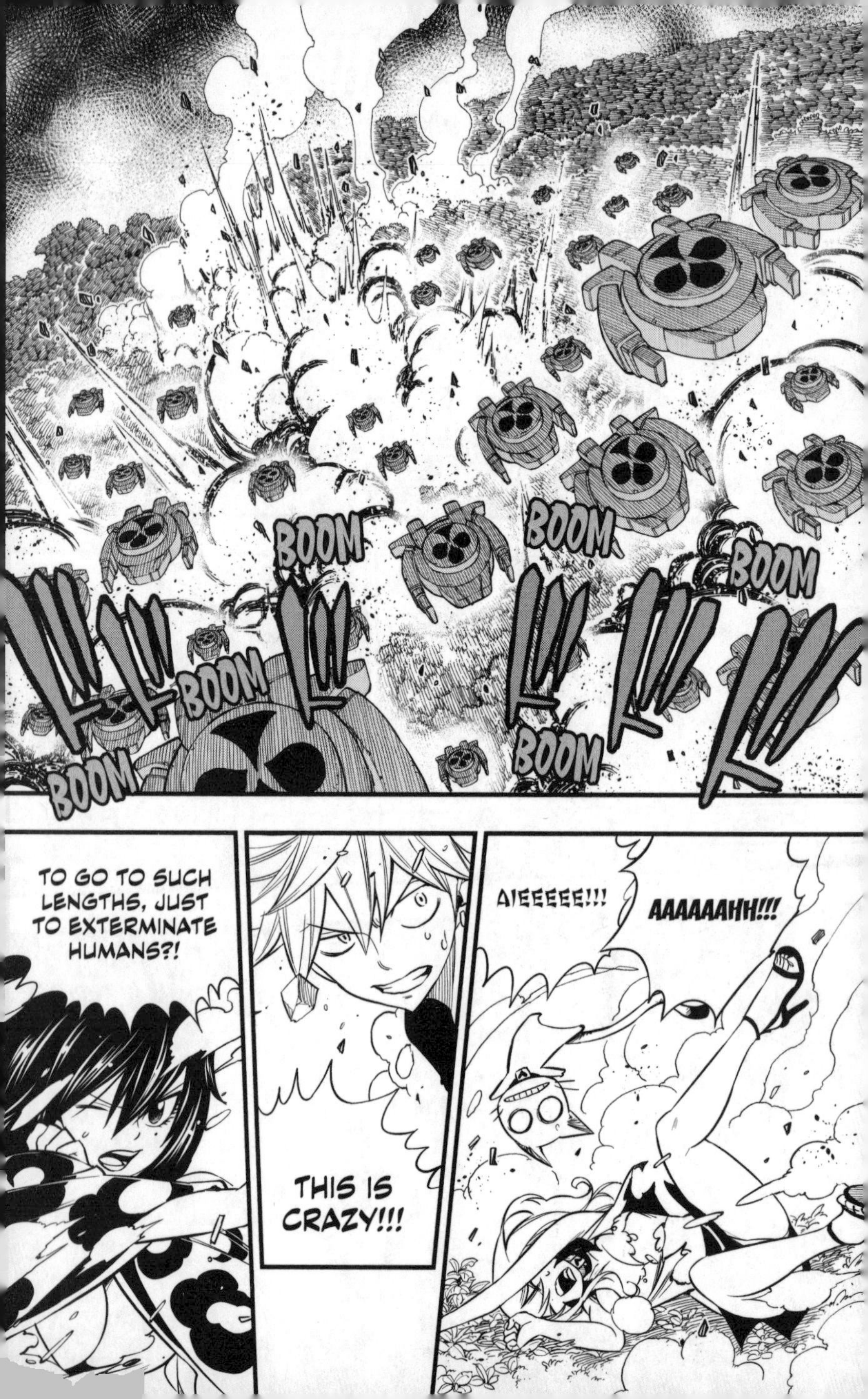
BOOM
BOOM
BOOM
BOOM
BOOM
BOOM
AAAAAAHH!!!
AIEEEEE!!!
THIS IS CRAZY!!!
TO GO TO SUCH LENGTHS, JUST TO EXTERMINATE HUMANS?!

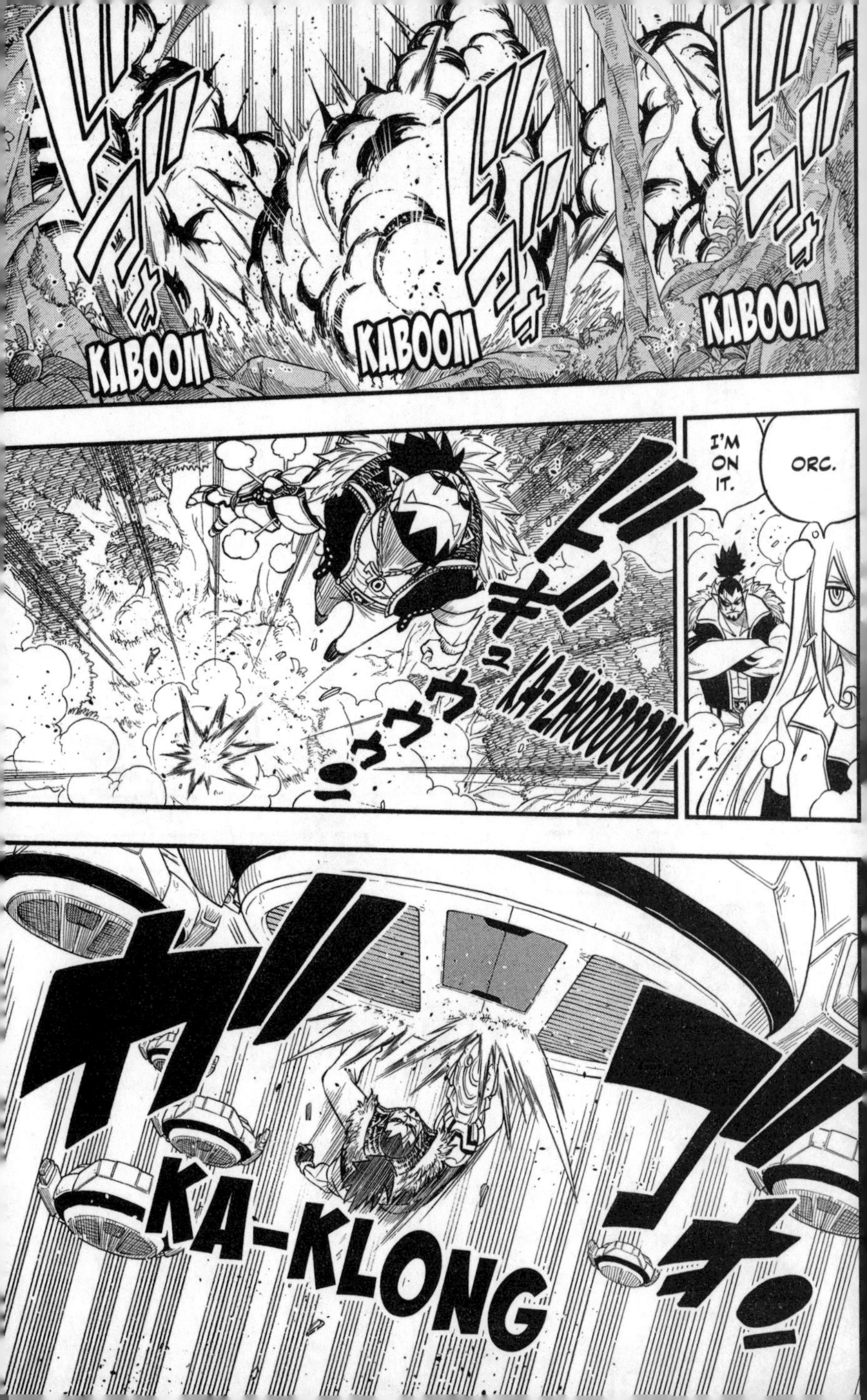
ドゴォ
KABOOM
ドゴォ
KABOOM
ドゴォ
KABOOM
ORC.
I'M ON IT.
ドキュウウン
KA-ZHOOOOOOM
ガゴーン
KA-KLONG

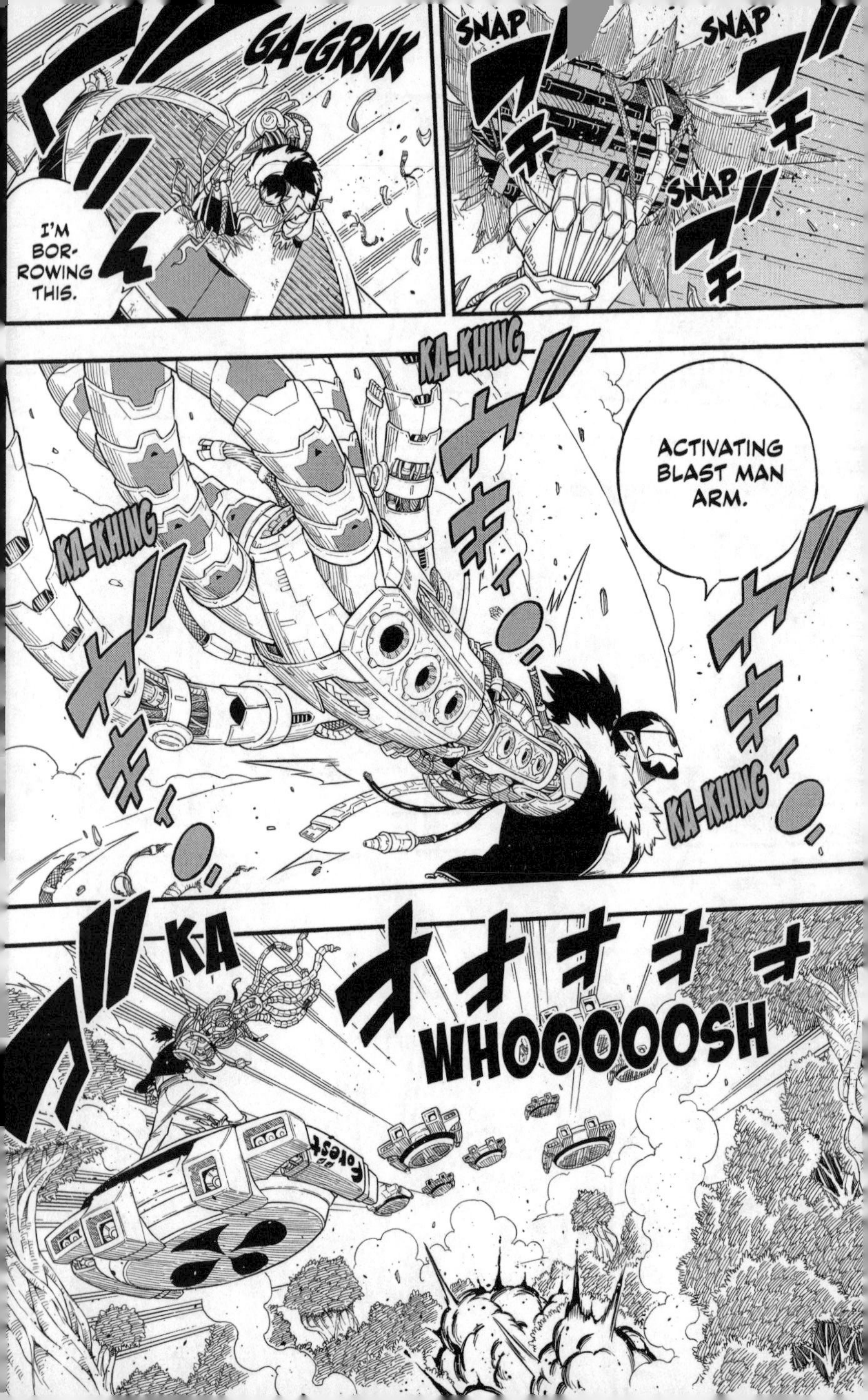

SNAP
SNAP
SNAP
GA-GRNK
I'M BOR-ROWING THIS.
KA-KHING
ACTIVATING BLAST MAN ARM.
KA-KHING
KA-KHING
KA
WHOOOOOSH
Forest

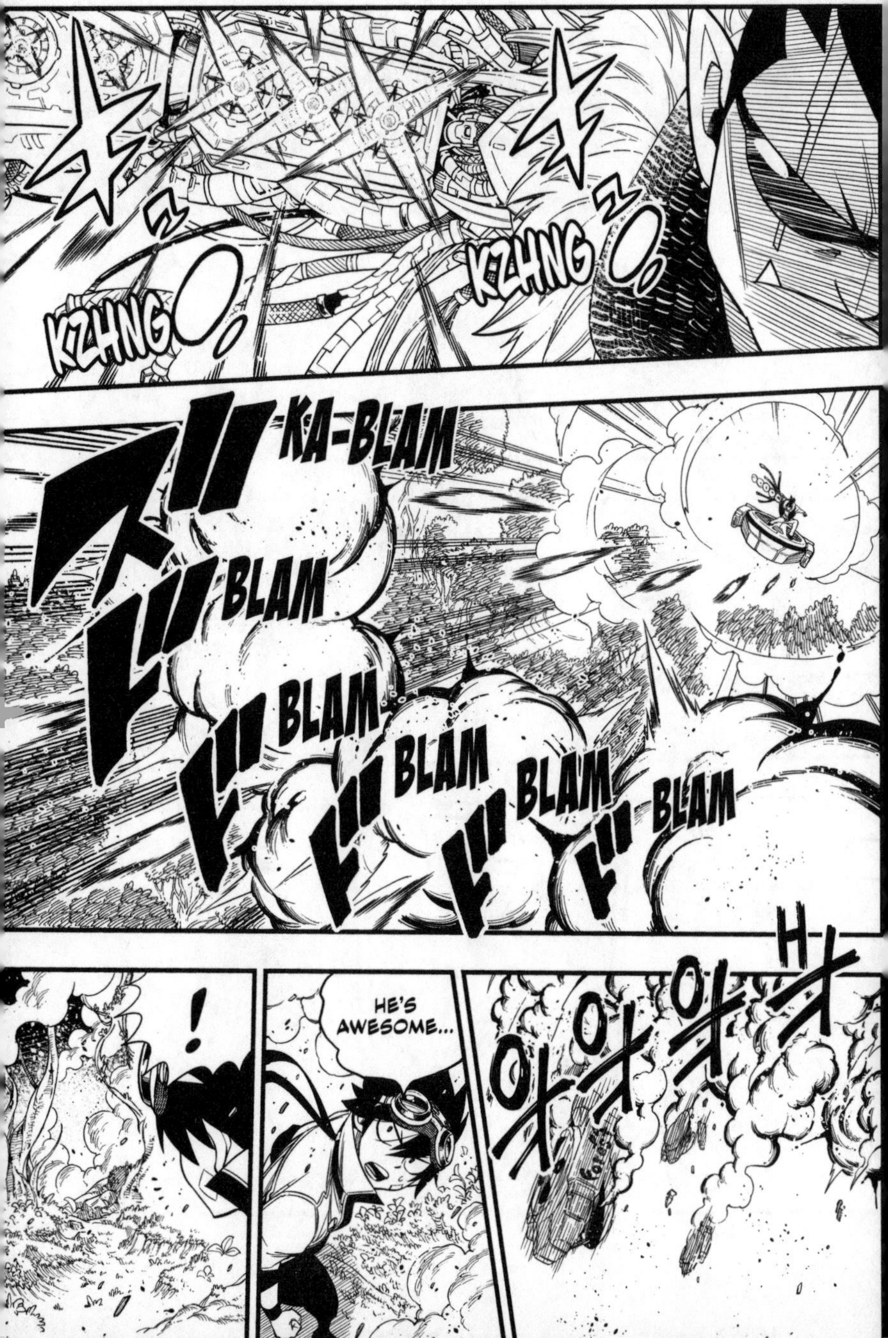
KZHNG
KZHNG
KA-BLAM
BLAM
BLAM
BLAM
BLAM
BLAM
OOOH
HE'S AWESOME...
!

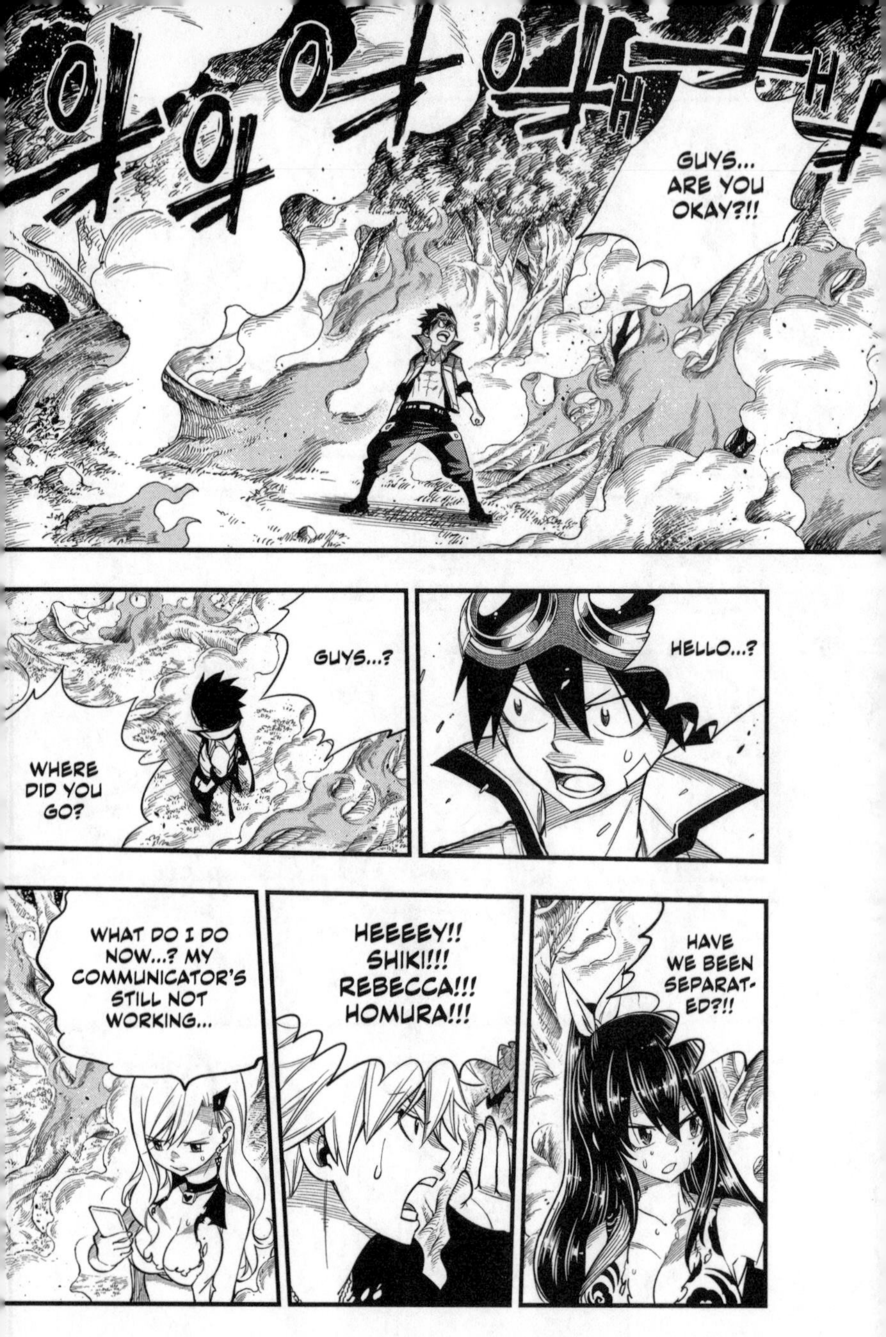
GUYS... ARE YOU OKAY?!!
HELLO...?
GUYS...?
WHERE DID YOU GO?
HAVE WE BEEN SEPARAT-ED?!!
HEEEEY!! SHIKI!!!! REBECCA!!! HOMURA!!!
WHAT DO I DO NOW...? MY COMMUNICATOR'S STILL NOT WORKING...

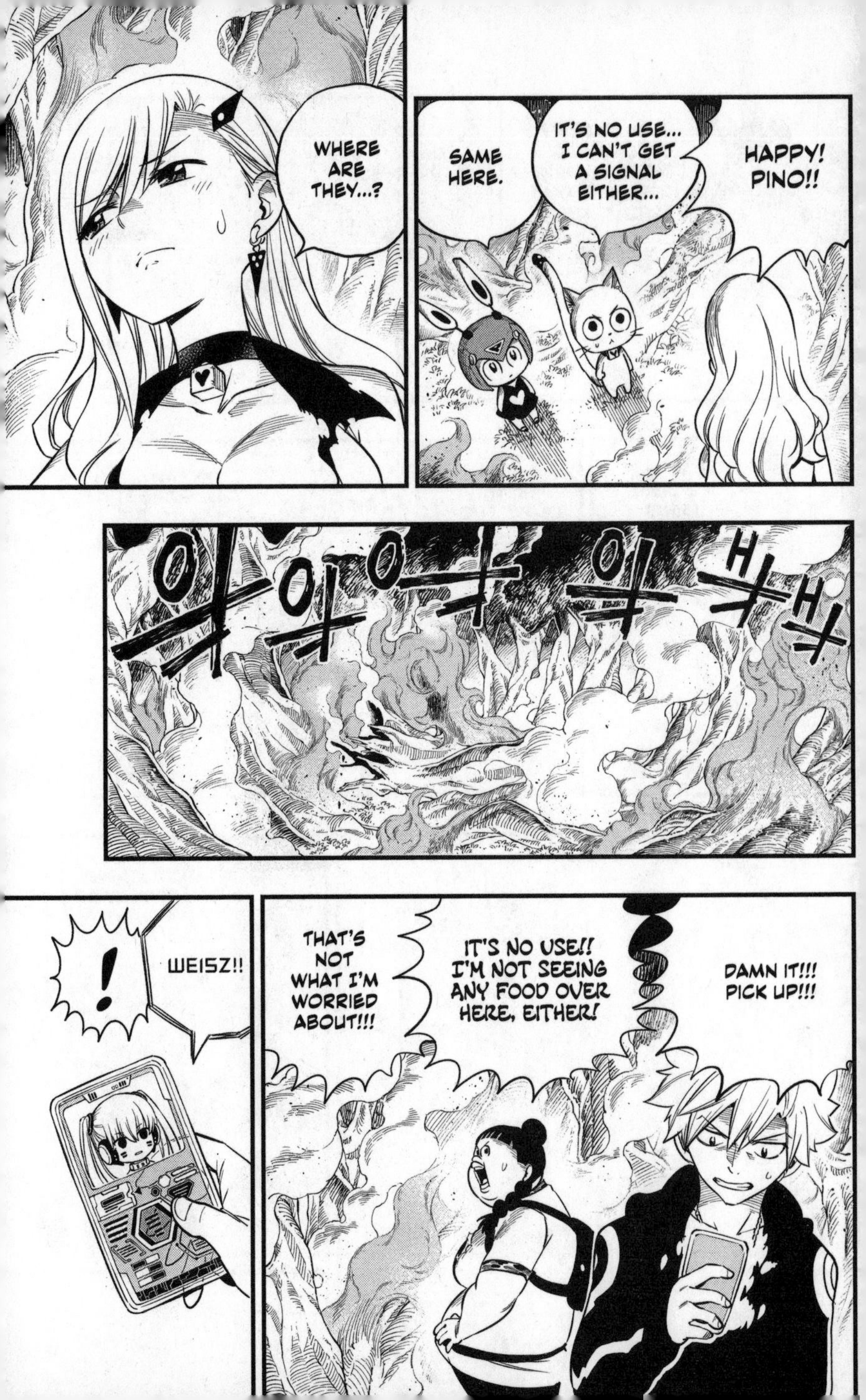
HAPPY! PINO!!
IT'S NO USE... I CAN'T GET A SIGNAL EITHER...
SAME HERE.
WHERE ARE THEY...?
OOOOHH
DAMN IT!!! PICK UP!!!
IT'S NO USE!! I'M NOT SEEING ANY FOOD OVER HERE, EITHER!
THAT'S NOT WHAT I'M WORRIED ABOUT!!!
!
WEISZ!!

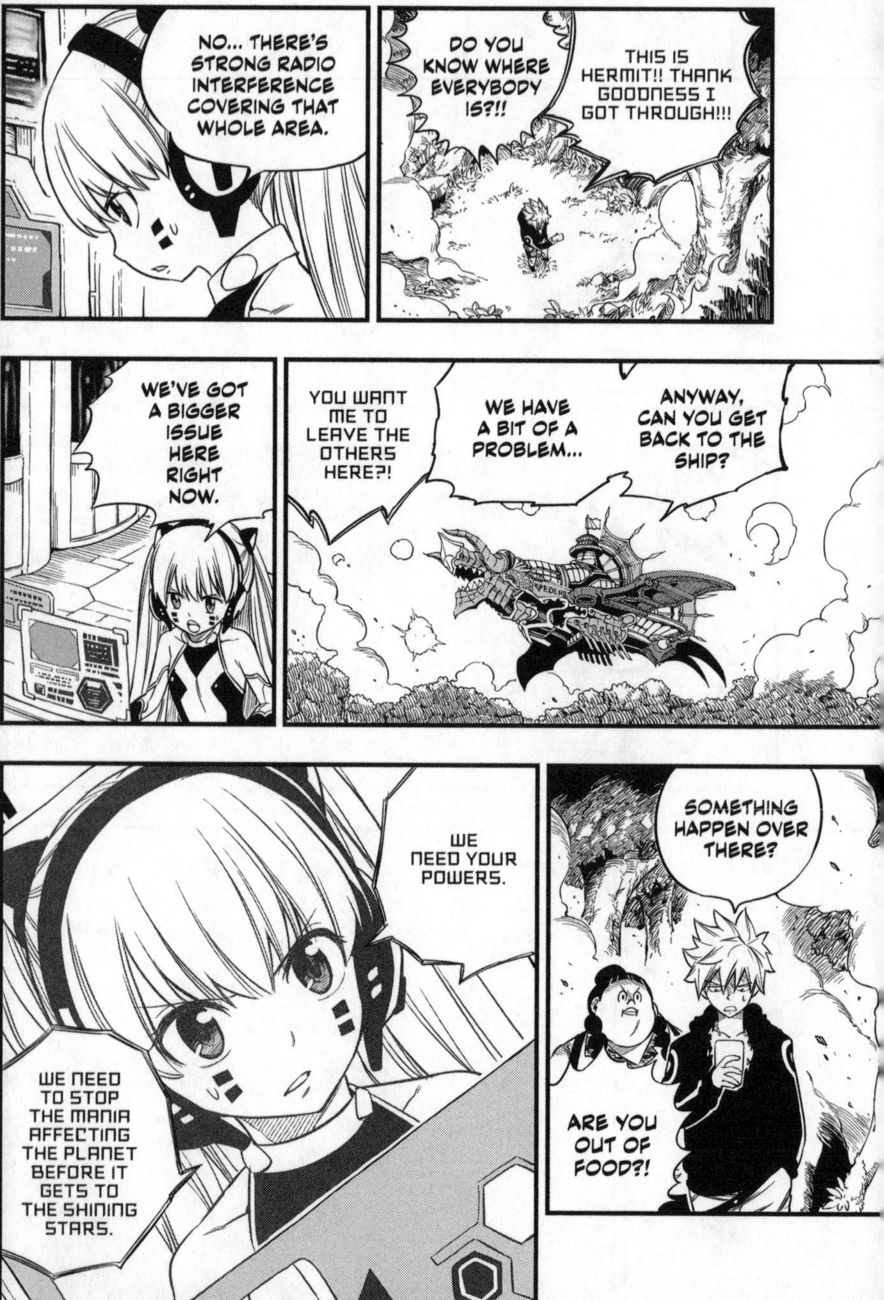
THIS IS HERMIT!! THANK GOODNESS I GOT THROUGH!!!
DO YOU KNOW WHERE EVERYBODY IS?!!
NO... THERE'S STRONG RADIO INTERFERENCE COVERING THAT WHOLE AREA.
ANYWAY, CAN YOU GET BACK TO THE SHIP?
WE HAVE A BIT OF A PROBLEM...
YOU WANT ME TO LEAVE THE OTHERS HERE?!
WE'VE GOT A BIGGER ISSUE HERE RIGHT NOW.
SOMETHING HAPPEN OVER THERE?
ARE YOU OUT OF FOOD?!
WE NEED YOUR POWERS.
WE NEED TO STOP THE MANIA AFFECTING THE PLANET BEFORE IT GETS TO THE SHINING STARS.

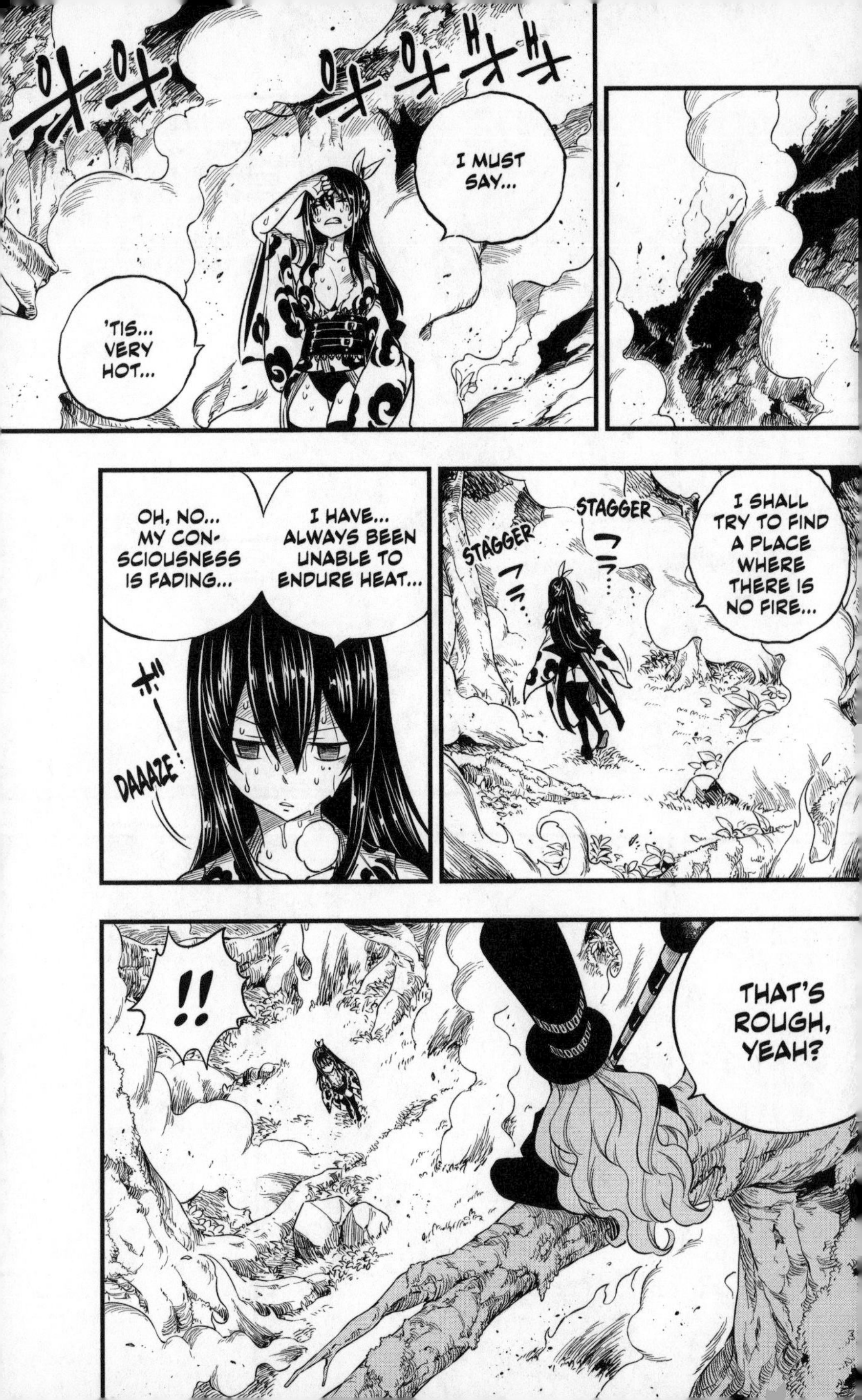
I MUST SAY...
'TIS... VERY HOT...
STAGGER
STAGGER
I SHALL TRY TO FIND A PLACE WHERE THERE IS NO FIRE...
I HAVE... ALWAYS BEEN UNABLE TO ENDURE HEAT...
OH, NO... MY CONSCIOUSNESS IS FADING...
DAAAZE
THAT'S ROUGH, YEAH?
!!

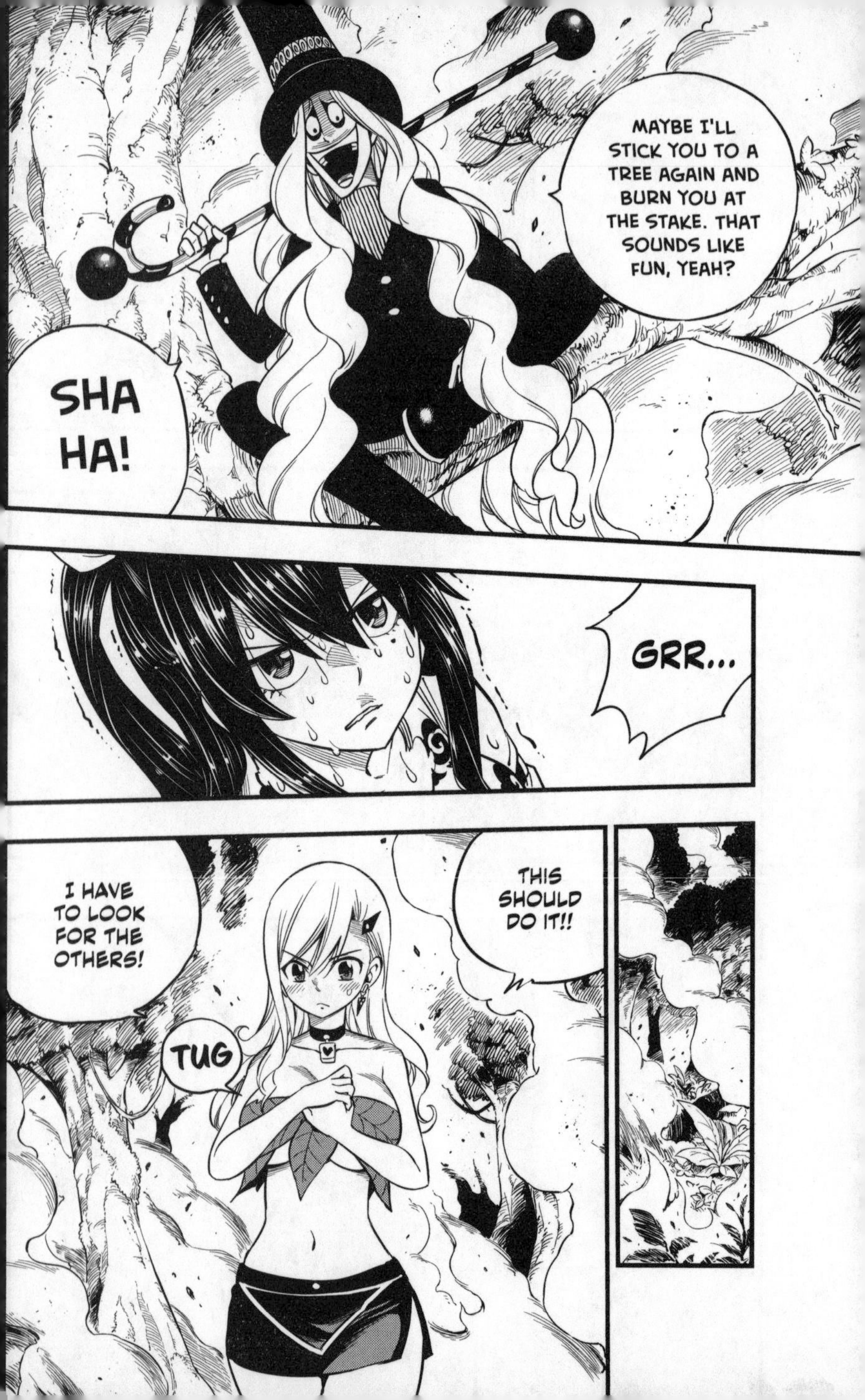
MAYBE I'LL STICK YOU TO A TREE AGAIN AND BURN YOU AT THE STAKE. THAT SOUNDS LIKE FUN, YEAH?
SHA HA!
GRR...
THIS SHOULD DO IT!!
I HAVE TO LOOK FOR THE OTHERS!
TUG

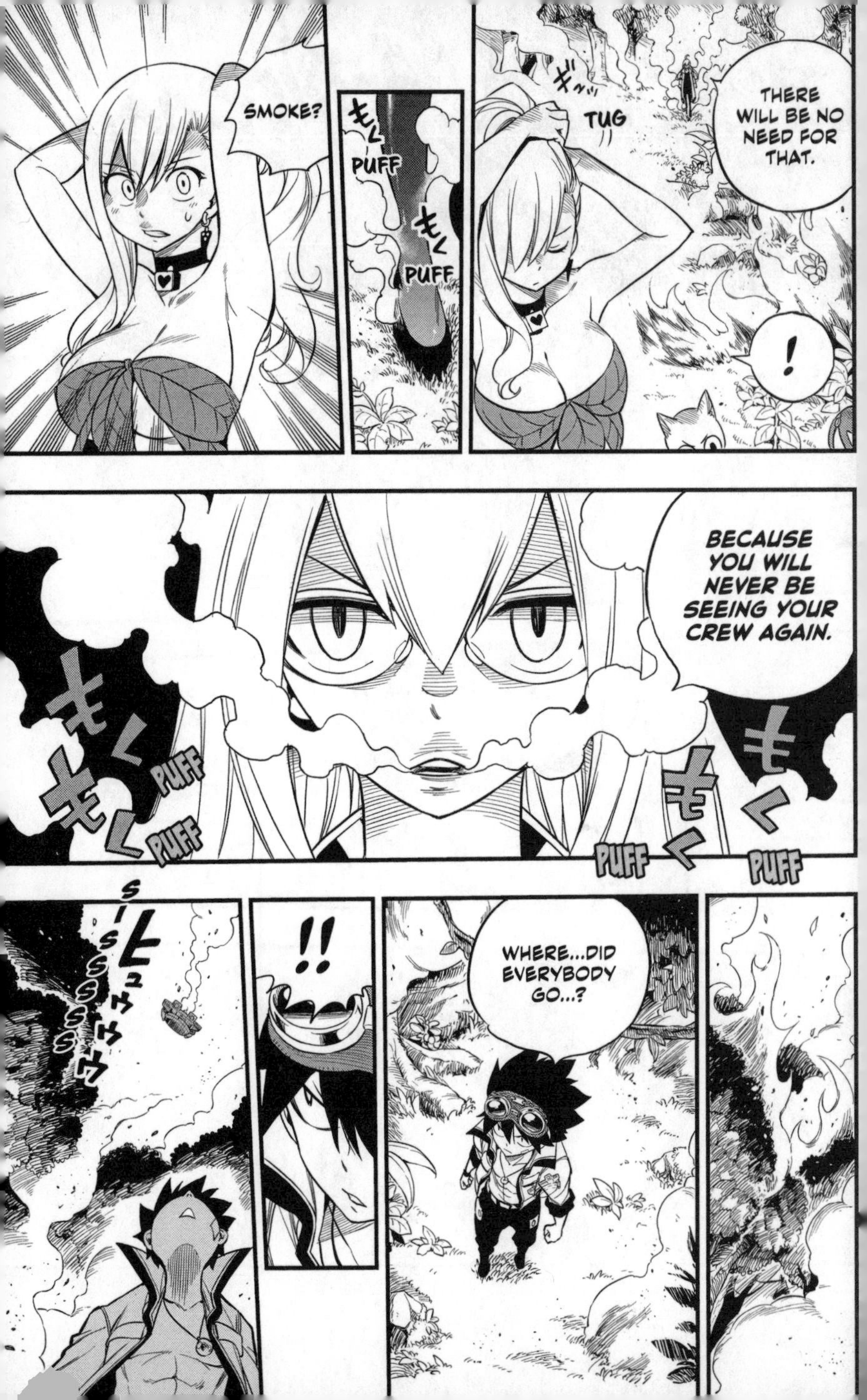
THERE WILL BE NO NEED FOR THAT.
TUG
!
PUFF
PUFF
SMOKE?
BECAUSE YOU WILL NEVER BE SEEING YOUR CREW AGAIN.
PUFF
PUFF
PUFF
PUFF
WHERE...DID EVERYBODY GO...?
!!
SSSSSS

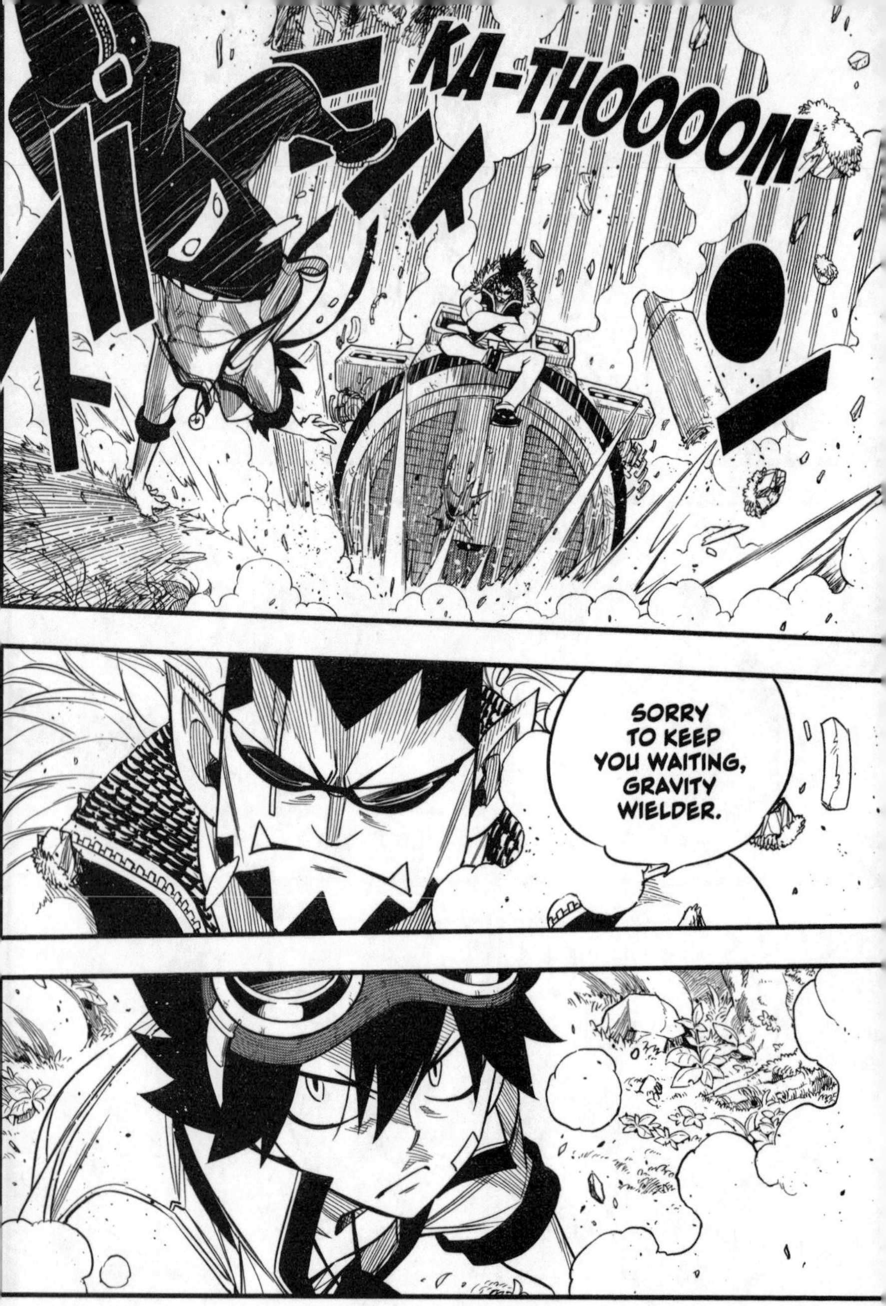
KA-THOOOOM
SORRY TO KEEP YOU WAITING, GRAVITY WIELDER.

EDENS ZERO

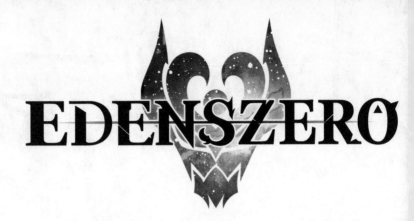

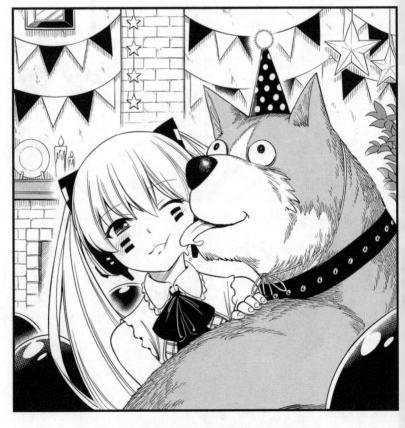

CHAPTER 117: SHIKI VS. ORC

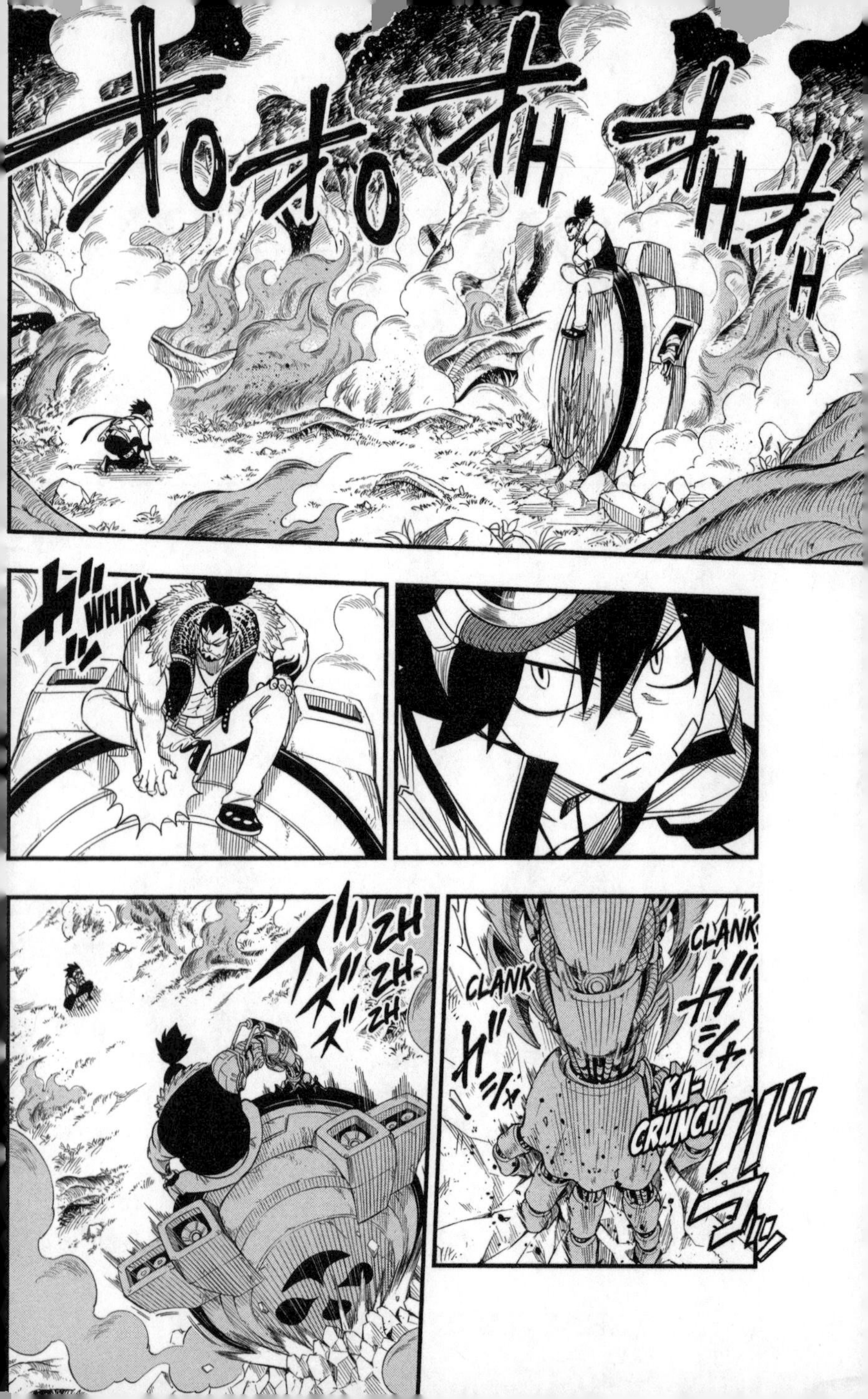
WHAK
CLANK
CLANK
KA-CRUNCH
ZH ZH ZH

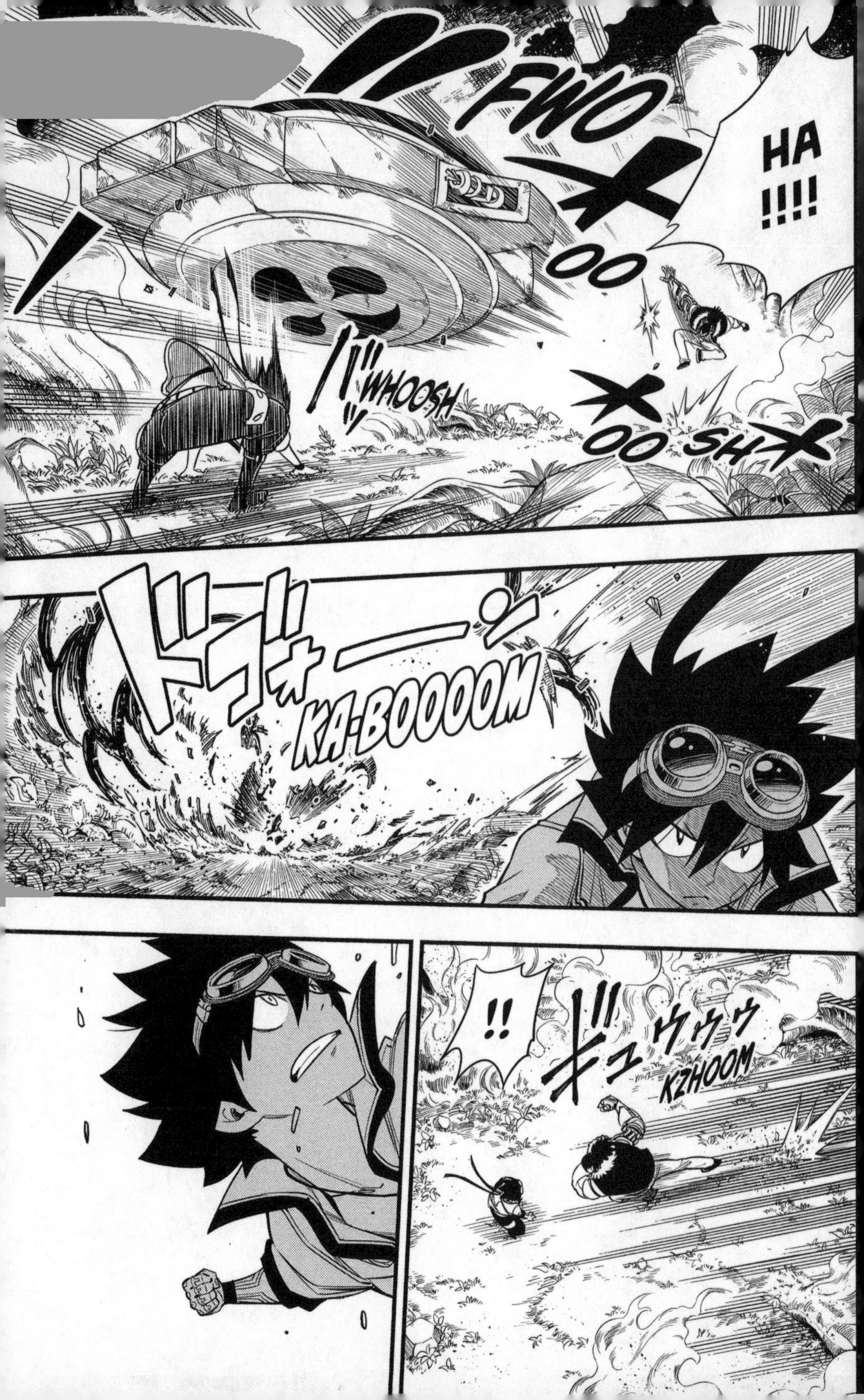
HA !!!!
FWOOO
WHOOSH
WHOOSH
ドゴォーン
KA-BOOOOM
!!
ギュウウウ
KZHOOM

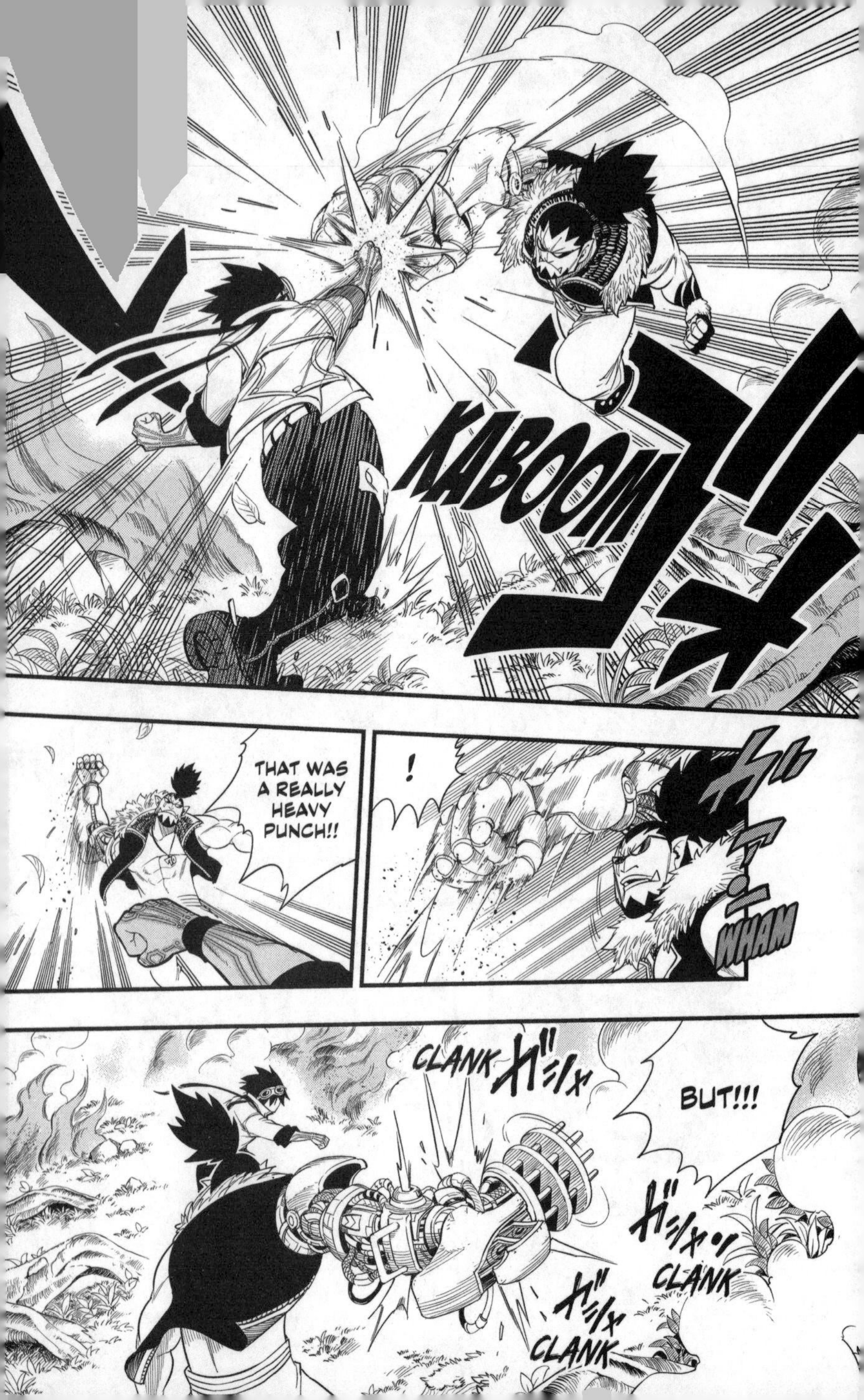
KABOOM
!
WHAM
THAT WAS A REALLY HEAVY PUNCH!!
BUT!!!
CLANK
CLANK
CLANK

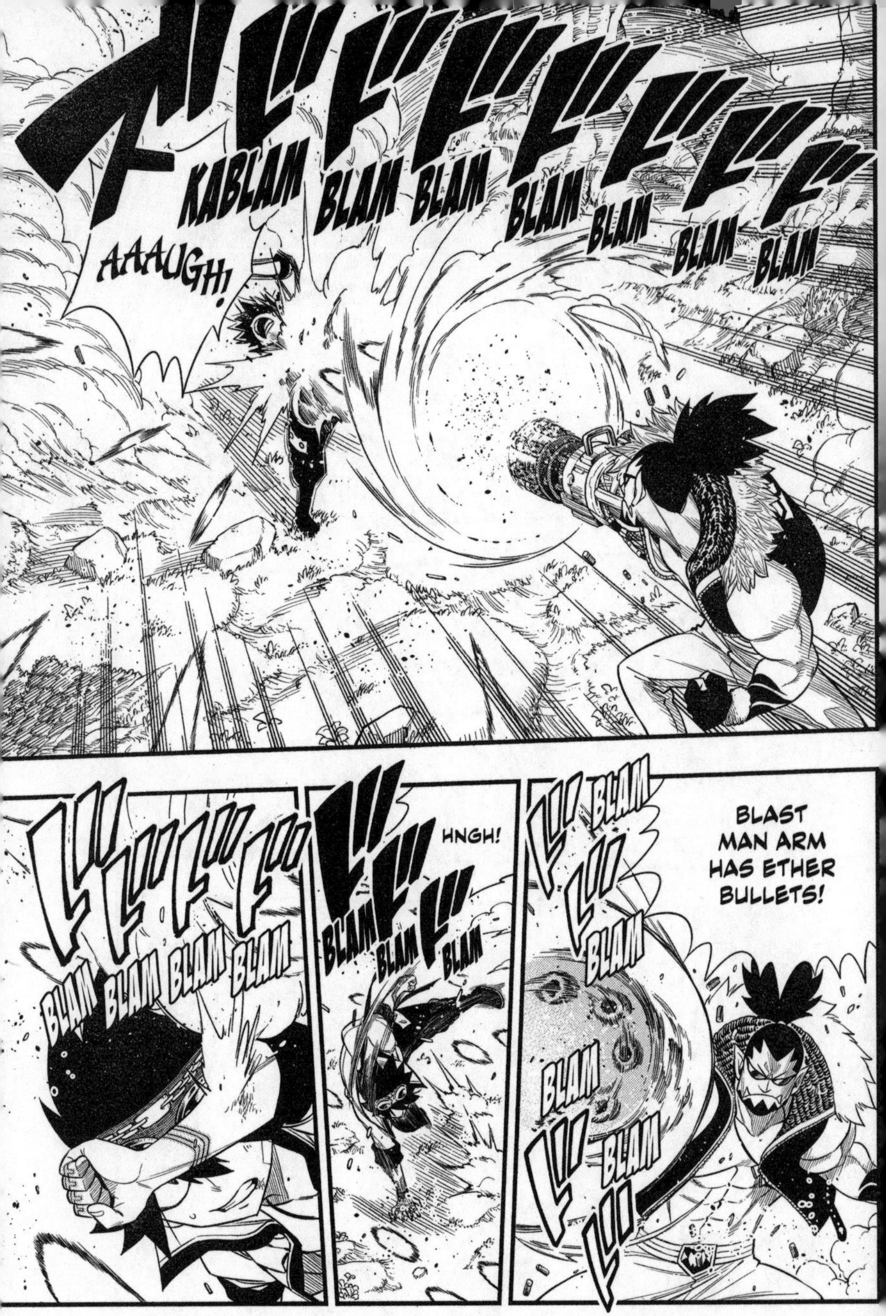
KABLAM BLAM BLAM BLAM BLAM BLAM BLAM
AAAUGH!
BLAST MAN ARM HAS ETHER BULLETS!
BLAM BLAM BLAM BLAM
HNGH!
BLAM BLAM BLAM
BLAM BLAM BLAM BLAM

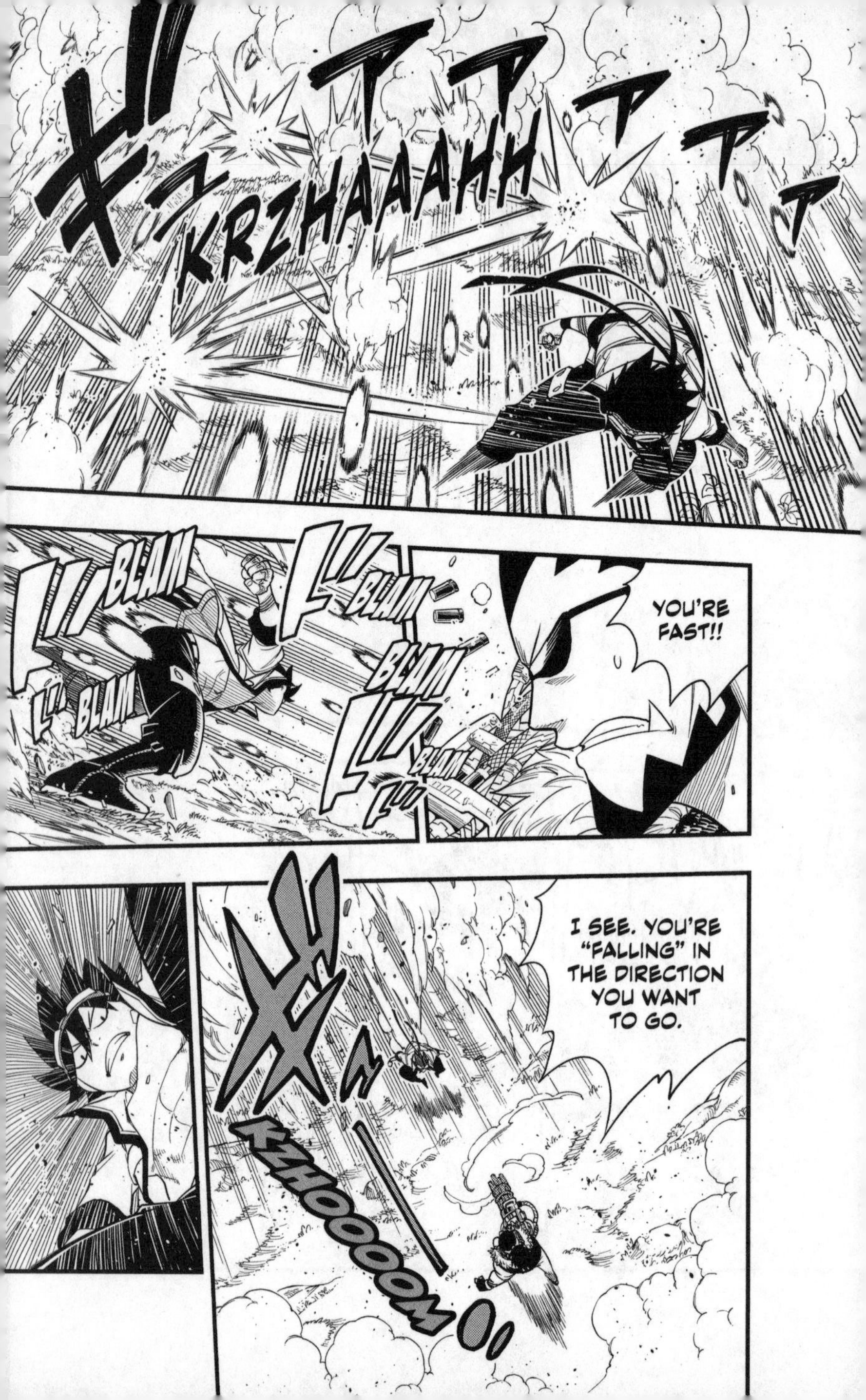
KRZHAAAHH
YOU'RE FAST!!
BLAM
BLAM
BLAM
BLAM
BLAM
I SEE. YOU'RE "FALLING" IN THE DIRECTION YOU WANT TO GO.
KZHOOOOM

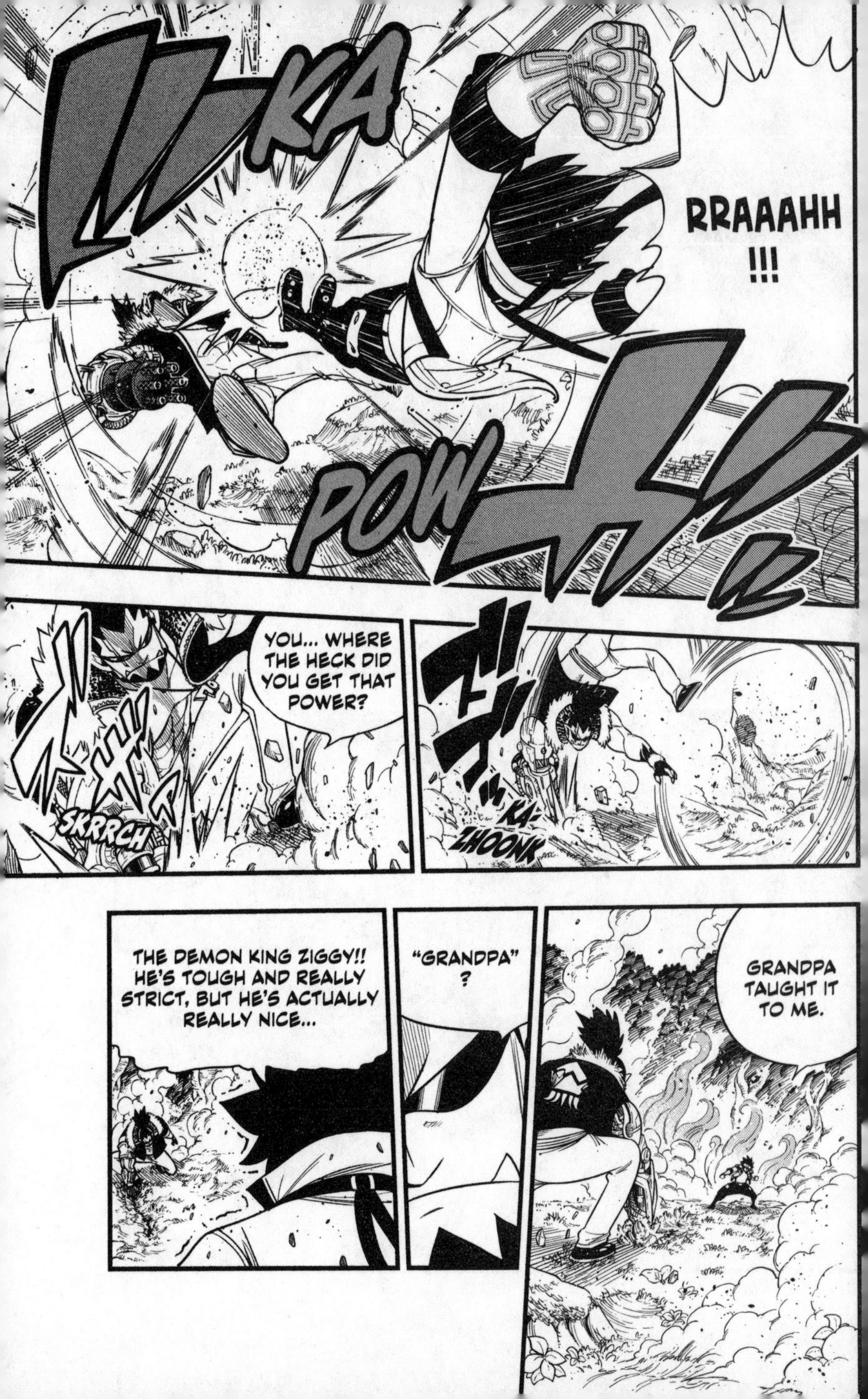
KA
RRAAAHH !!!
POW
KA-ZHOONK
YOU... WHERE THE HECK DID YOU GET THAT POWER?
SKRRCH
GRANDPA TAUGHT IT TO ME.
"GRANDPA" ?
THE DEMON KING ZIGGY!! HE'S TOUGH AND REALLY STRICT, BUT HE'S ACTUALLY REALLY NICE...

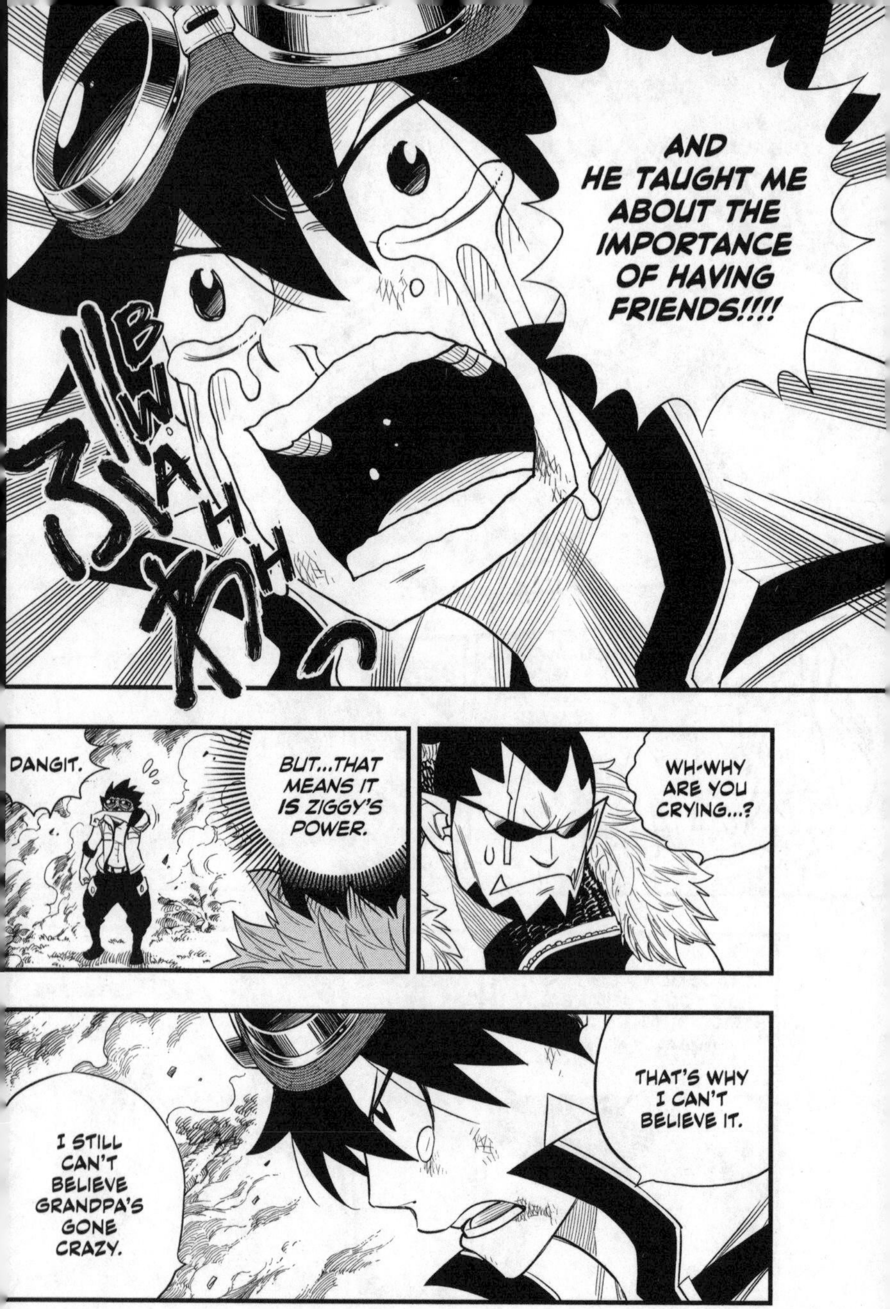
AND HE TAUGHT ME ABOUT THE IMPORTANCE OF HAVING FRIENDS!!!!
BWAHH
WH-WHY ARE YOU CRYING...?
BUT...THAT MEANS IT IS ZIGGY'S POWER.
DANGIT.
THAT'S WHY I CAN'T BELIEVE IT.
I STILL CAN'T BELIEVE GRANDPA'S GONE CRAZY.

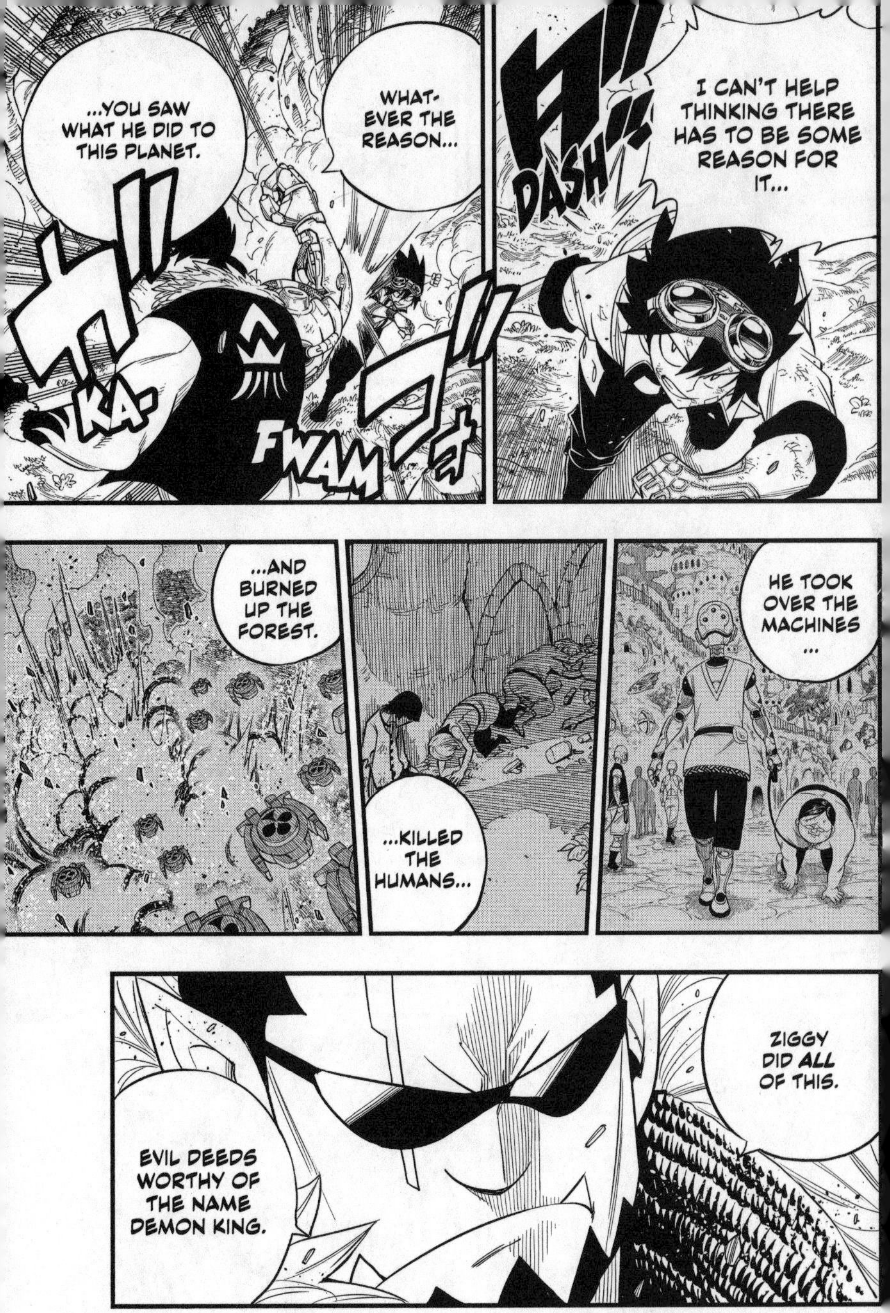
I CAN'T HELP THINKING THERE HAS TO BE SOME REASON FOR IT...
DASH
WHAT-EVER THE REASON...
...YOU SAW WHAT HE DID TO THIS PLANET.
FWAM
KA-
HE TOOK OVER THE MACHINES ...
...KILLED THE HUMANS...
...AND BURNED UP THE FOREST.
ZIGGY DID **ALL** OF THIS.
EVIL DEEDS WORTHY OF THE NAME DEMON KING.

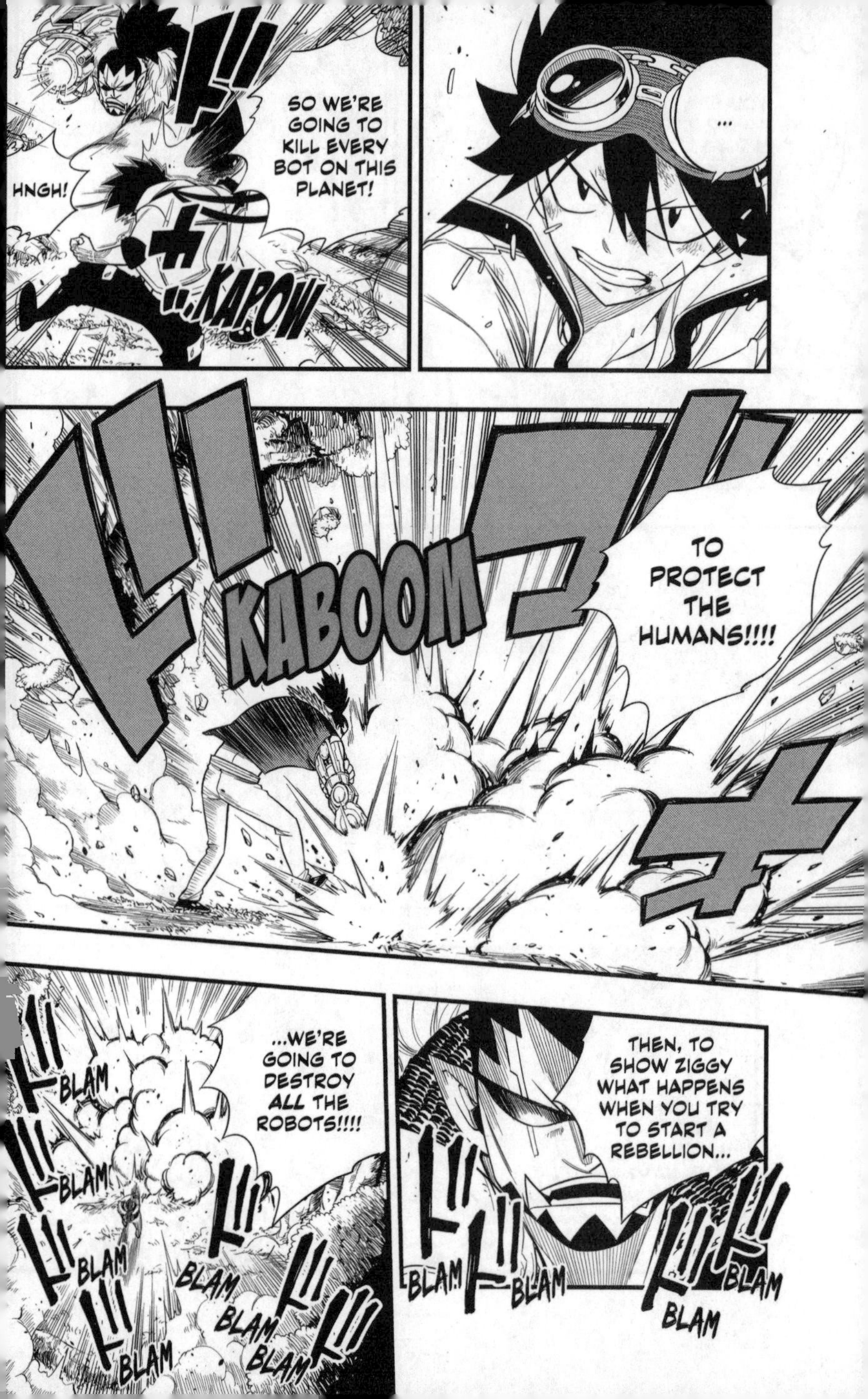
...
SO WE'RE GOING TO KILL EVERY BOT ON THIS PLANET!
HNGH!
KAPOW
KABOOM
TO PROTECT THE HUMANS!!!!
THEN, TO SHOW ZIGGY WHAT HAPPENS WHEN YOU TRY TO START A REBELLION...
BLAM
BLAM
BLAM
BLAM
BLAM
...WE'RE GOING TO DESTROY ALL THE ROBOTS!!!!
BLAM
BLAM
BLAM
BLAM
BLAM
BLAM
BLAM

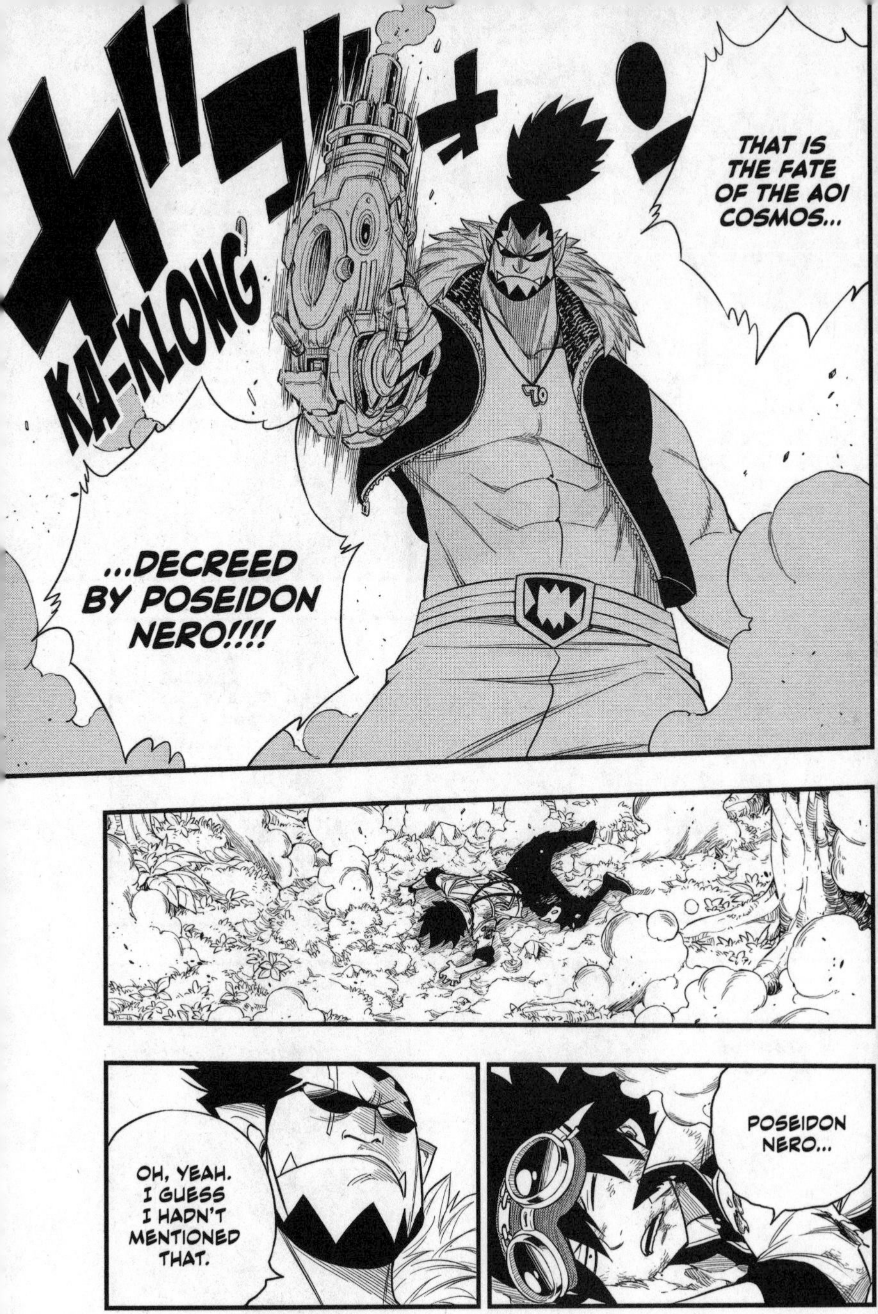
KA-KLONG
THAT IS THE FATE OF THE AOI COSMOS...
...DECREED BY POSEIDON NERO!!!!
POSEIDON NERO...
OH, YEAH. I GUESS I HADN'T MENTIONED THAT.

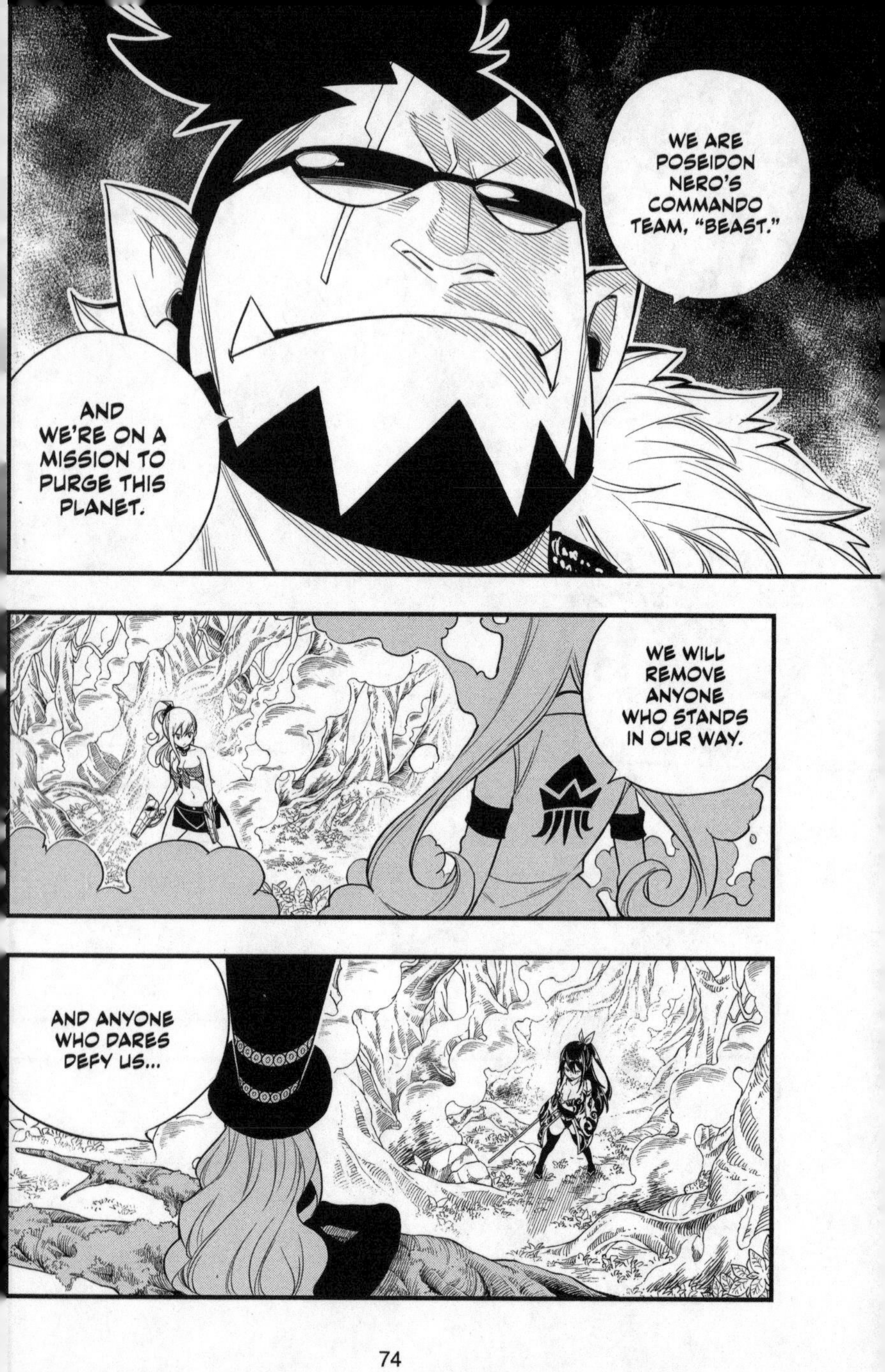
WE ARE POSEIDON NERO'S COMMANDO TEAM, "BEAST."
AND WE'RE ON A MISSION TO PURGE THIS PLANET.
WE WILL REMOVE ANYONE WHO STANDS IN OUR WAY.
AND ANYONE WHO DARES DEFY US...

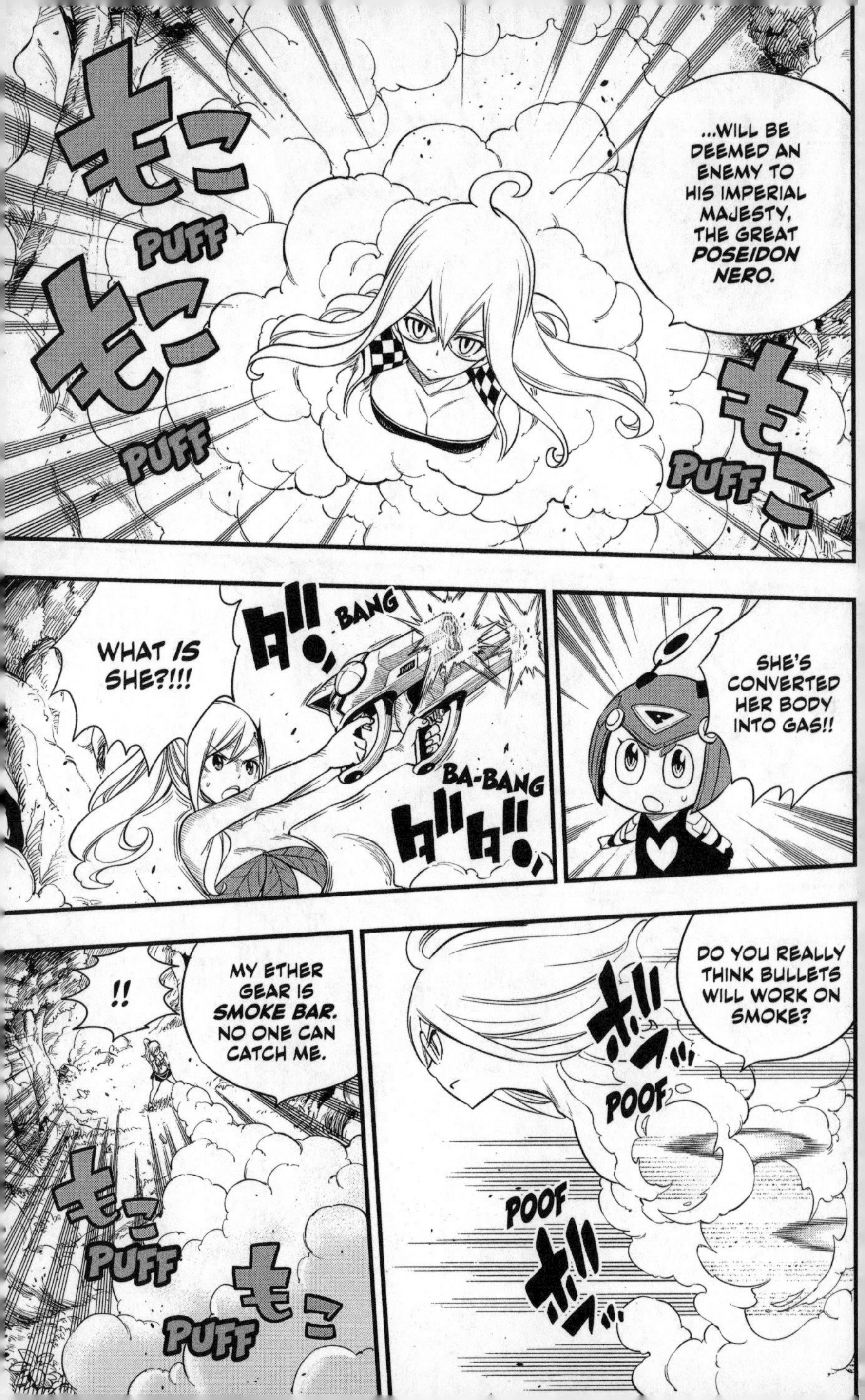
...WILL BE DEEMED AN ENEMY TO HIS IMPERIAL MAJESTY, THE GREAT *POSEIDON NERO.*
もこ
PUFF
もこ
PUFF
もこ
PUFF
SHE'S CONVERTED HER BODY INTO GAS!!
ガッ
BANG
WHAT *IS* SHE?!!!
BA-BANG
ガガッ
DO YOU REALLY THINK BULLETS WILL WORK ON SMOKE?
ボフッ
POOF
POOF
ボフッ
MY ETHER GEAR IS *SMOKE BAR.* NO ONE CAN CATCH ME.
!!
もこ
PUFF
もこ
PUFF

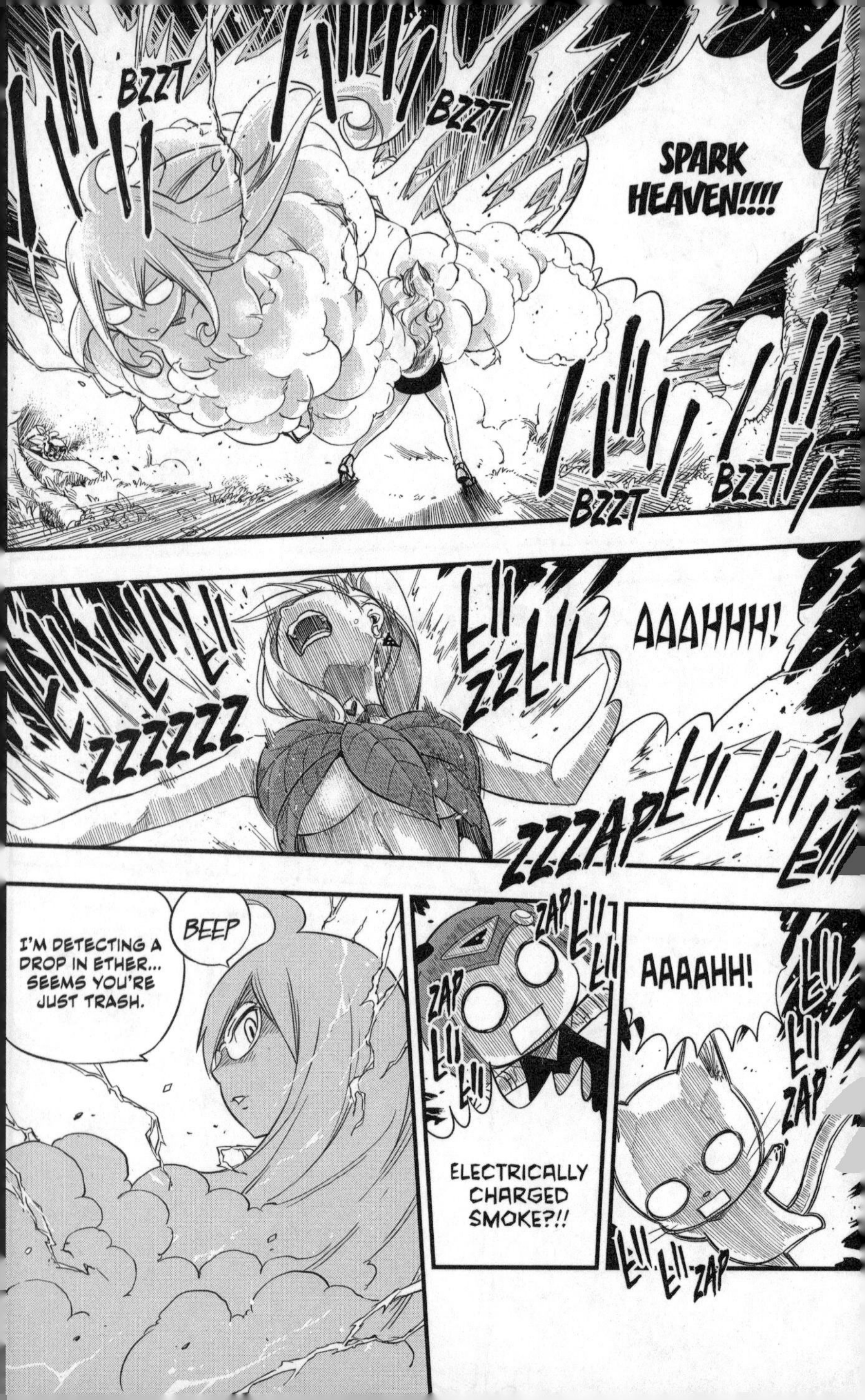

SPARK HEAVEN!!!!
BZZT
BZZT
BZZT
BZZT
AAAHHH!
ZZZAP
ZZZZZZ
AAAAHH!
ZAP
ZAP
ZAP
ZAP
ELECTRICALLY CHARGED SMOKE?!!
BEEP
I'M DETECTING A DROP IN ETHER... SEEMS YOU'RE JUST TRASH.

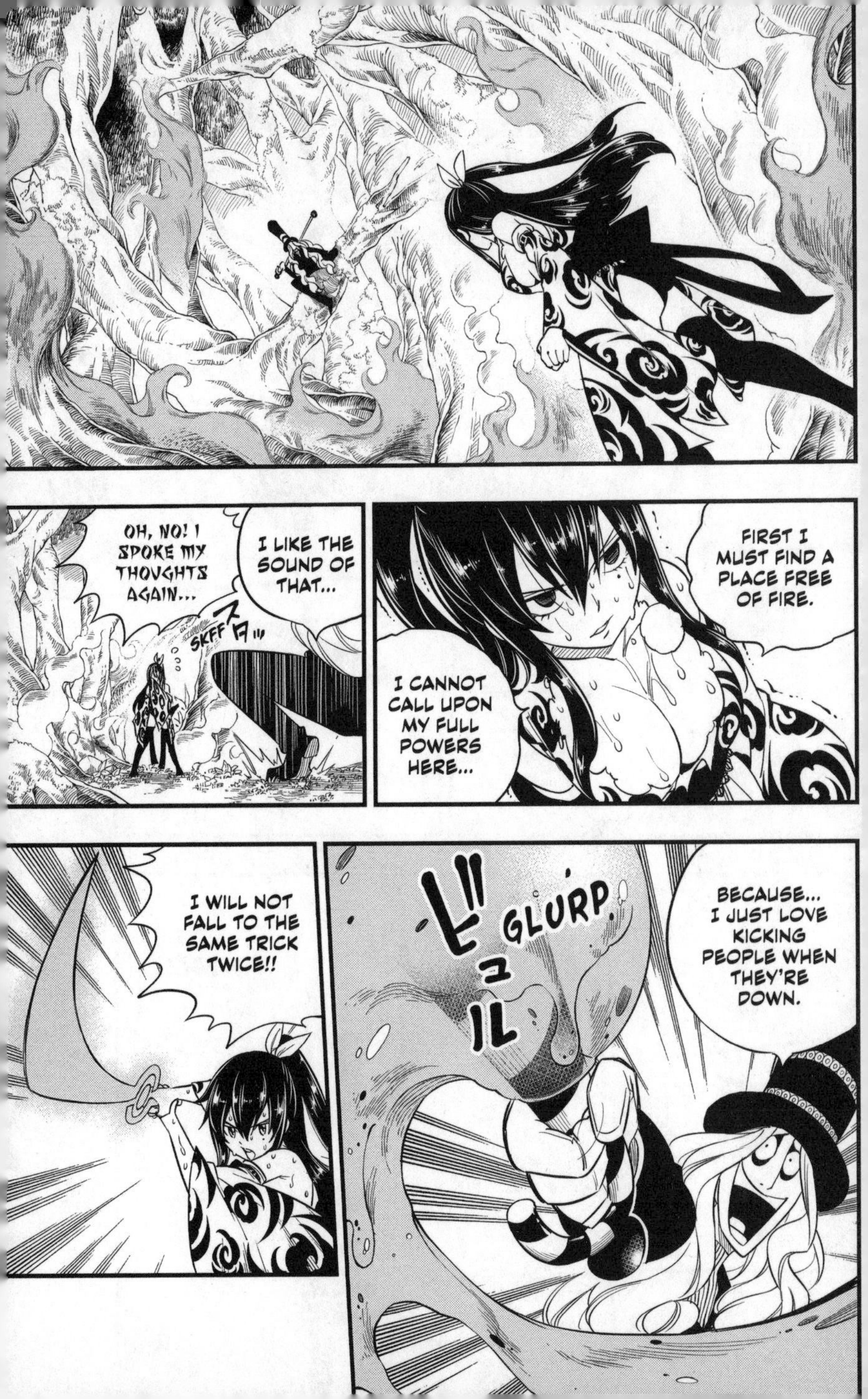
FIRST I MUST FIND A PLACE FREE OF FIRE.
I CANNOT CALL UPON MY FULL POWERS HERE...
I LIKE THE SOUND OF THAT...
OH, NO! I SPOKE MY THOUGHTS AGAIN...
SKFF
BECAUSE... I JUST LOVE KICKING PEOPLE WHEN THEY'RE DOWN.
GLURP
I WILL NOT FALL TO THE SAME TRICK TWICE!!

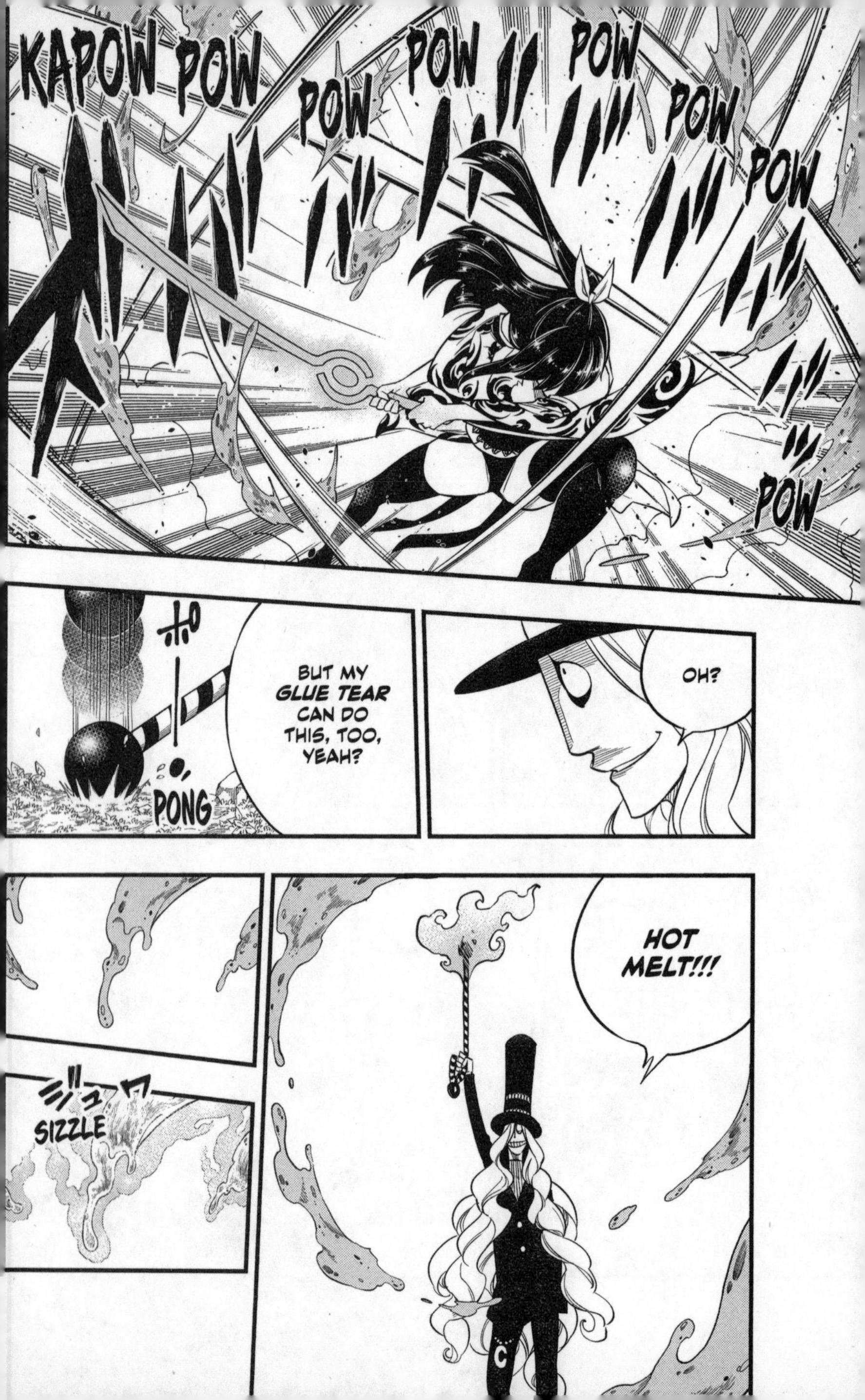
POW
POW
POW
POW
POW
POW
KAPOW POW
POW
OH?
BUT MY GLUE TEAR CAN DO THIS, TOO, YEAH?
PONG
HOT MELT!!!
SIZZLE

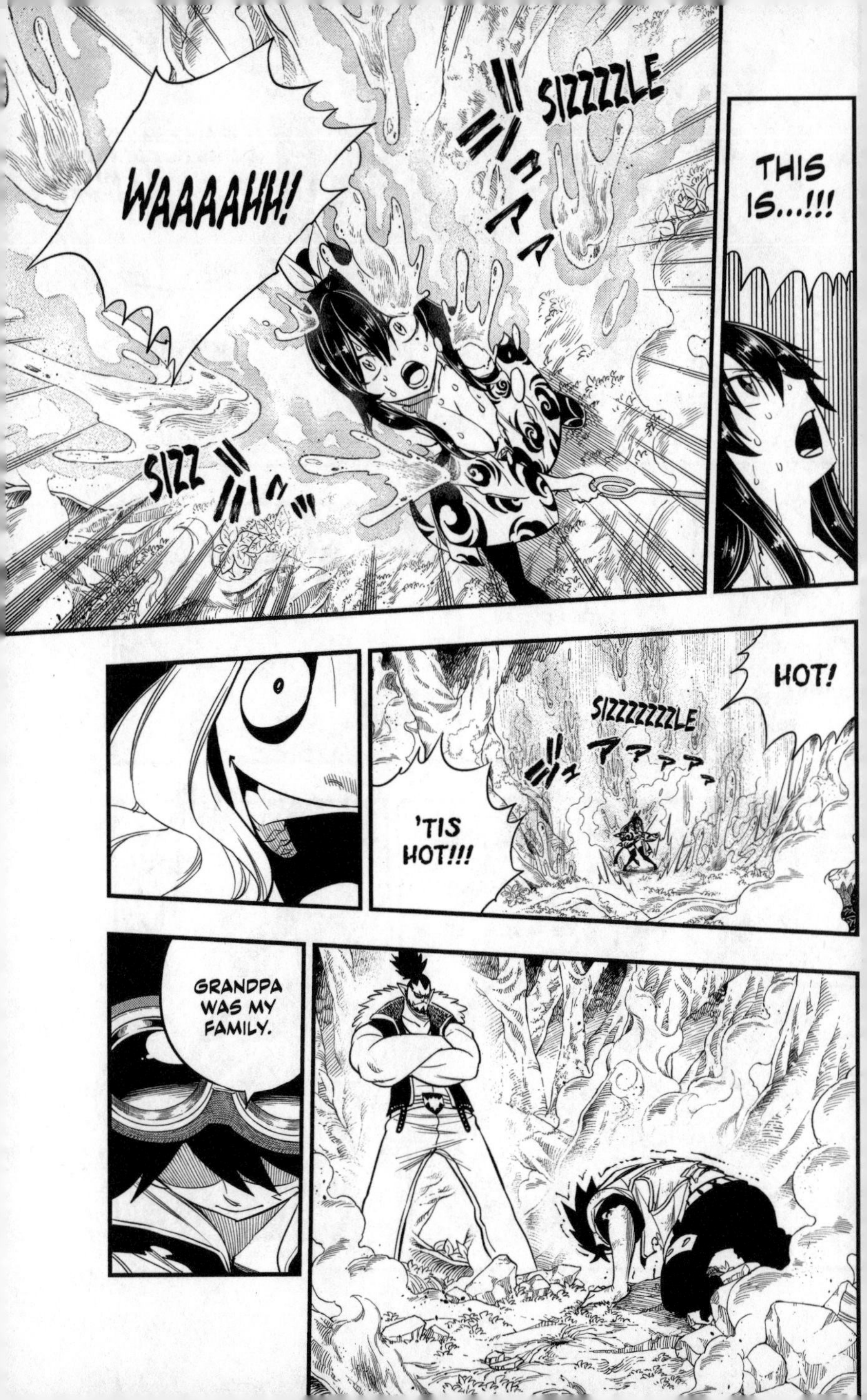
THIS IS...!!!
SIZZZZZLE
WAAAAHH!
SIZZ
HOT!
SIZZZZZZZLE
'TIS HOT!!!
GRANDPA WAS MY FAMILY.

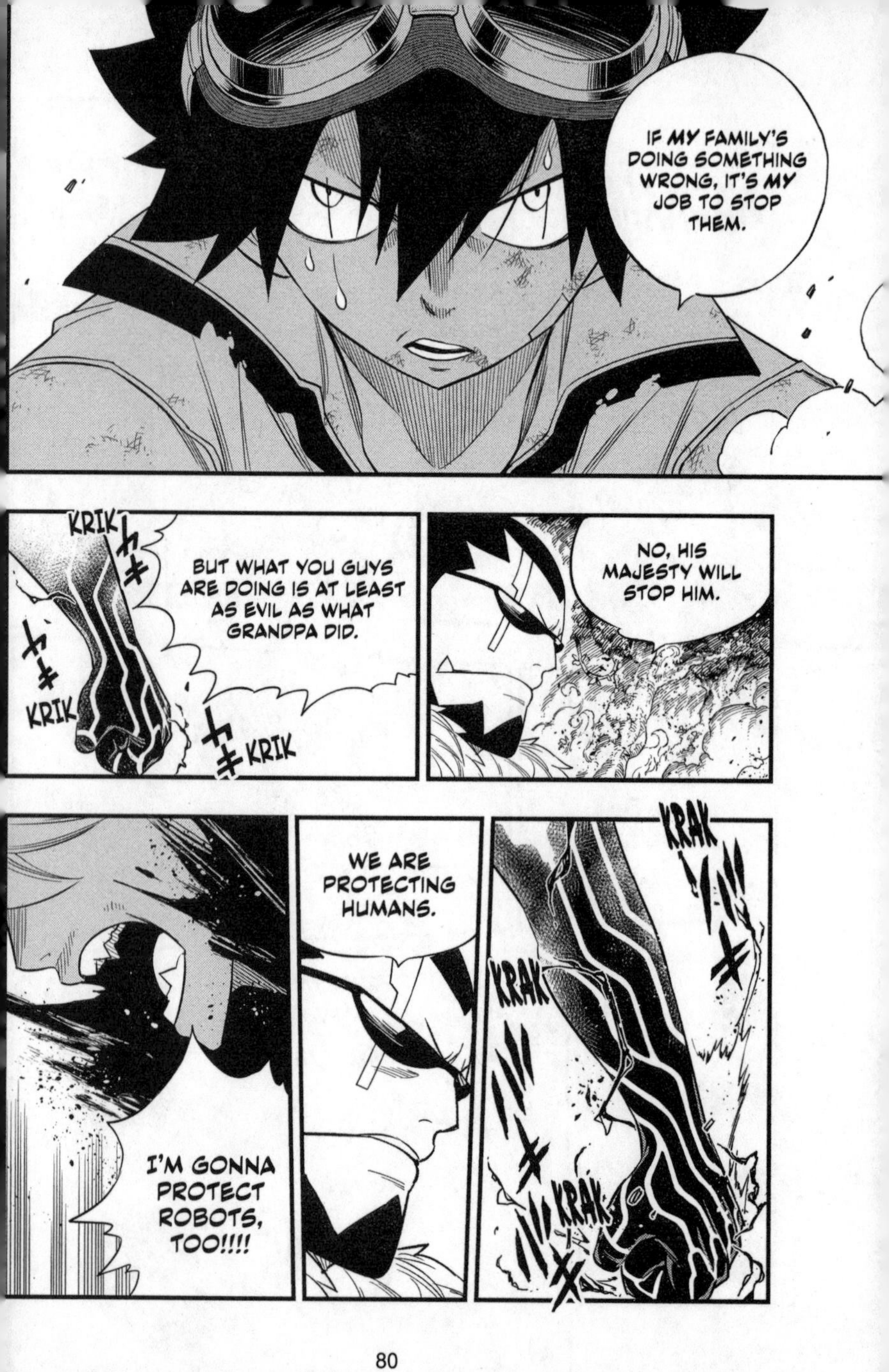
IF MY FAMILY'S DOING SOMETHING WRONG, IT'S MY JOB TO STOP THEM.
NO, HIS MAJESTY WILL STOP HIM.
KRIK
BUT WHAT YOU GUYS ARE DOING IS AT LEAST AS EVIL AS WHAT GRANDPA DID.
KRIK
KRIK
KRAK
KRAK
KRAK
WE ARE PROTECTING HUMANS.
I'M GONNA PROTECT ROBOTS, TOO!!!!

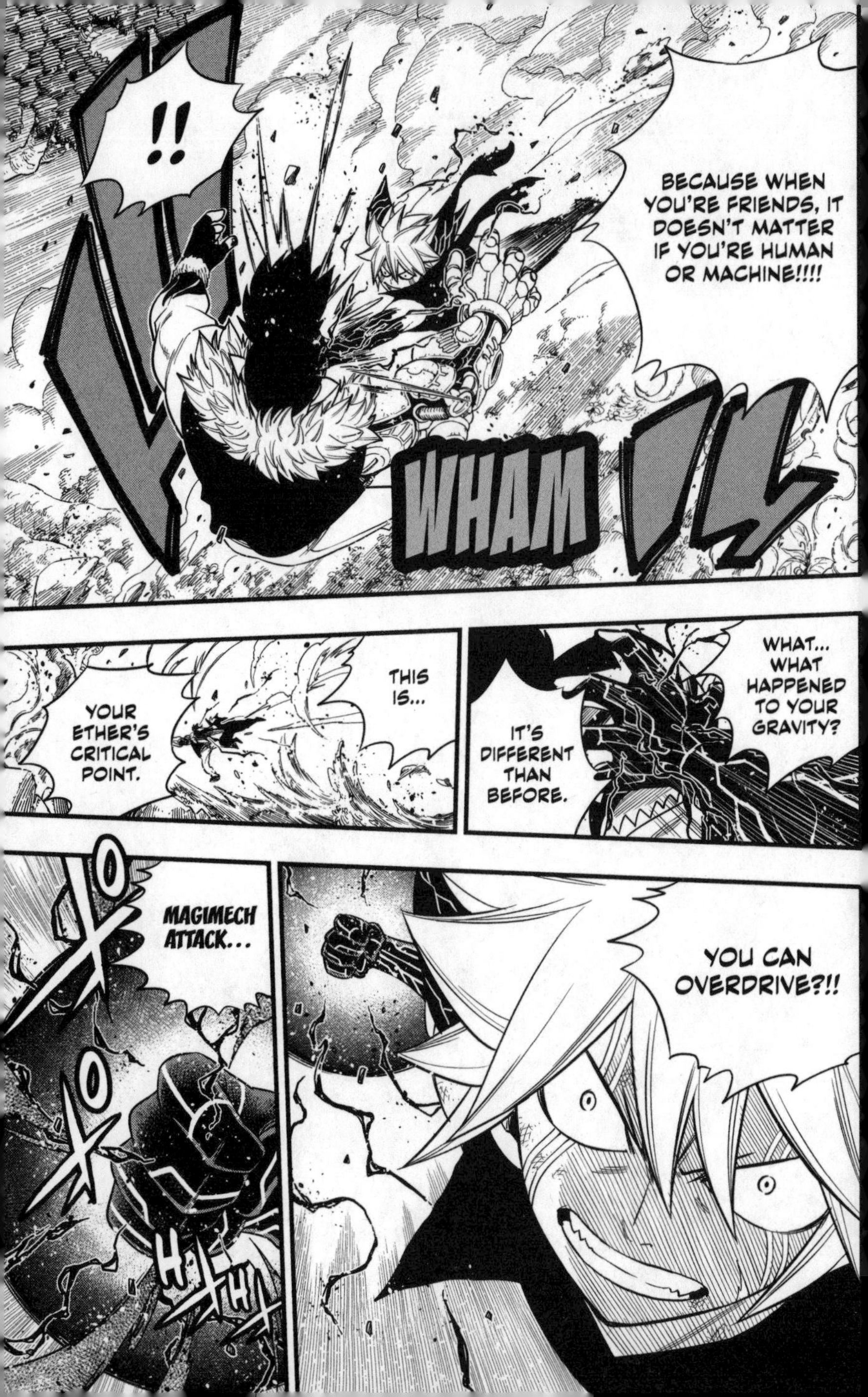
BECAUSE WHEN YOU'RE FRIENDS, IT DOESN'T MATTER IF YOU'RE HUMAN OR MACHINE!!!!
!!
WHAM
WHAT... WHAT HAPPENED TO YOUR GRAVITY?
IT'S DIFFERENT THAN BEFORE.
THIS IS...
YOUR ETHER'S CRITICAL POINT.
YOU CAN OVERDRIVE?!!
MAGIMECH ATTACK...

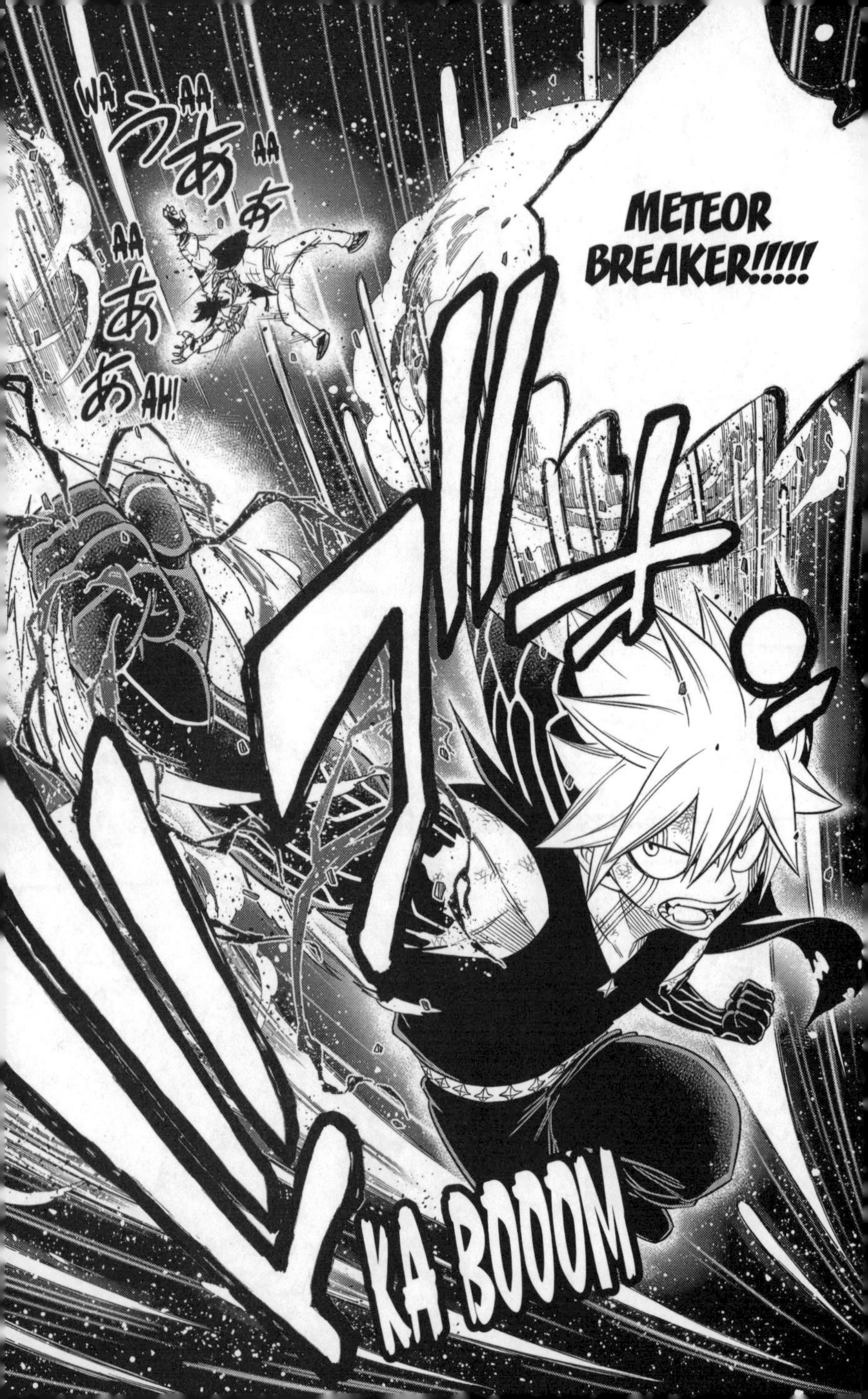
METEOR BREAKER!!!!!
WA うAA あAA ぁ AA うあああ AH!
KA BOOOM

EDENS ZERO

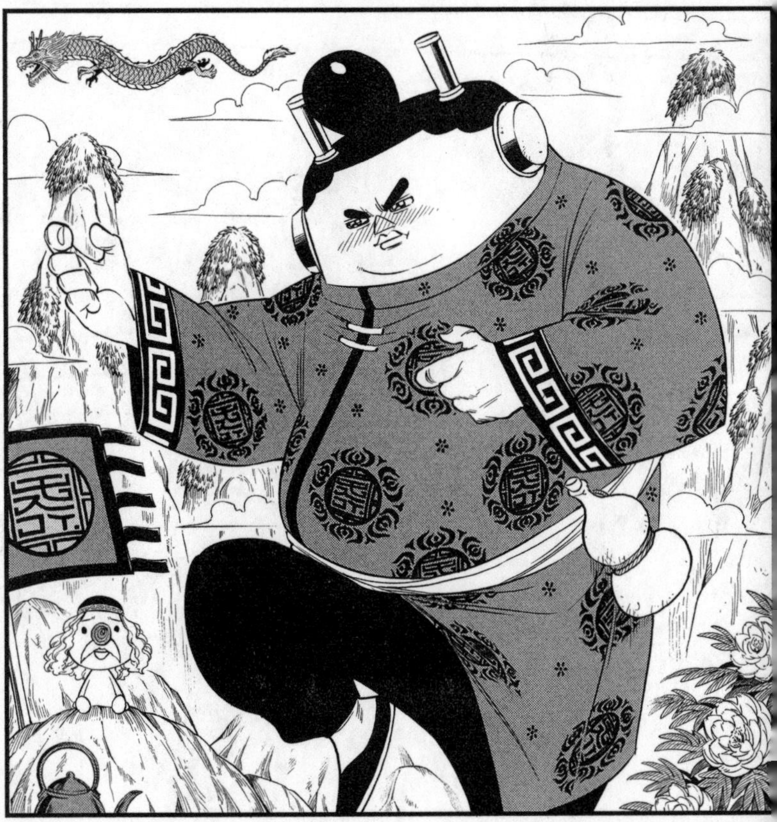

CHAPTER 118: STAR DRAIN

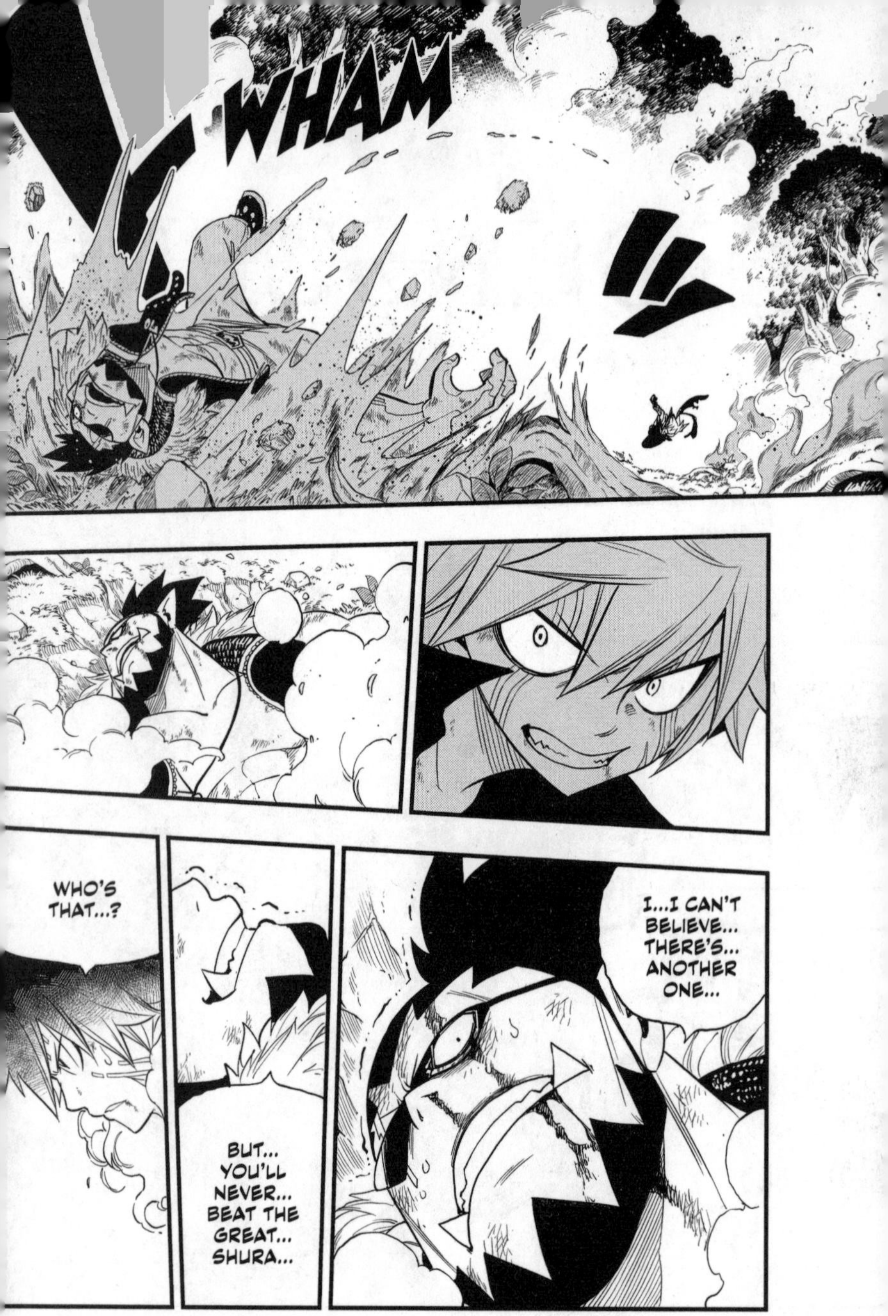
WHAM
I...I CAN'T BELIEVE... THERE'S... ANOTHER ONE...
BUT... YOU'LL NEVER... BEAT THE GREAT... SHURA...
WHO'S THAT...?

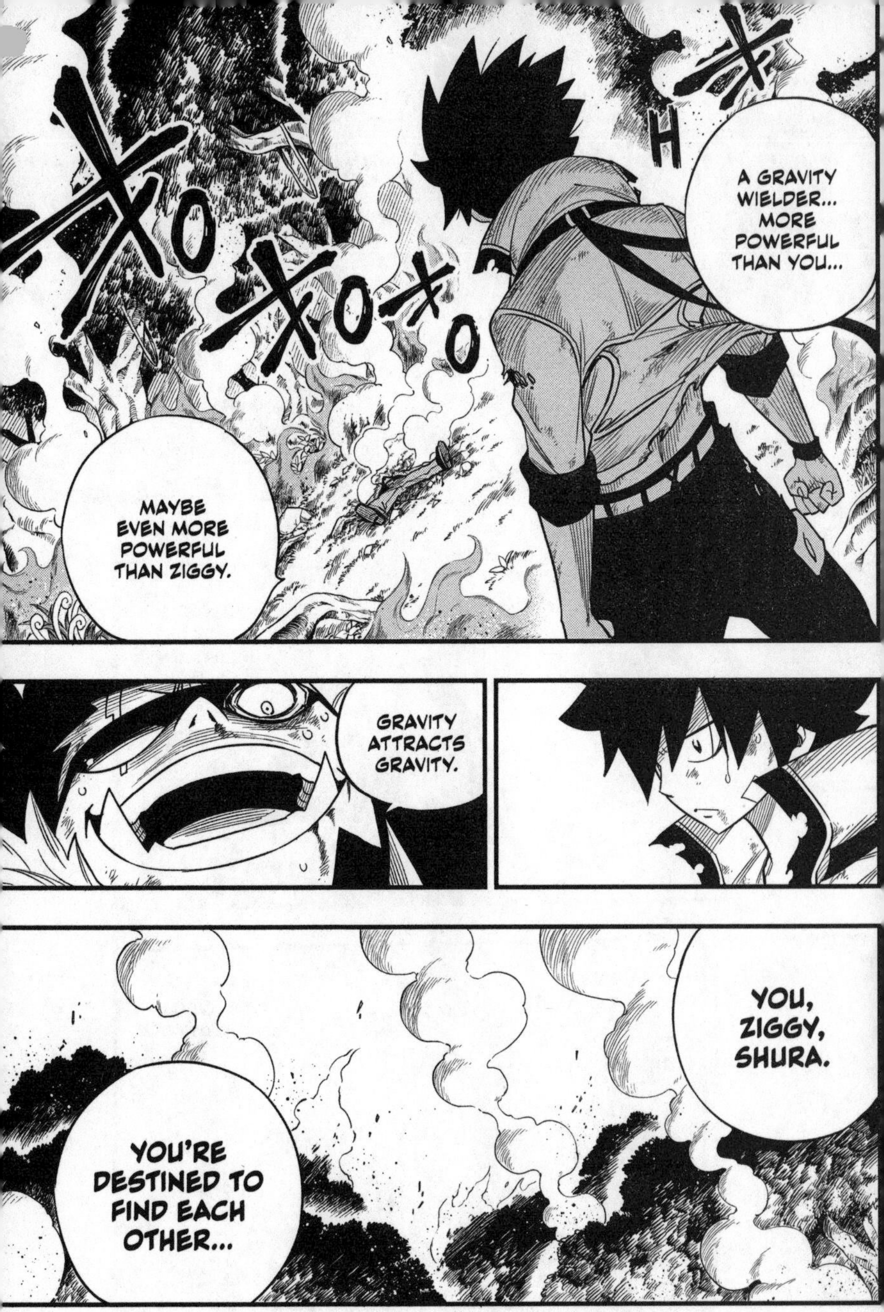
A GRAVITY WIELDER... MORE POWERFUL THAN YOU...
MAYBE EVEN MORE POWERFUL THAN ZIGGY.
GRAVITY ATTRACTS GRAVITY.
YOU, ZIGGY, SHURA.
YOU'RE DESTINED TO FIND EACH OTHER...

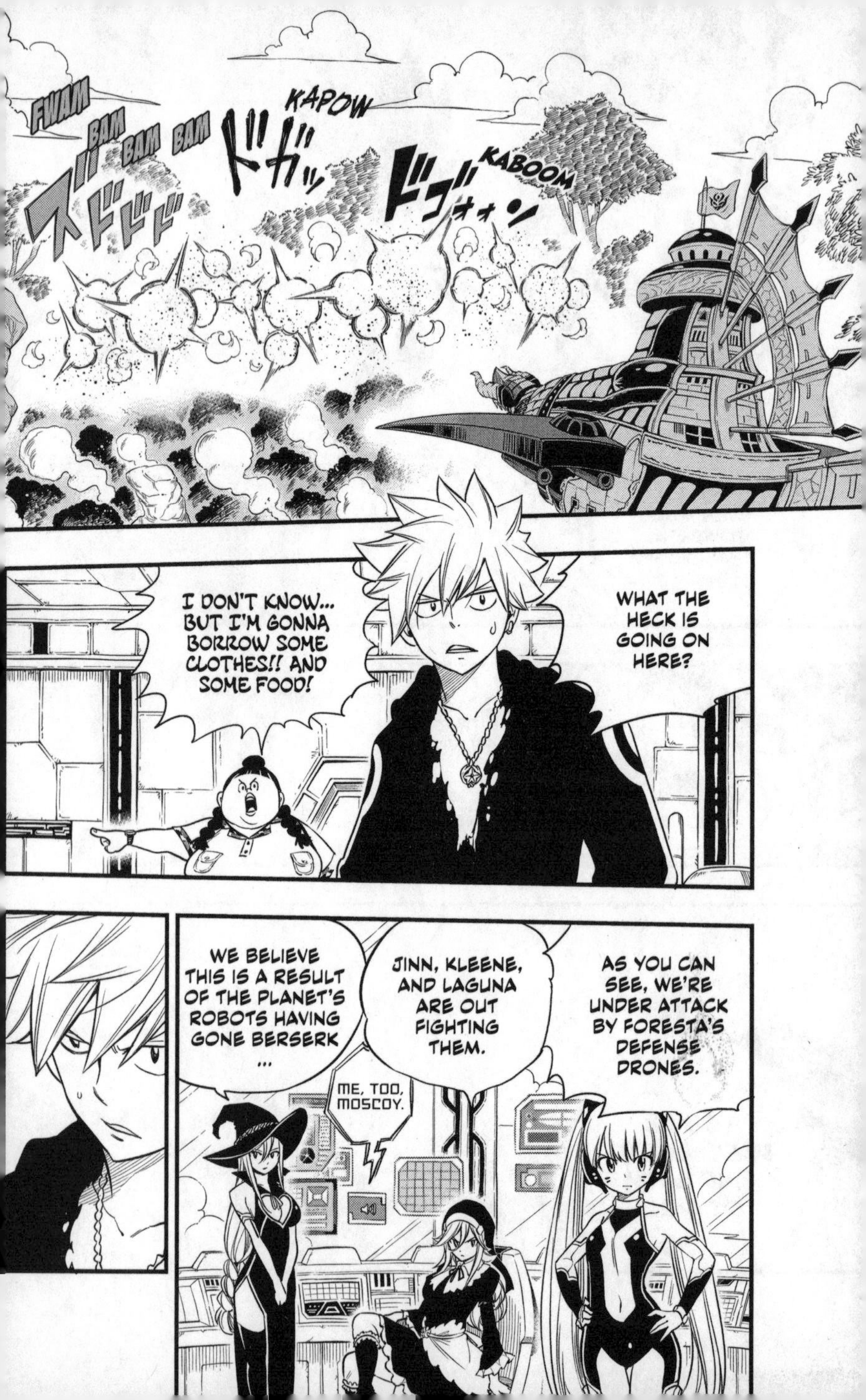
KABOOM
ドゴォォン
KAPOW
ドガッ
BAM BAM
BAM
FWAM
スドドドド
WHAT THE HECK IS GOING ON HERE?
I DON'T KNOW... BUT I'M GONNA BORROW SOME CLOTHES!! AND SOME FOOD!
AS YOU CAN SEE, WE'RE UNDER ATTACK BY FORESTA'S DEFENSE DRONES.
JINN, KLEENE, AND LAGUNA ARE OUT FIGHTING THEM.
ME, TOO, MOSCOY.
WE BELIEVE THIS IS A RESULT OF THE PLANET'S ROBOTS HAVING GONE BERSERK ...

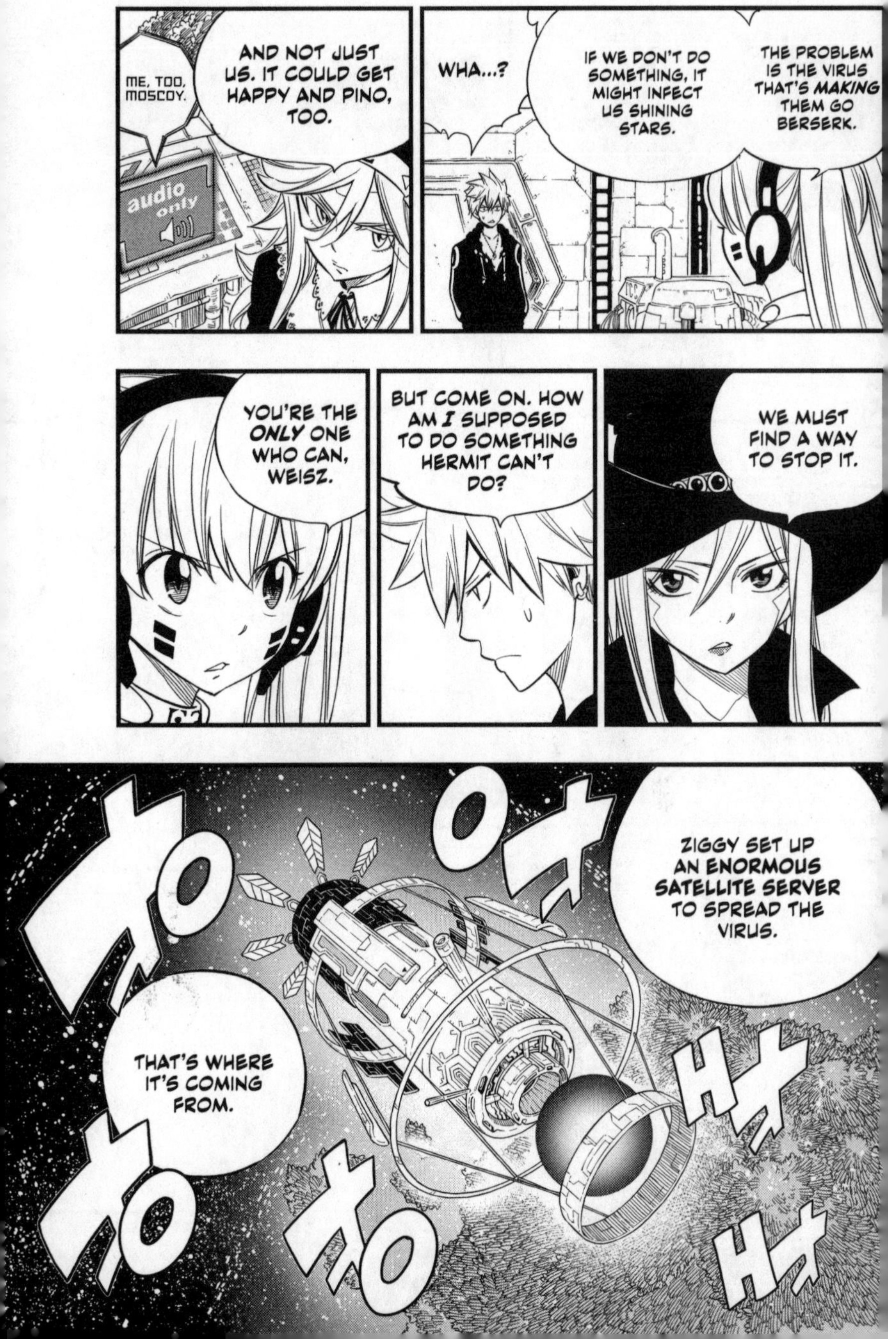
THE PROBLEM IS THE VIRUS THAT'S *MAKING* THEM GO BERSERK.
IF WE DON'T DO SOMETHING, IT MIGHT INFECT US SHINING STARS.
WHA...?
AND NOT JUST US. IT COULD GET HAPPY AND PINO, TOO.
ME, TOO, MOSCOY.
audio only
WE MUST FIND A WAY TO STOP IT.
BUT COME ON. HOW AM *I* SUPPOSED TO DO SOMETHING HERMIT CAN'T DO?
YOU'RE THE *ONLY* ONE WHO CAN, WEISZ.
ZIGGY SET UP AN ENORMOUS SATELLITE SERVER TO SPREAD THE VIRUS.
THAT'S WHERE IT'S COMING FROM.

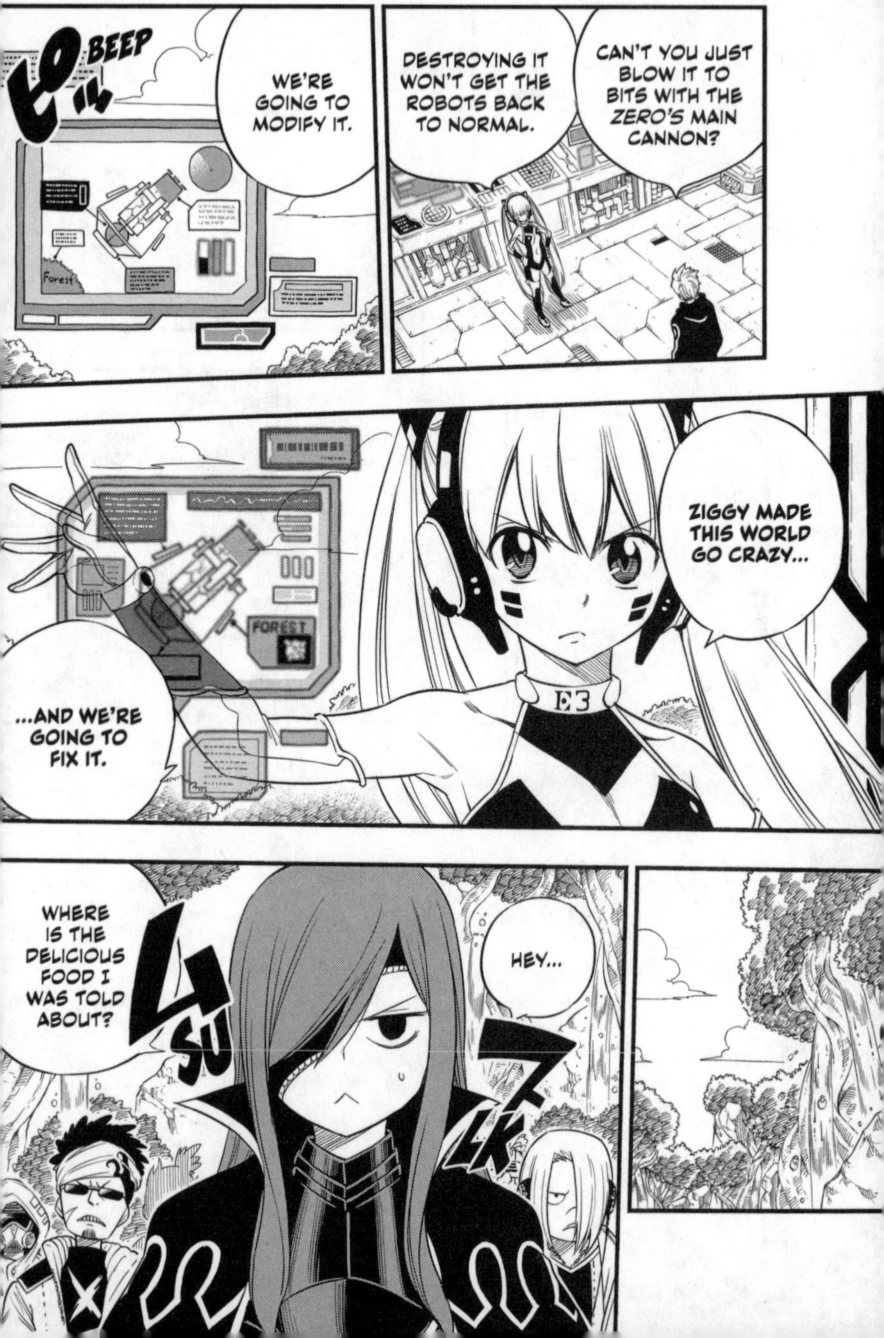
CAN'T YOU JUST BLOW IT TO BITS WITH THE ZERO'S MAIN CANNON?
DESTROYING IT WON'T GET THE ROBOTS BACK TO NORMAL.
BEEP
WE'RE GOING TO MODIFY IT.
Forest
ZIGGY MADE THIS WORLD GO CRAZY...
FOREST
...AND WE'RE GOING TO FIX IT.
HEY...
SU
WHERE IS THE DELICIOUS FOOD I WAS TOLD ABOUT?

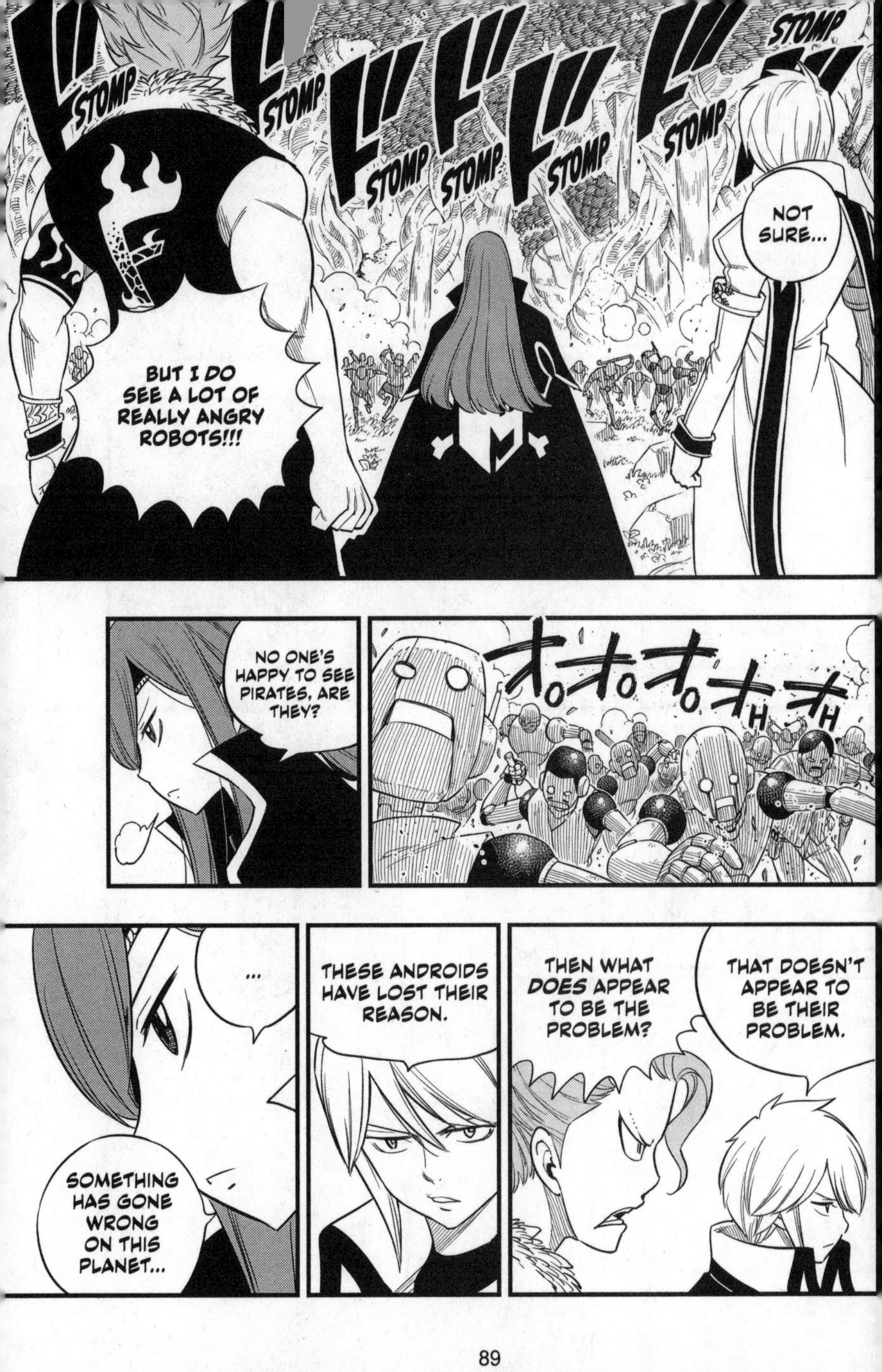
STOMP
STOMP
STOMP
STOMP
STOMP
STOMP
STOMP
NOT SURE...
BUT I DO SEE A LOT OF REALLY ANGRY ROBOTS!!!
NO ONE'S HAPPY TO SEE PIRATES, ARE THEY?
THAT DOESN'T APPEAR TO BE THEIR PROBLEM.
THEN WHAT DOES APPEAR TO BE THE PROBLEM?
THESE ANDROIDS HAVE LOST THEIR REASON.
...
SOMETHING HAS GONE WRONG ON THIS PLANET...

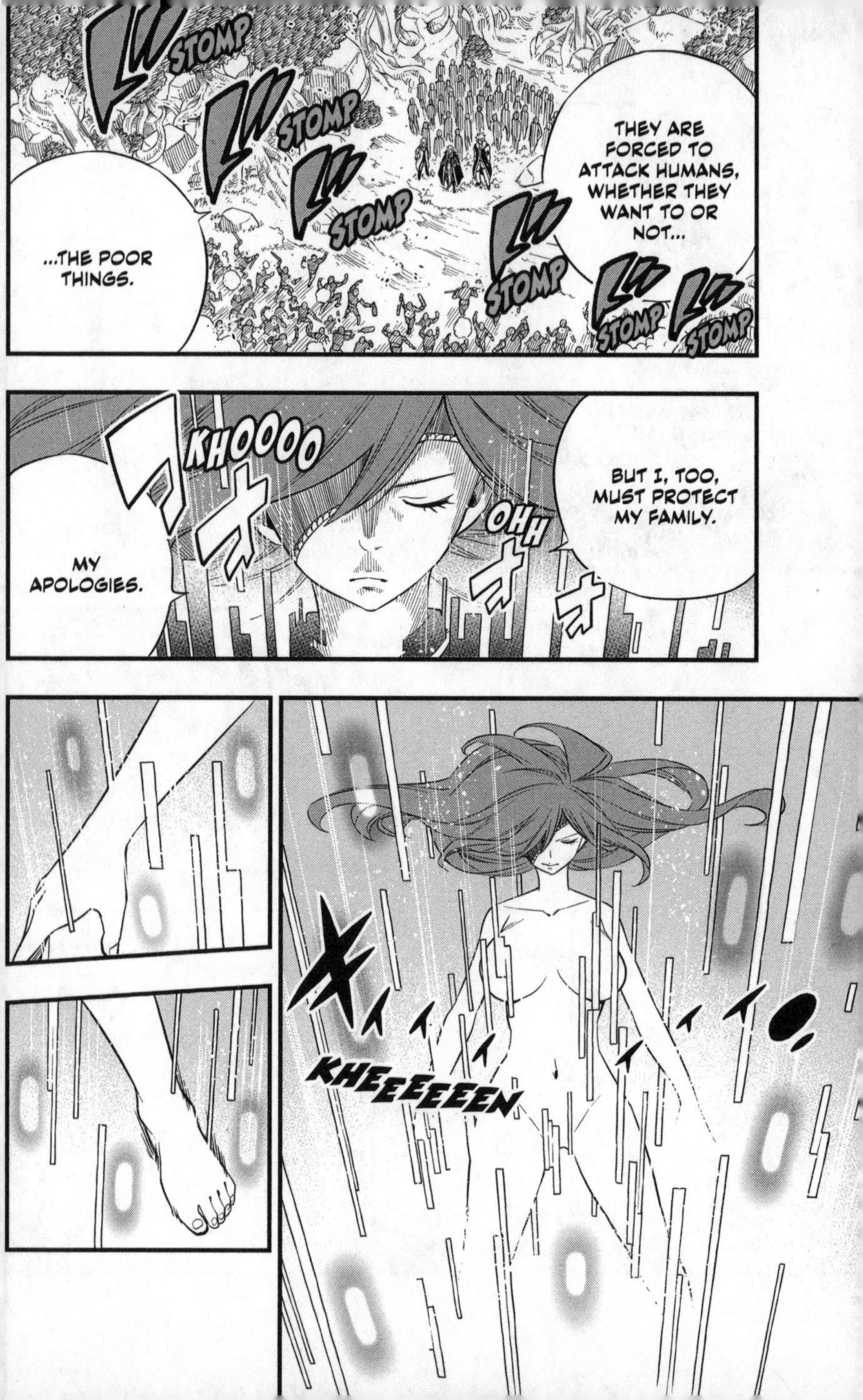
THEY ARE FORCED TO ATTACK HUMANS, WHETHER THEY WANT TO OR NOT...
STOMP
STOMP
STOMP
STOMP
STOMP
STOMP
STOMP
...THE POOR THINGS.
BUT I, TOO, MUST PROTECT MY FAMILY.
OHH
KHOOOO
MY APOLOGIES.
KHEEEEEEEN

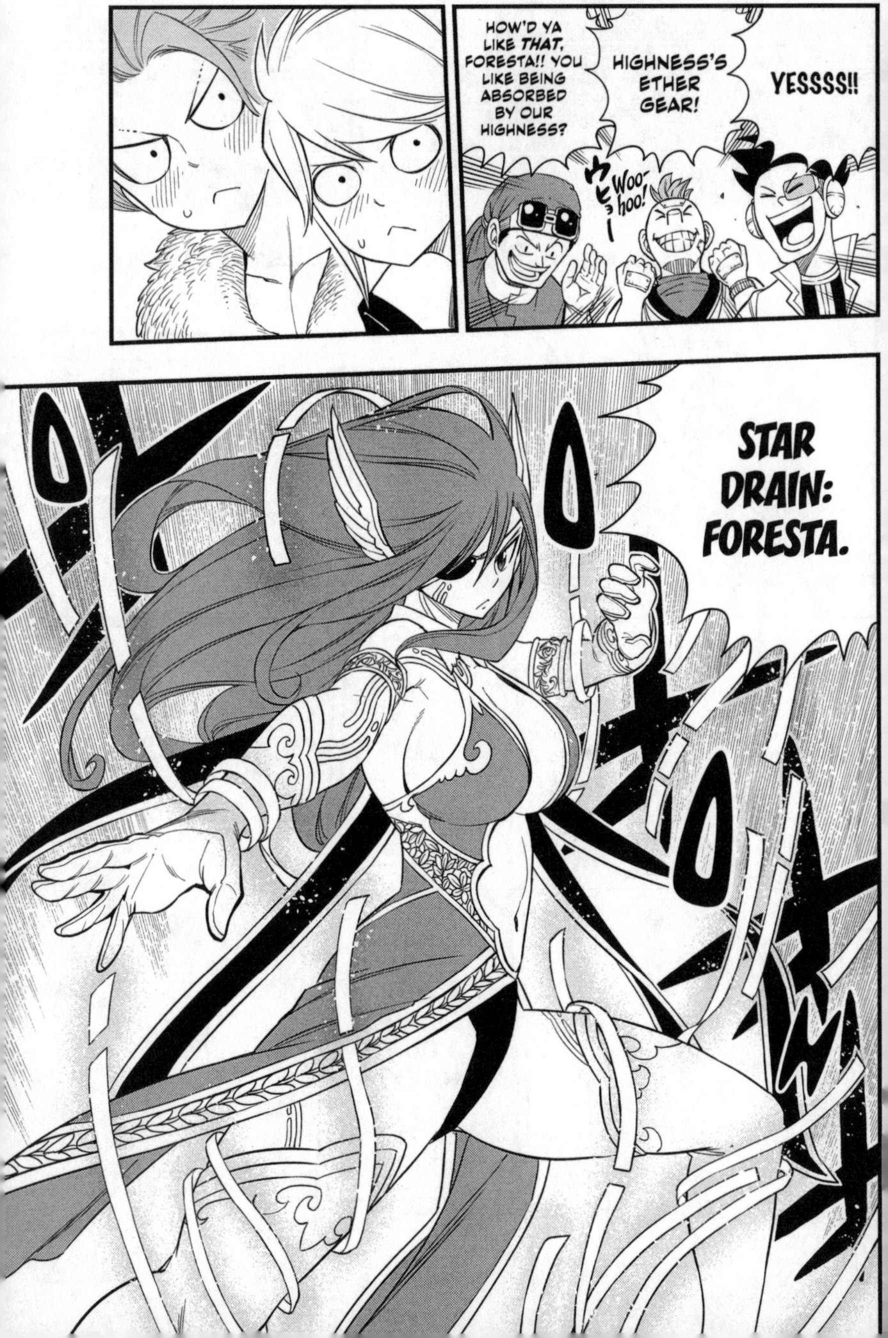
YESSSS!!
HIGHNESS'S ETHER GEAR!
HOW'D YA LIKE *THAT*, FORESTA!! YOU LIKE BEING ABSORBED BY OUR HIGHNESS?
Woo-hoo!
STAR DRAIN: FORESTA.

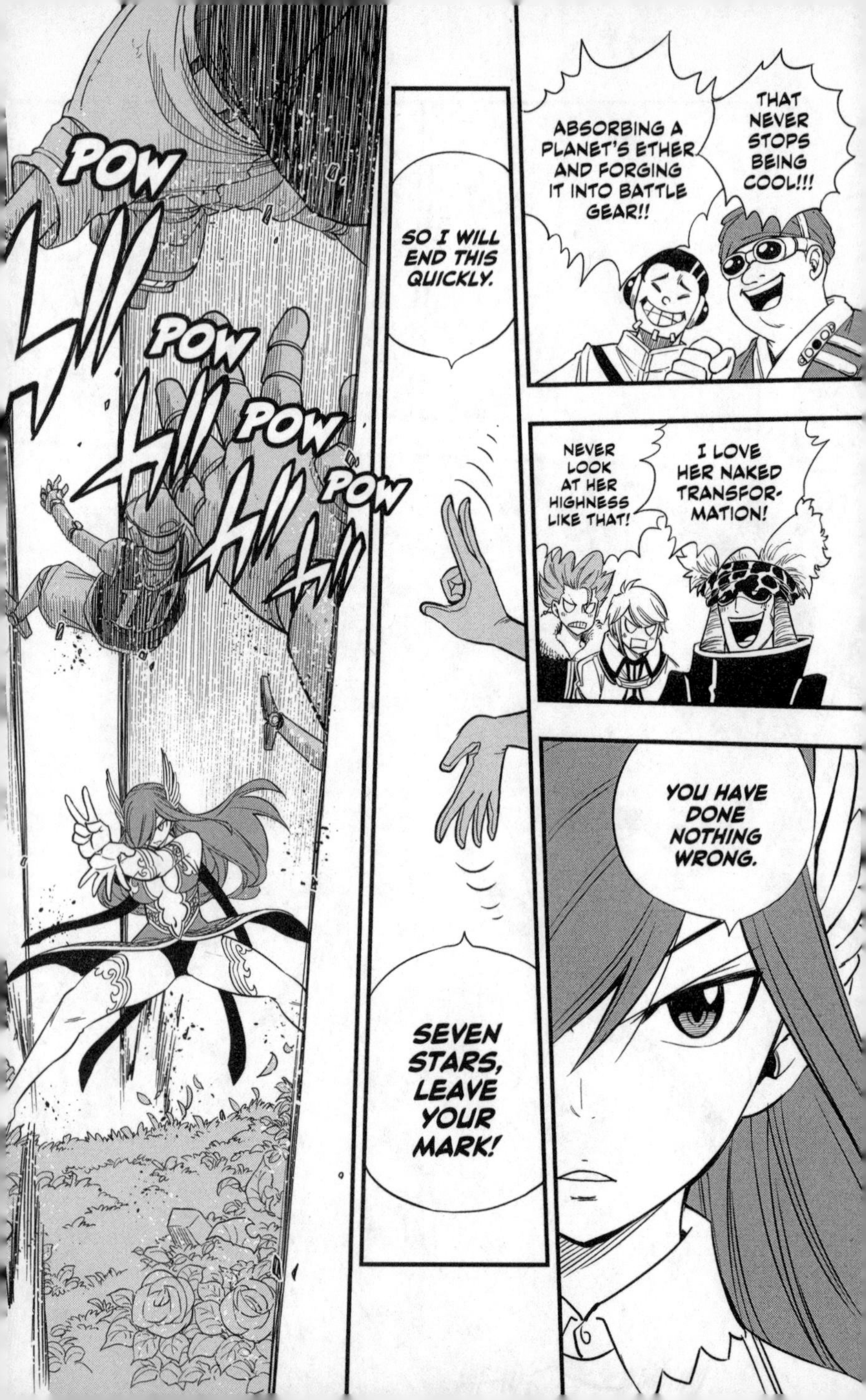
THAT NEVER STOPS BEING COOL!!!
ABSORBING A PLANET'S ETHER AND FORGING IT INTO BATTLE GEAR!!
I LOVE HER NAKED TRANSFORMATION!
NEVER LOOK AT HER HIGHNESS LIKE THAT!
YOU HAVE DONE NOTHING WRONG.
SO I WILL END THIS QUICKLY.
SEVEN STARS, LEAVE YOUR MARK!
POW
POW
POW
POW

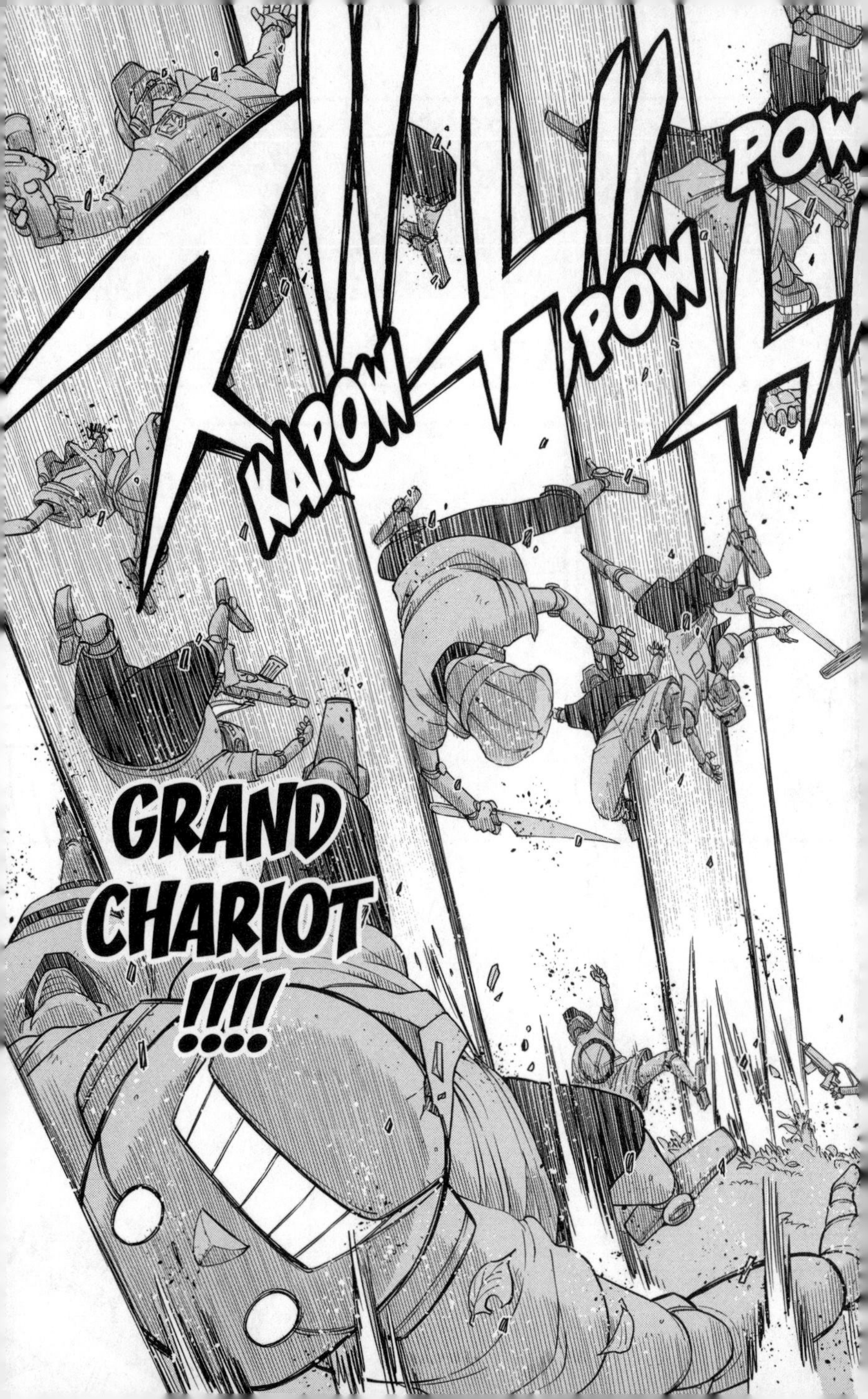
POW
POW
KAPOW
GRAND CHARIOT !!!!

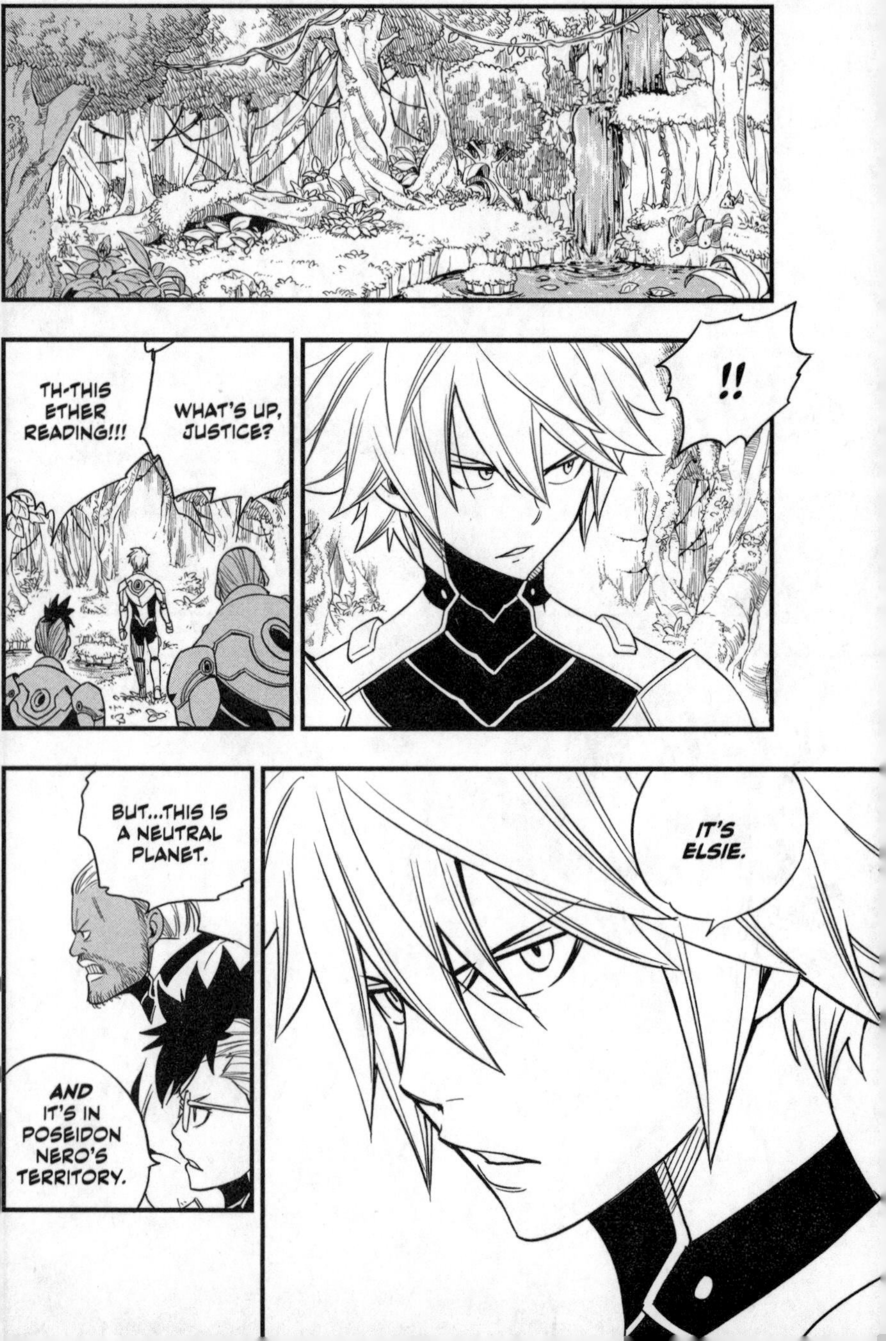
!!
WHAT'S UP, JUSTICE?
TH-THIS ETHER READING!!!
IT'S ELSIE.
BUT...THIS IS A NEUTRAL PLANET.
AND IT'S IN POSEIDON NERO'S TERRITORY.

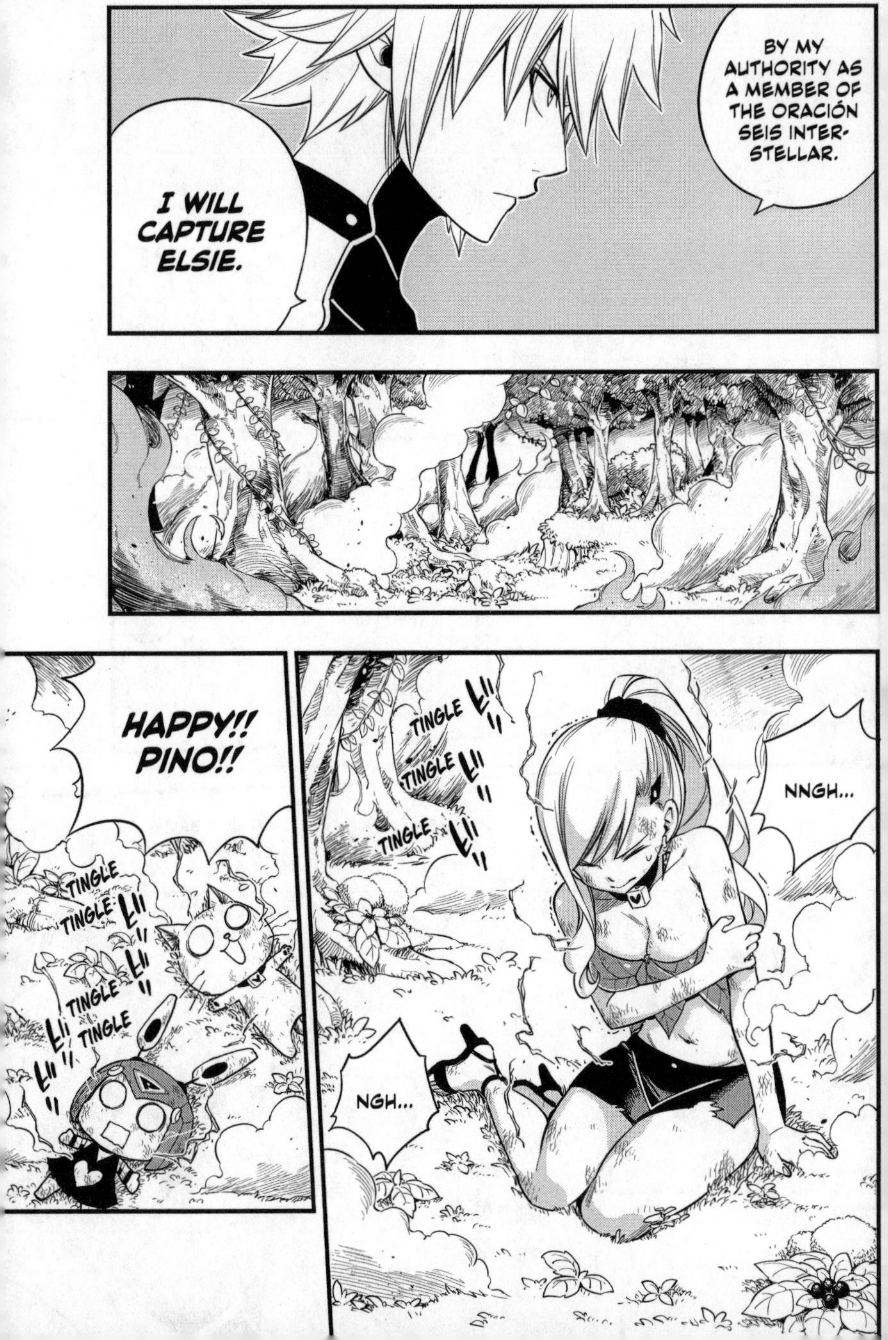
BY MY AUTHORITY AS A MEMBER OF THE ORACIÓN SEIS INTER-STELLAR.
I WILL CAPTURE ELSIE.
TINGLE
TINGLE
TINGLE
NNGH...
NGH...
HAPPY!! PINO!!
TINGLE
TINGLE
TINGLE
TINGLE

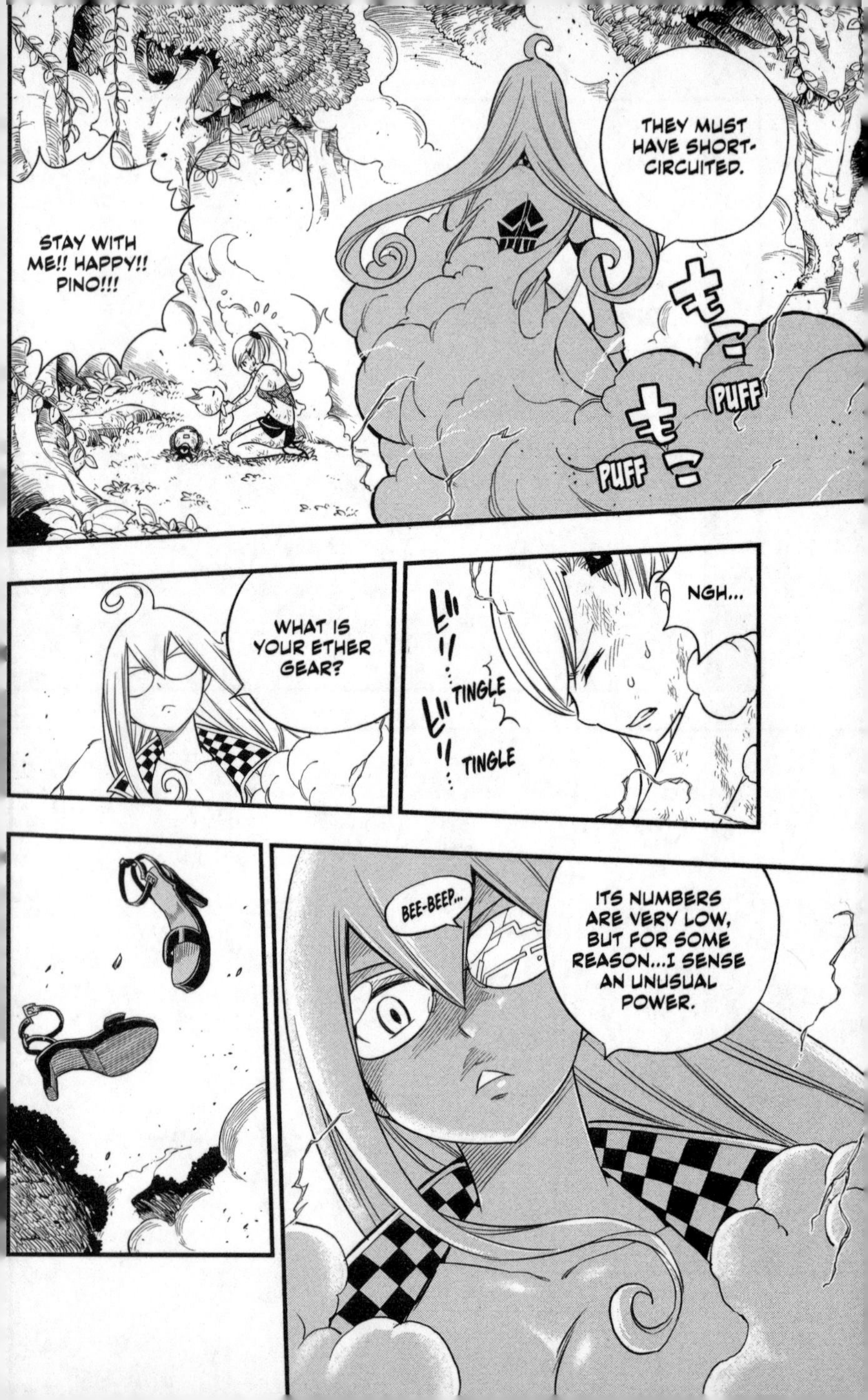
THEY MUST HAVE SHORT-CIRCUITED.
PUFF
PUFF
STAY WITH ME!! HAPPY!! PINO!!!
NGH...
TINGLE
TINGLE
WHAT IS YOUR ETHER GEAR?
BEE-BEEP...
ITS NUMBERS ARE VERY LOW, BUT FOR SOME REASON...I SENSE AN UNUSUAL POWER.

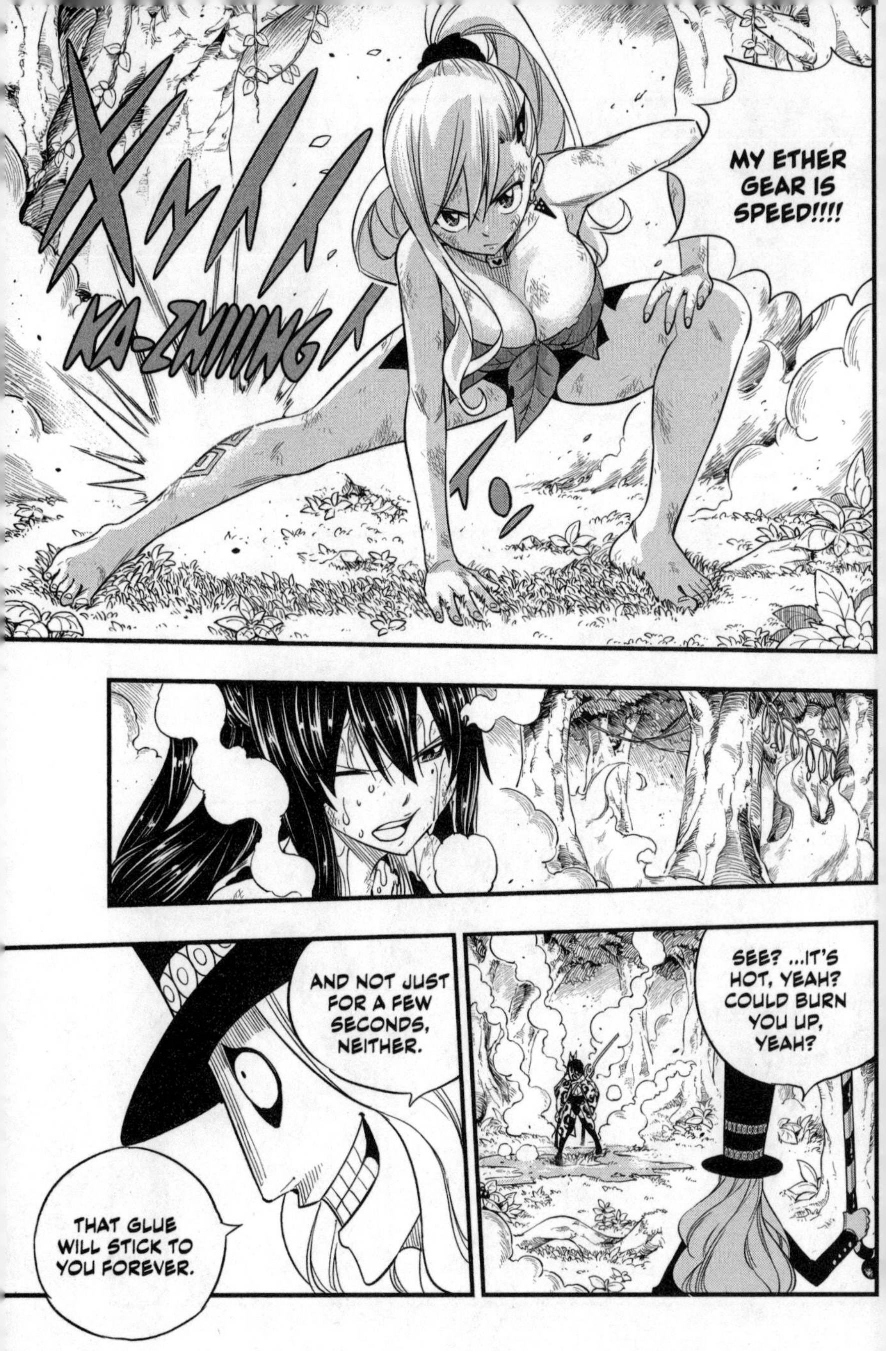
MY ETHER GEAR IS SPEED!!!!
KA-ZHIIING
SEE? ...IT'S HOT, YEAH? COULD BURN YOU UP, YEAH?
AND NOT JUST FOR A FEW SECONDS, NEITHER.
THAT GLUE WILL STICK TO YOU FOREVER.

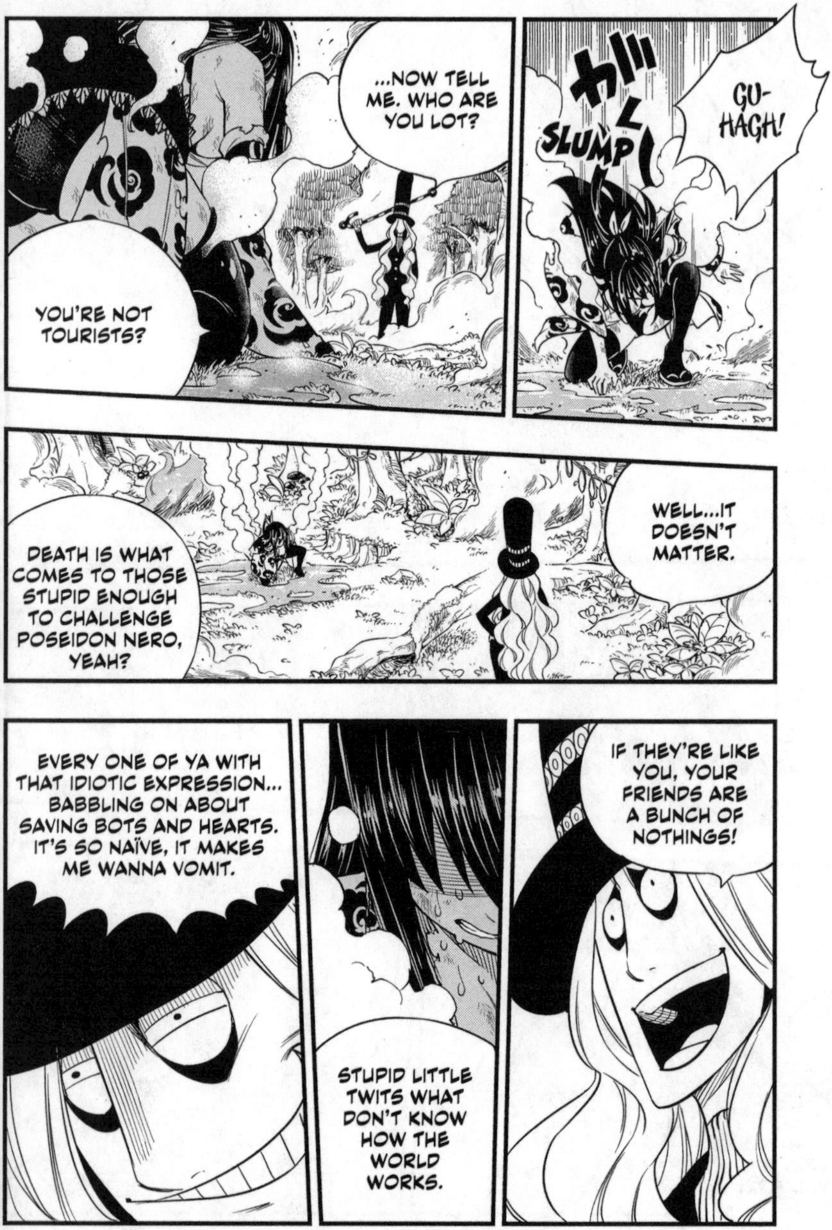
GU-HAGH!
SLUMP
...NOW TELL ME. WHO ARE YOU LOT?
YOU'RE NOT TOURISTS?
WELL...IT DOESN'T MATTER.
DEATH IS WHAT COMES TO THOSE STUPID ENOUGH TO CHALLENGE POSEIDON NERO, YEAH?
IF THEY'RE LIKE YOU, YOUR FRIENDS ARE A BUNCH OF NOTHINGS!
STUPID LITTLE TWITS WHAT DON'T KNOW HOW THE WORLD WORKS.
EVERY ONE OF YA WITH THAT IDIOTIC EXPRESSION... BABBLING ON ABOUT SAVING BOTS AND HEARTS. IT'S SO NAÏVE, IT MAKES ME WANNA VOMIT.

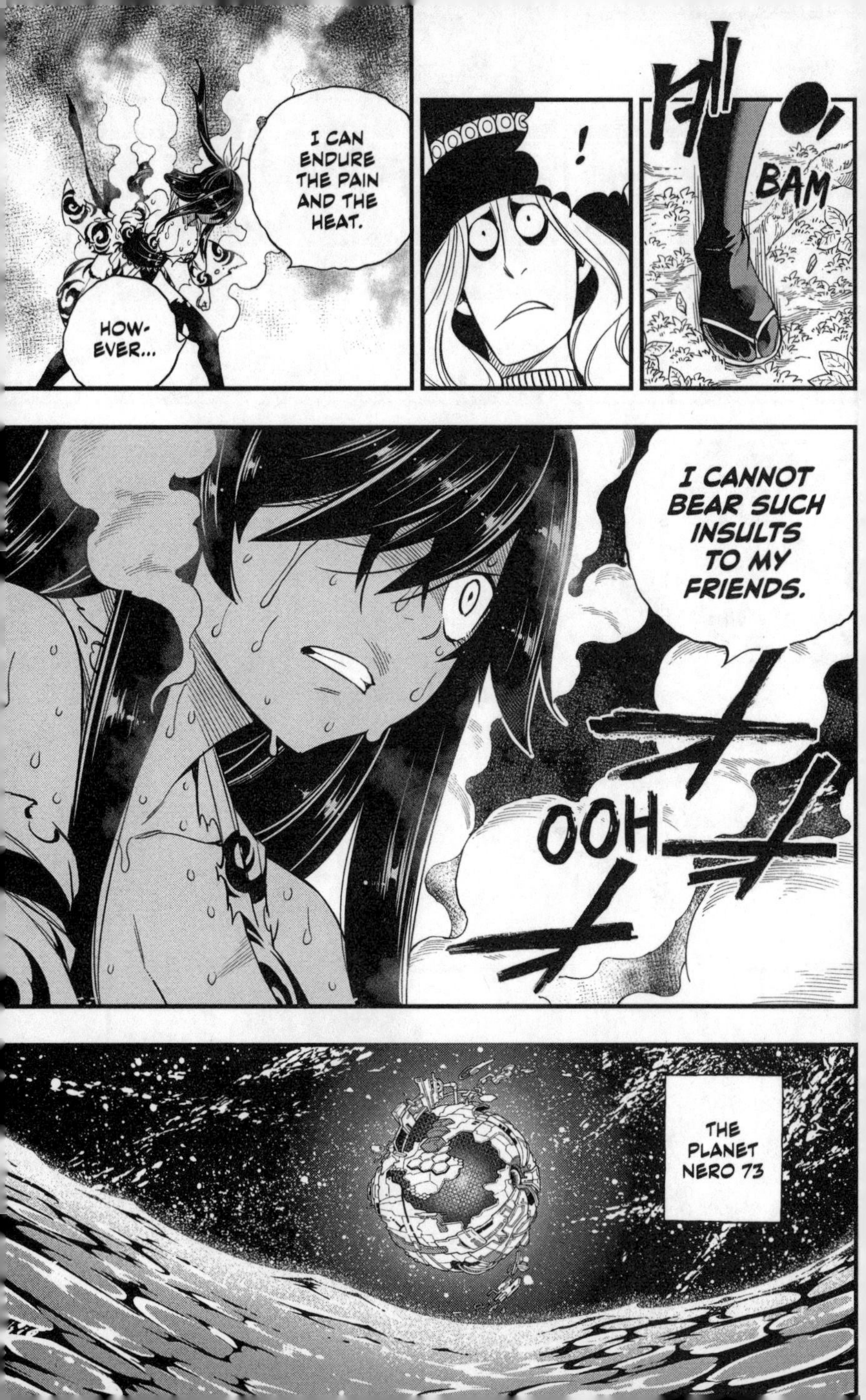
BAM
!
I CAN ENDURE THE PAIN AND THE HEAT.
HOW-EVER...
I CANNOT BEAR SUCH INSULTS TO MY FRIENDS.
OOH
THE PLANET NERO 73

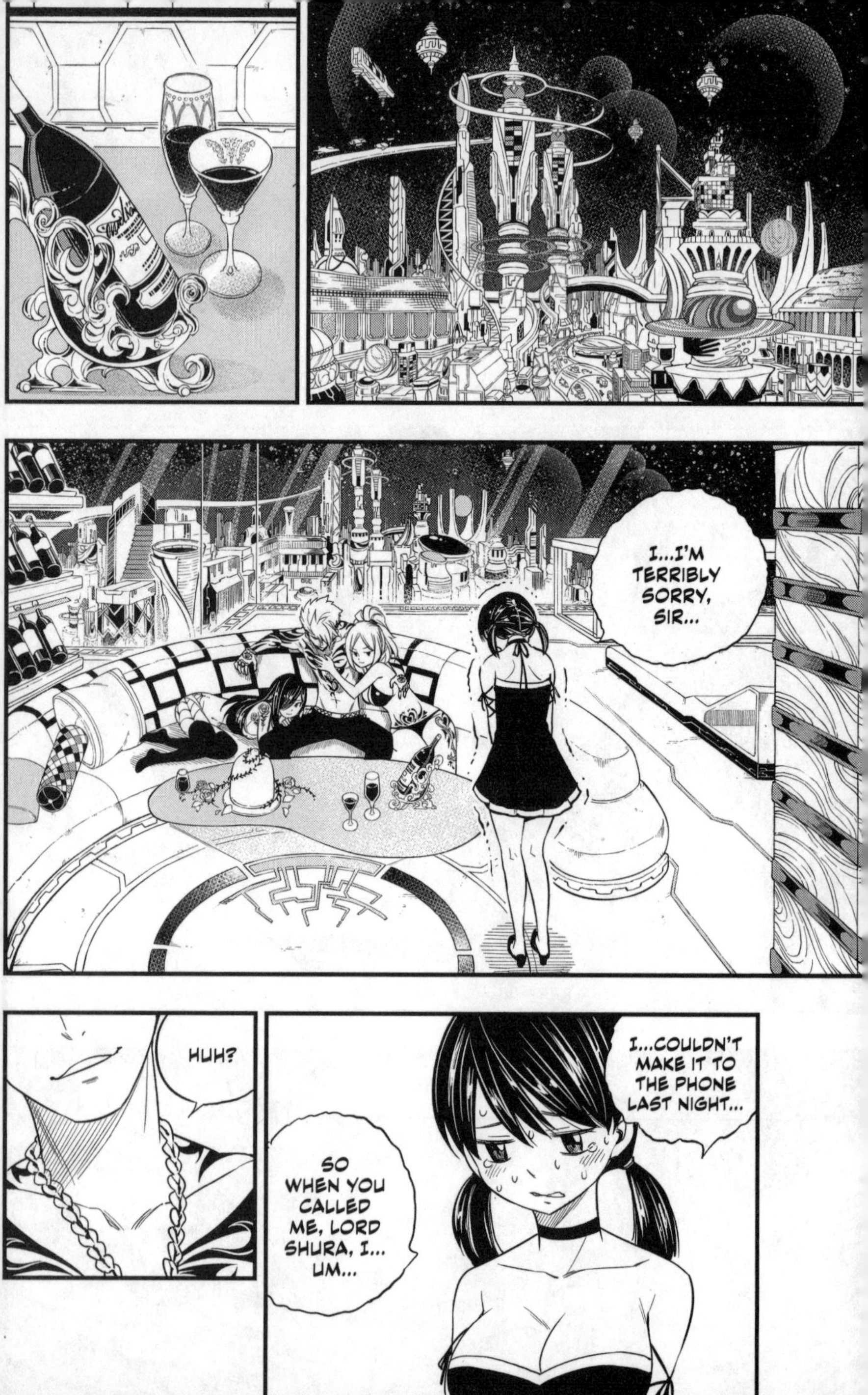
I...I'M TERRIBLY SORRY, SIR...
I...COULDN'T MAKE IT TO THE PHONE LAST NIGHT...
SO WHEN YOU CALLED ME, LORD SHURA, I... UM...
HUH?

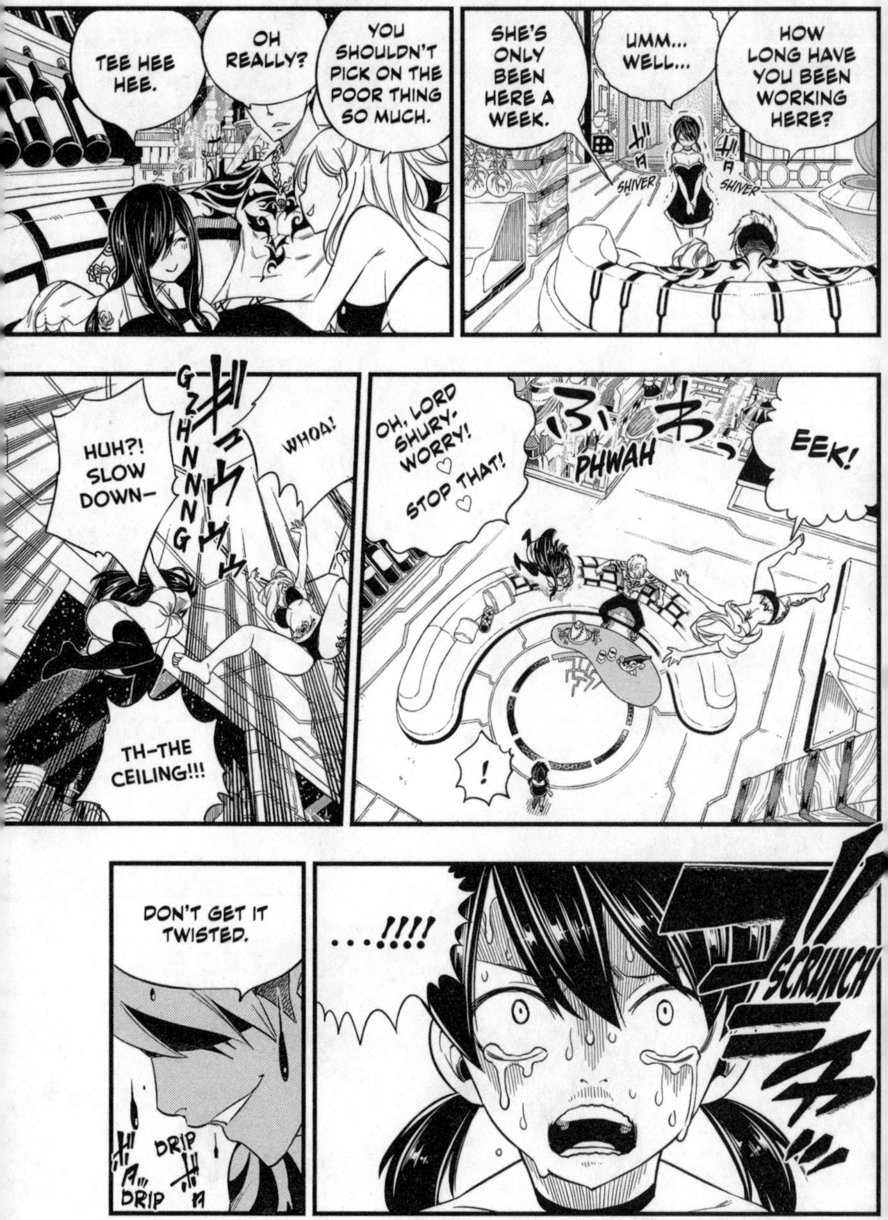
HOW LONG HAVE YOU BEEN WORKING HERE?
UMM... WELL...
SHIVER
SHIVER
SHE'S ONLY BEEN HERE A WEEK.
YOU SHOULDN'T PICK ON THE POOR THING SO MUCH.
OH REALLY?
TEE HEE HEE.
EEK!
PHWAH
OH, LORD SHURY. WORRY! ♡
STOP THAT! ♡
!
WHOA!
GZHNNNNG
HUH?! SLOW DOWN—
TH-THE CEILING!!!
SCRUNCH!!!!
...!!!!
DON'T GET IT TWISTED.
DRIP
DRIP

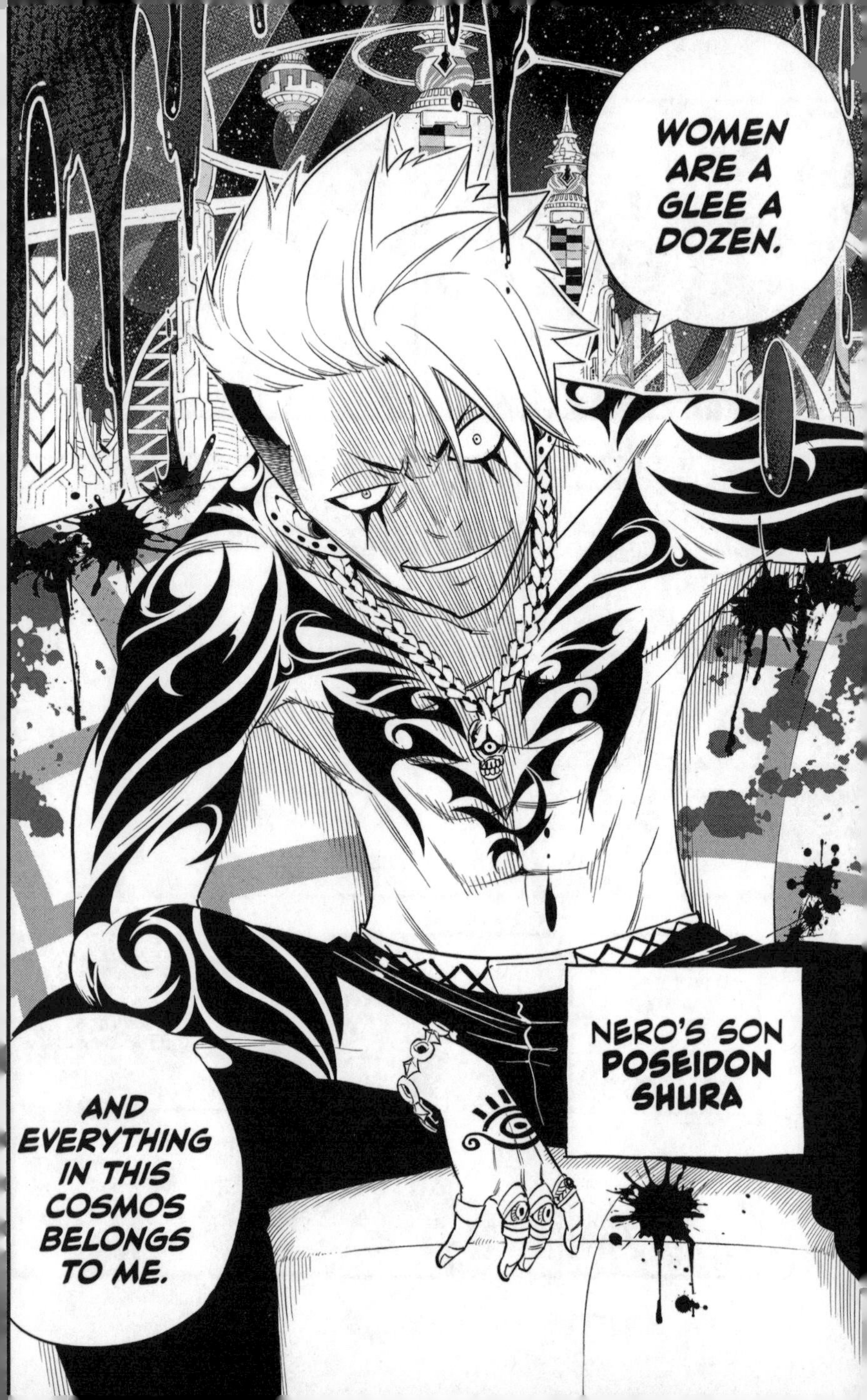
WOMEN ARE A GLEE A DOZEN.
NERO'S SON POSEIDON SHURA
AND EVERYTHING IN THIS COSMOS BELONGS TO ME.

EDENS ZERO

CHAPTER 119: HOMURA VS. MORA

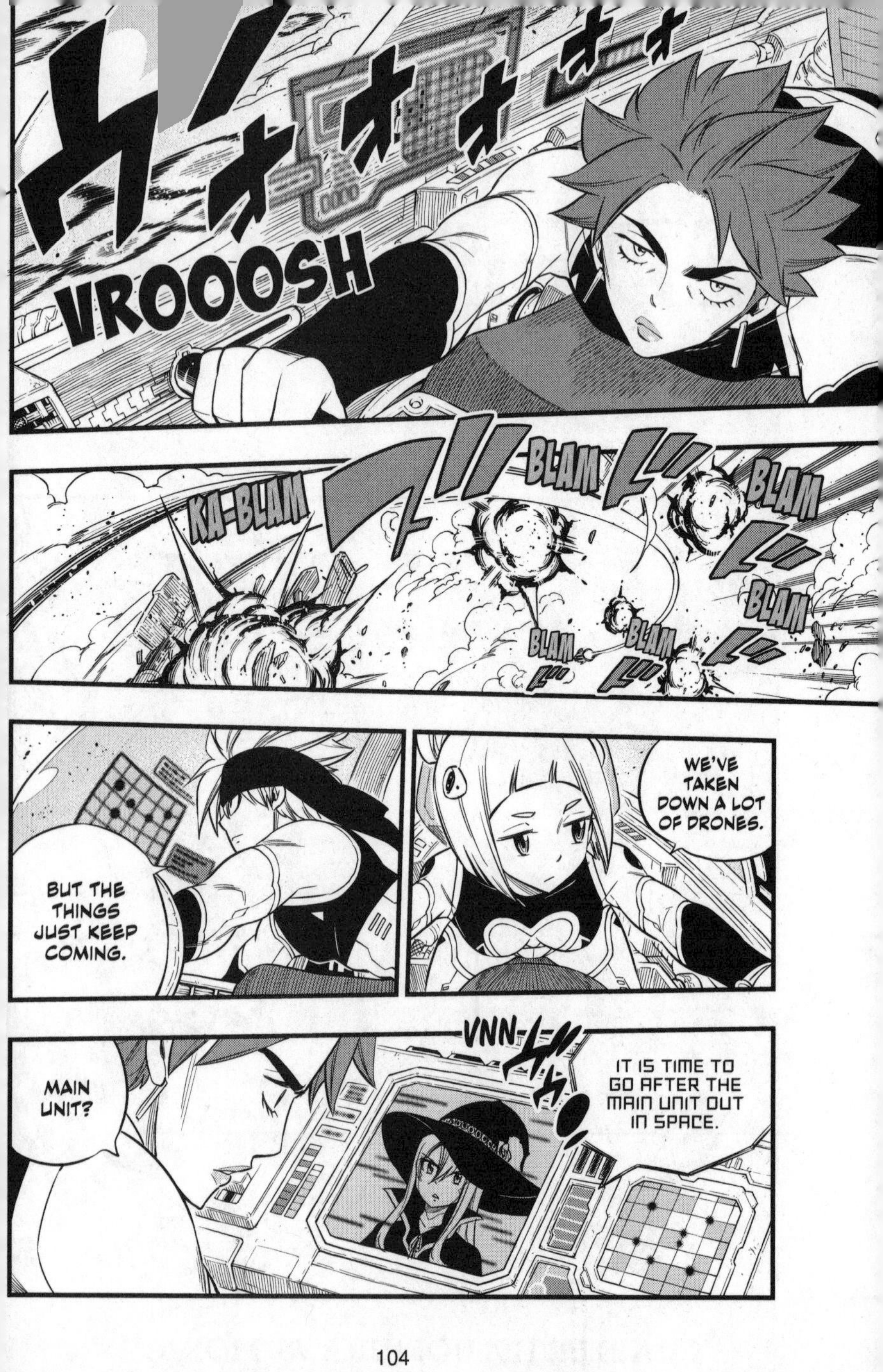
VROOOSH
BLAM
BLAM
BLAM
BLAM
BLAM
KA-BLAM
WE'VE TAKEN DOWN A LOT OF DRONES.
BUT THE THINGS JUST KEEP COMING.
VNN
IT IS TIME TO GO AFTER THE MAIN UNIT OUT IN SPACE.
MAIN UNIT?

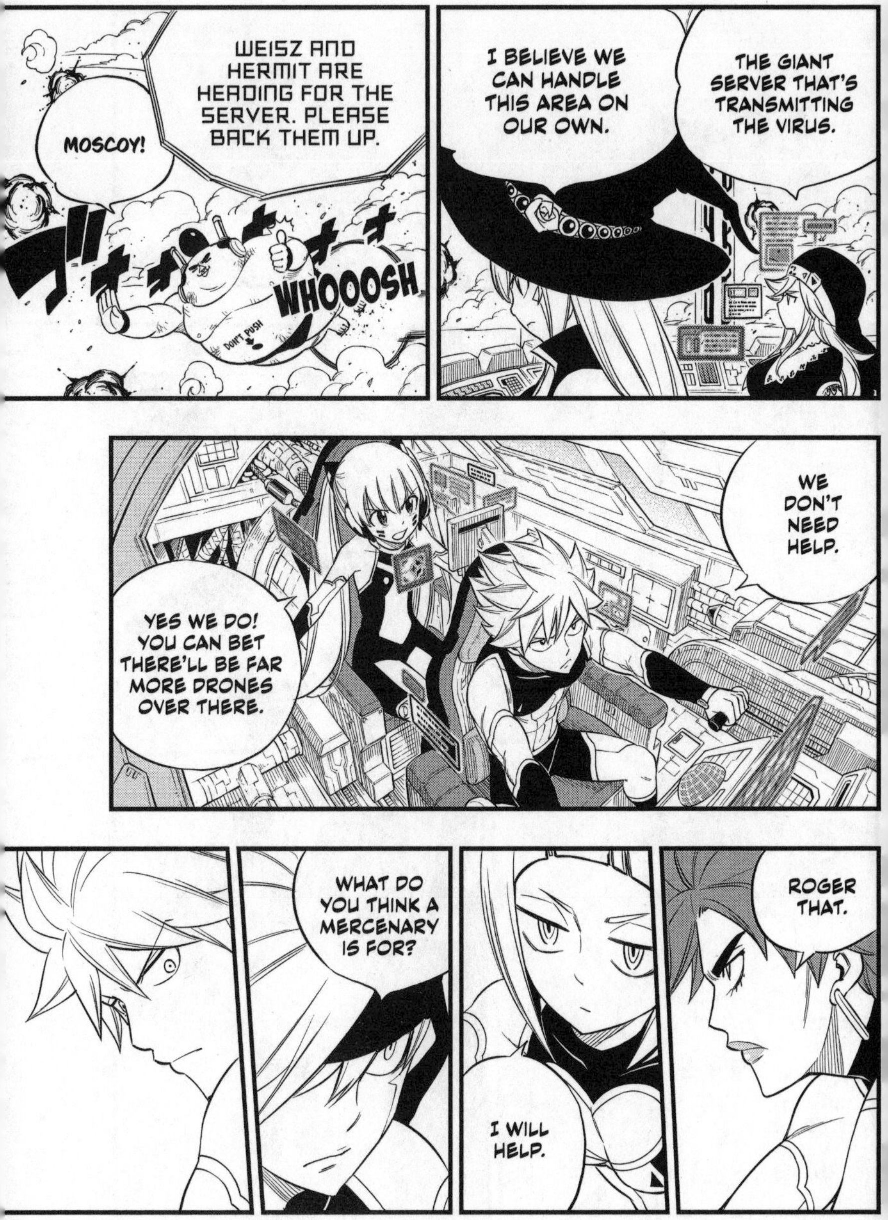
THE GIANT SERVER THAT'S TRANSMITTING THE VIRUS.
I BELIEVE WE CAN HANDLE THIS AREA ON OUR OWN.
WEISZ AND HERMIT ARE HEADING FOR THE SERVER. PLEASE BACK THEM UP.
MOSCOY!
WHOOOSH
DON'T PUSH
WE DON'T NEED HELP.
YES WE DO! YOU CAN BET THERE'LL BE FAR MORE DRONES OVER THERE.
ROGER THAT.
I WILL HELP.
WHAT DO YOU THINK A MERCENARY IS FOR?

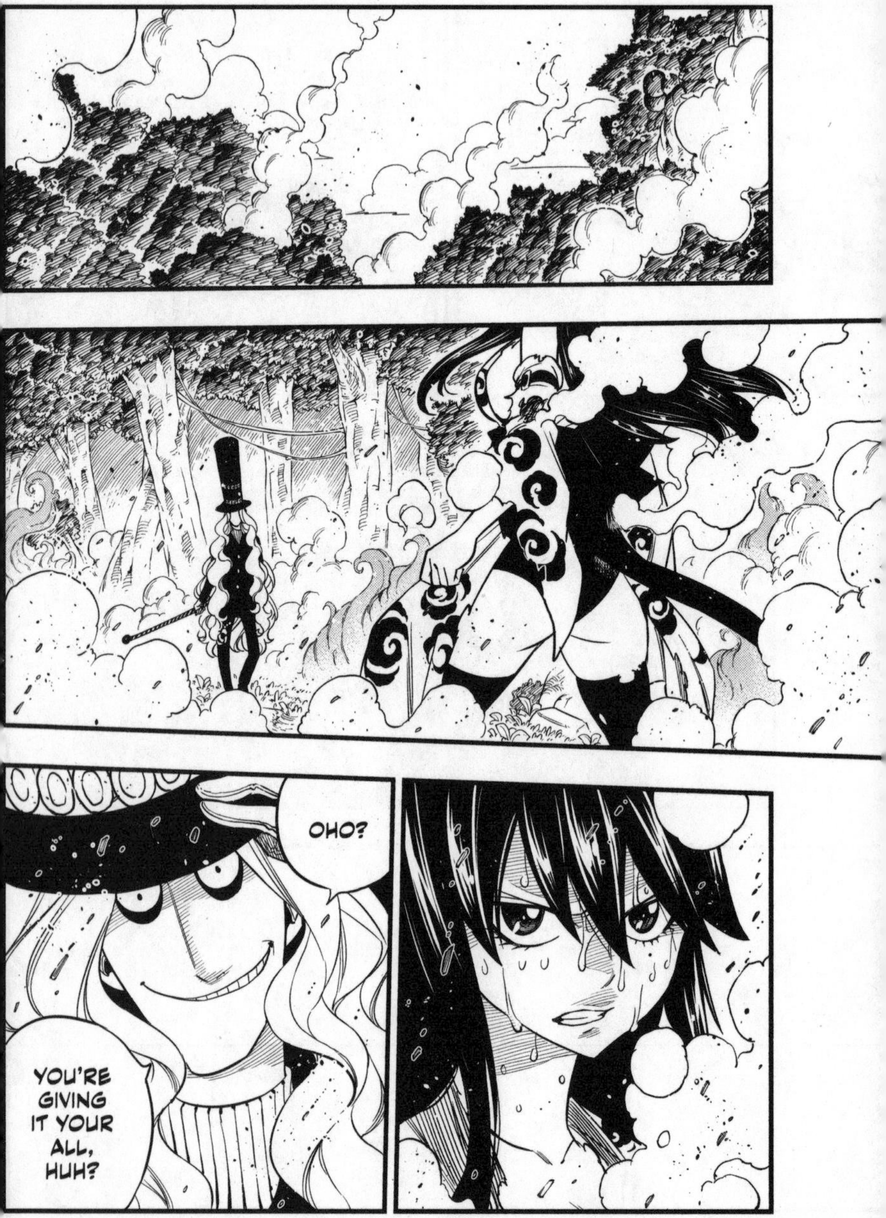
OHO?
YOU'RE GIVING IT YOUR ALL, HUH?

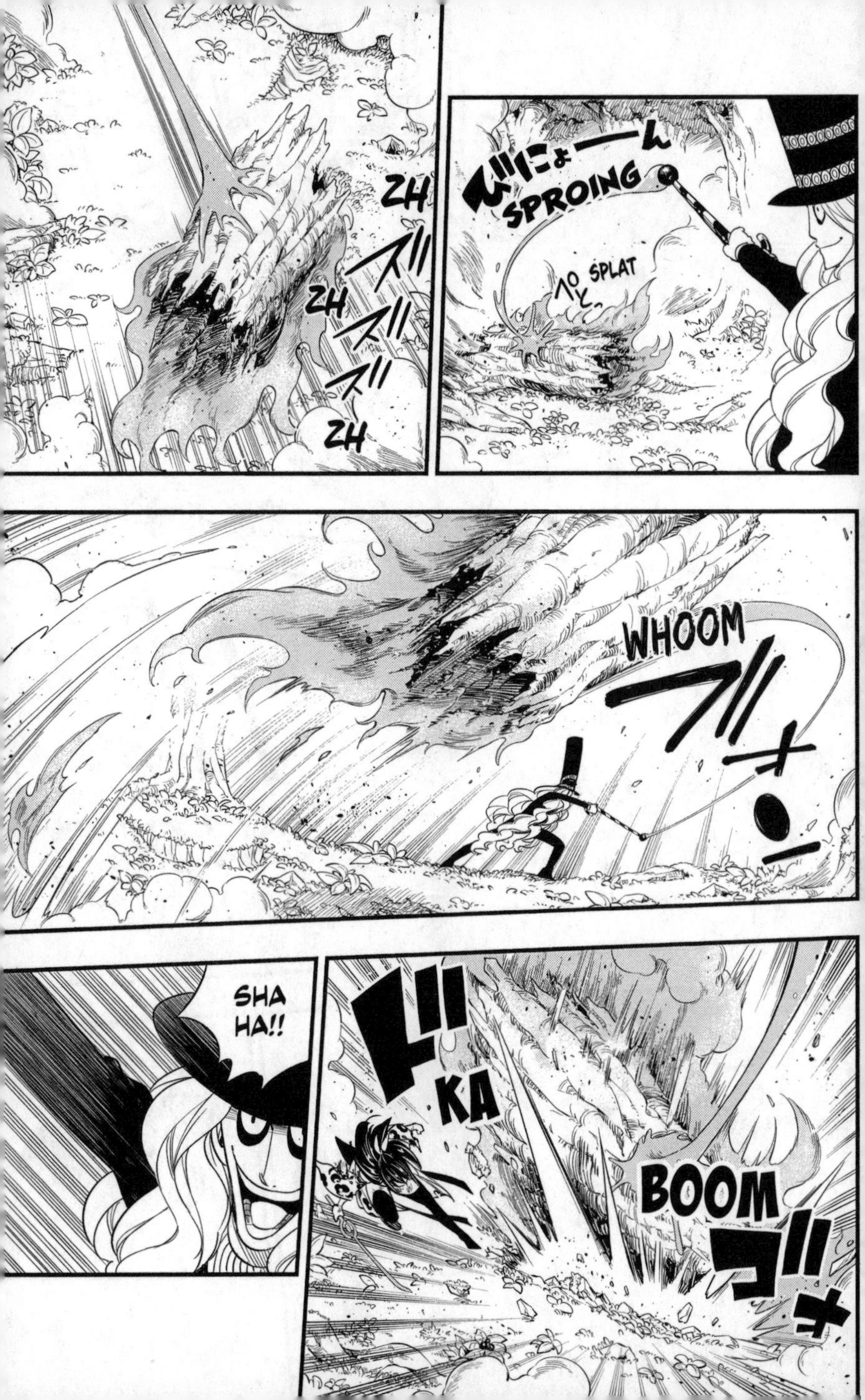
SPROING
SPLAT
ZH
ZH
ZH
WHOOM
KA
BOOM
SHA HA!!

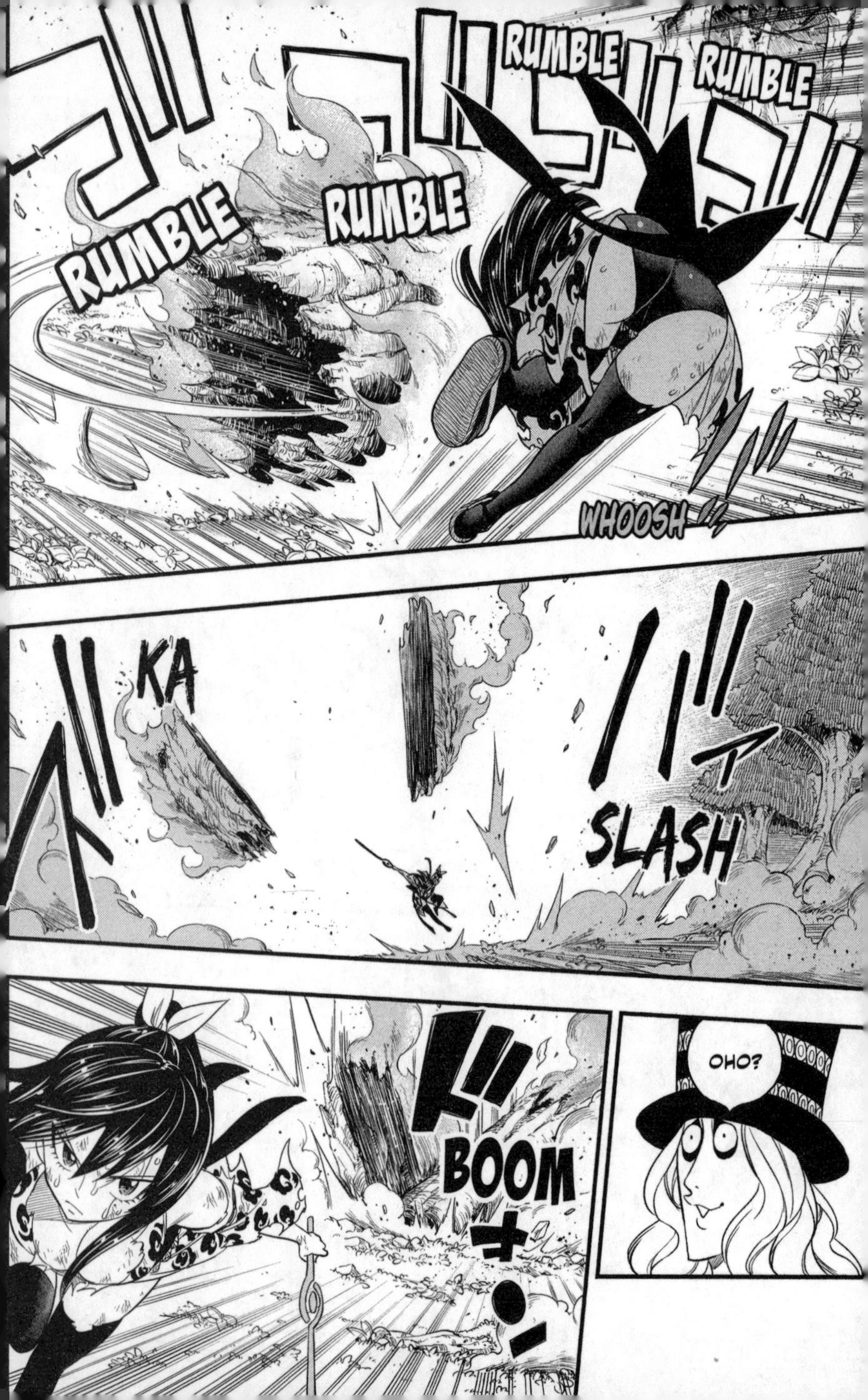
RUMBLE
RUMBLE
RUMBLE
RUMBLE
WHOOSH
SLASH
KA
OHO?
BOOM

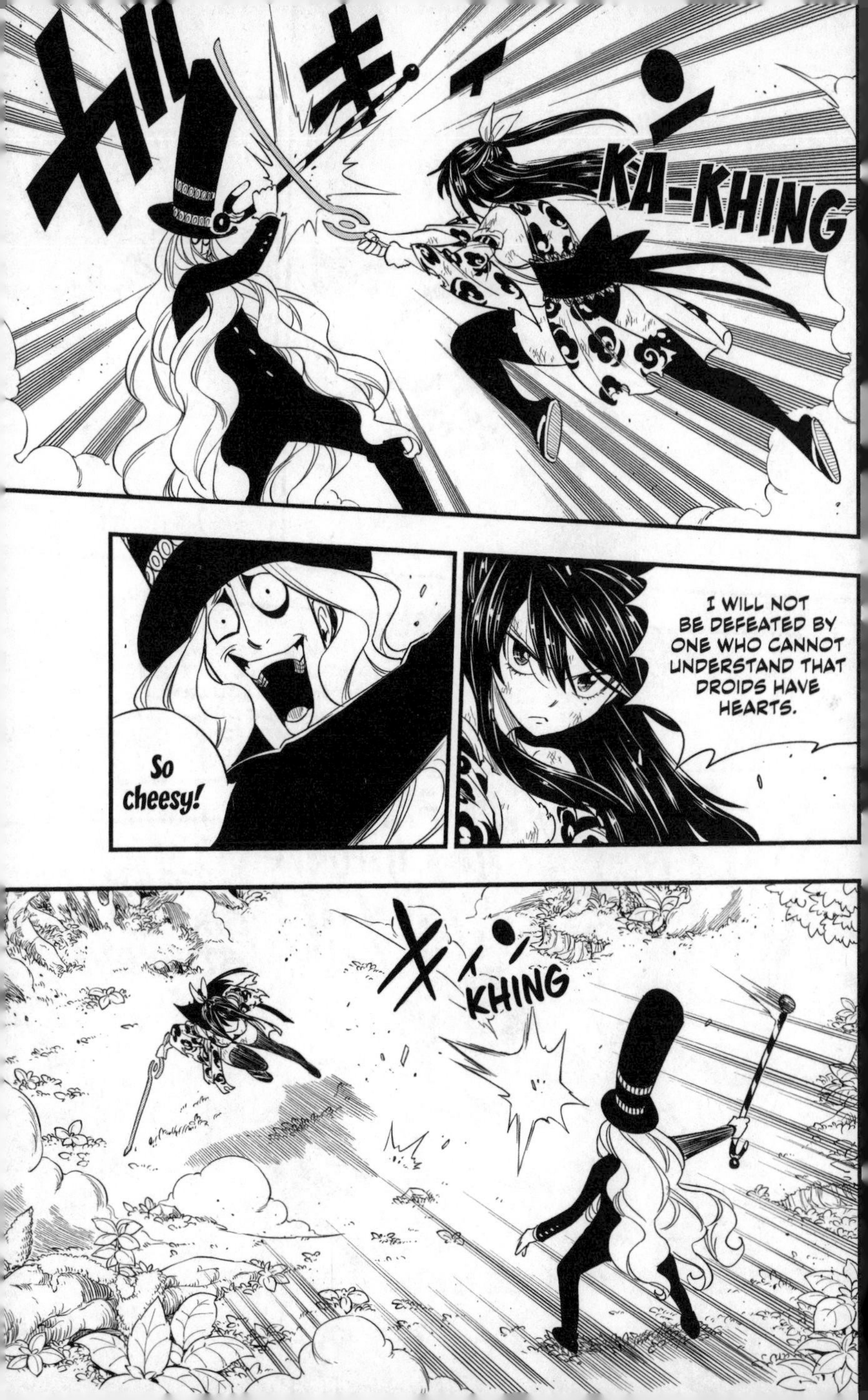
KA-KHING
I WILL NOT BE DEFEATED BY ONE WHO CANNOT UNDERSTAND THAT DROIDS HAVE HEARTS.
So cheesy!
KHING

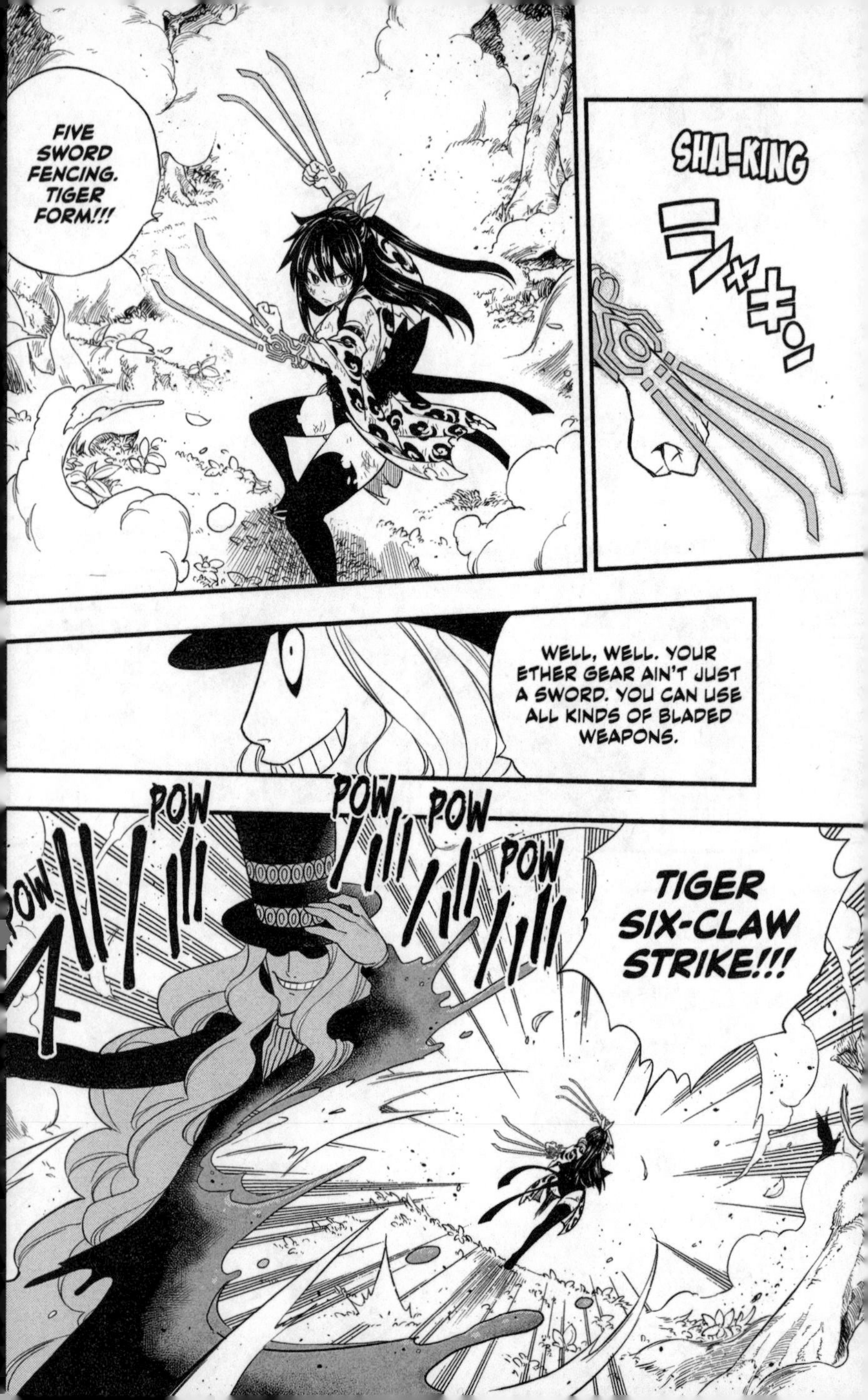
SHA-KING
FIVE SWORD FENCING. TIGER FORM!!!
WELL, WELL. YOUR ETHER GEAR AIN'T JUST A SWORD. YOU CAN USE ALL KINDS OF BLADED WEAPONS.
TIGER SIX-CLAW STRIKE!!!
POW
POW
POW
POW
POW

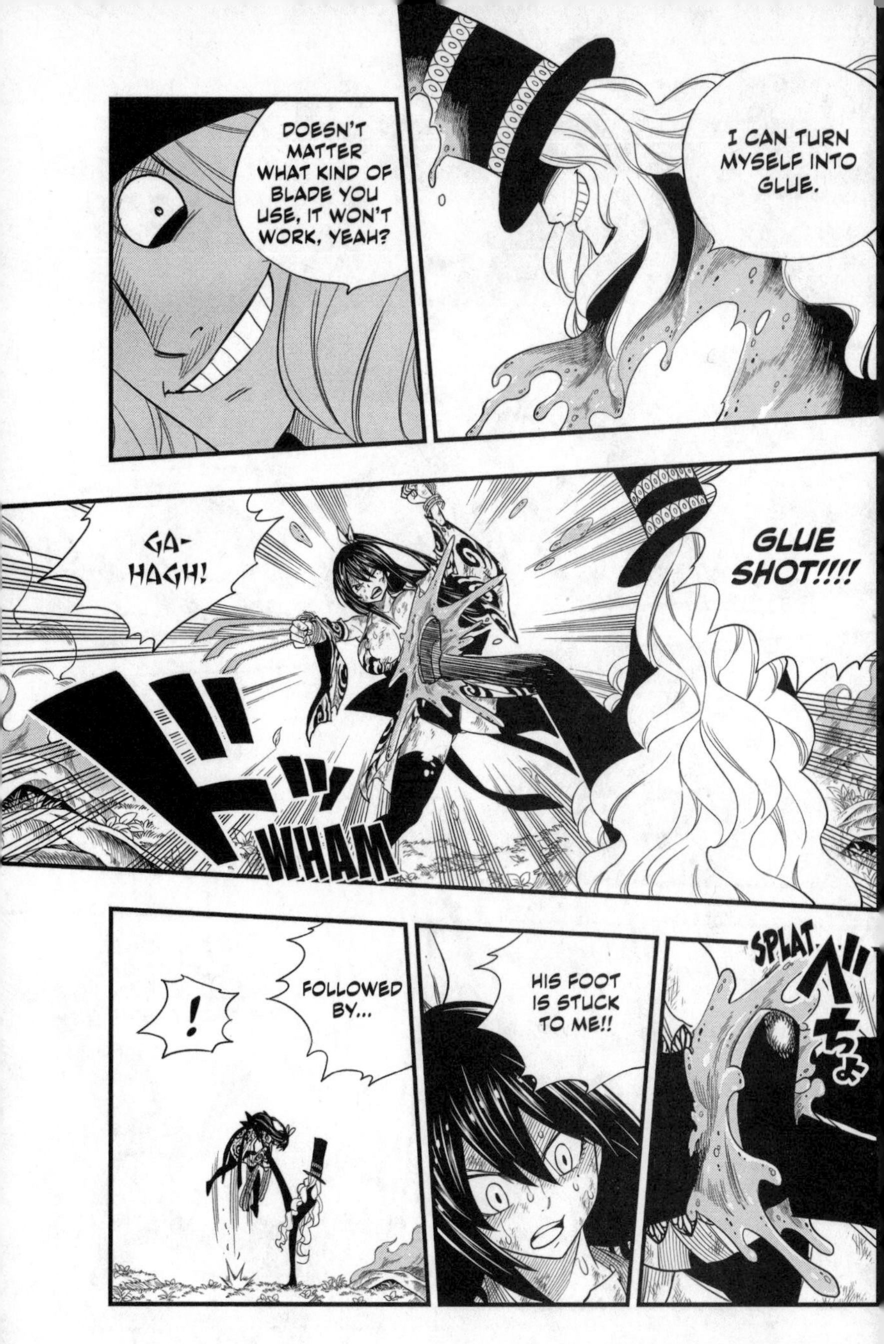
I CAN TURN MYSELF INTO GLUE.
DOESN'T MATTER WHAT KIND OF BLADE YOU USE, IT WON'T WORK, YEAH?
GLUE SHOT!!!!
GA-HAGH!
ドッ
WHAM
SPLAT
べちょ
HIS FOOT IS STUCK TO ME!!
FOLLOWED BY...
!

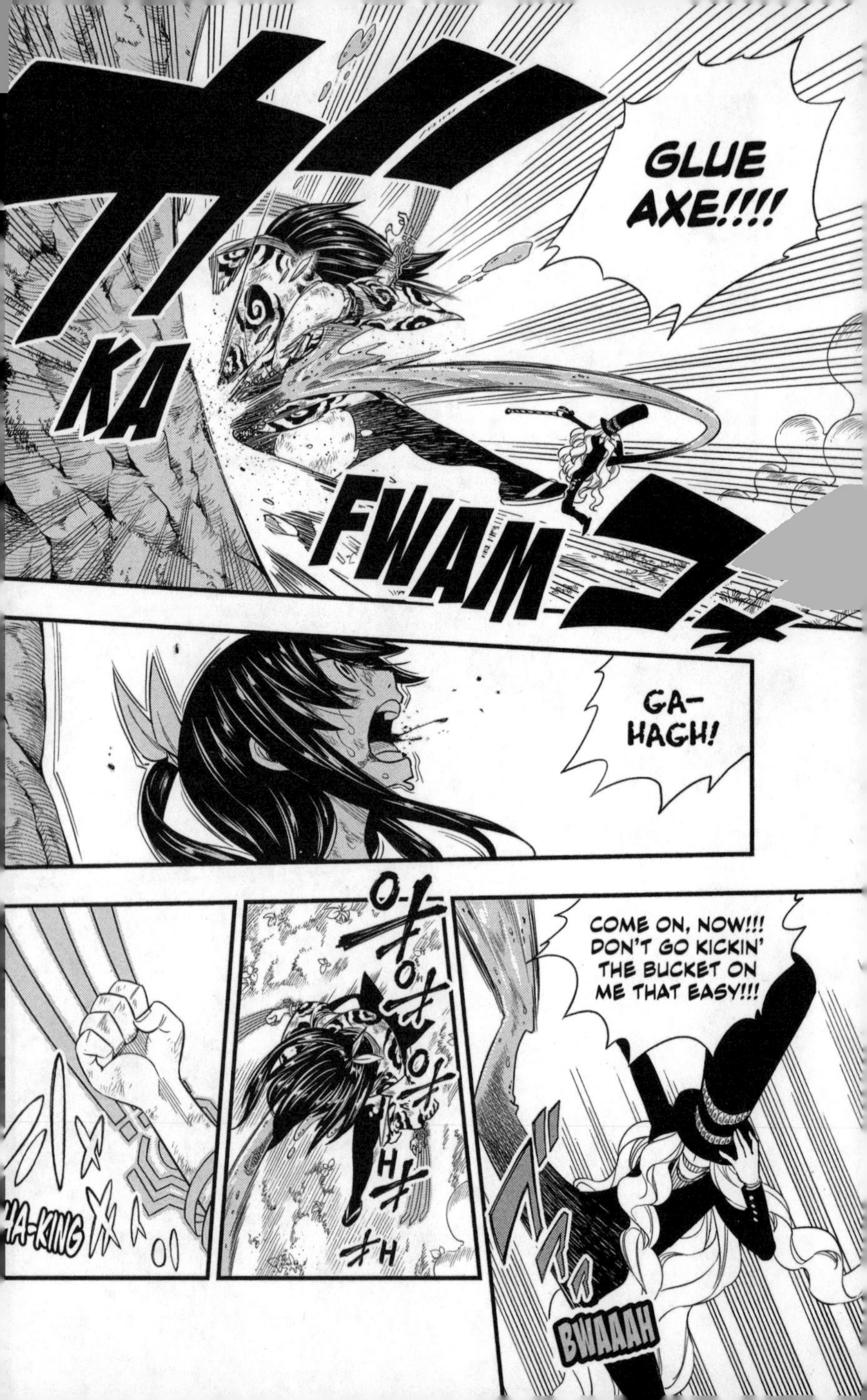
GLUE AXE!!!!
KA
FWAM
GA-HAGH!
COME ON, NOW!!! DON'T GO KICKIN' THE BUCKET ON ME THAT EASY!!!
BWAAAH
HA-KING

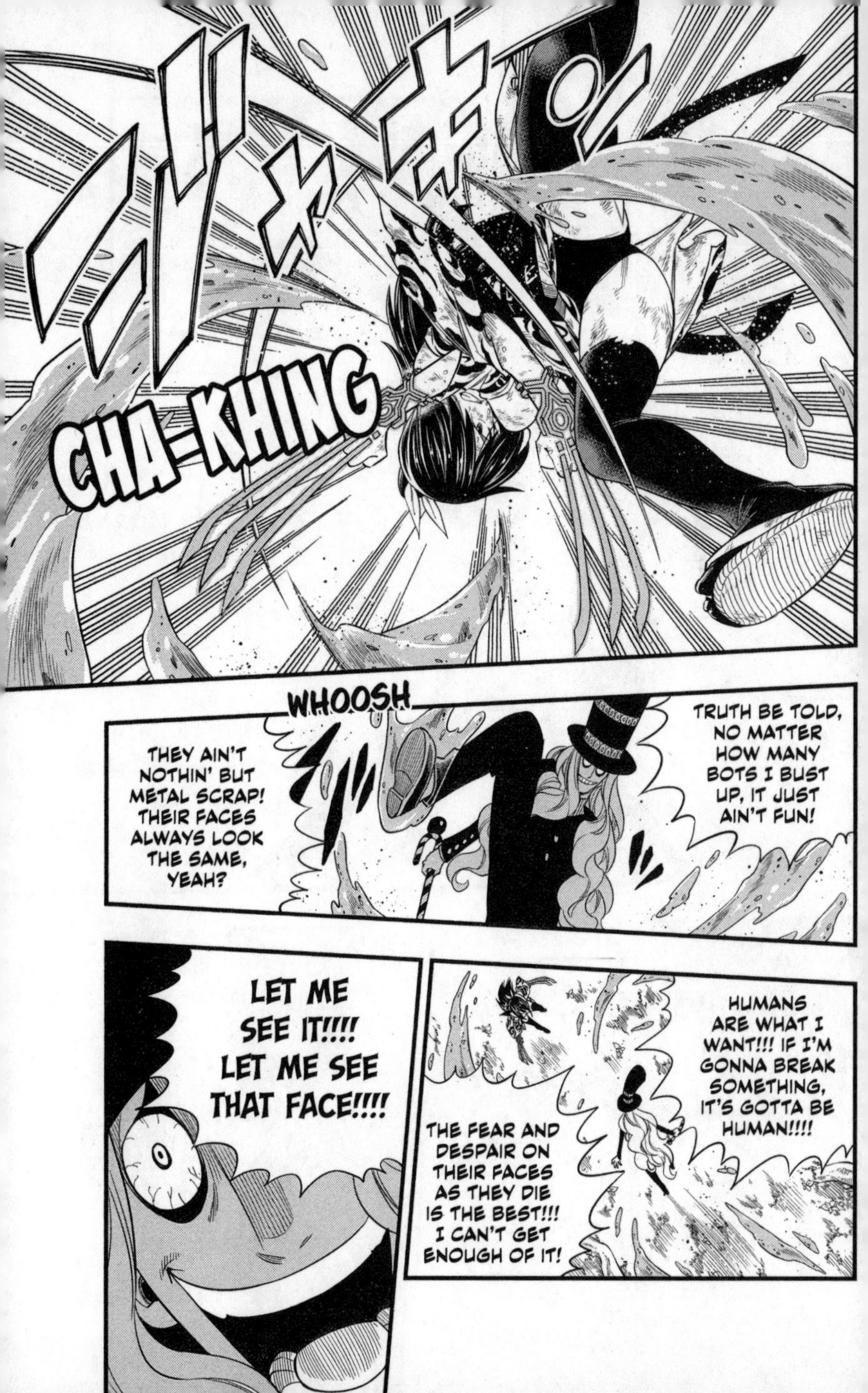
CHA-KHING
WHOOSH
TRUTH BE TOLD, NO MATTER HOW MANY BOTS I BUST UP, IT JUST AIN'T FUN!
THEY AIN'T NOTHIN' BUT METAL SCRAP! THEIR FACES ALWAYS LOOK THE SAME, YEAH?
HUMANS ARE WHAT I WANT!!! IF I'M GONNA BREAK SOMETHING, IT'S GOTTA BE HUMAN!!!!
THE FEAR AND DESPAIR ON THEIR FACES AS THEY DIE IS THE BEST!!! I CAN'T GET ENOUGH OF IT!
LET ME SEE IT!!!! LET ME SEE THAT FACE!!!!

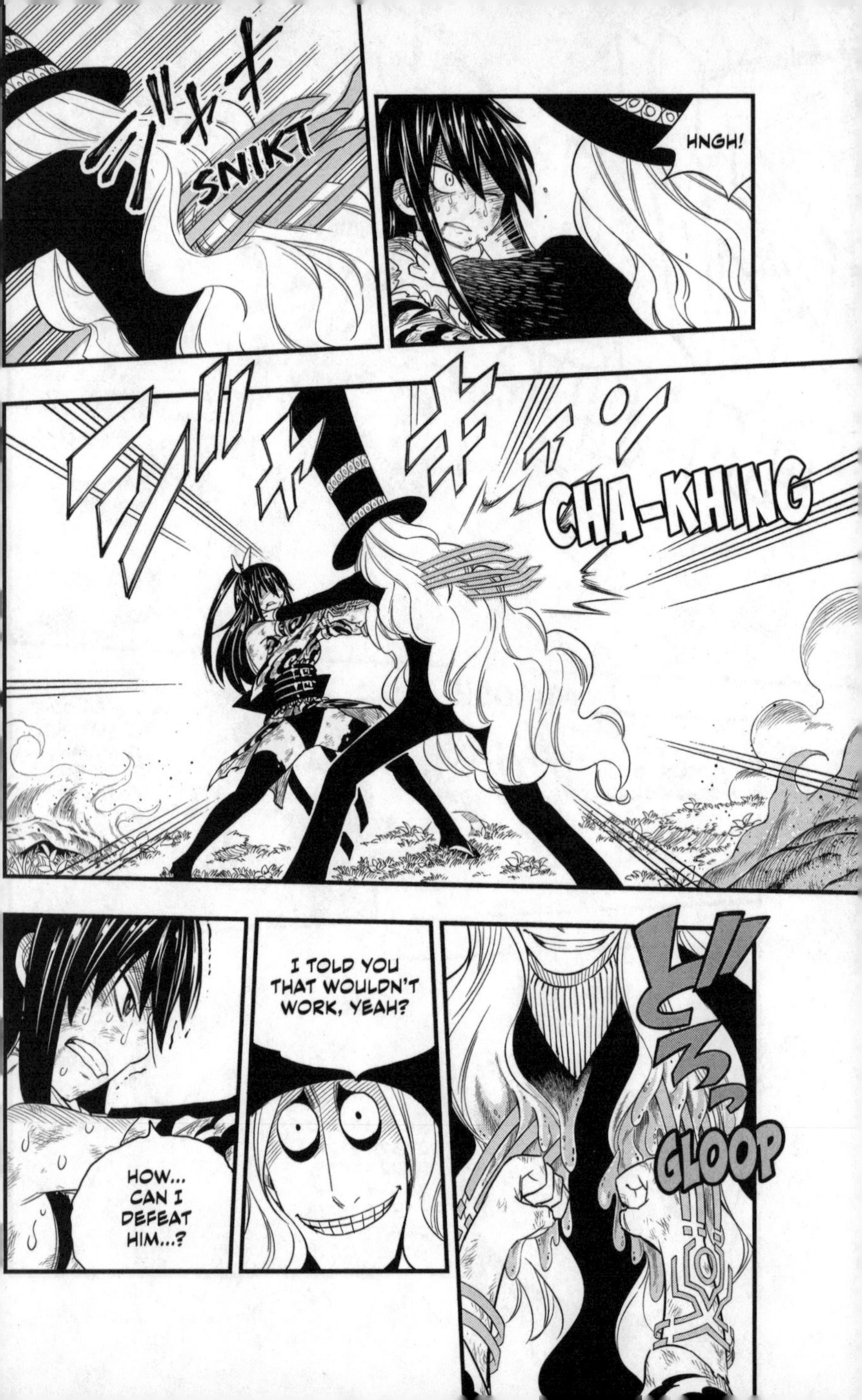
HNGH!
SNIKT
CHA-KHING
GLOOP
I TOLD YOU THAT WOULDN'T WORK, YEAH?
HOW... CAN I DEFEAT HIM...?

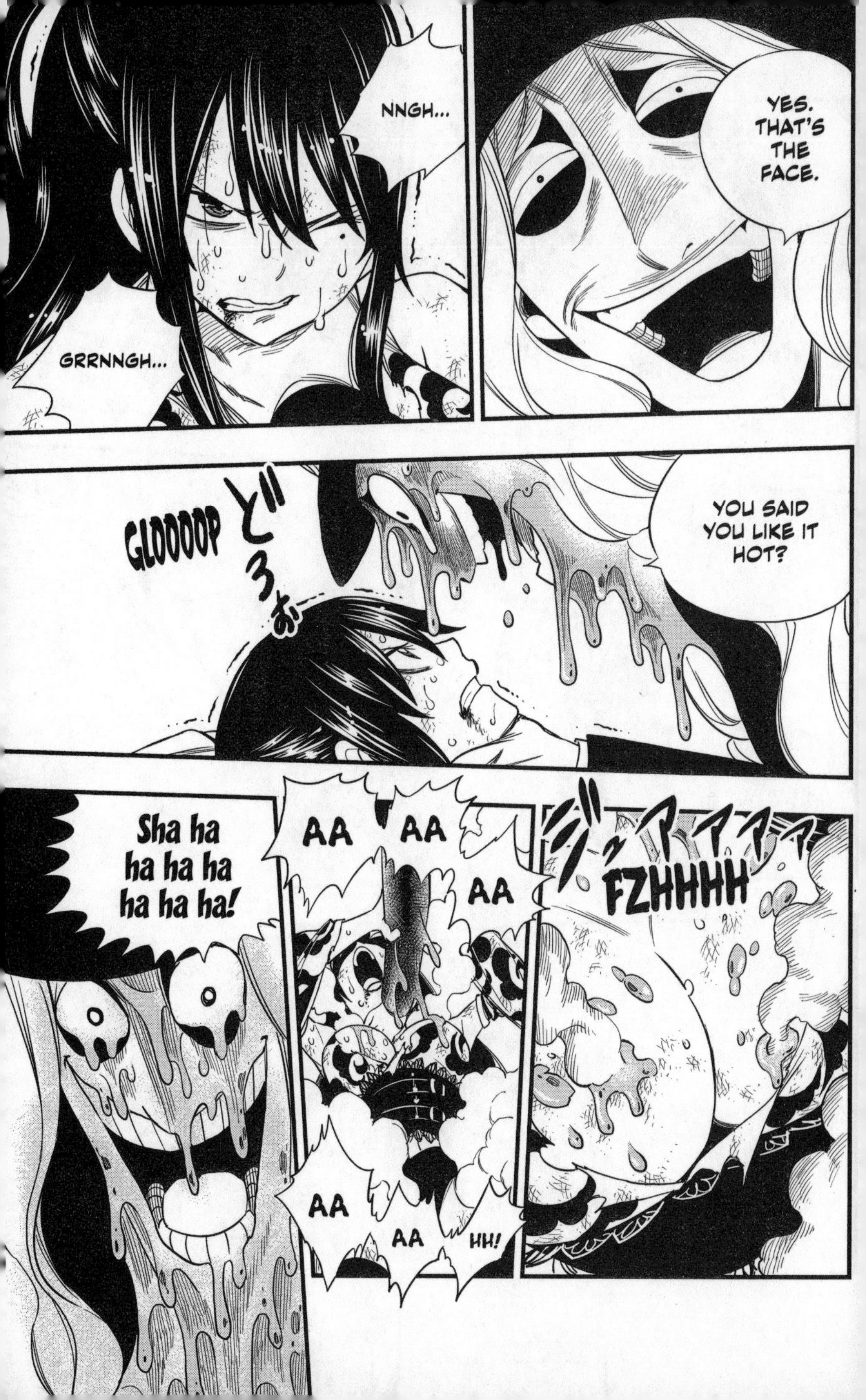
YES. THAT'S THE FACE.
NNGH...
GRRNNGH...
YOU SAID YOU LIKE IT HOT?
どろぉ
GLOOOOP
ジュアアアア
FZHHHH
AA AA AA AA AA HH!
Sha ha ha ha ha ha ha ha ha!

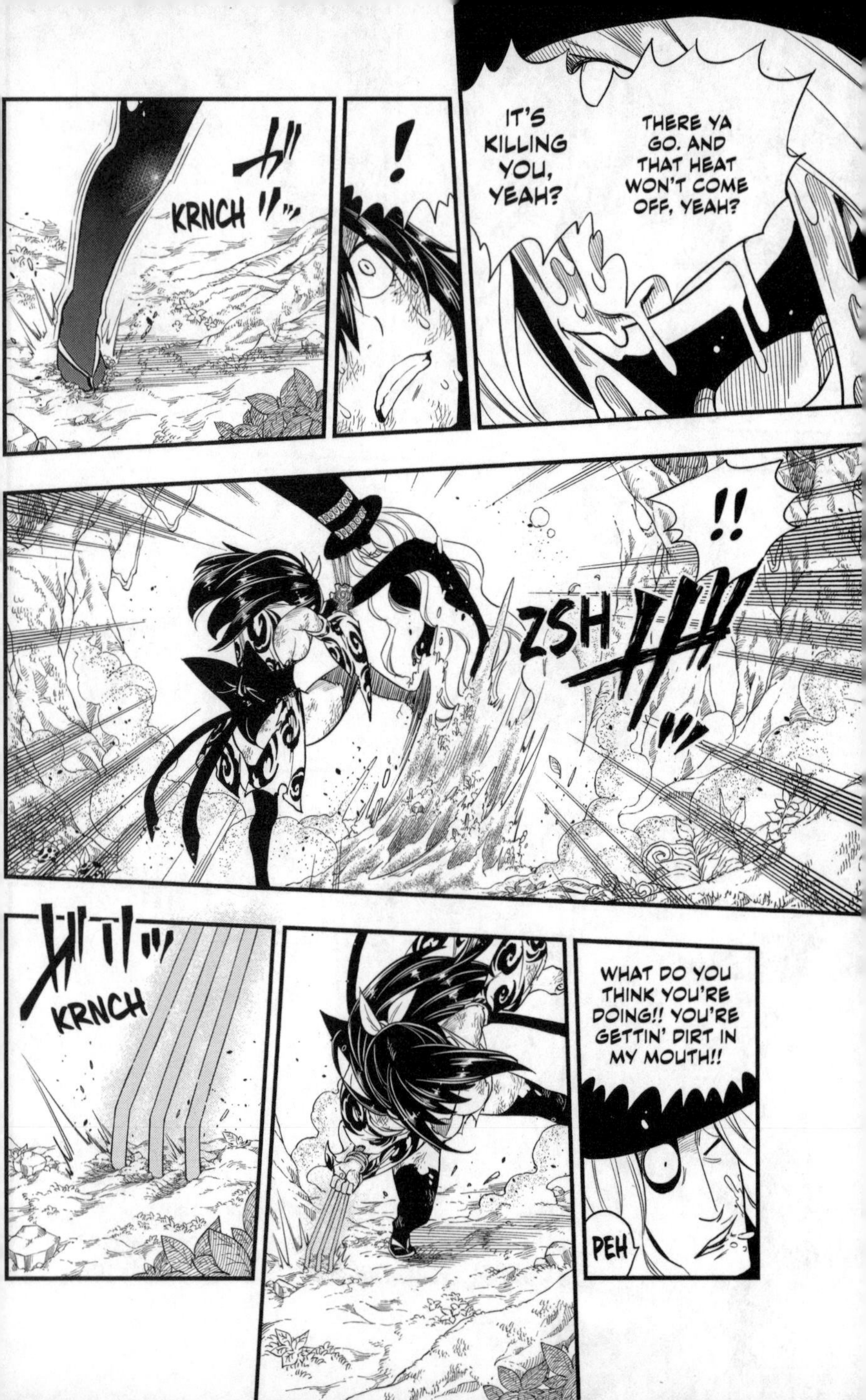
THERE YA GO. AND THAT HEAT WON'T COME OFF, YEAH?
IT'S KILLING YOU, YEAH?
!
KRNCH
!!
ZSH
WHAT DO YOU THINK YOU'RE DOING!! YOU'RE GETTIN' DIRT IN MY MOUTH!!
PEH
KRNCH

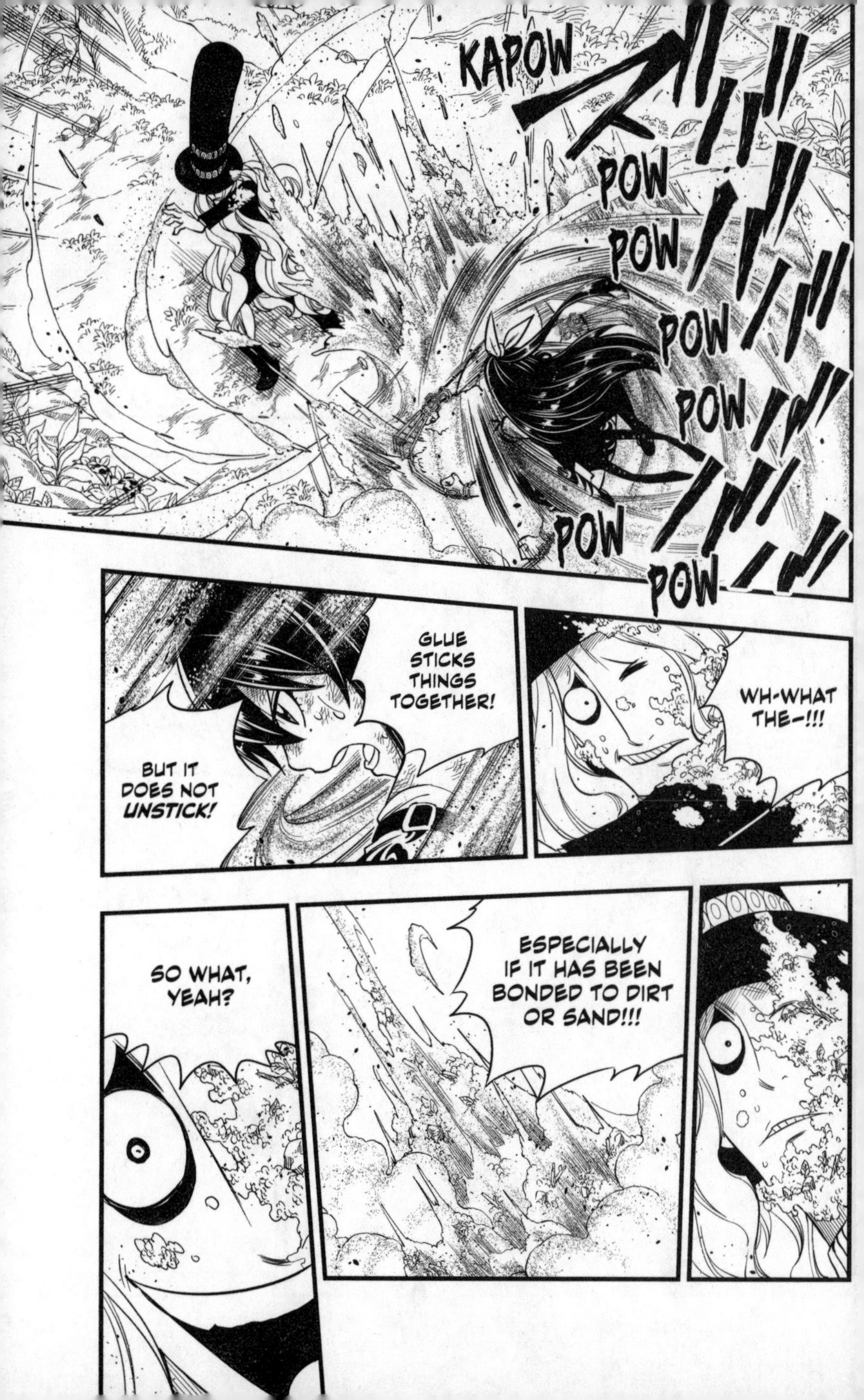
KAPOW
POW
POW
POW
POW
POW
POW
WH-WHAT THE-!!!
GLUE STICKS THINGS TOGETHER!
BUT IT DOES NOT *UNSTICK!*
ESPECIALLY IF IT HAS BEEN BONDED TO DIRT OR SAND!!!
SO WHAT, YEAH?

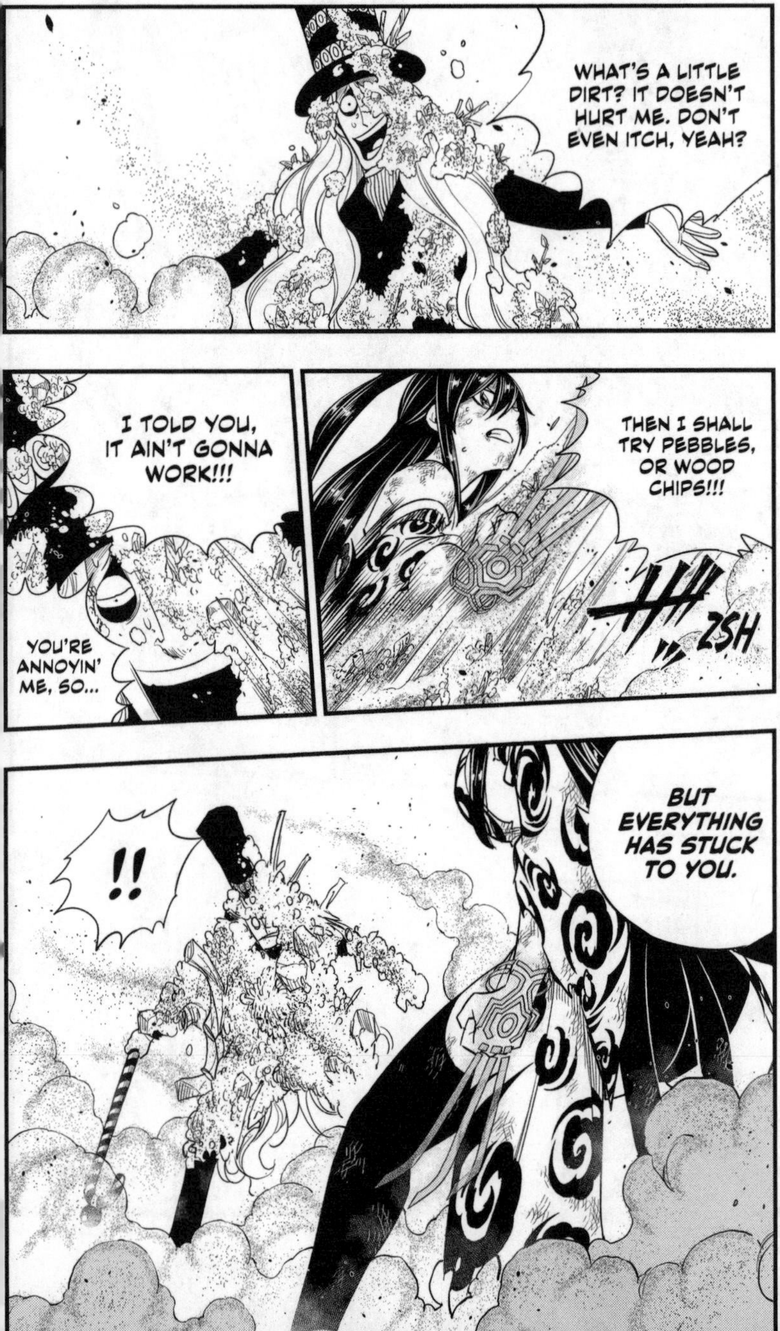
WHAT'S A LITTLE DIRT? IT DOESN'T HURT ME. DON'T EVEN ITCH, YEAH?
THEN I SHALL TRY PEBBLES, OR WOOD CHIPS!!!
ZSH
I TOLD YOU, IT AIN'T GONNA WORK!!!
YOU'RE ANNOYIN' ME, SO...
BUT EVERYTHING HAS STUCK TO YOU.
!!

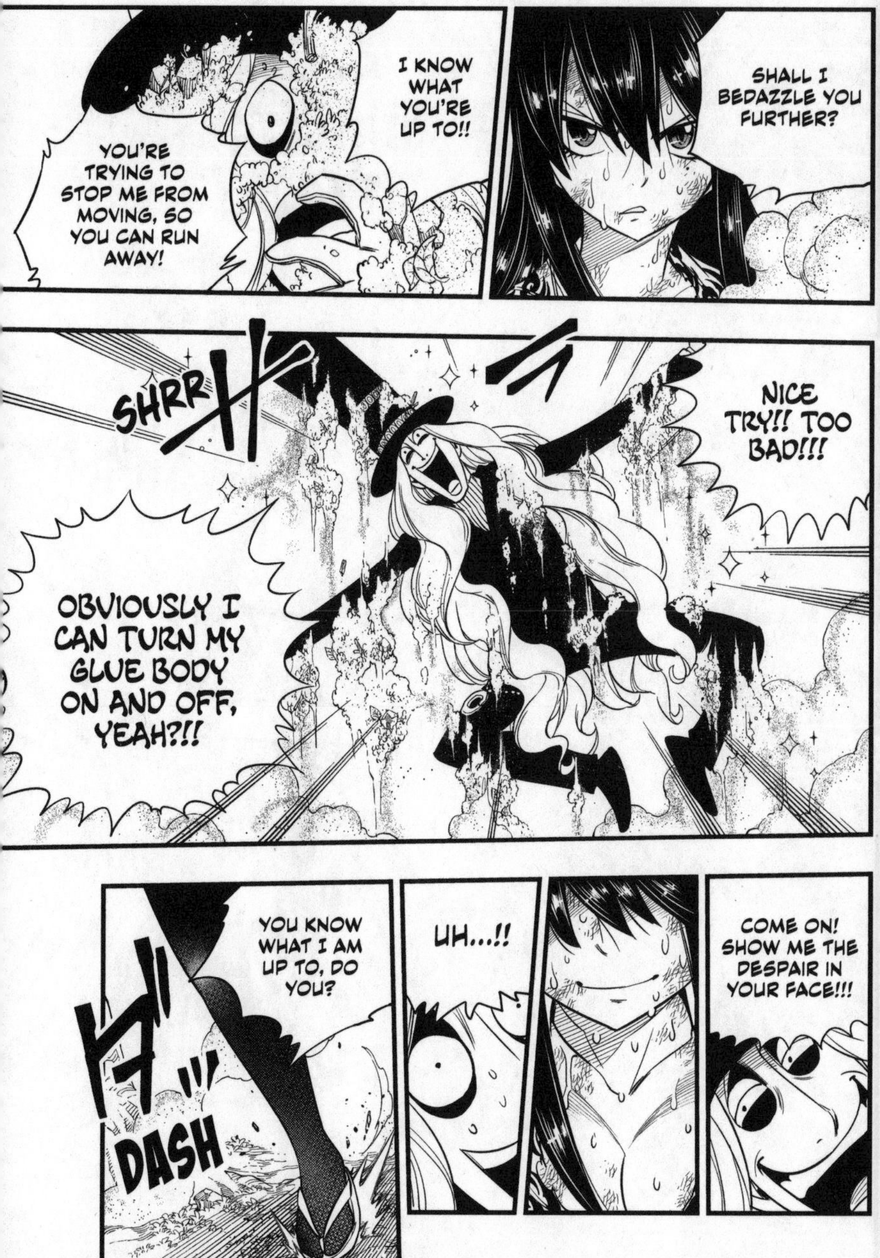
SHALL I BEDAZZLE YOU FURTHER?
I KNOW WHAT YOU'RE UP TO!!
YOU'RE TRYING TO STOP ME FROM MOVING, SO YOU CAN RUN AWAY!
NICE TRY!! TOO BAD!!!
SHRR
OBVIOUSLY I CAN TURN MY GLUE BODY ON AND OFF, YEAH?!!
COME ON! SHOW ME THE DESPAIR IN YOUR FACE!!!
UH...!!
YOU KNOW WHAT I AM UP TO, DO YOU?
ダッ
DASH

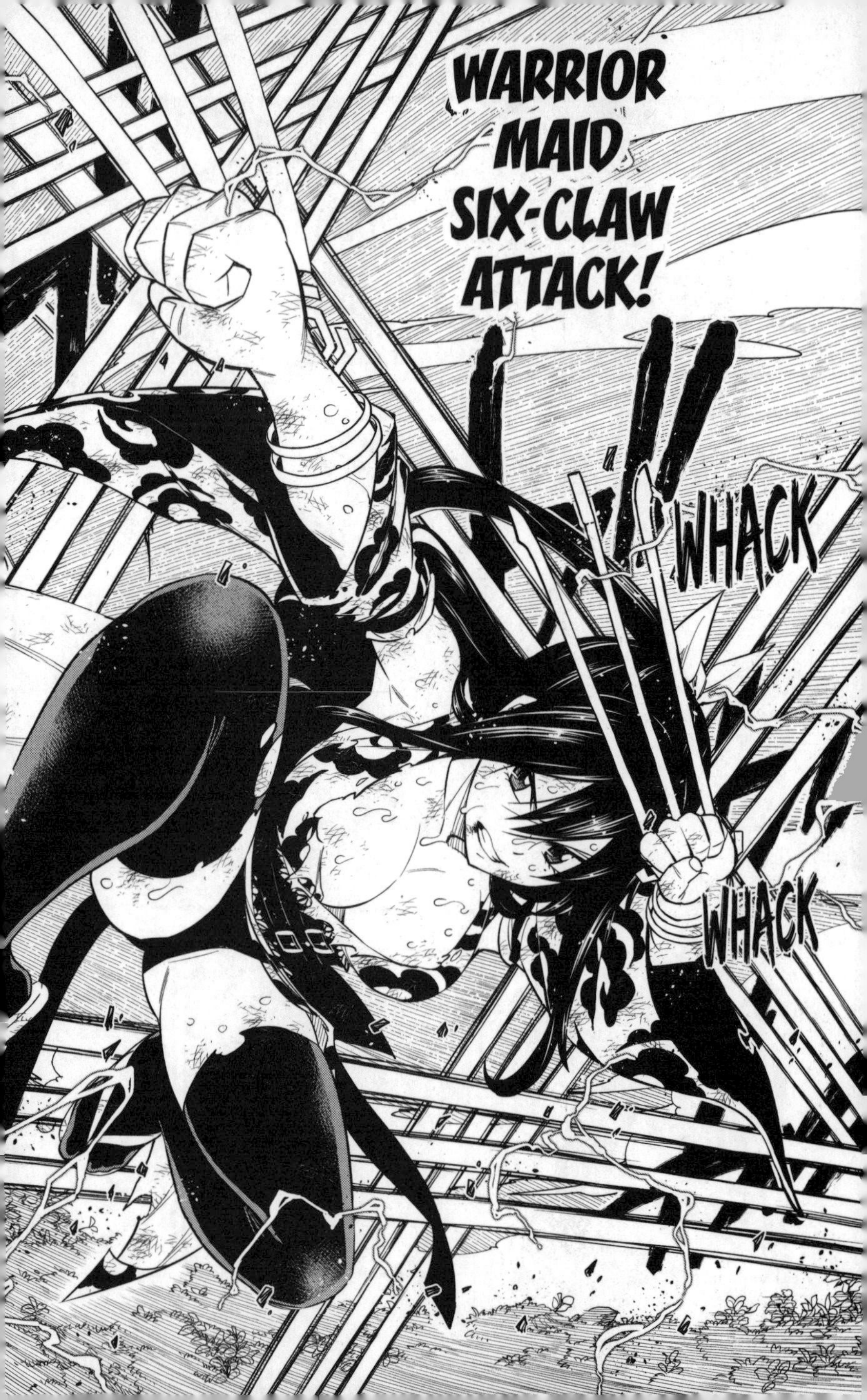
WARRIOR MAID SIX-CLAW ATTACK!
WHACK
WHACK

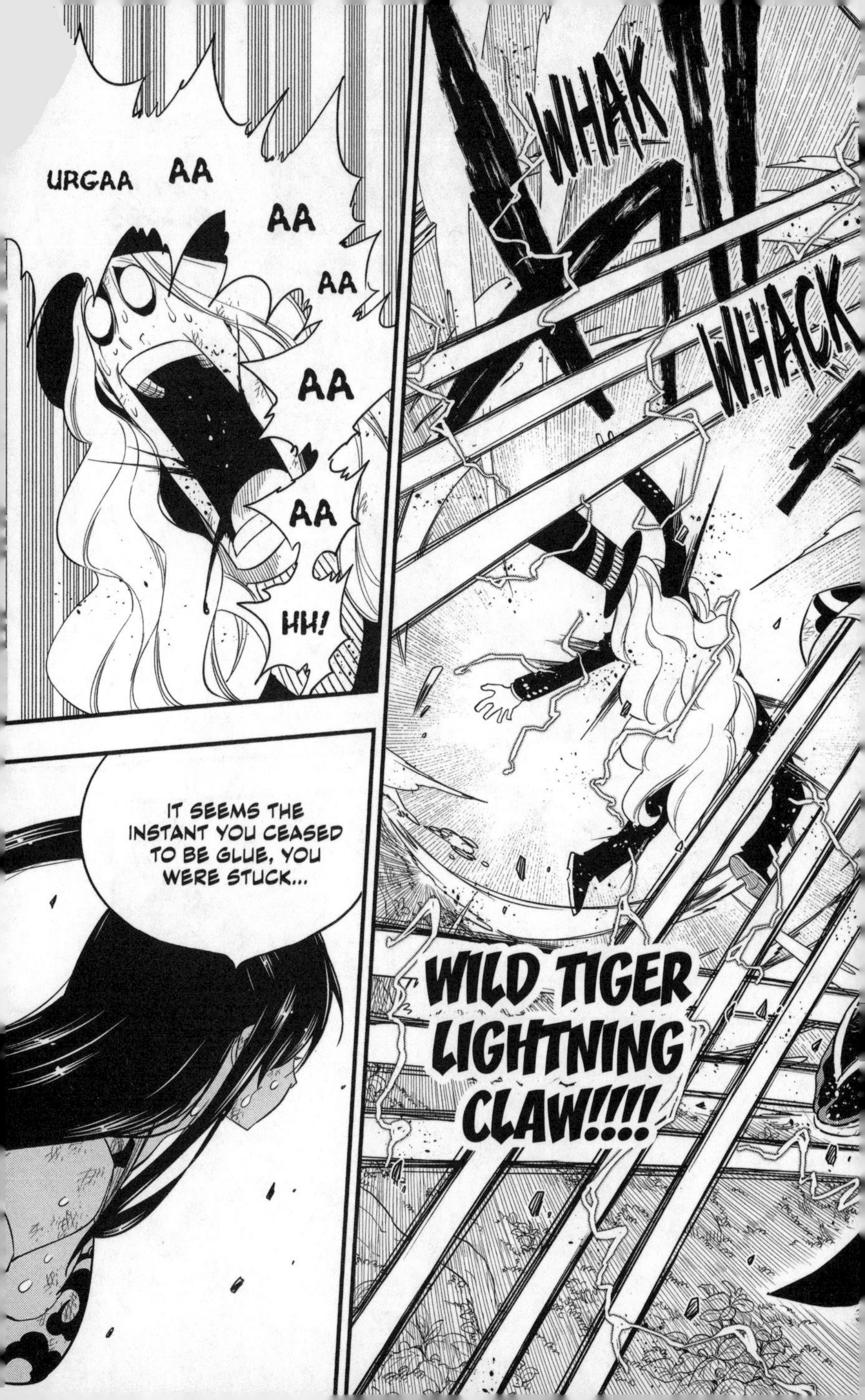
WHAK
WHACK
WILD TIGER LIGHTNING CLAW!!!!
URGAA AA AA AA AA AA HH!
IT SEEMS THE INSTANT YOU CEASED TO BE GLUE, YOU WERE STUCK...

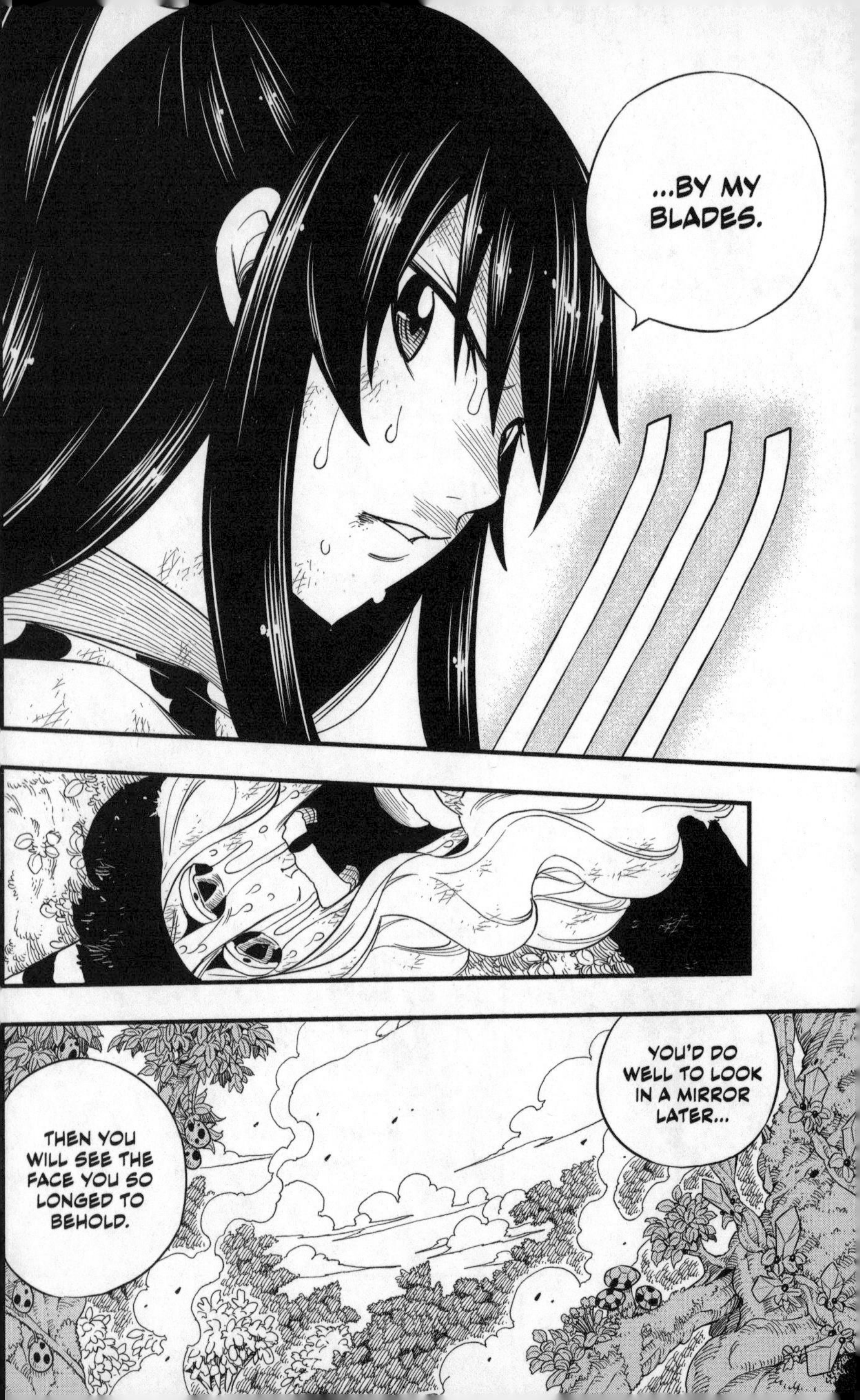
...BY MY BLADES.
YOU'D DO WELL TO LOOK IN A MIRROR LATER...
THEN YOU WILL SEE THE FACE YOU SO LONGED TO BEHOLD.

EDENS ZERO

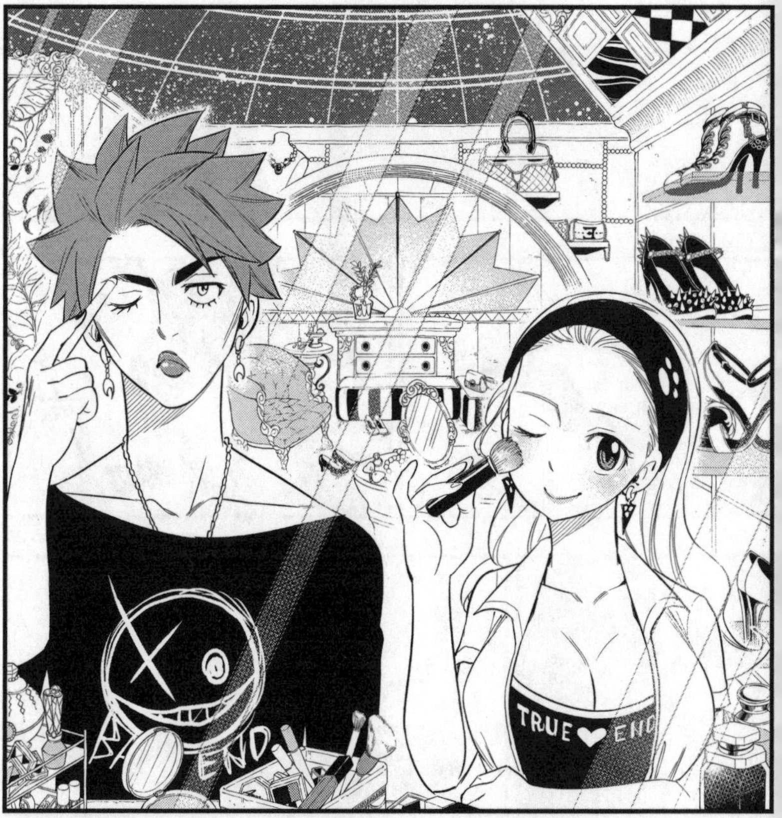
TRUE

CHAPTER 120: REBECCA VS. BRITNEY

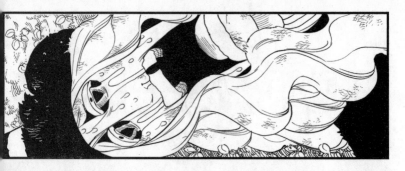

SWOON

'TIS... HOT.

I MUST SAY...

DAAAZE!

GRIMP

...

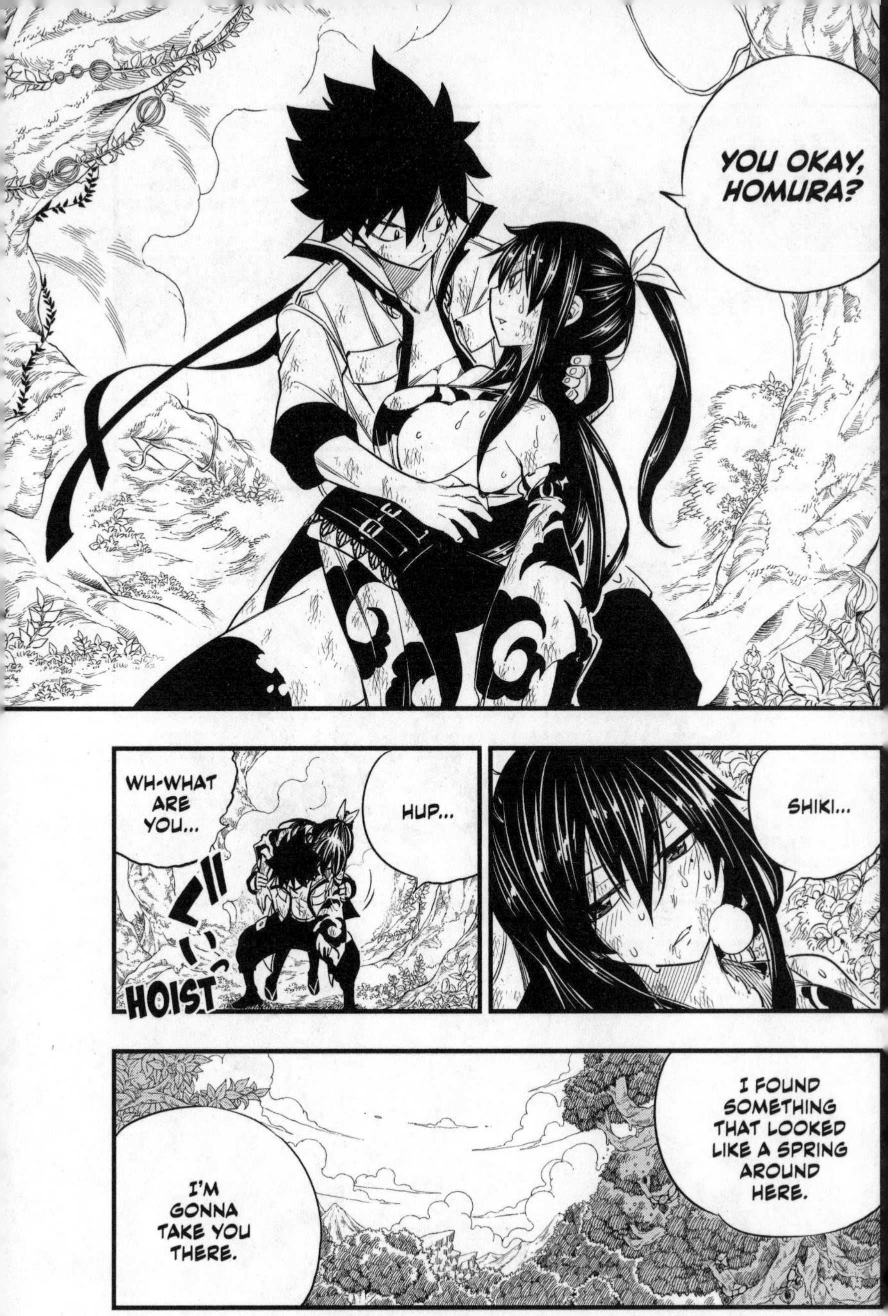
YOU OKAY, HOMURA?
SHIKI...
HUP...
WH-WHAT ARE YOU...
HOIST
I FOUND SOMETHING THAT LOOKED LIKE A SPRING AROUND HERE.
I'M GONNA TAKE YOU THERE.

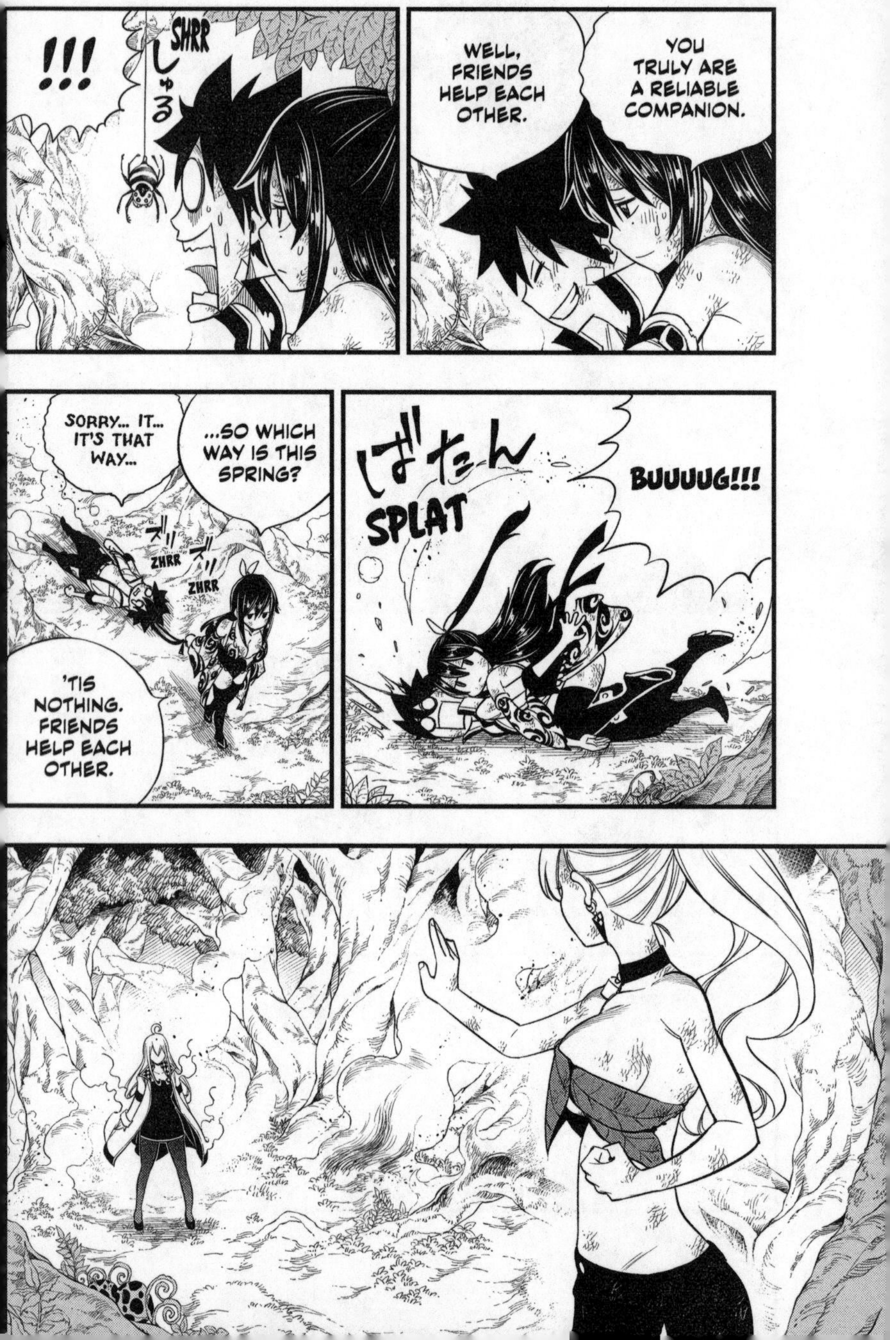
YOU TRULY ARE A RELIABLE COMPANION.
WELL, FRIENDS HELP EACH OTHER.
SHRR
しゅる
!!!
BUUUUG!!!
ばたん
SPLAT
...SO WHICH WAY IS THIS SPRING?
SORRY... IT... IT'S THAT WAY...
ズリ
ZHRR
ズリ
ZHRR
'TIS NOTHING. FRIENDS HELP EACH OTHER.

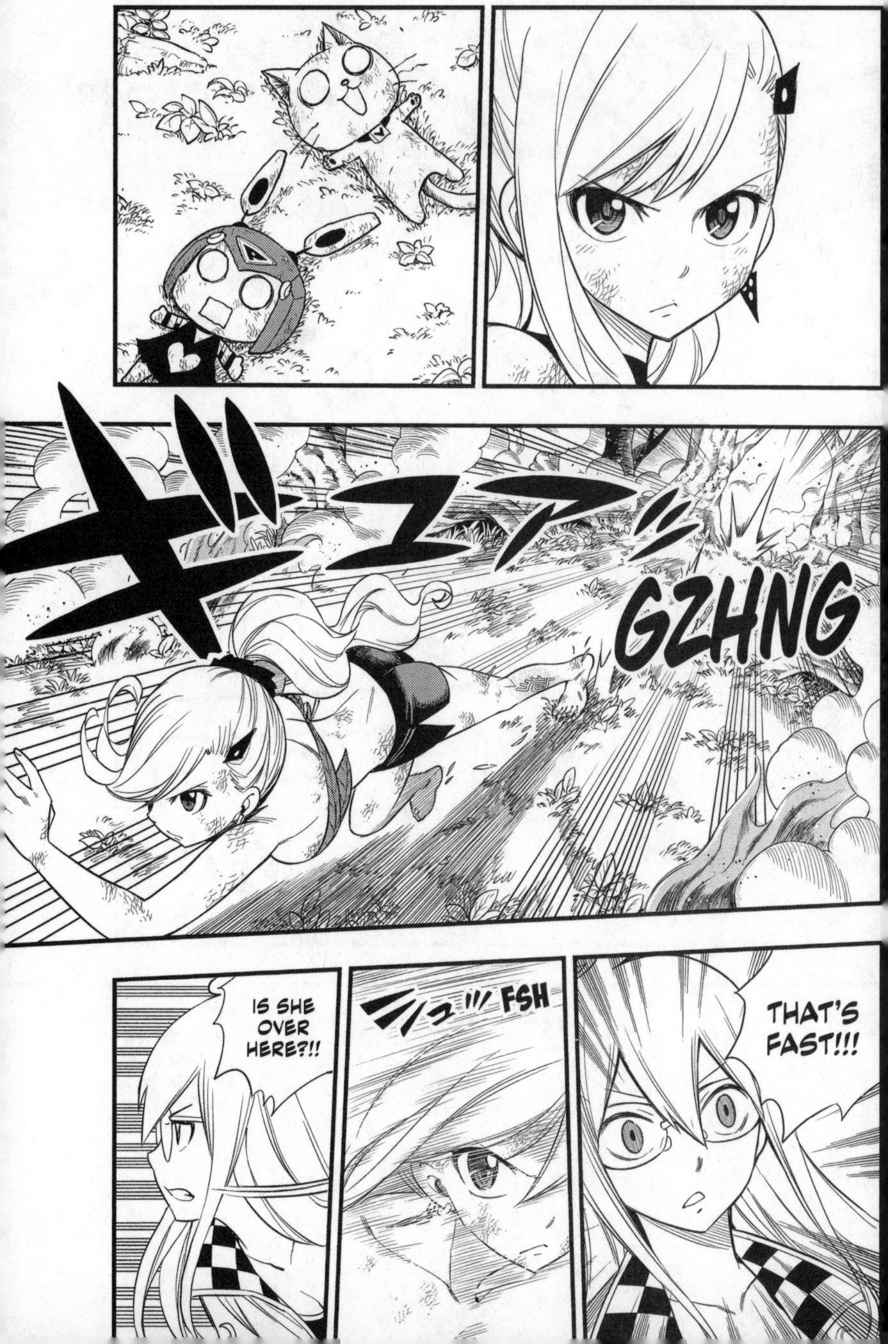
GZHNG
THAT'S FAST!!!
FSH
IS SHE OVER HERE?!!

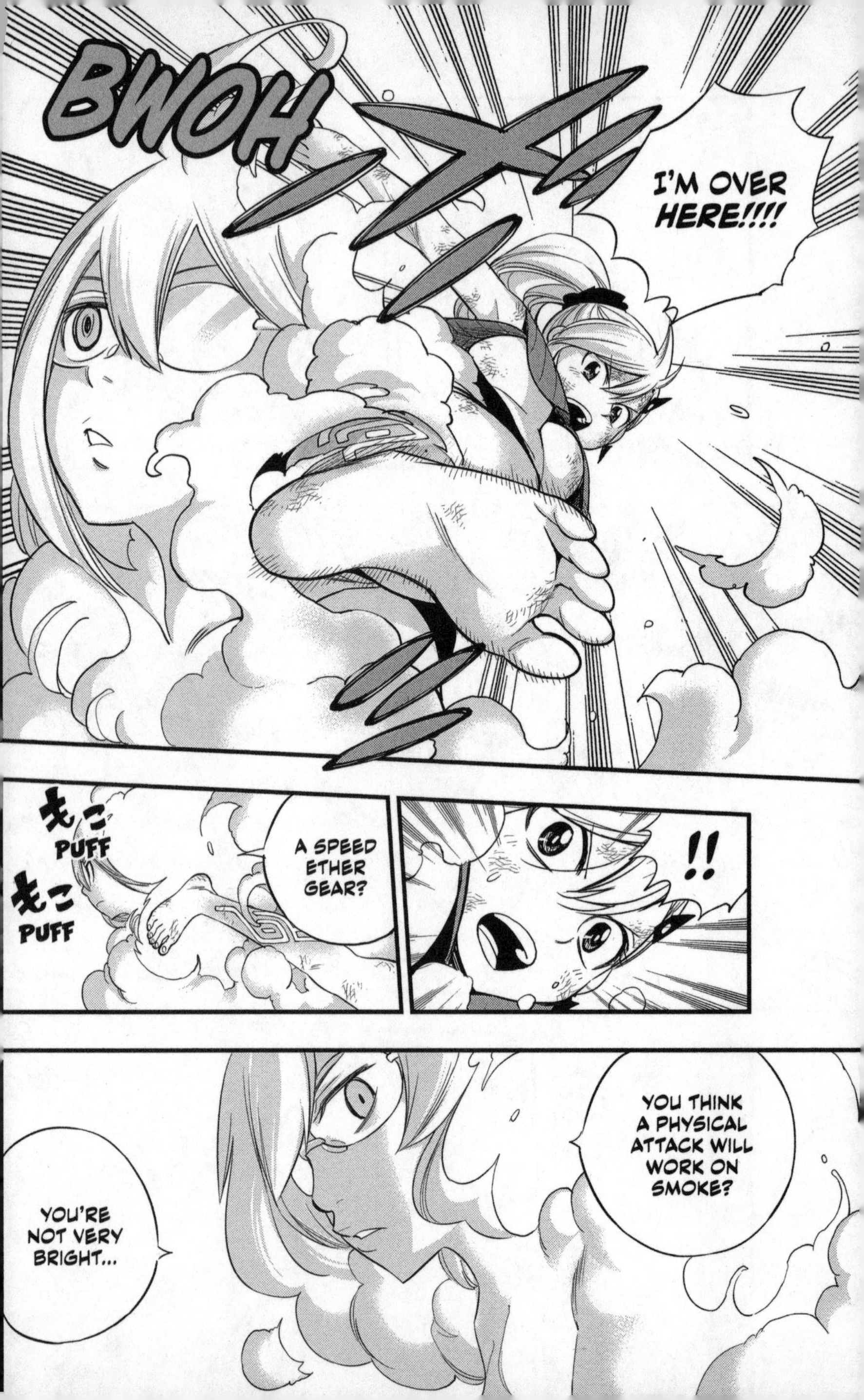
I'M OVER HERE!!!!
BWOH
!!
A SPEED ETHER GEAR?
もこ PUFF
もこ PUFF
YOU THINK A PHYSICAL ATTACK WILL WORK ON SMOKE?
YOU'RE NOT VERY BRIGHT...

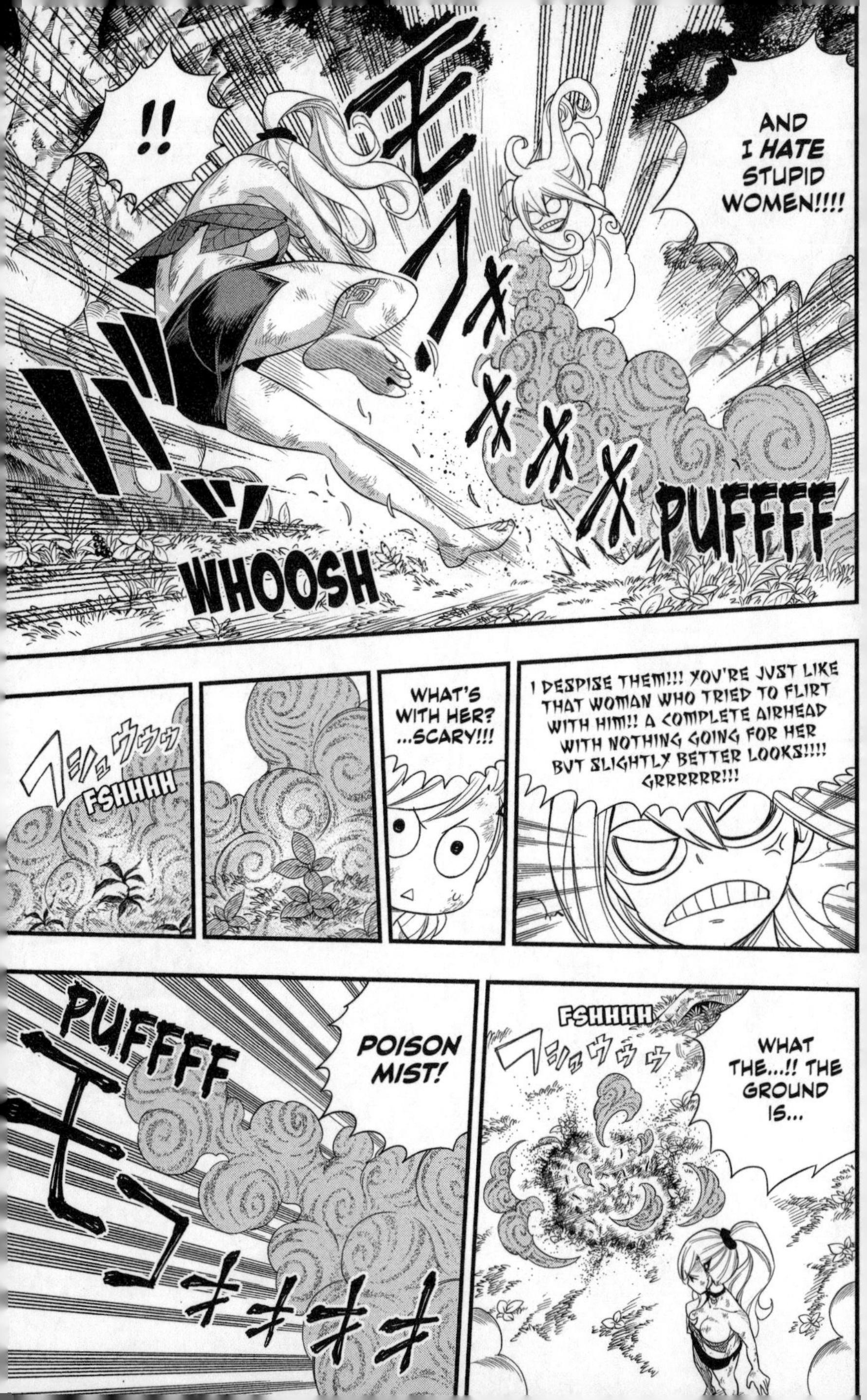

AND I HATE STUPID WOMEN!!!!
PUFFFF
!!
WHOOSH
I DESPISE THEM!!! YOU'RE JUST LIKE THAT WOMAN WHO TRIED TO FLIRT WITH HIM!! A COMPLETE AIRHEAD WITH NOTHING GOING FOR HER BUT SLIGHTLY BETTER LOOKS!!!! GRRRRRR!!!
WHAT'S WITH HER? ...SCARY!!!
FSHHHH
FSHHHH
WHAT THE...!! THE GROUND IS...
POISON MIST!
PUFFFF

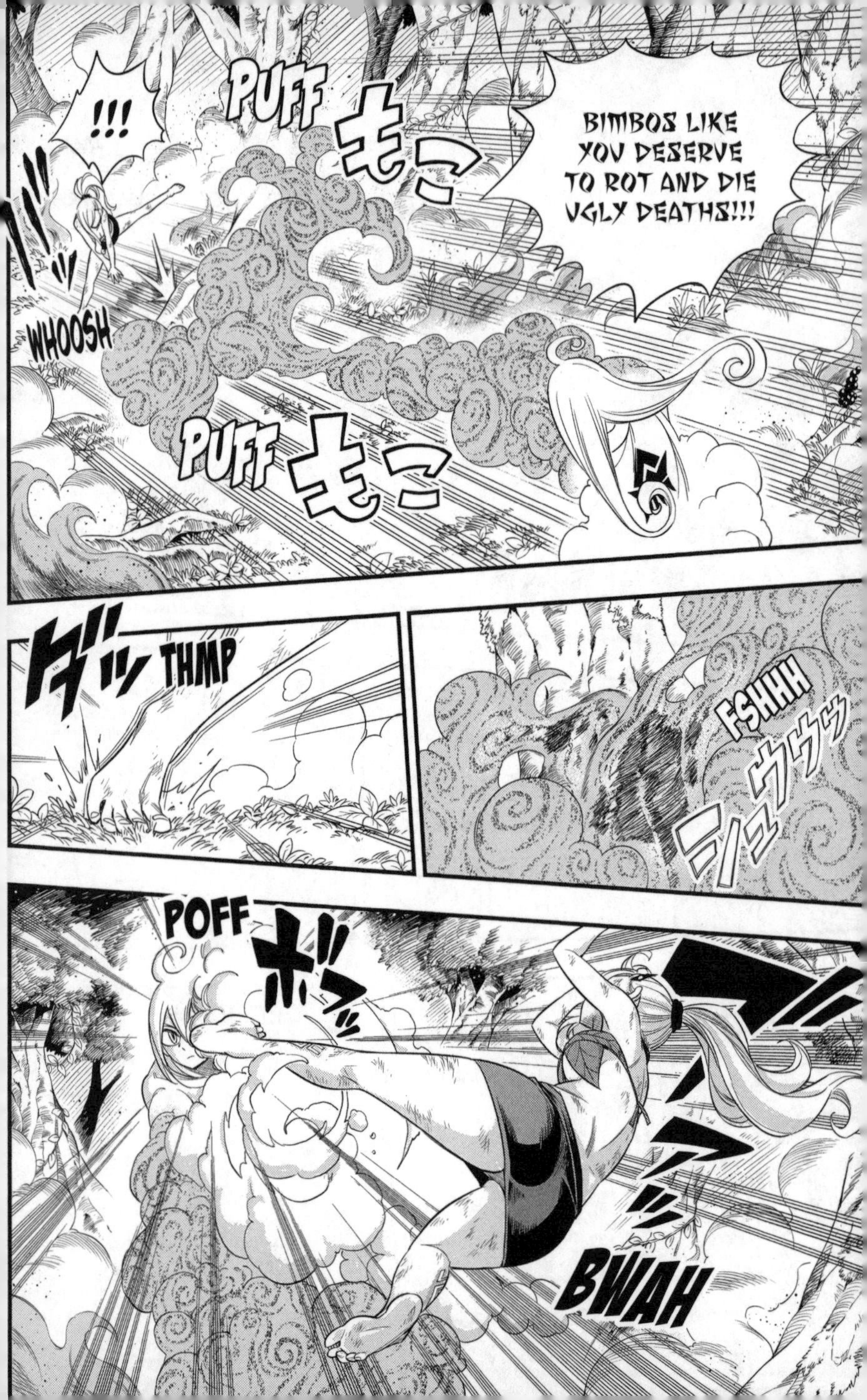

BIMBOS LIKE YOU DESERVE TO ROT AND DIE UGLY DEATHS!!!
PUFF もこ
!!!
WHOOSH
PUFF もこ
FSHHH シュウウウ
THMP
BWAH
POFF ボフッ

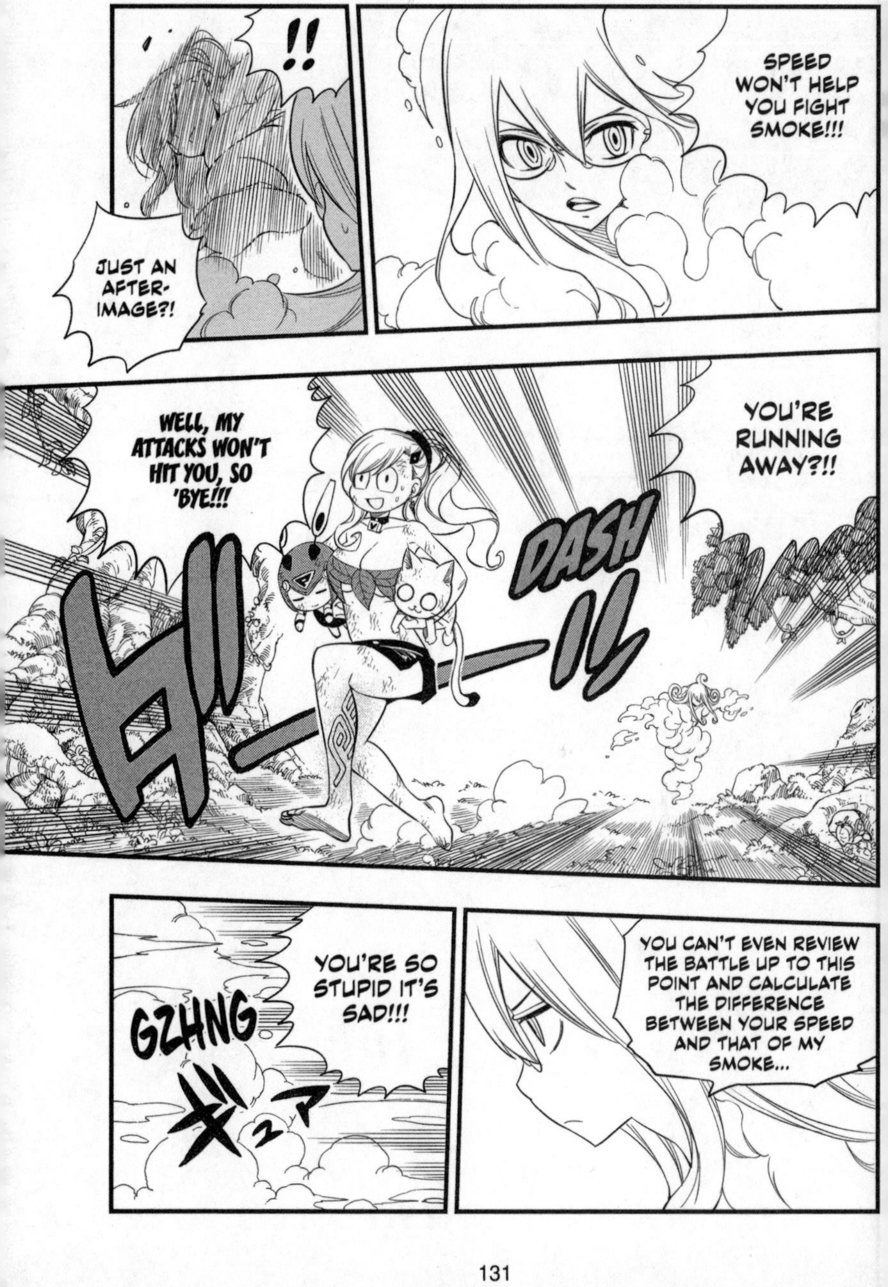
SPEED WON'T HELP YOU FIGHT SMOKE!!!
!!
JUST AN AFTER-IMAGE?!
YOU'RE RUNNING AWAY?!!
DASH
WELL, MY ATTACKS WON'T HIT YOU, SO 'BYE!!!
YOU CAN'T EVEN REVIEW THE BATTLE UP TO THIS POINT AND CALCULATE THE DIFFERENCE BETWEEN YOUR SPEED AND THAT OF MY SMOKE...
YOU'RE SO STUPID IT'S SAD!!!
GZHNG

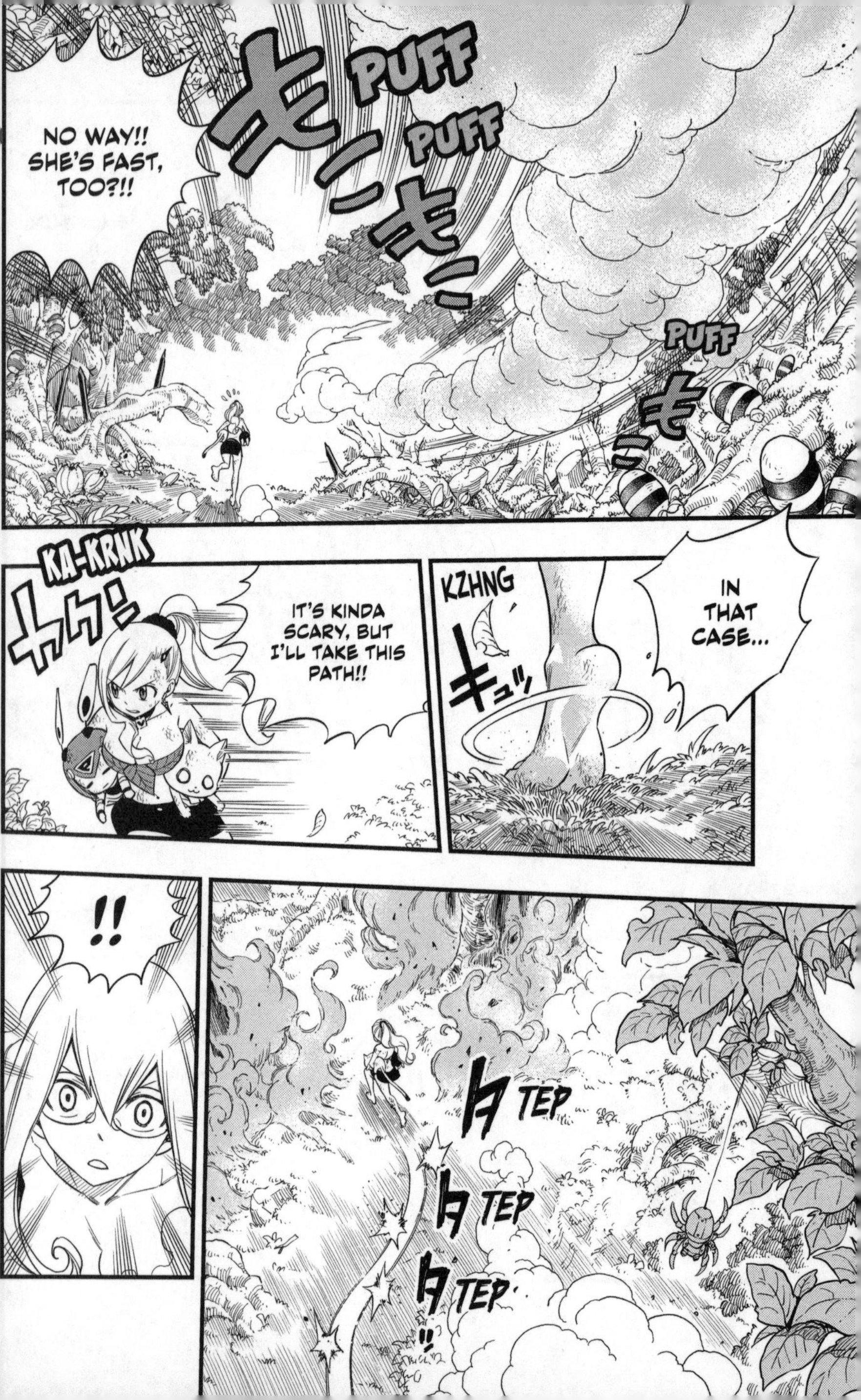
PUFF
PUFF
NO WAY!! SHE'S FAST, TOO?!!
PUFF
IN THAT CASE...
KZHNG
IT'S KINDA SCARY, BUT I'LL TAKE THIS PATH!!
KA-KRNK
TEP
TEP
TEP
!!

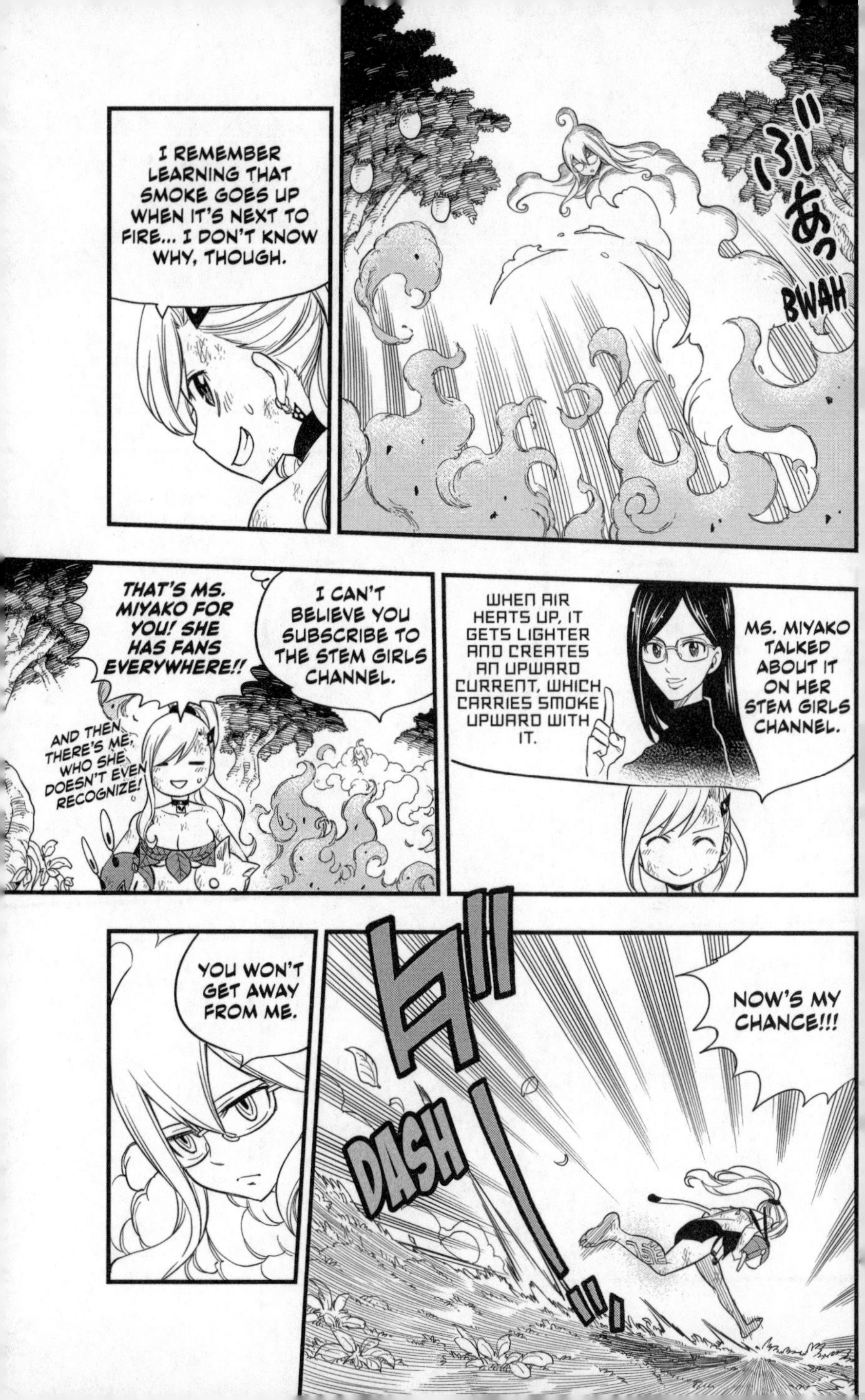
ぶぁっ
BWAH
I REMEMBER LEARNING THAT SMOKE GOES UP WHEN IT'S NEXT TO FIRE... I DON'T KNOW WHY, THOUGH.
MS. MIYAKO TALKED ABOUT IT ON HER STEM GIRLS CHANNEL.
WHEN AIR HEATS UP, IT GETS LIGHTER AND CREATES AN UPWARD CURRENT, WHICH CARRIES SMOKE UPWARD WITH IT.
I CAN'T BELIEVE YOU SUBSCRIBE TO THE STEM GIRLS CHANNEL.
THAT'S MS. MIYAKO FOR YOU! SHE HAS FANS EVERYWHERE!!
AND THEN, THERE'S ME, WHO SHE DOESN'T EVEN RECOGNIZE!
NOW'S MY CHANCE!!!
ダッ
DASH
YOU WON'T GET AWAY FROM ME.

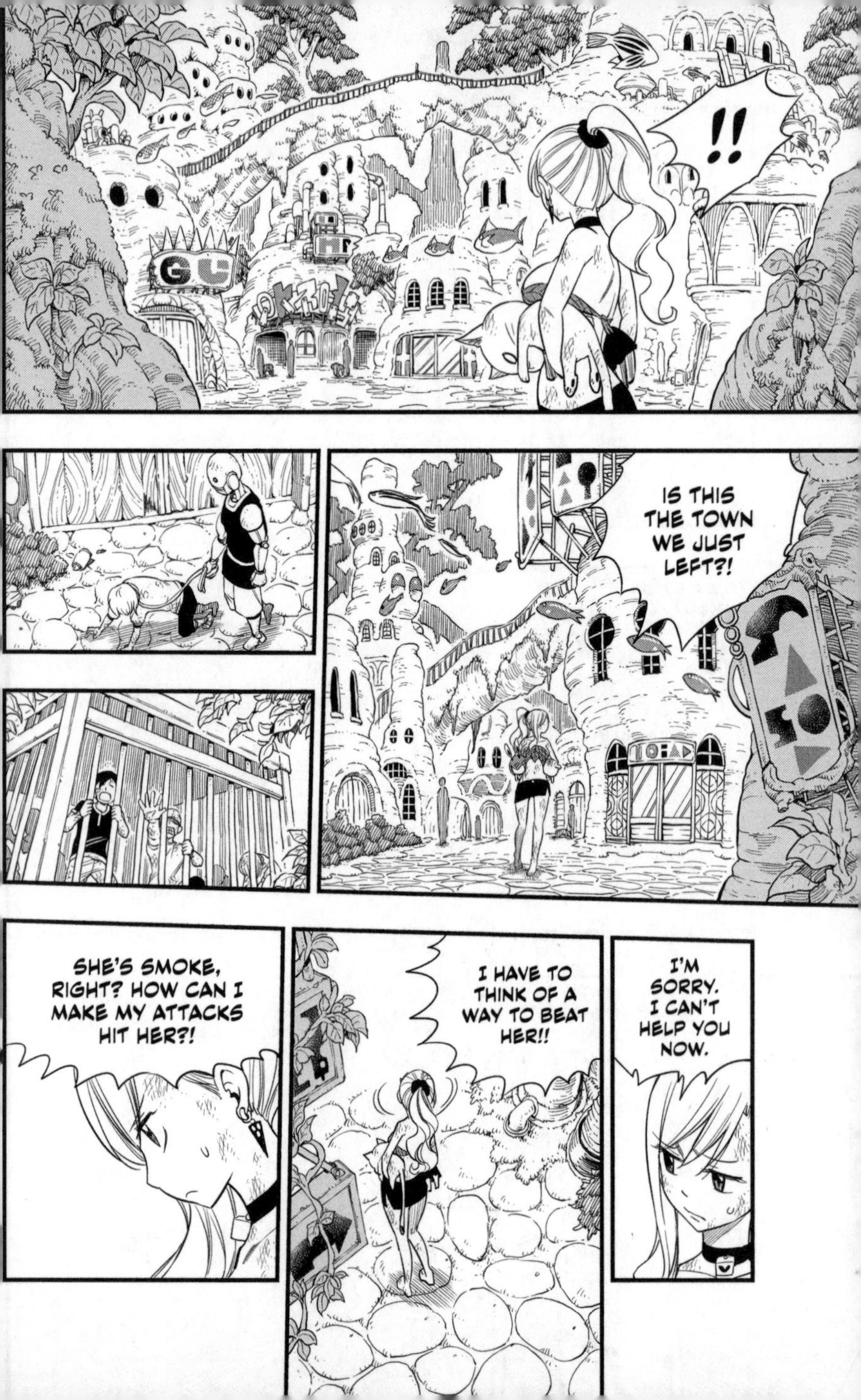
!!
IS THIS THE TOWN WE JUST LEFT?!
I'M SORRY. I CAN'T HELP YOU NOW.
I HAVE TO THINK OF A WAY TO BEAT HER!!
SHE'S SMOKE, RIGHT? HOW CAN I MAKE MY ATTACKS HIT HER?!

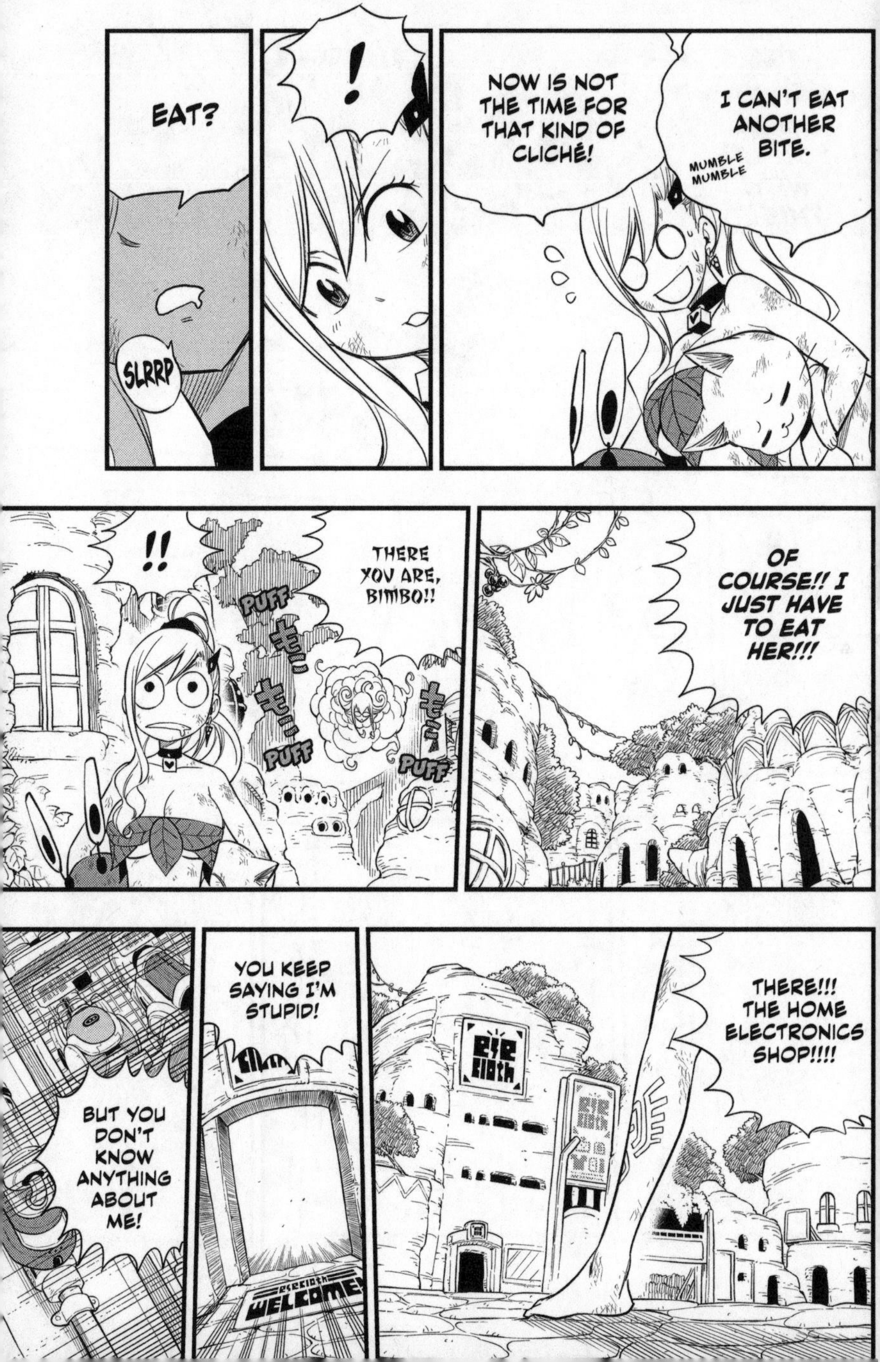
I CAN'T EAT ANOTHER BITE.
MUMBLE MUMBLE
NOW IS NOT THE TIME FOR THAT KIND OF CLICHÉ!
!
EAT?
SLRRP
OF COURSE!! I JUST HAVE TO EAT HER!!!
THERE YOU ARE, BIMBO!!
!!
PUFF
PUFF
PUFF
THERE!!! THE HOME ELECTRONICS SHOP!!!!
YOU KEEP SAYING I'M STUPID!
WELCOME!
BUT YOU DON'T KNOW ANYTHING ABOUT ME!

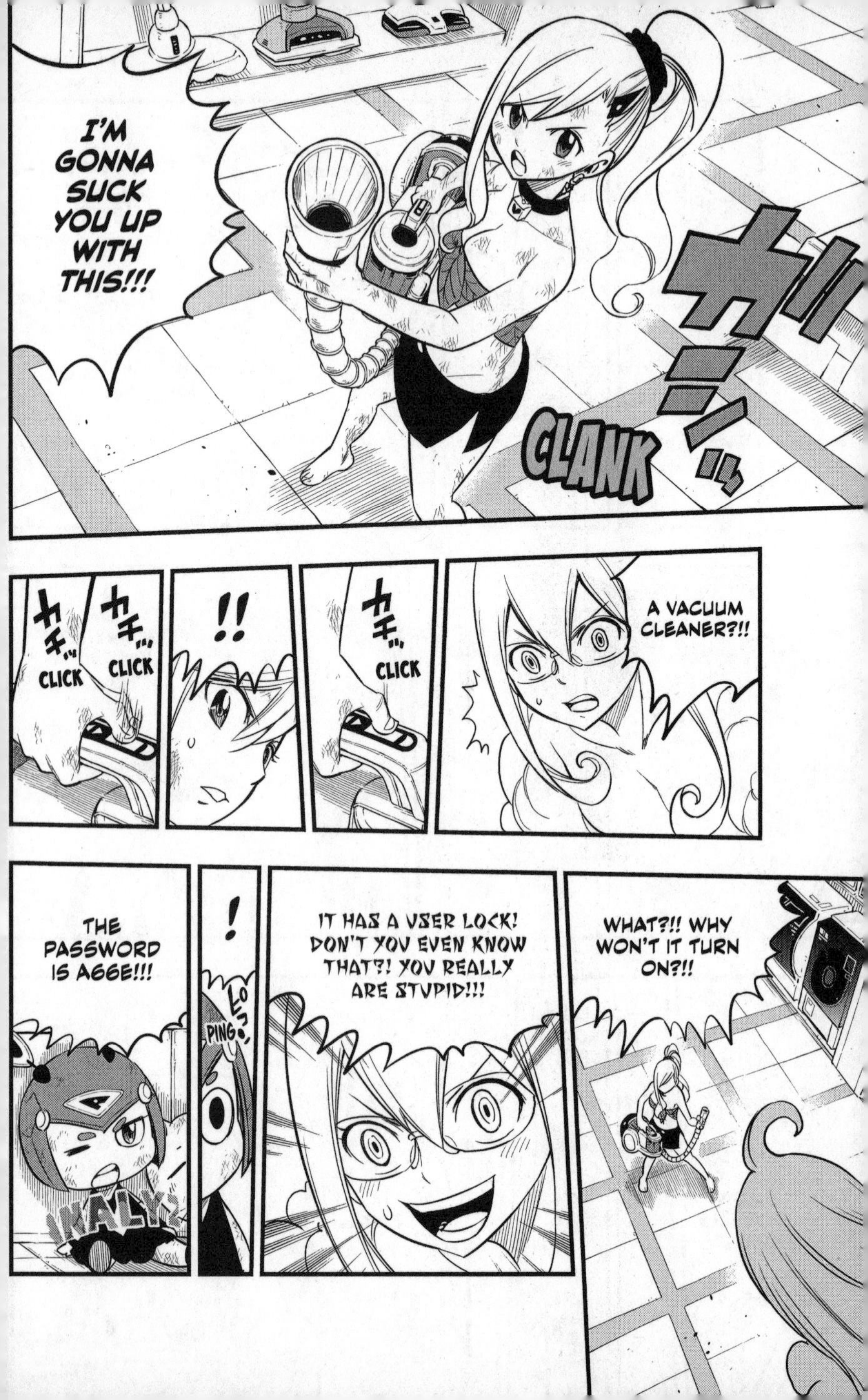
I'M GONNA SUCK YOU UP WITH THIS!!!
CLANK
A VACUUM CLEANER?!!
CLICK
!!
CLICK
CLICK
WHAT?!! WHY WON'T IT TURN ON?!!
IT HAS A USER LOCK! DON'T YOU EVEN KNOW THAT?! YOU REALLY ARE STUPID!!!
!
PING
THE PASSWORD IS A66E!!!

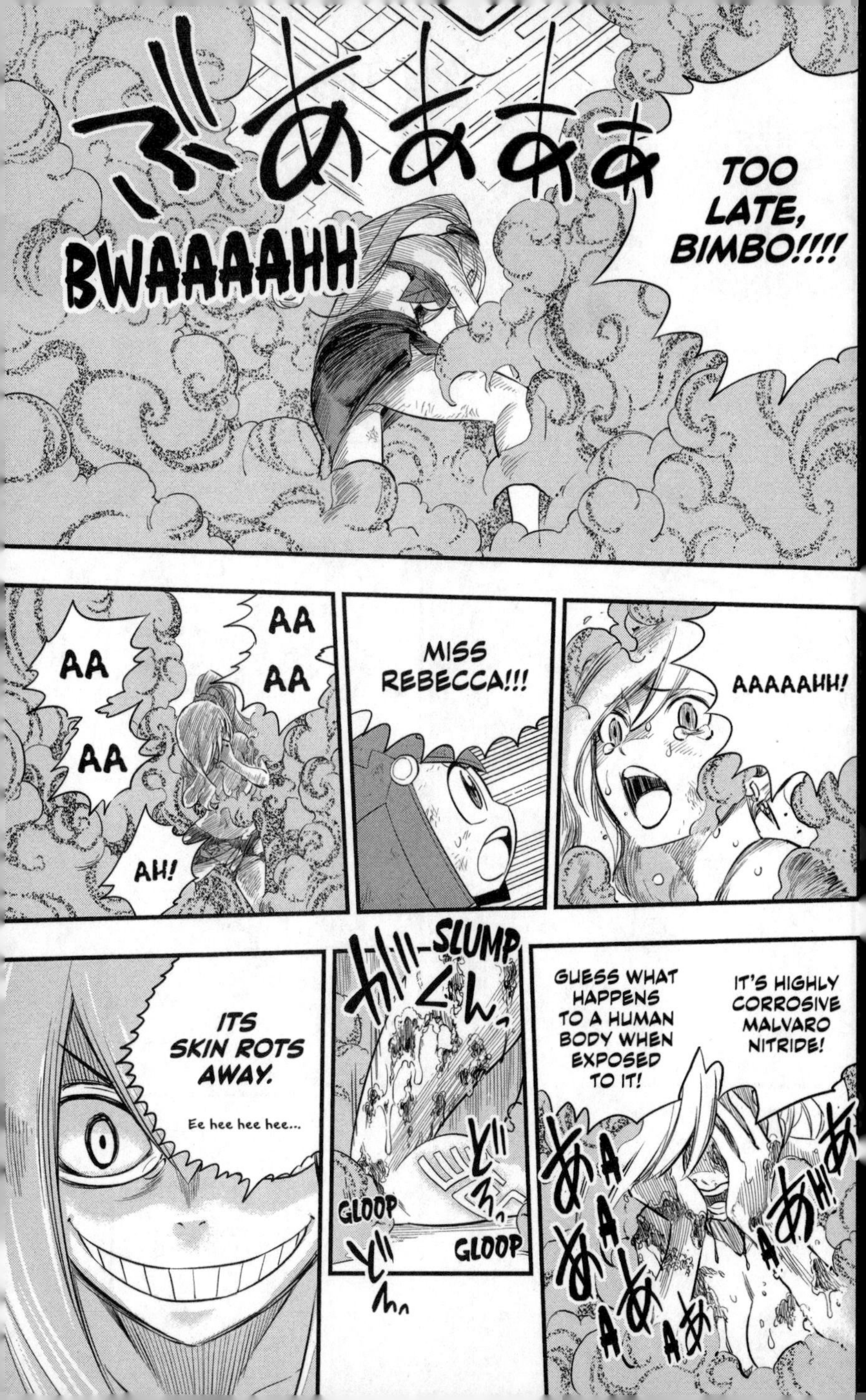
TOO LATE, BIMBO!!!!
ぶああああ
BWAAAAAHH
AAAAAHH!
MISS REBECCA!!!
AA
AA
AA
AA
AH!
IT'S HIGHLY CORROSIVE MALVARO NITRIDE!
GUESS WHAT HAPPENS TO A HUMAN BODY WHEN EXPOSED TO IT!
SLUMP
GLOOP
GLOOP
ITS SKIN ROTS AWAY.
Ee hee hee hee...

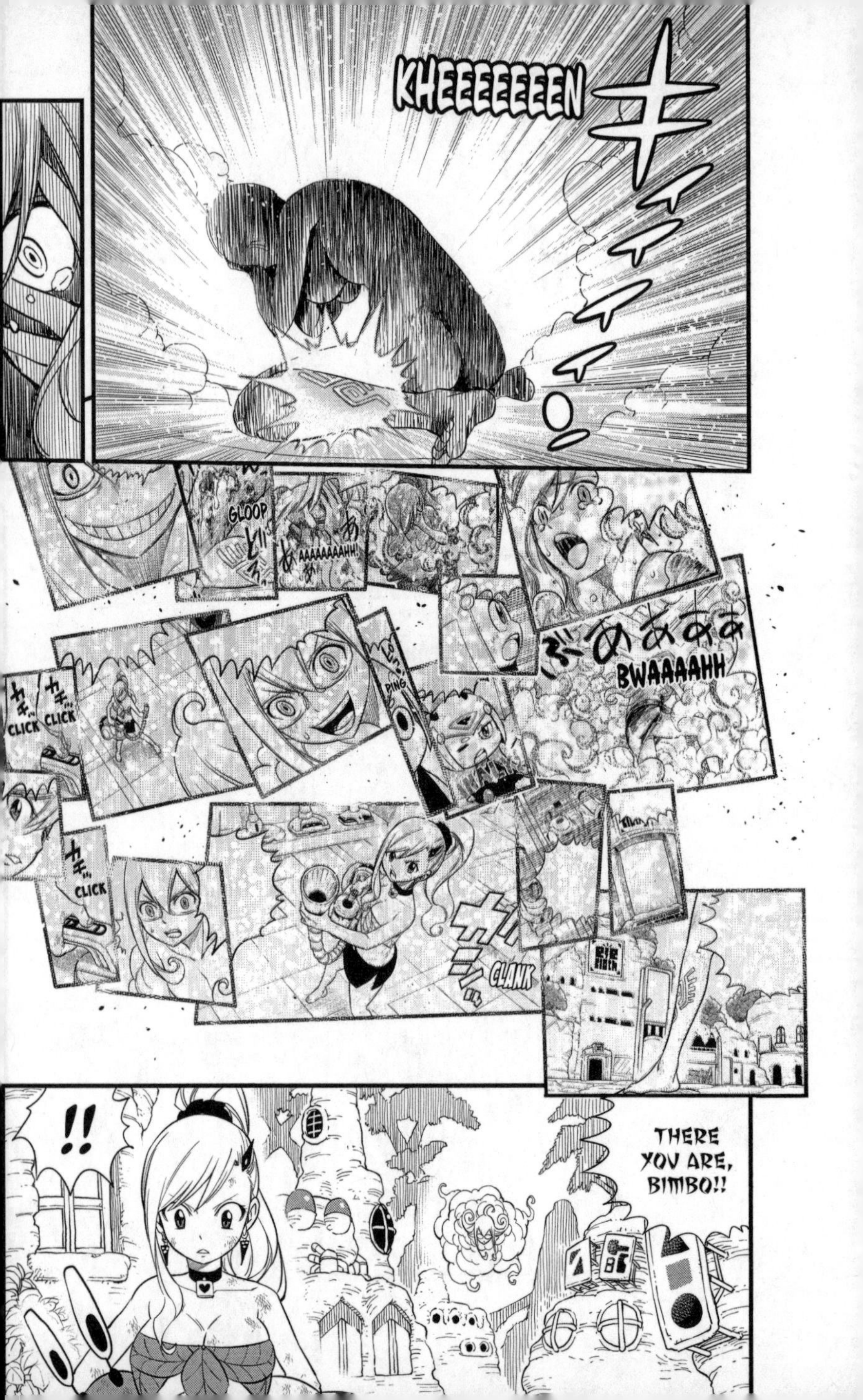
KHEEEEEEEEN
AAAAAAAAAH!
GLOOP
BWAAAAHH
PING
CLICK
CLICK
CLANK
CLICK
THERE YOU ARE, BIMBO!!
!!

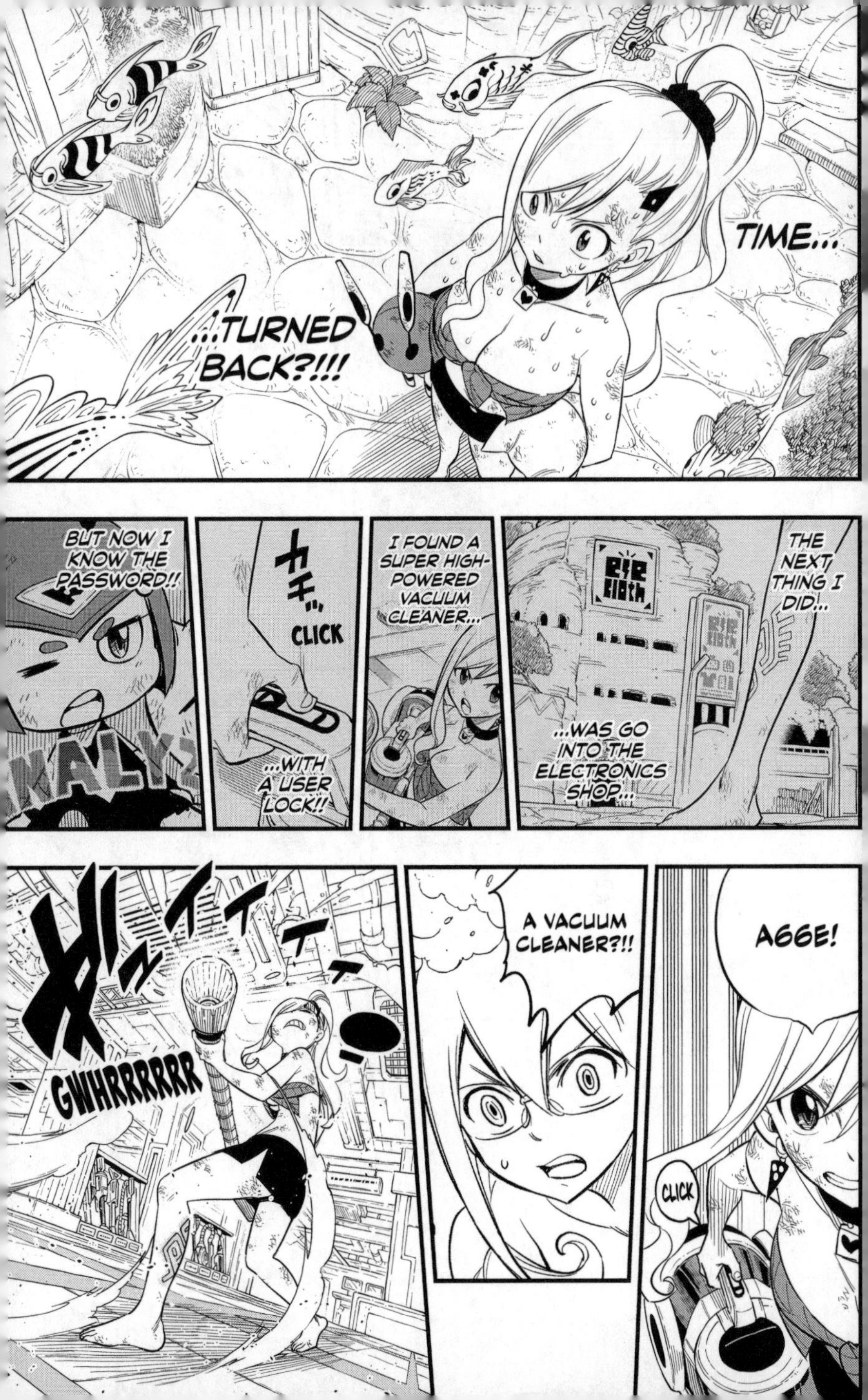
TIME...
...TURNED BACK?!!!
THE NEXT THING I DID...
...WAS GO INTO THE ELECTRONICS SHOP...
I FOUND A SUPER HIGH-POWERED VACUUM CLEANER...
カチッ
CLICK
...WITH A USER LOCK!!
BUT NOW I KNOW THE PASSWORD!!
A66E!
CLICK
A VACUUM CLEANER?!!
GWHRRRRR

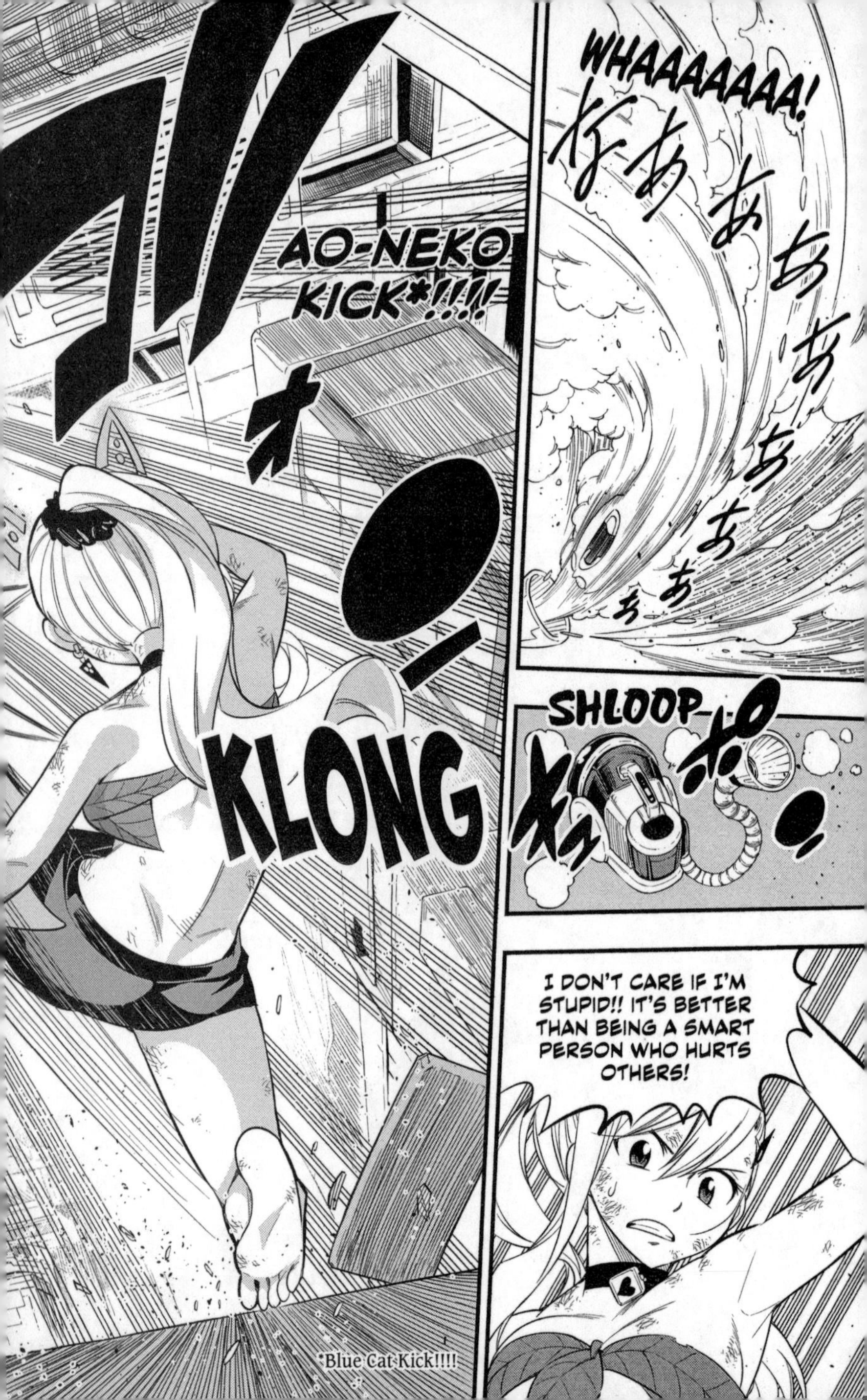
WHAAAAAAAA!
SHLOOP
I DON'T CARE IF I'M STUPID!! IT'S BETTER THAN BEING A SMART PERSON WHO HURTS OTHERS!
AO-NEKO KICK*!!!!
KLONG

*Blue Cat Kick!!!!

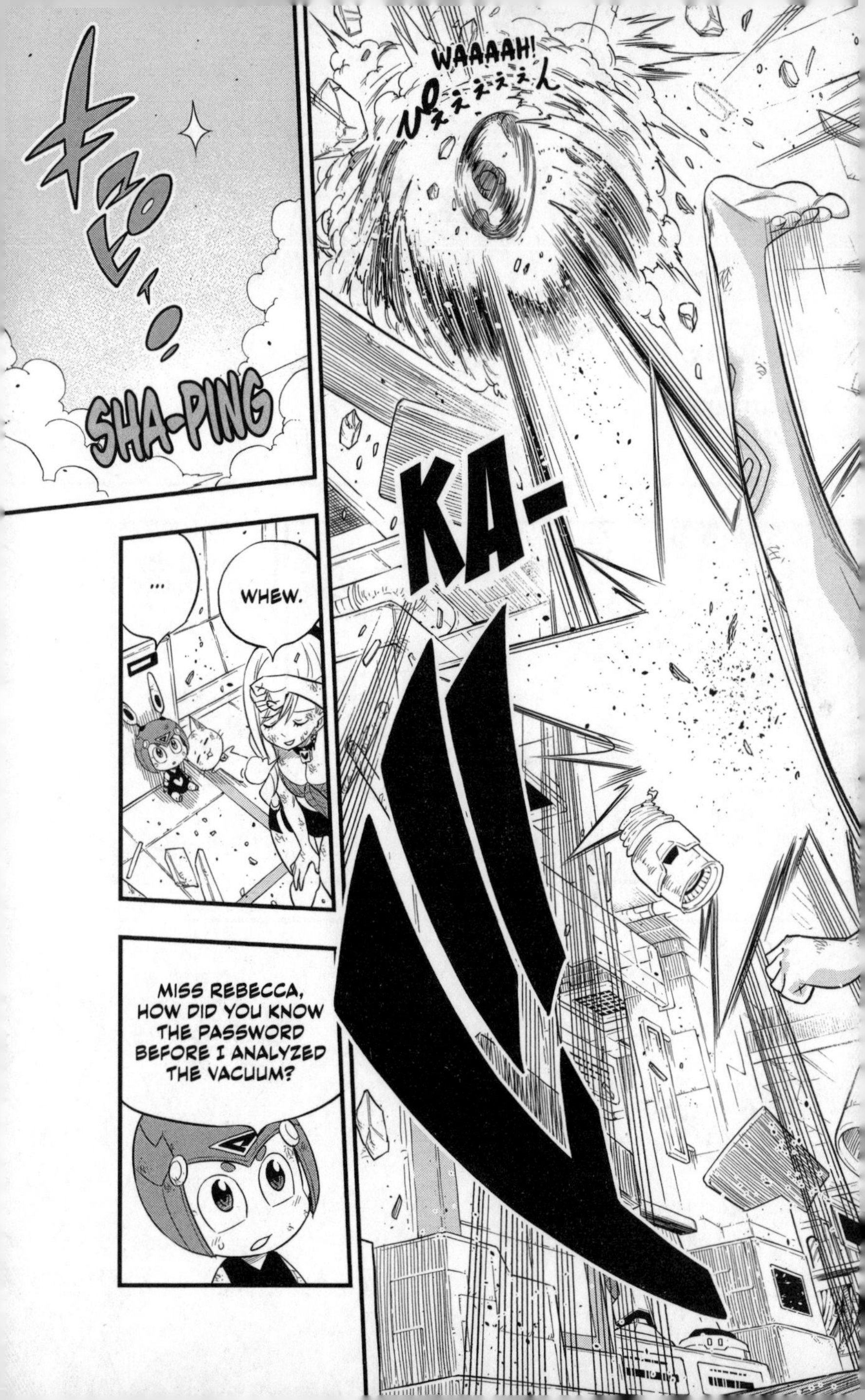
WAAAAH!
ぴえええええん
KA-
SHA-PING
WHEW.
...
MISS REBECCA, HOW DID YOU KNOW THE PASSWORD BEFORE I ANALYZED THE VACUUM?

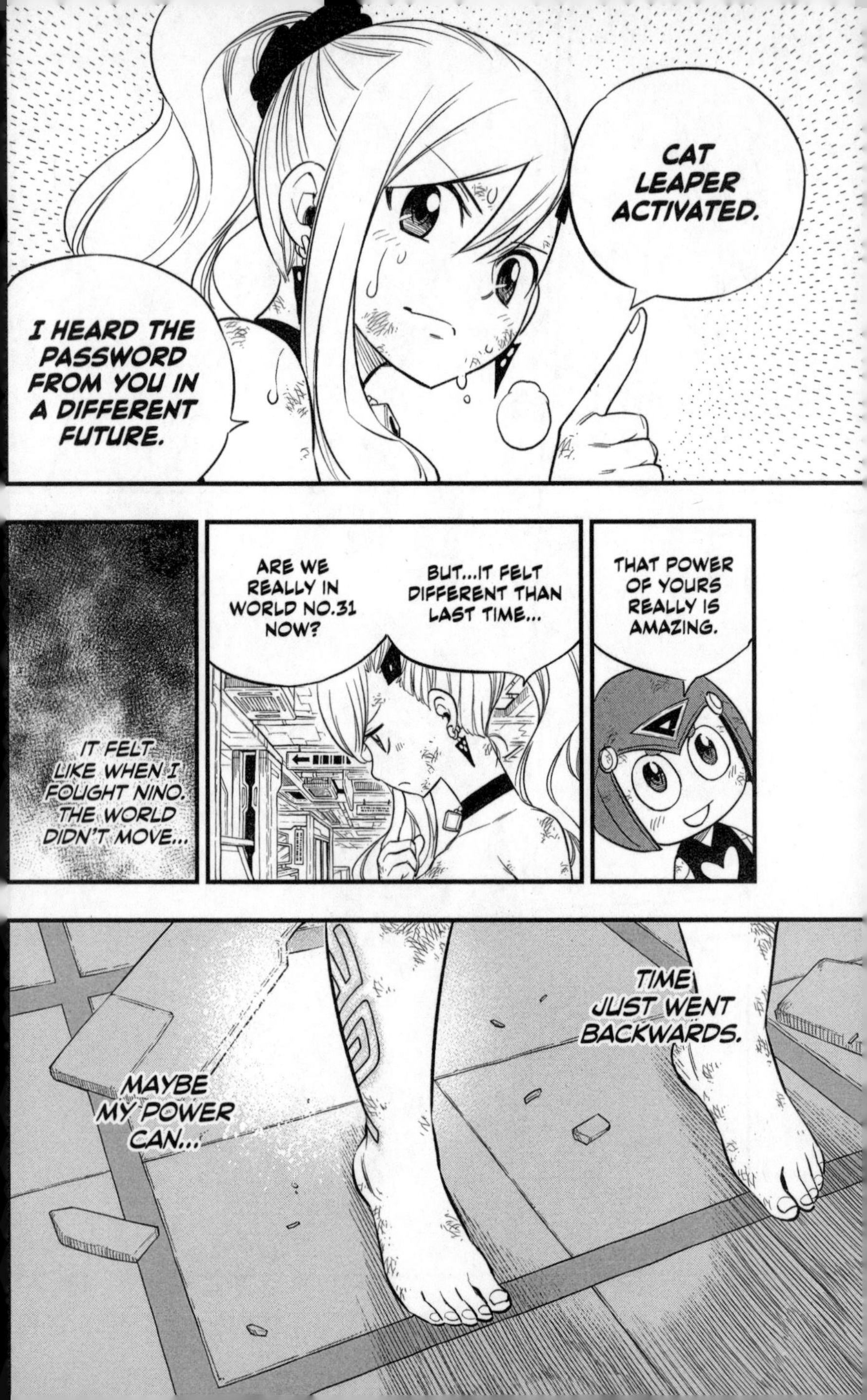
CAT LEAPER ACTIVATED.
I HEARD THE PASSWORD FROM YOU IN A DIFFERENT FUTURE.
THAT POWER OF YOURS REALLY IS AMAZING.
BUT...IT FELT DIFFERENT THAN LAST TIME...
ARE WE REALLY IN WORLD NO.31 NOW?
IT FELT LIKE WHEN I FOUGHT NINO. THE WORLD DIDN'T MOVE...
TIME JUST WENT BACKWARDS.
MAYBE MY POWER CAN...

EDENS ZERO

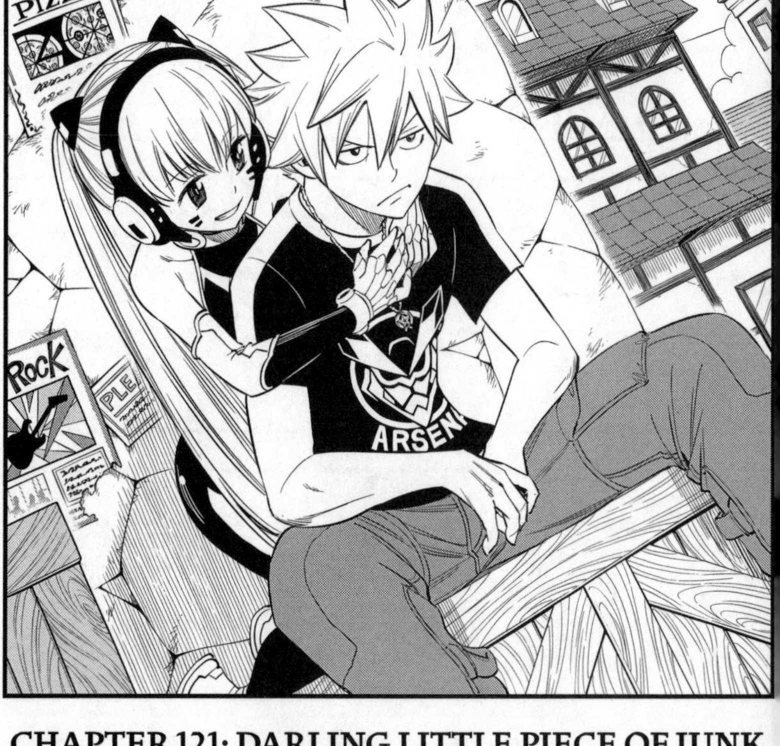
PIZZA
ROCK
PLE
ARSEN

CHAPTER 121: DARLING LITTLE PIECE OF JUNK

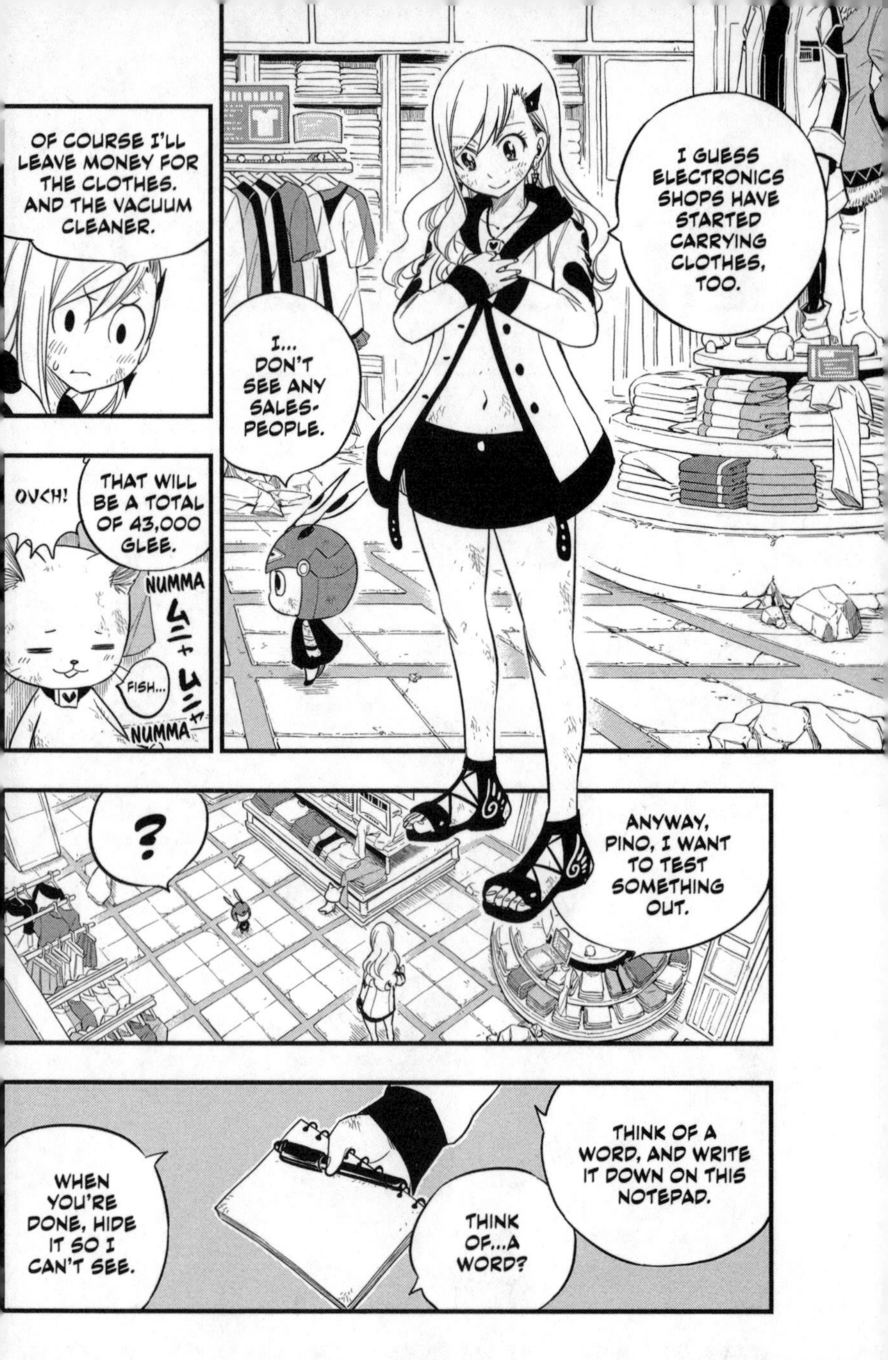
I GUESS ELECTRONICS SHOPS HAVE STARTED CARRYING CLOTHES, TOO.
I... DON'T SEE ANY SALES-PEOPLE.
OF COURSE I'LL LEAVE MONEY FOR THE CLOTHES. AND THE VACUUM CLEANER.
THAT WILL BE A TOTAL OF 43,000 GLEE.
OUCH!
NUMMA
ムニャ
FISH...
ムニャ
NUMMA
ANYWAY, PINO, I WANT TO TEST SOMETHING OUT.
?
THINK OF A WORD, AND WRITE IT DOWN ON THIS NOTEPAD.
THINK OF...A WORD?
WHEN YOU'RE DONE, HIDE IT SO I CAN'T SEE.

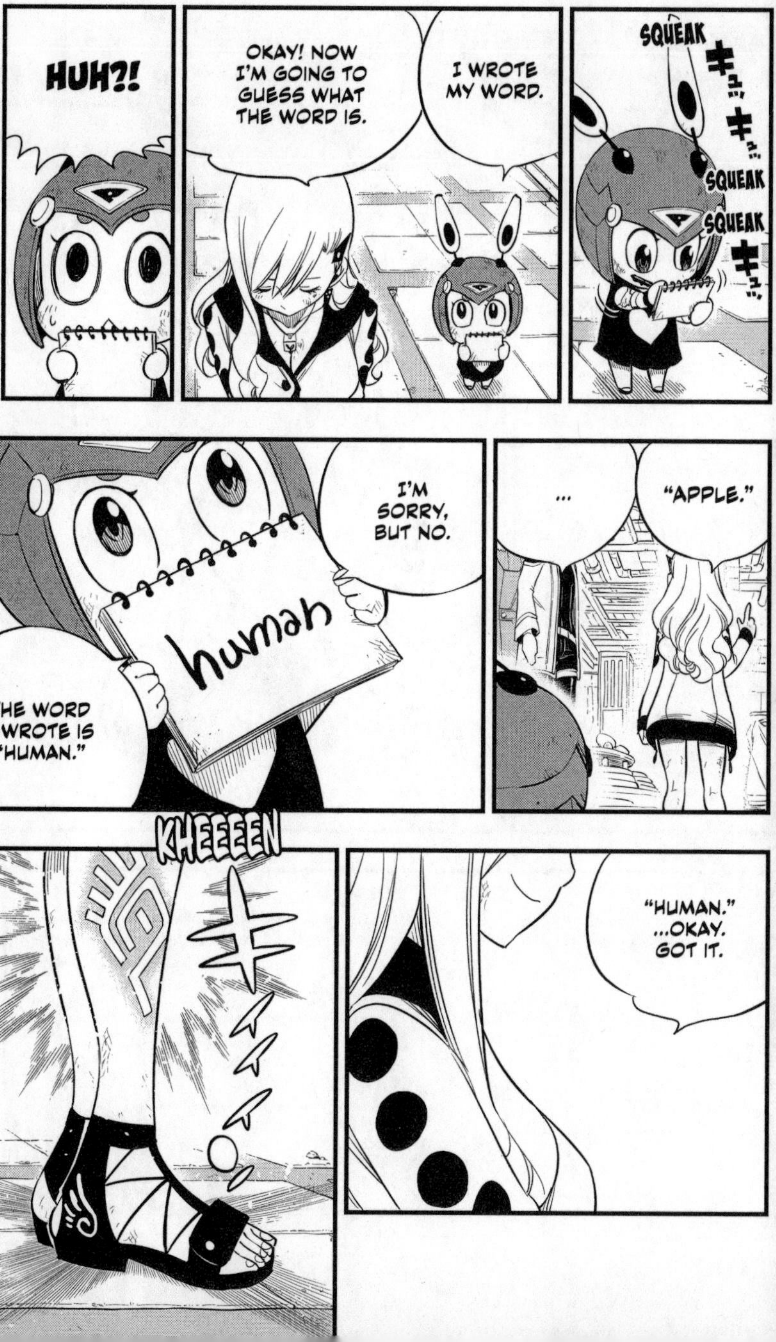
SQUEAK
キュッ
キュッ
SQUEAK
SQUEAK
キュッ
I WROTE MY WORD.
OKAY! NOW I'M GOING TO GUESS WHAT THE WORD IS.
HUH?!
"APPLE."
...
I'M SORRY, BUT NO.
human
THE WORD I WROTE IS "HUMAN."
"HUMAN." ...OKAY. GOT IT.
KHEEEEN
キーン

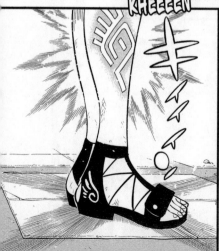

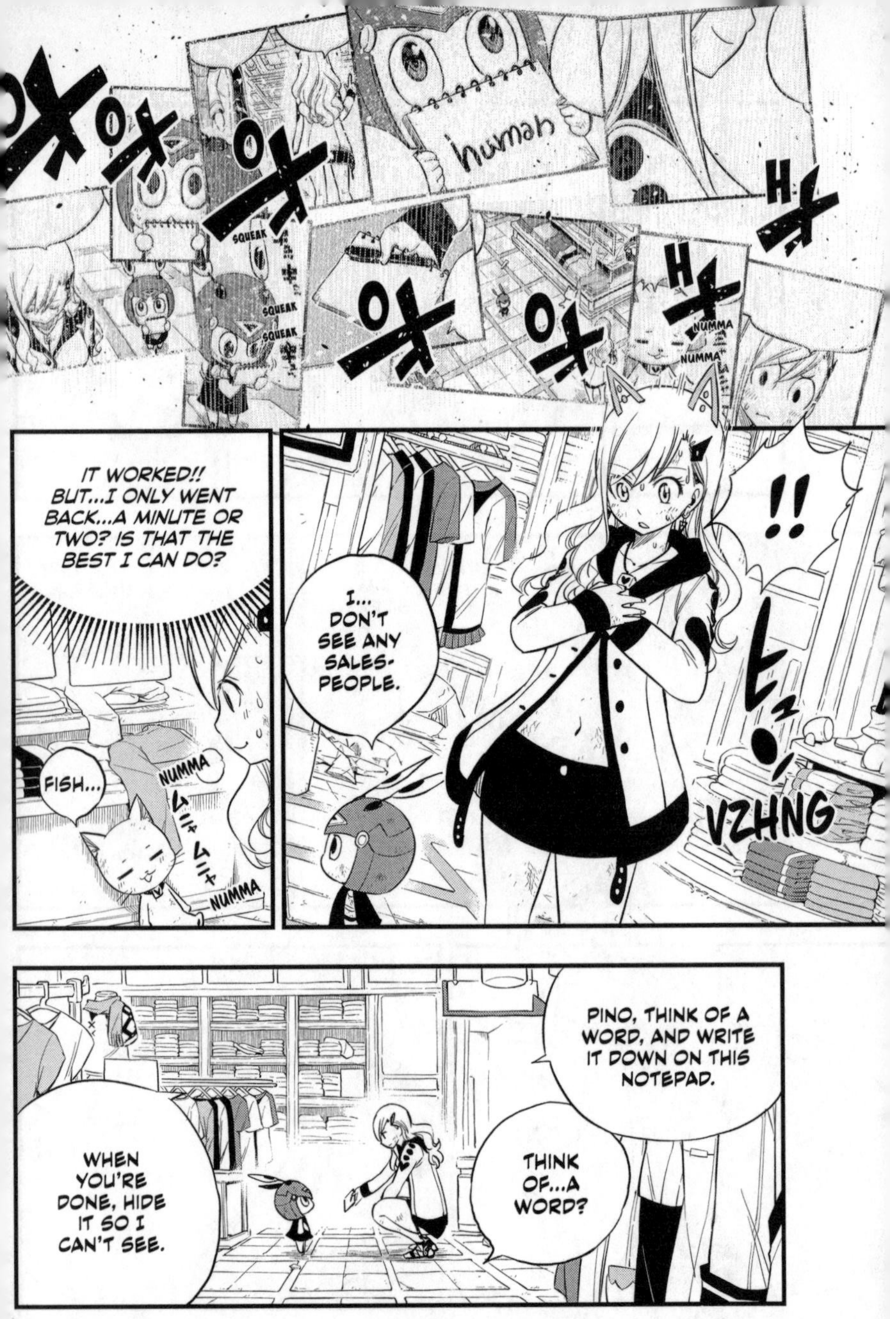
NUMMA
NUMMA
humah
SQUEAK
SQUEAK
SQUEAK
!!
VZHNG
I... DON'T SEE ANY SALES-PEOPLE.
IT WORKED!! BUT...I ONLY WENT BACK...A MINUTE OR TWO? IS THAT THE BEST I CAN DO?
NUMMA
FISH...
NUMMA
PINO, THINK OF A WORD, AND WRITE IT DOWN ON THIS NOTEPAD.
THINK OF...A WORD?
WHEN YOU'RE DONE, HIDE IT SO I CAN'T SEE.

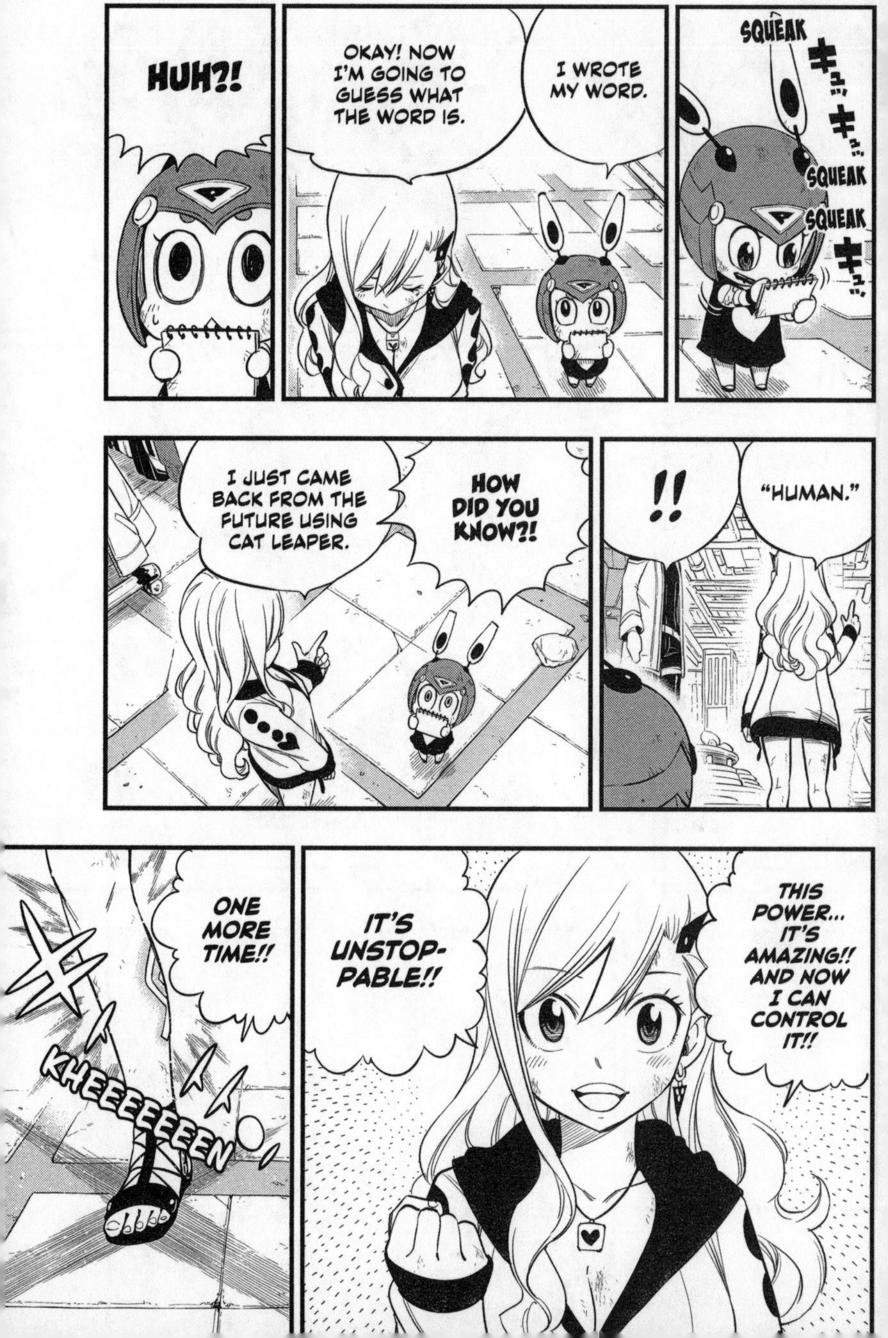
SQUEAK
キュッ
キュッ
SQUEAK
SQUEAK
キュッ
I WROTE MY WORD.
OKAY! NOW I'M GOING TO GUESS WHAT THE WORD IS.
HUH?!
"HUMAN."
!!
HOW DID YOU KNOW?!
I JUST CAME BACK FROM THE FUTURE USING CAT LEAPER.
THIS POWER... IT'S AMAZING!! AND NOW I CAN CONTROL IT!!
IT'S UNSTOP-PABLE!!
ONE MORE TIME!!
KHEEEEEEEEN

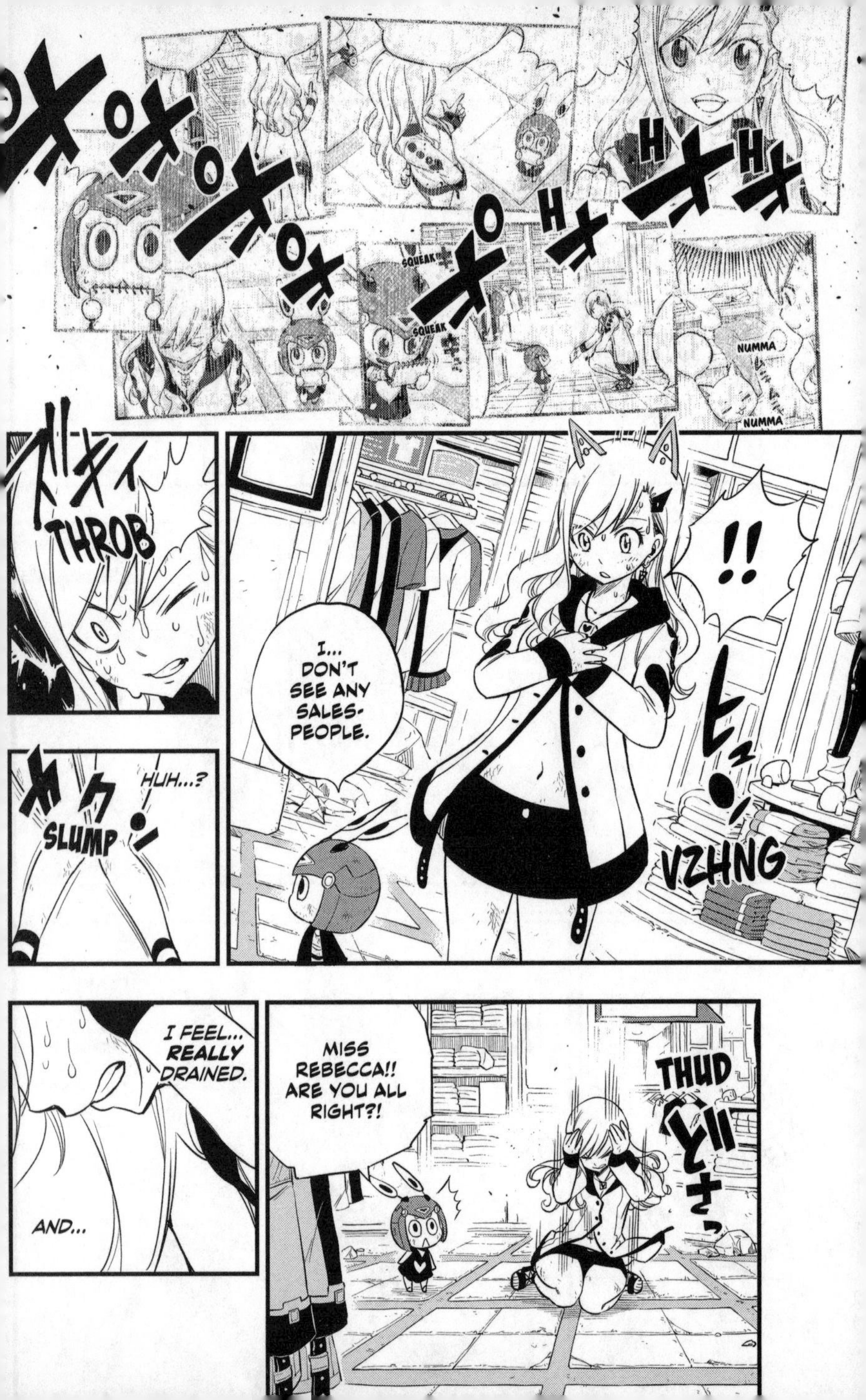
NUMMA
NUMMA
SQUEAK!!
SQUEAK
!!
I... DON'T SEE ANY SALES-PEOPLE.
VZHNG
THROB
HUH...?
SLUMP
THUD
MISS REBECCA!! ARE YOU ALL RIGHT?!
I FEEL... REALLY DRAINED.
AND...

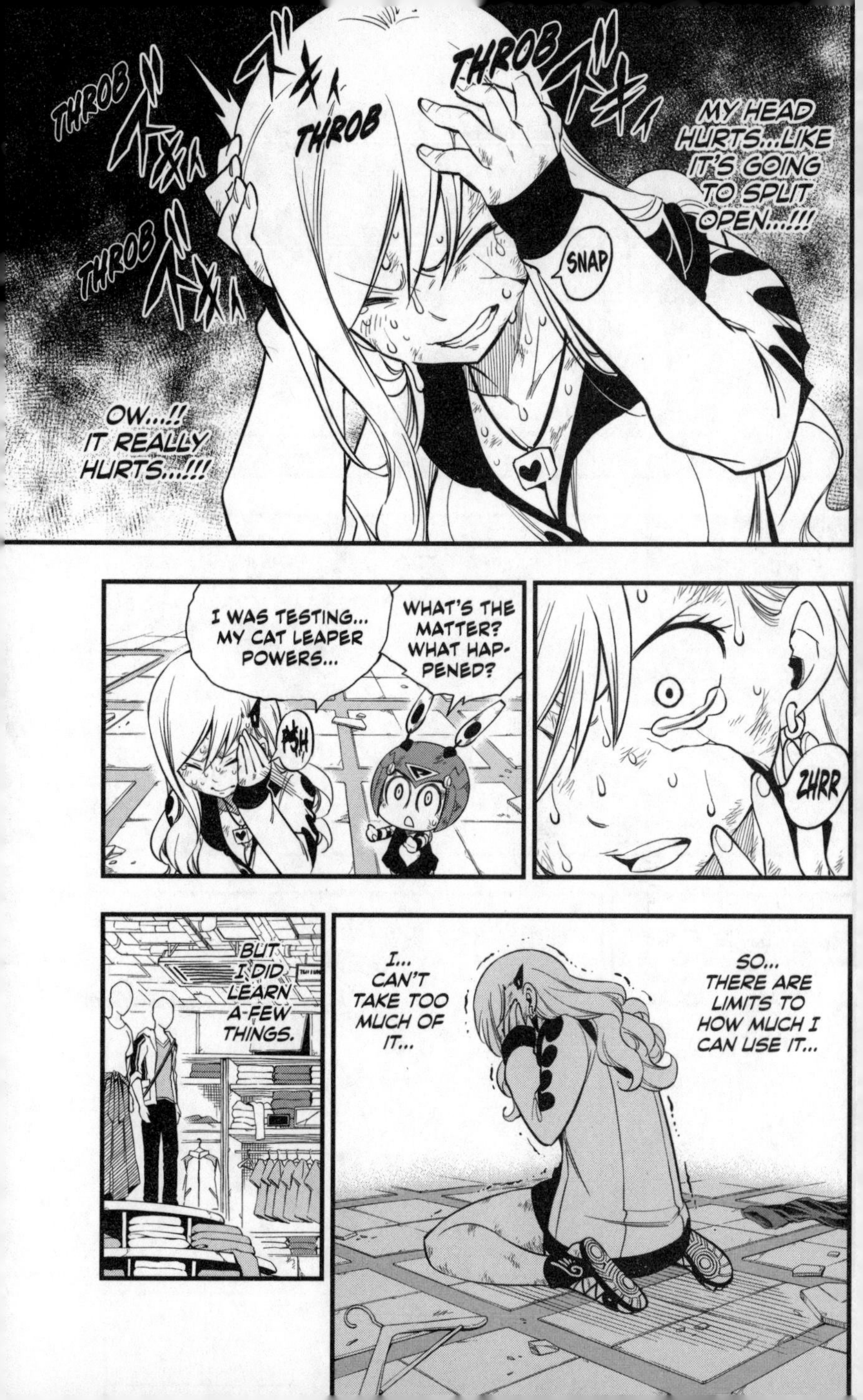
THROB
MY HEAD HURTS...LIKE IT'S GOING TO SPLIT OPEN...!!!
THROB
SNAP
THROB
THROB
OW...!! IT REALLY HURTS...!!!
ZHRR
WHAT'S THE MATTER? WHAT HAP-PENED?
I WAS TESTING... MY CAT LEAPER POWERS...
PSH
SO... THERE ARE LIMITS TO HOW MUCH I CAN USE IT...
I... CAN'T TAKE TOO MUCH OF IT...
BUT I DID LEARN A FEW THINGS.

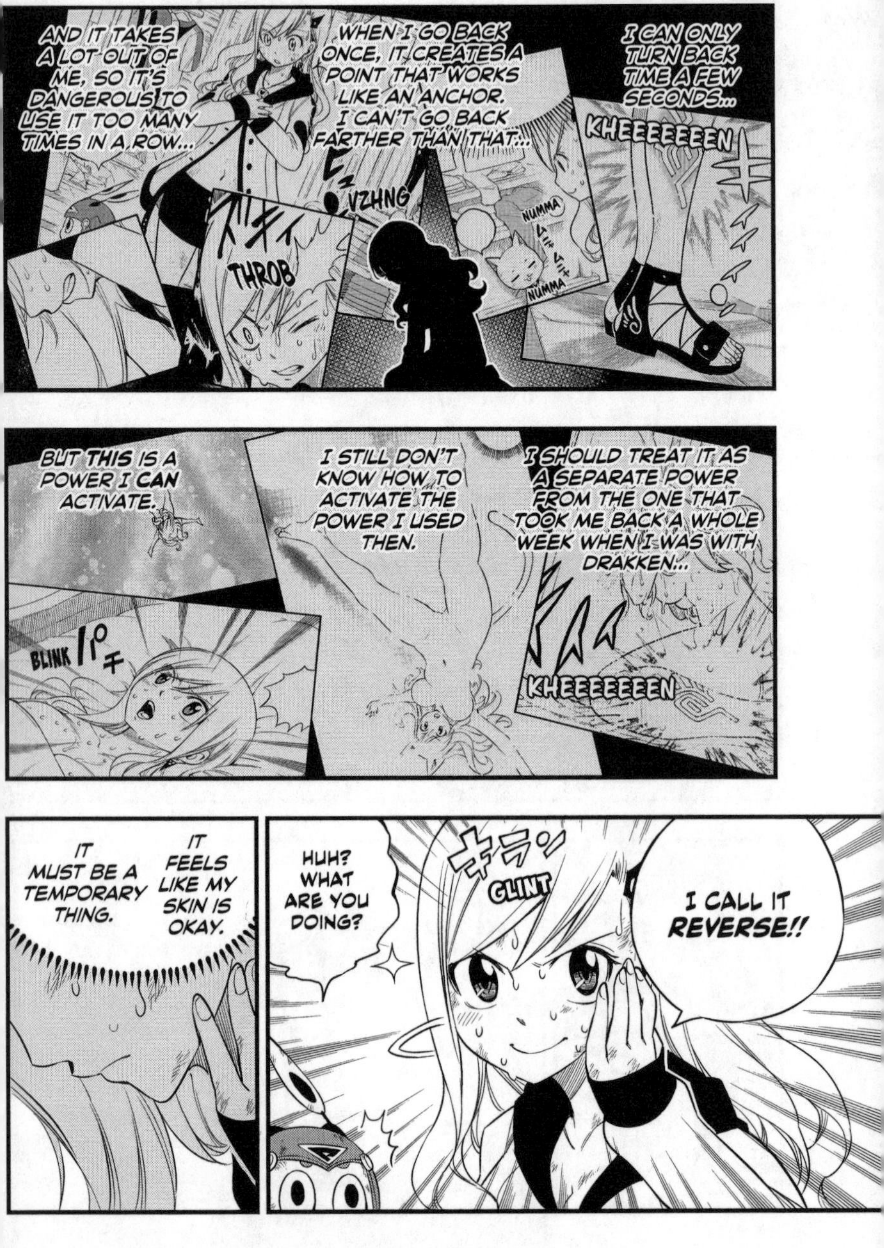
I CAN ONLY TURN BACK TIME A FEW SECONDS...
KHEEEEEEEEN
WHEN I GO BACK ONCE, IT CREATES A POINT THAT WORKS LIKE AN ANCHOR. I CAN'T GO BACK FARTHER THAN THAT...
NUMMA
NUMMA
AND IT TAKES A LOT OUT OF ME, SO IT'S DANGEROUS TO USE IT TOO MANY TIMES IN A ROW...
VZHNG
THROB
I SHOULD TREAT IT AS A SEPARATE POWER FROM THE ONE THAT TOOK ME BACK A WHOLE WEEK WHEN I WAS WITH DRAKKEN...
KHEEEEEEEEN
I STILL DON'T KNOW HOW TO ACTIVATE THE POWER I USED THEN.
BUT THIS IS A POWER I CAN ACTIVATE.
BLINK
I CALL IT REVERSE!!
GLINT
HUH? WHAT ARE YOU DOING?
IT FEELS LIKE MY SKIN IS OKAY.
IT MUST BE A TEMPORARY THING.

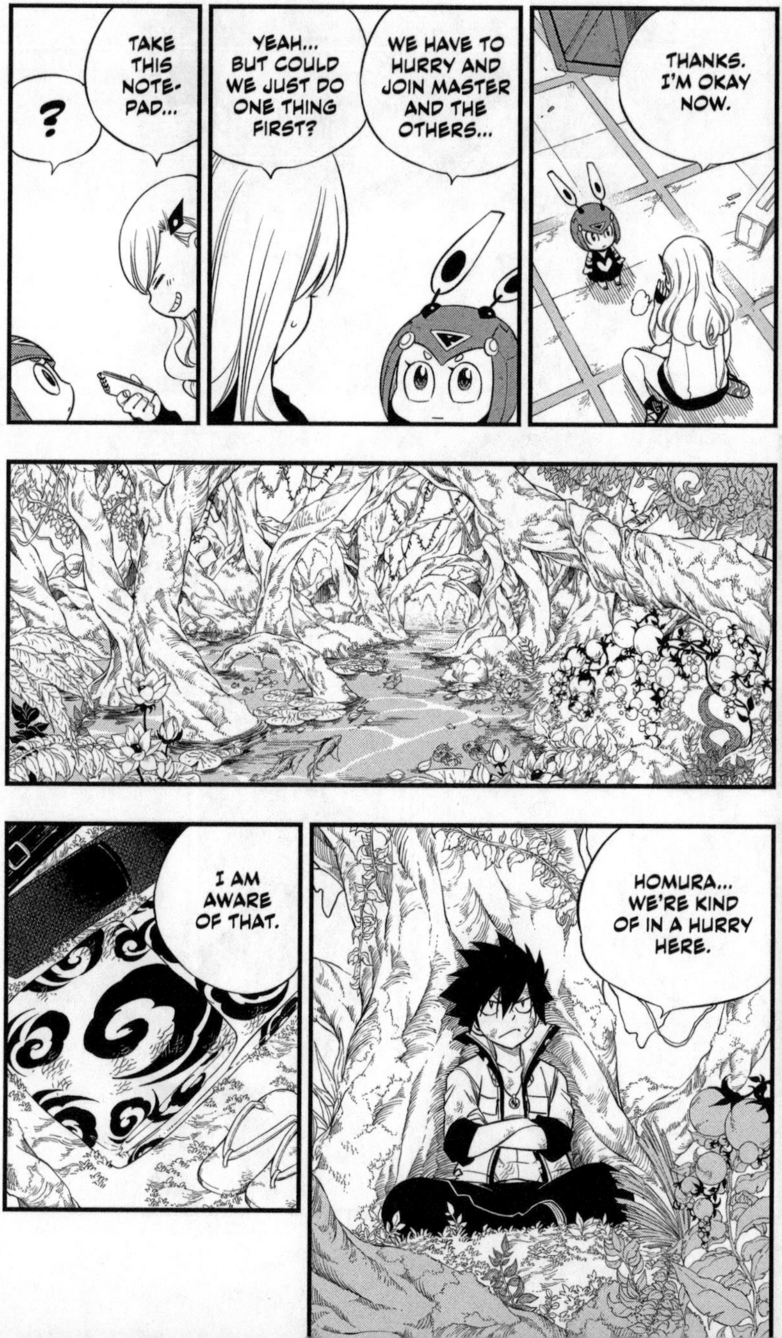
THANKS. I'M OKAY NOW.
WE HAVE TO HURRY AND JOIN MASTER AND THE OTHERS...
YEAH... BUT COULD WE JUST DO ONE THING FIRST?
TAKE THIS NOTE-PAD...
?
HOMURA... WE'RE KIND OF IN A HURRY HERE.
I AM AWARE OF THAT.

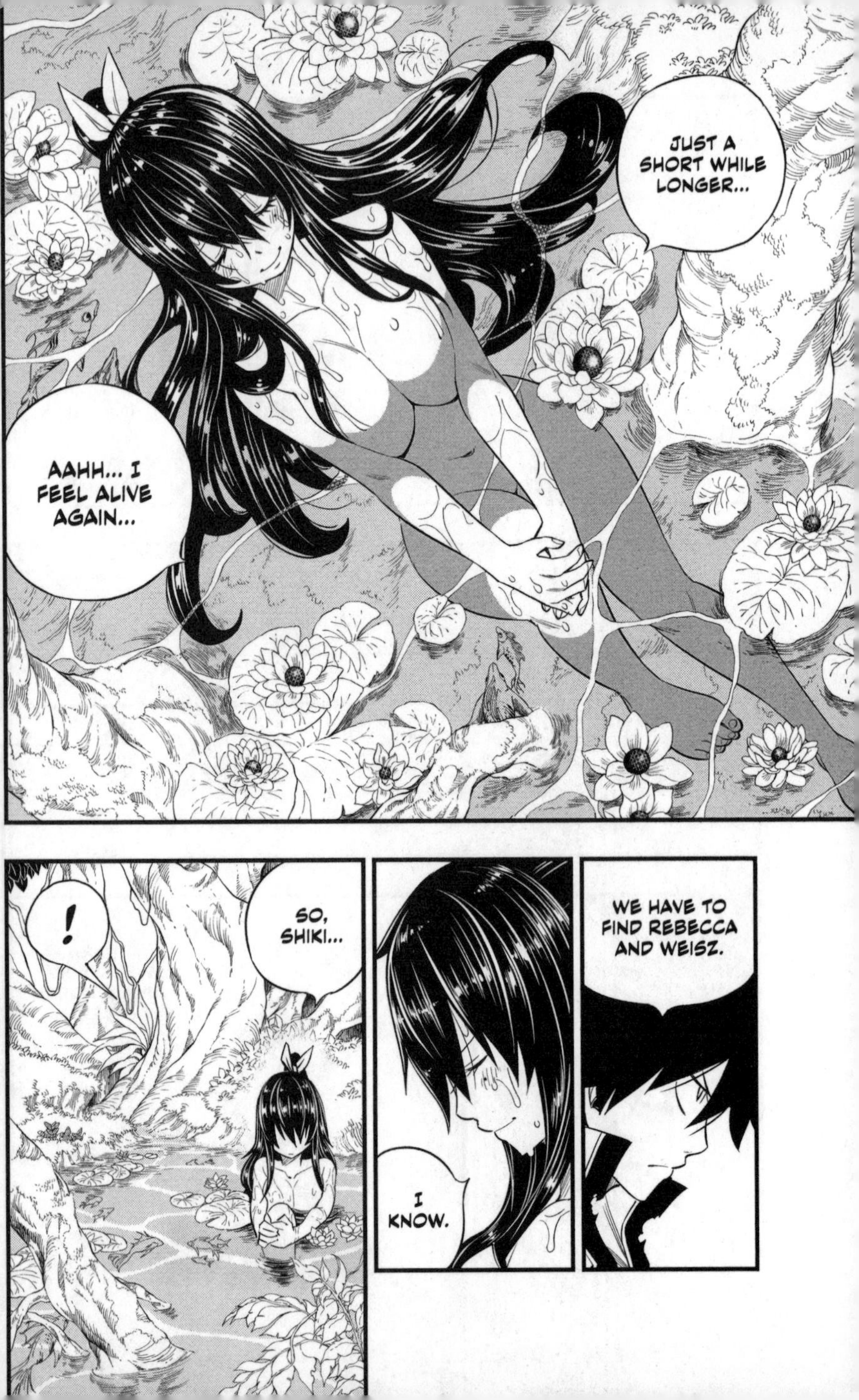
JUST A SHORT WHILE LONGER...
AAHH... I FEEL ALIVE AGAIN...
WE HAVE TO FIND REBECCA AND WEISZ.
I KNOW.
SO, SHIKI...
!

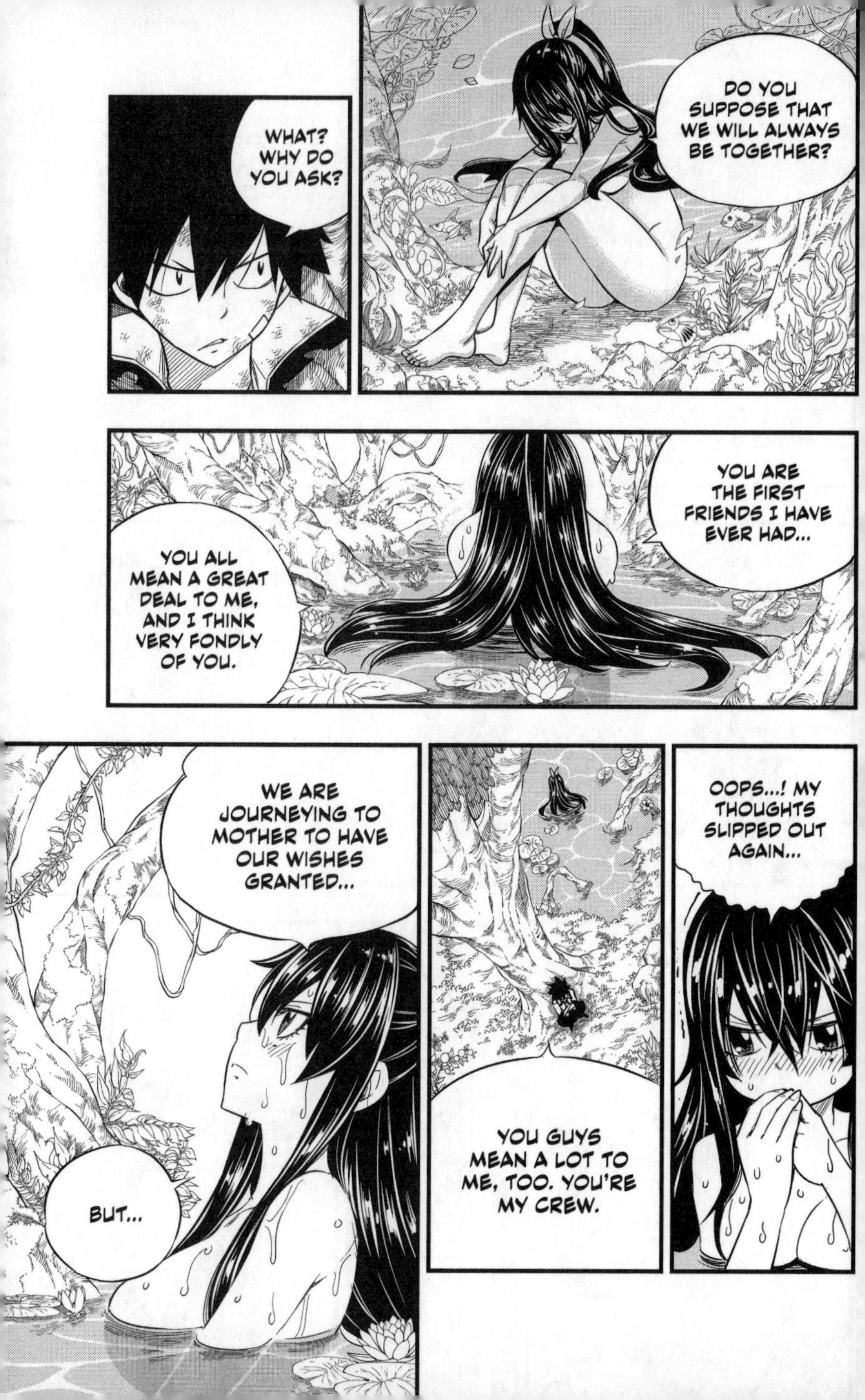
DO YOU SUPPOSE THAT WE WILL ALWAYS BE TOGETHER?
WHAT? WHY DO YOU ASK?
YOU ARE THE FIRST FRIENDS I HAVE EVER HAD...
YOU ALL MEAN A GREAT DEAL TO ME, AND I THINK VERY FONDLY OF YOU.
OOPS...! MY THOUGHTS SLIPPED OUT AGAIN...
YOU GUYS MEAN A LOT TO ME, TOO. YOU'RE MY CREW.
WE ARE JOURNEYING TO MOTHER TO HAVE OUR WISHES GRANTED...
BUT...

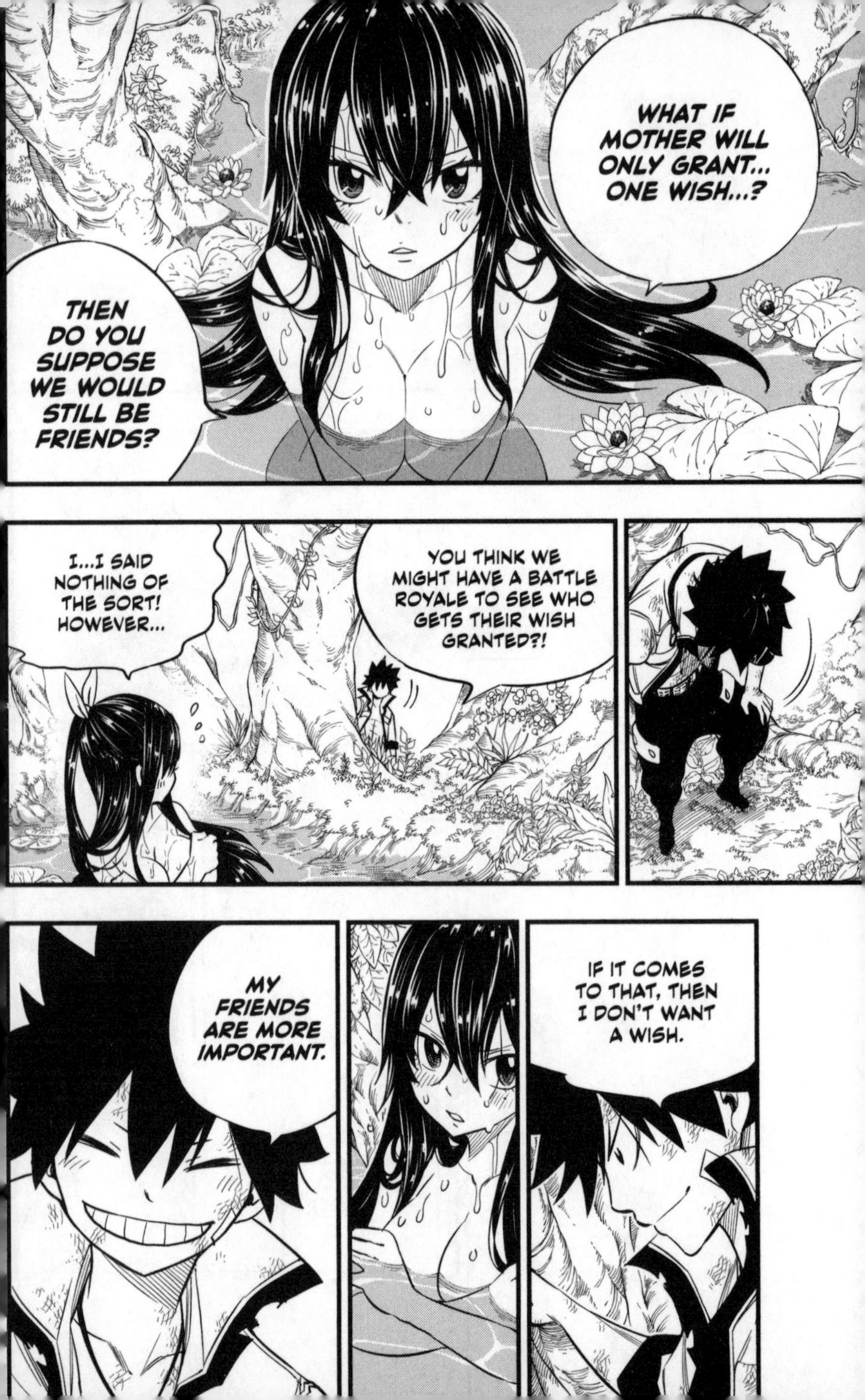
WHAT IF MOTHER WILL ONLY GRANT... ONE WISH...?
THEN DO YOU SUPPOSE WE WOULD STILL BE FRIENDS?
YOU THINK WE MIGHT HAVE A BATTLE ROYALE TO SEE WHO GETS THEIR WISH GRANTED?!
I...I SAID NOTHING OF THE SORT! HOWEVER...
IF IT COMES TO THAT, THEN I DON'T WANT A WISH.
MY FRIENDS ARE MORE IMPORTANT.

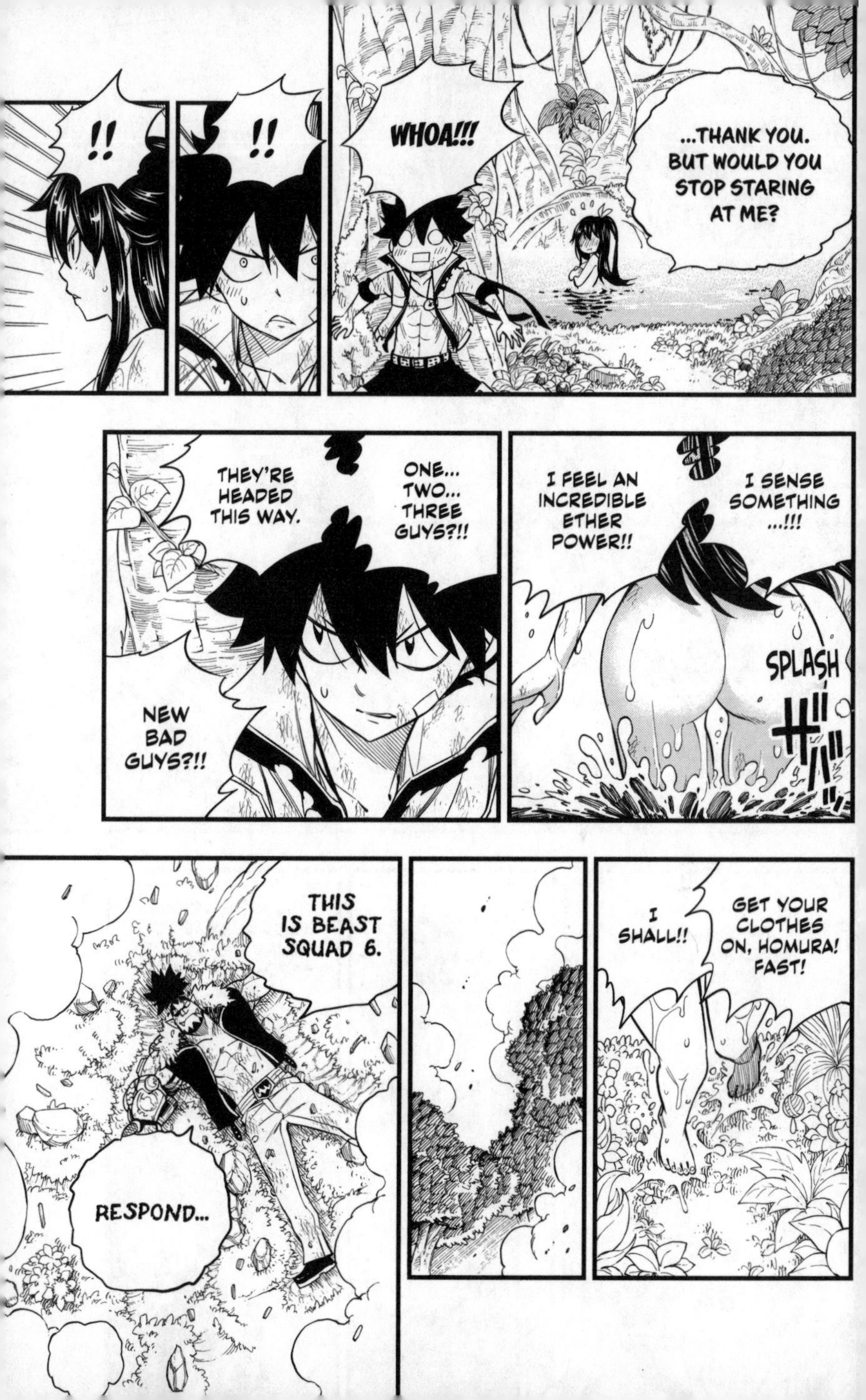
...THANK YOU. BUT WOULD YOU STOP STARING AT ME?
WHOA!!!
!!
!!
I SENSE SOMETHING ...!!!
I FEEL AN INCREDIBLE ETHER POWER!!
SPLASH
ONE... TWO... THREE GUYS?!!
THEY'RE HEADED THIS WAY.
NEW BAD GUYS?!!
GET YOUR CLOTHES ON, HOMURA! FAST!
I SHALL!!
THIS IS BEAST SQUAD 6.
RESPOND...

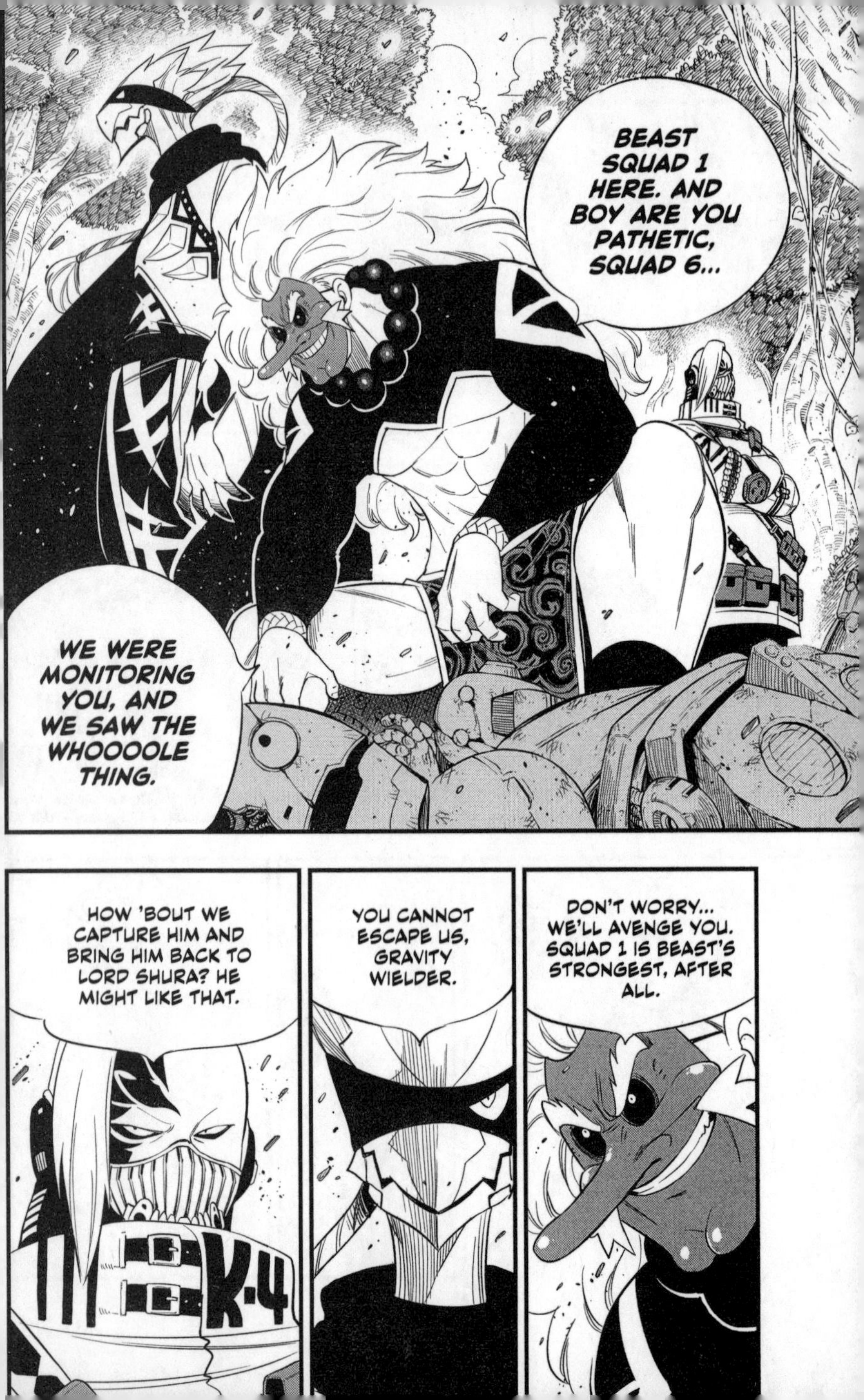
BEAST SQUAD 1 HERE. AND BOY ARE YOU PATHETIC, SQUAD 6...
WE WERE MONITORING YOU, AND WE SAW THE WHOOOOLE THING.
DON'T WORRY... WE'LL AVENGE YOU. SQUAD 1 IS BEAST'S STRONGEST, AFTER ALL.
YOU CANNOT ESCAPE US, GRAVITY WIELDER.
HOW 'BOUT WE CAPTURE HIM AND BRING HIM BACK TO LORD SHURA? HE MIGHT LIKE THAT.
K-4

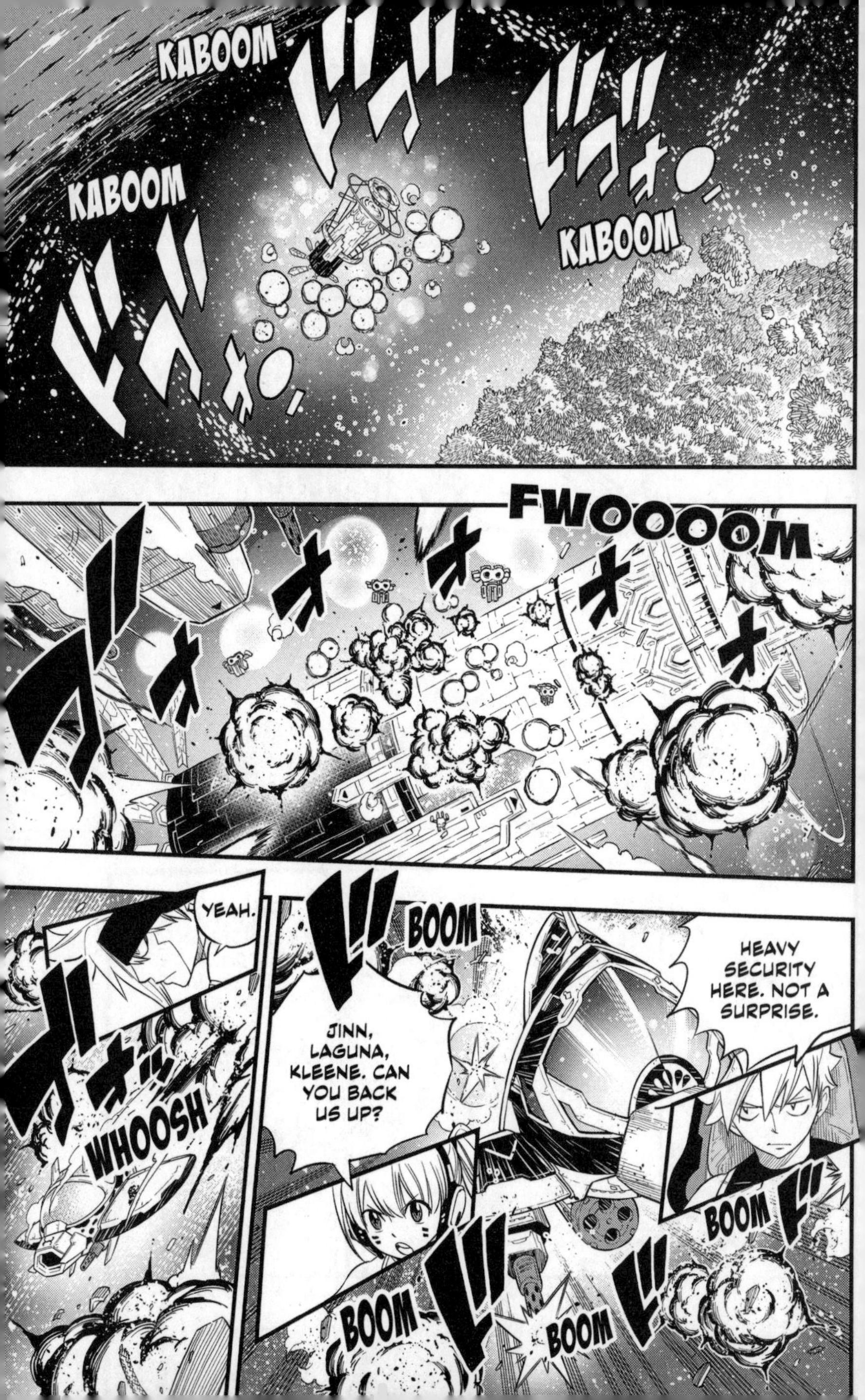
KABOOM
KABOOM
KABOOM
FWOOOOM
HEAVY SECURITY HERE. NOT A SURPRISE.
BOOM
BOOM
JINN, LAGUNA, KLEENE. CAN YOU BACK US UP?
BOOM
BOOM
YEAH.
WHOOSH

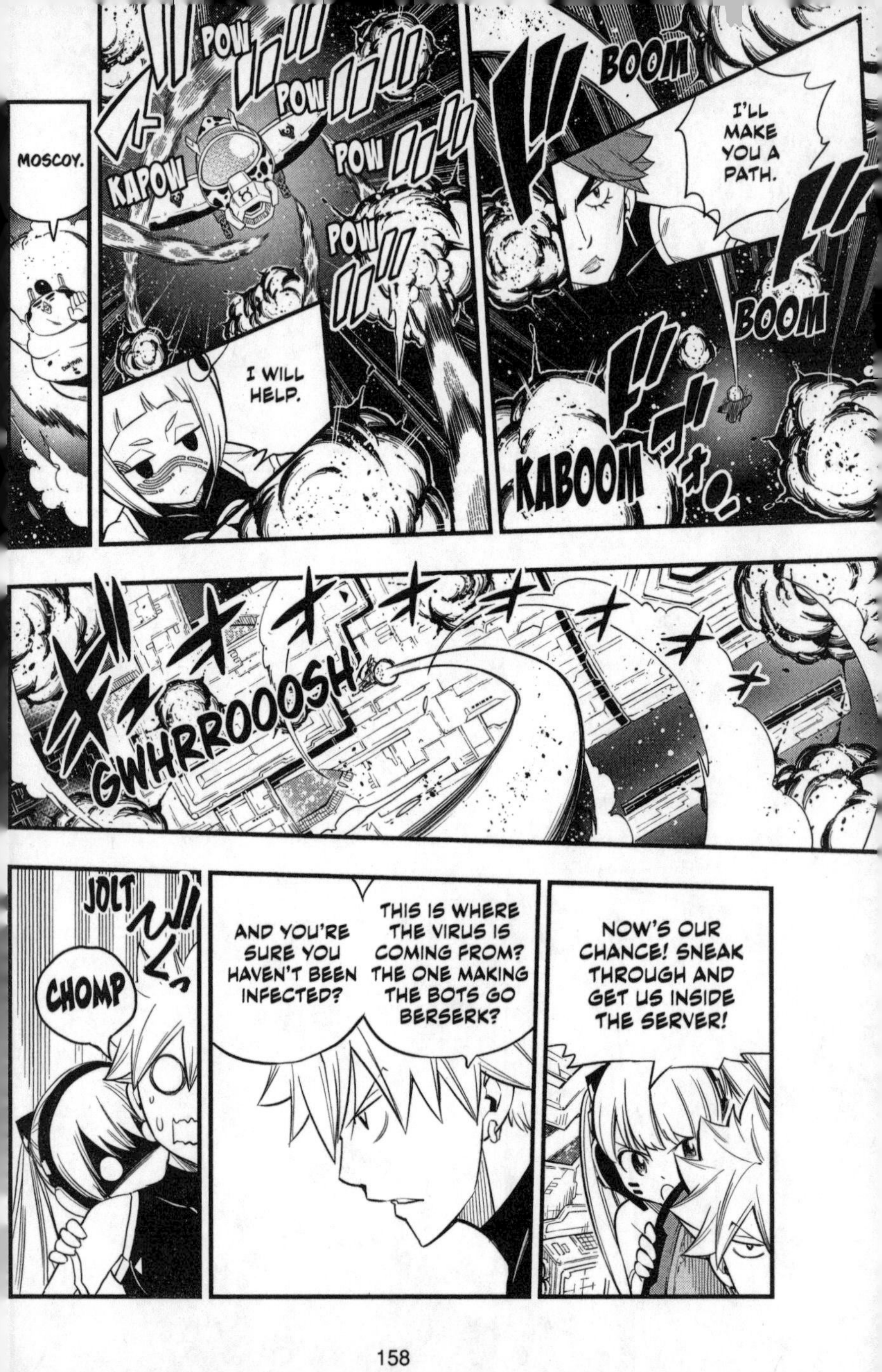
BOOM
I'LL MAKE YOU A PATH.
BOOM
KABOOM
POW
POW
POW
KAPOW
POW
I WILL HELP.
MOSCOY.
GWHRROOOSH
NOW'S OUR CHANCE! SNEAK THROUGH AND GET US INSIDE THE SERVER!
THIS IS WHERE THE VIRUS IS COMING FROM? THE ONE MAKING THE BOTS GO BERSERK?
AND YOU'RE SURE YOU HAVEN'T BEEN INFECTED?
JOLT
CHOMP

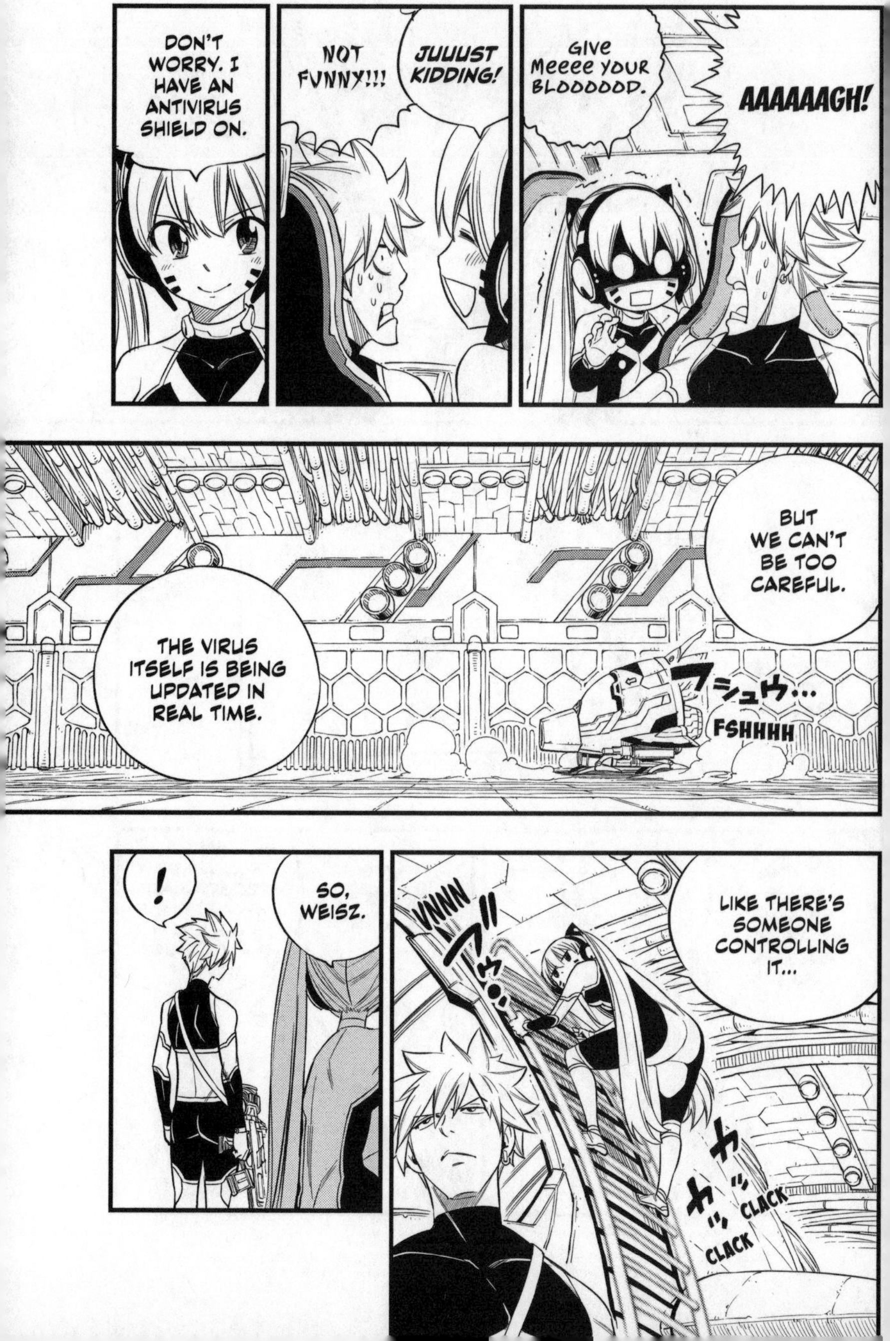
GIVE MEEEE YOUR BLOOOOOD.
AAAAAAGH!
JUUUST KIDDING!
NOT FUNNY!!!
DON'T WORRY. I HAVE AN ANTIVIRUS SHIELD ON.
BUT WE CAN'T BE TOO CAREFUL.
フシュウ…
FSHHHH
THE VIRUS ITSELF IS BEING UPDATED IN REAL TIME.
LIKE THERE'S SOMEONE CONTROLLING IT...
ヴゥゥ…
VNNN
カッ
CLACK
カッ
CLACK
SO, WEISZ.
!

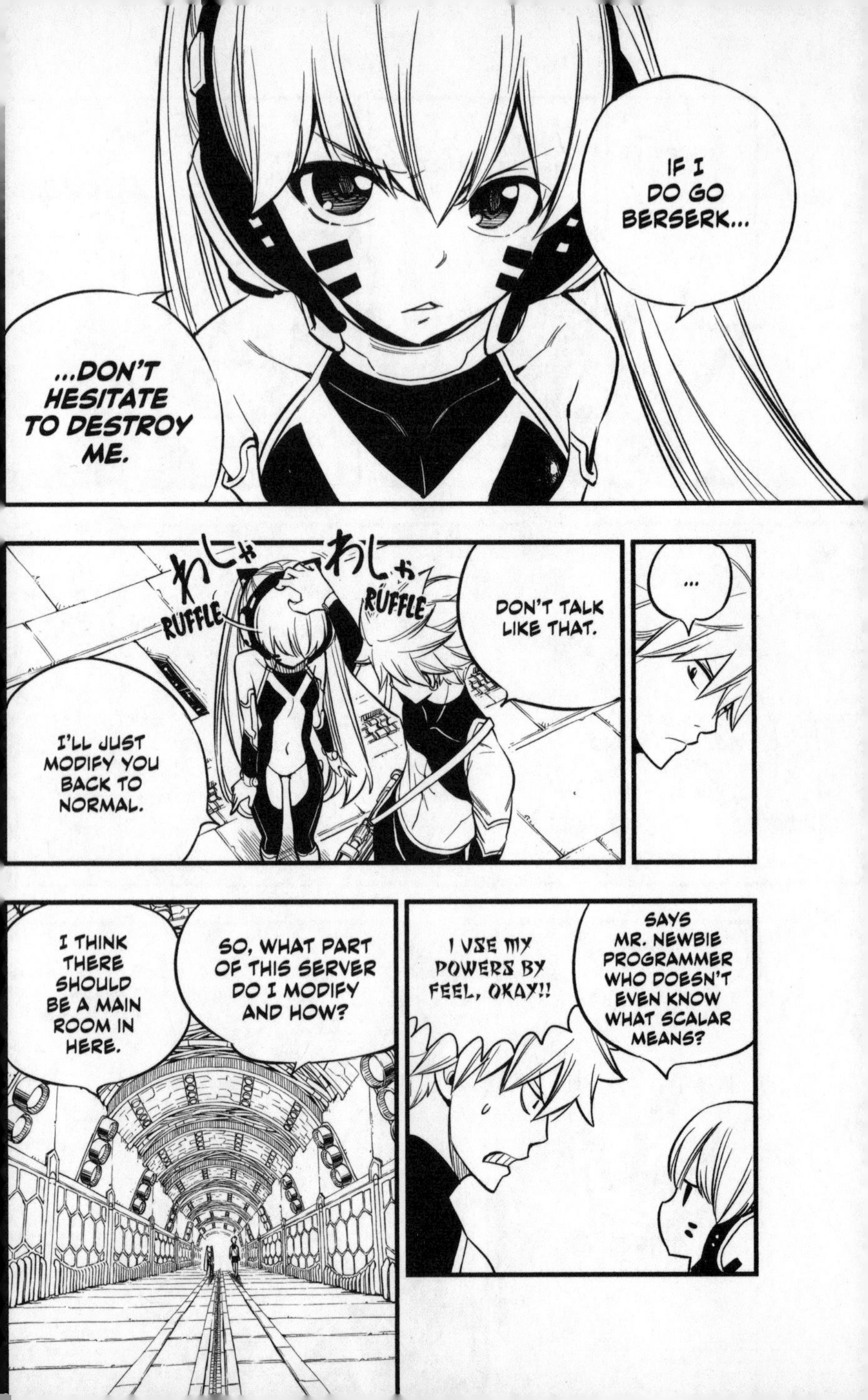
IF I DO GO BERSERK...
...DON'T HESITATE TO DESTROY ME.
...
DON'T TALK LIKE THAT.
RUFFLE
RUFFLE
I'LL JUST MODIFY YOU BACK TO NORMAL.
SAYS MR. NEWBIE PROGRAMMER WHO DOESN'T EVEN KNOW WHAT SCALAR MEANS?
I USE MY POWERS BY FEEL, OKAY!!
SO, WHAT PART OF THIS SERVER DO I MODIFY AND HOW?
I THINK THERE SHOULD BE A MAIN ROOM IN HERE.

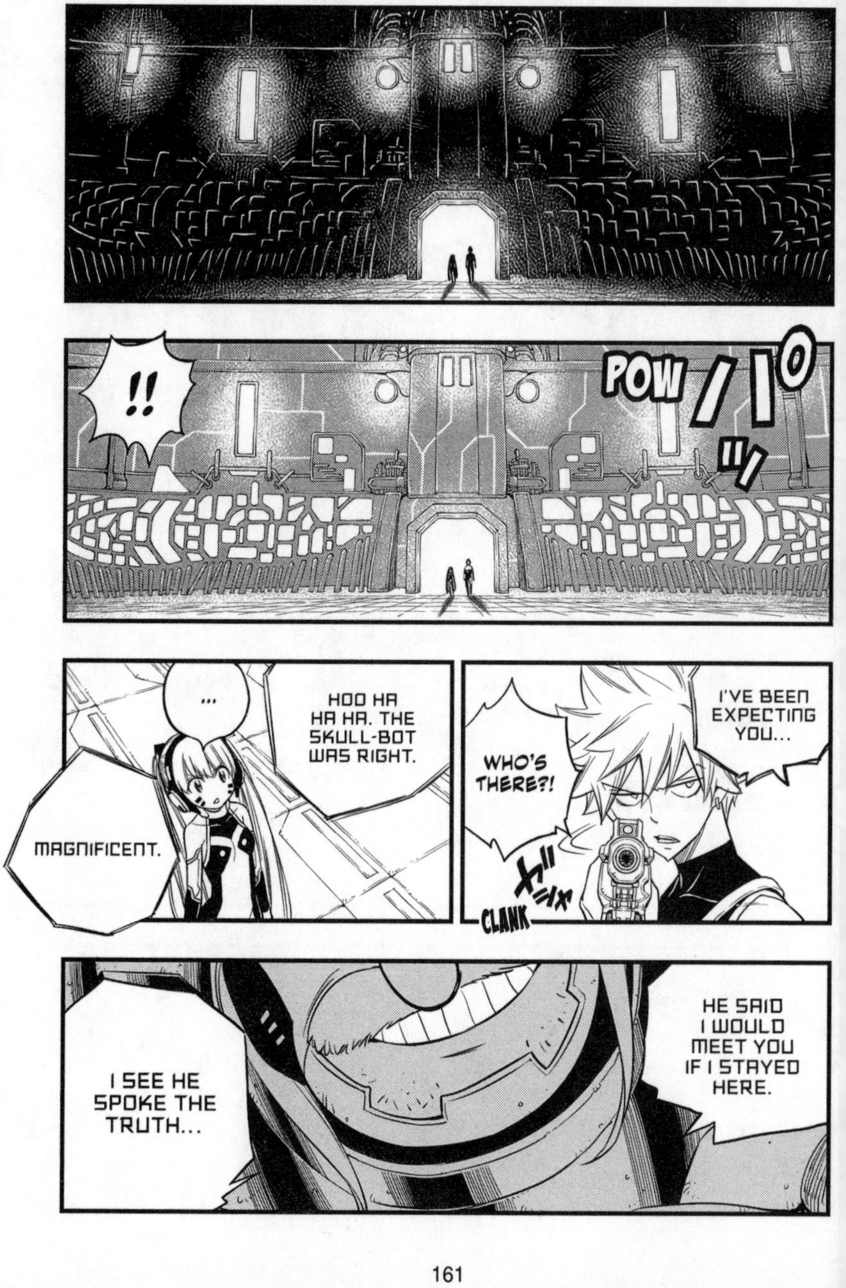
POW
!!
I'VE BEEN EXPECTING YOU...
WHO'S THERE?!
CLANK
HOO HA HA HA. THE SKULL-BOT WAS RIGHT.
...
MAGNIFICENT.
HE SAID I WOULD MEET YOU IF I STAYED HERE.
I SEE HE SPOKE THE TRUTH...

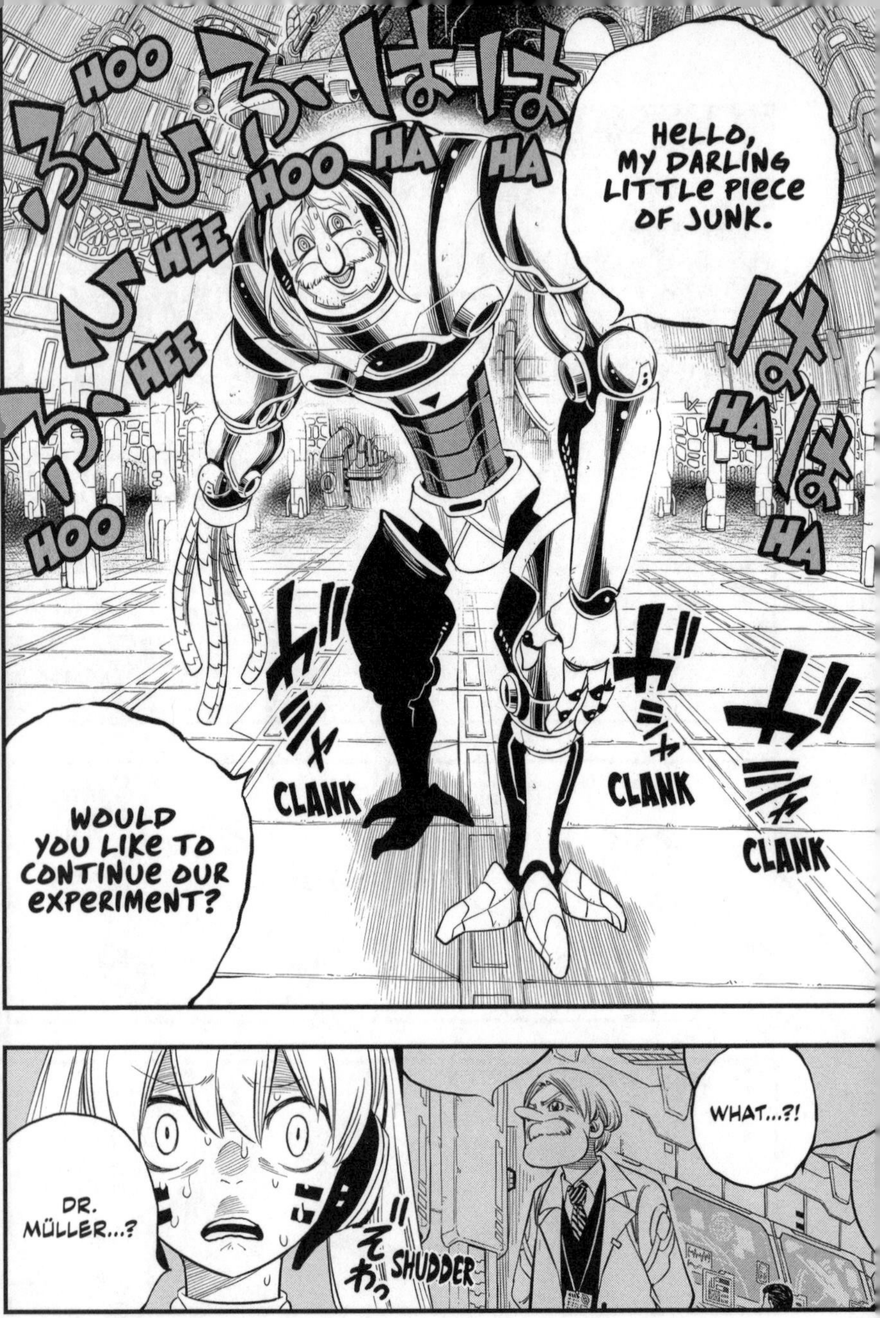
HELLO, MY DARLING LITTLE PIECE OF JUNK.
ははは
HA HA
ふひふふはは
HOO HEE HOO HA HA
ふふ
HEE HOO
ガシャ
CLANK
ガシャ
CLANK
ガシャ
CLANK
WOULD YOU LIKE TO CONTINUE OUR EXPERIMENT?
WHAT...?!
ぞわっ
SHUDDER
DR. MÜLLER...?

EDENS ZERO

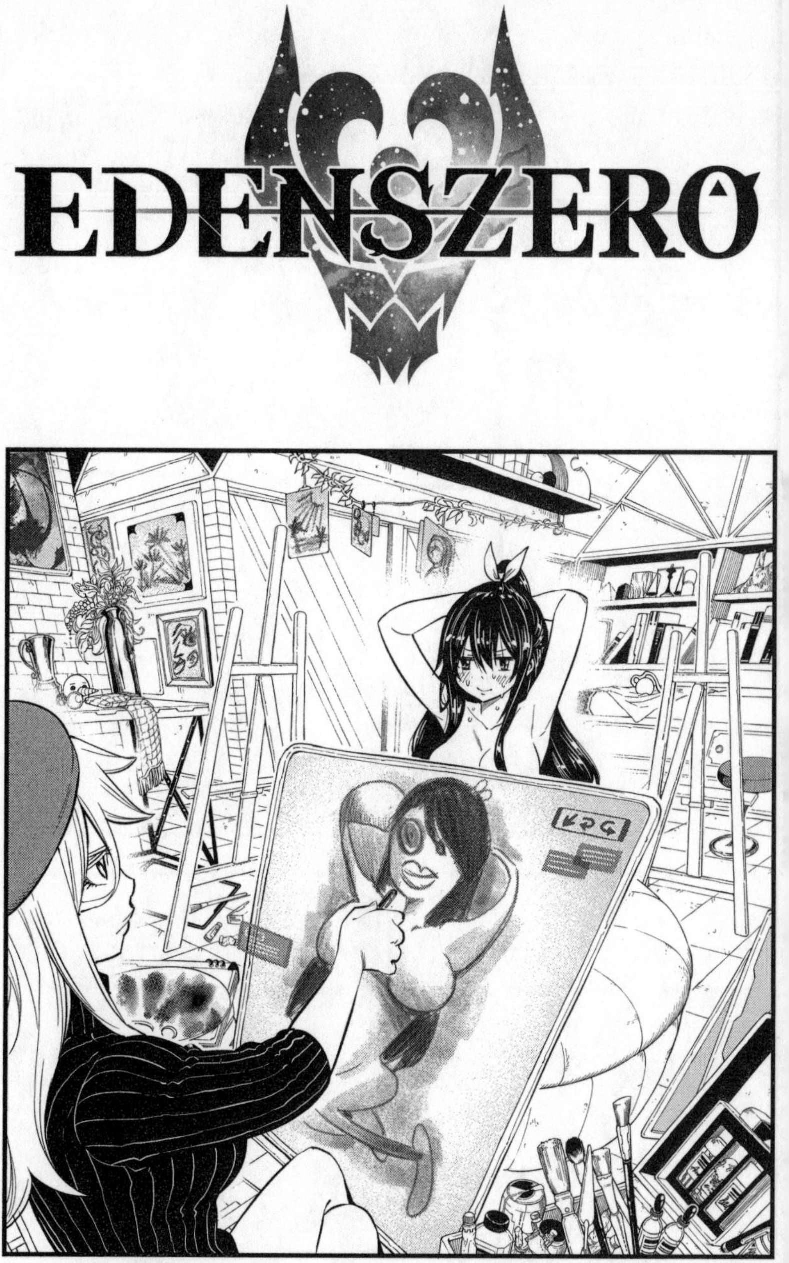

CHAPTER 122: TITAN OF VICTORY

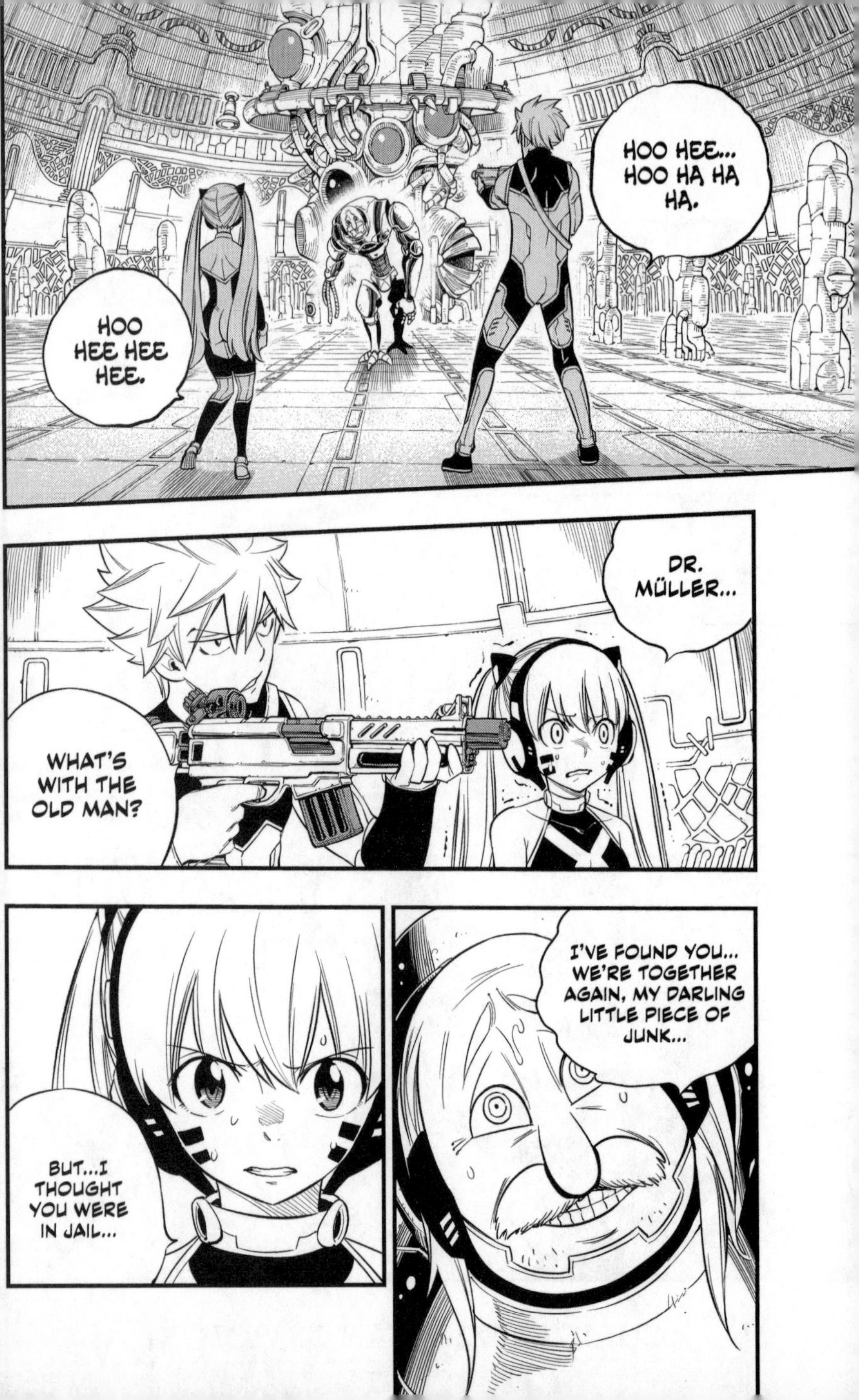
HOO HEE... HOO HA HA HA.
HOO HEE HEE HEE.
DR. MÜLLER...
WHAT'S WITH THE OLD MAN?
I'VE FOUND YOU... WE'RE TOGETHER AGAIN, MY DARLING LITTLE PIECE OF JUNK...
BUT...I THOUGHT YOU WERE IN JAIL...

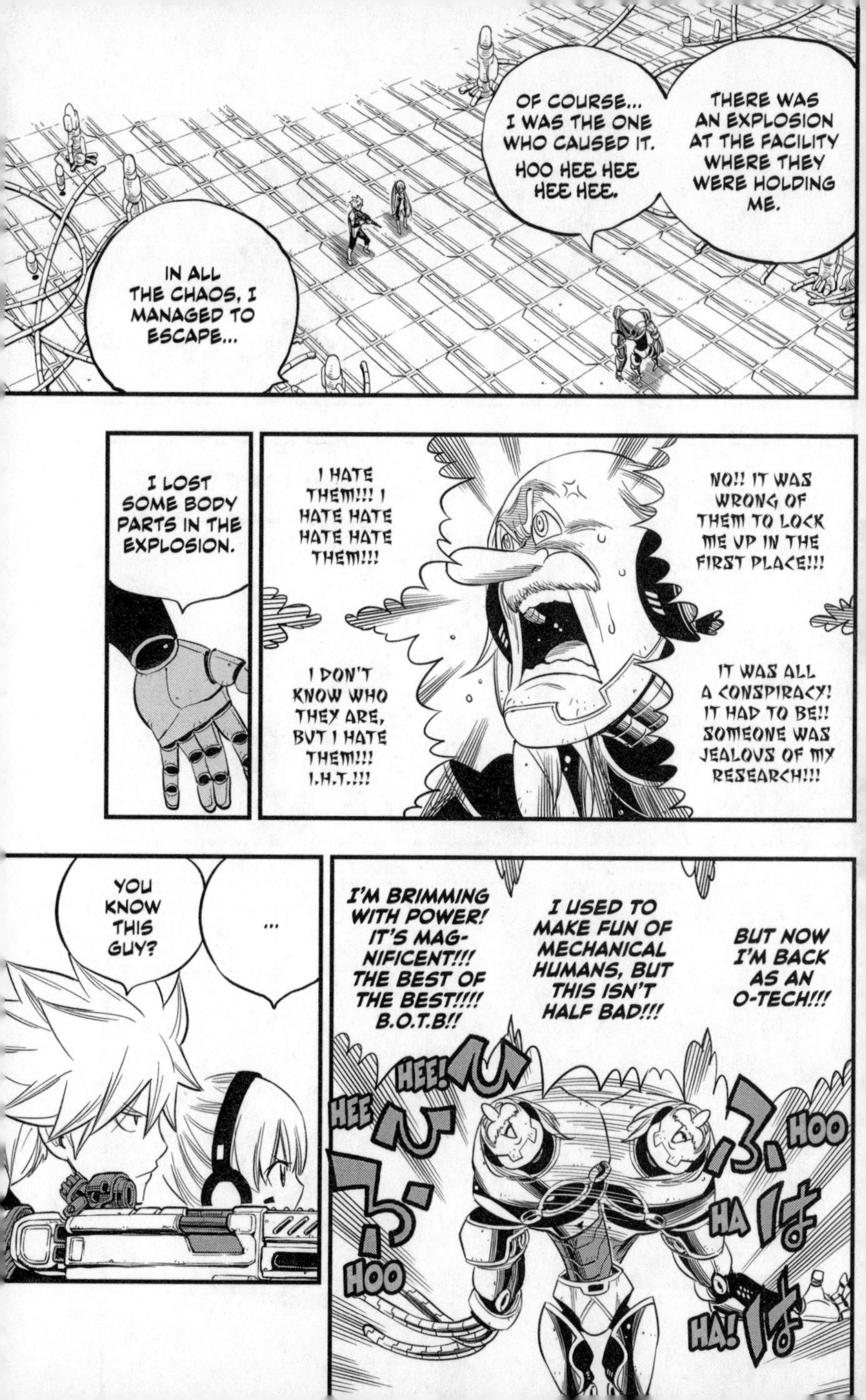
THERE WAS AN EXPLOSION AT THE FACILITY WHERE THEY WERE HOLDING ME.
OF COURSE... I WAS THE ONE WHO CAUSED IT.
HOO HEE HEE HEE HEE.
IN ALL THE CHAOS, I MANAGED TO ESCAPE...
NO!! IT WAS WRONG OF THEM TO LOCK ME UP IN THE FIRST PLACE!!!
I HATE THEM!!! I HATE HATE HATE HATE THEM!!!
IT WAS ALL A CONSPIRACY! IT HAD TO BE!! SOMEONE WAS JEALOUS OF MY RESEARCH!!!
I DON'T KNOW WHO THEY ARE, BUT I HATE THEM!!! I.H.T.!!!
I LOST SOME BODY PARTS IN THE EXPLOSION.
BUT NOW I'M BACK AS AN O-TECH!!!
I USED TO MAKE FUN OF MECHANICAL HUMANS, BUT THIS ISN'T HALF BAD!!!
I'M BRIMMING WITH POWER! IT'S MAG-NIFICENT!!! THE BEST OF THE BEST!!!! B.O.T.B!!
HOO
HEE!
HEE
HA
HOO
HA!
...
YOU KNOW THIS GUY?

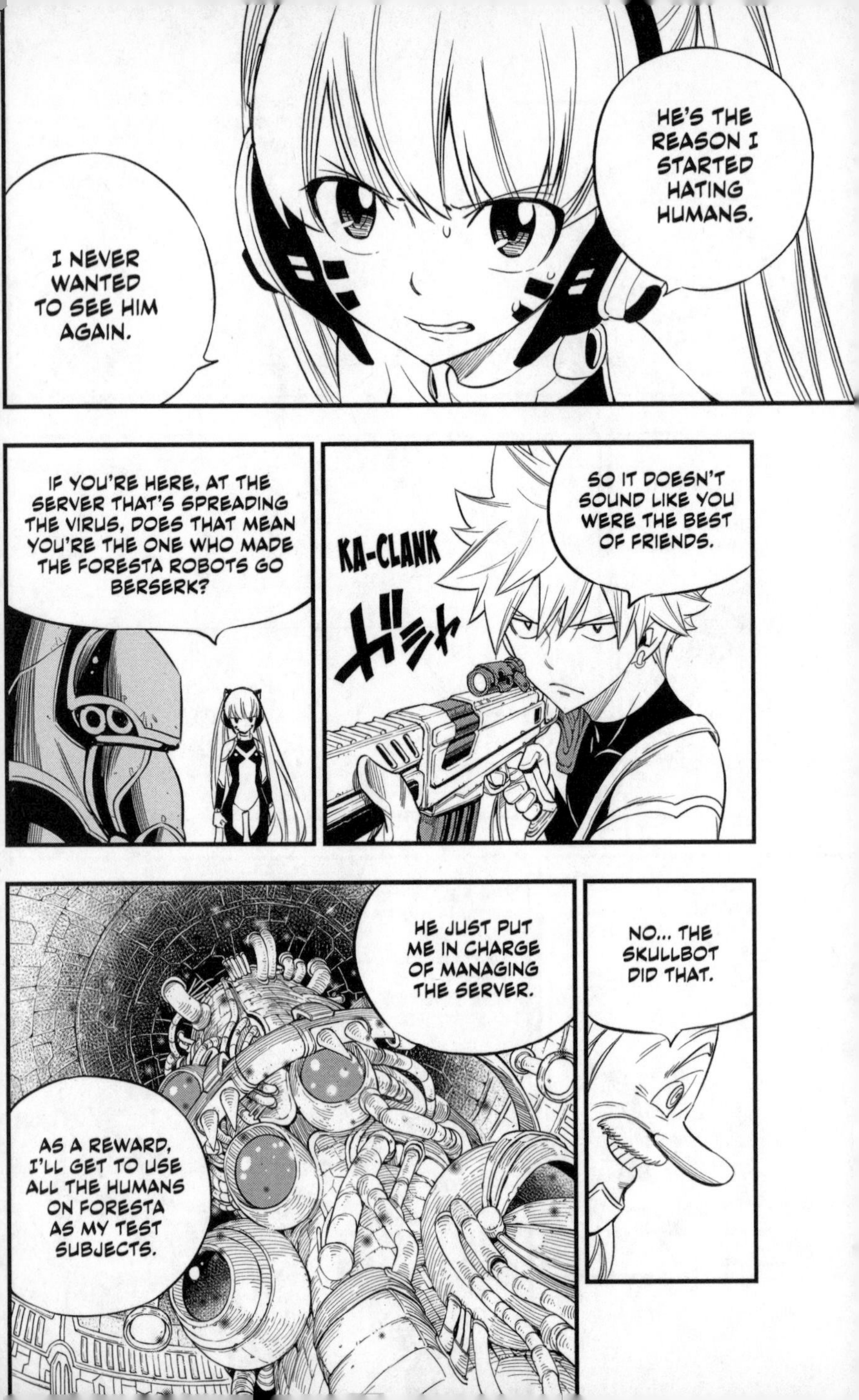
HE'S THE REASON I STARTED HATING HUMANS.
I NEVER WANTED TO SEE HIM AGAIN.
SO IT DOESN'T SOUND LIKE YOU WERE THE BEST OF FRIENDS.
KA-CLANK
ガシャ
IF YOU'RE HERE, AT THE SERVER THAT'S SPREADING THE VIRUS, DOES THAT MEAN YOU'RE THE ONE WHO MADE THE FORESTA ROBOTS GO BERSERK?
NO... THE SKULLBOT DID THAT.
HE JUST PUT ME IN CHARGE OF MANAGING THE SERVER.
AS A REWARD, I'LL GET TO USE ALL THE HUMANS ON FORESTA AS MY TEST SUBJECTS.

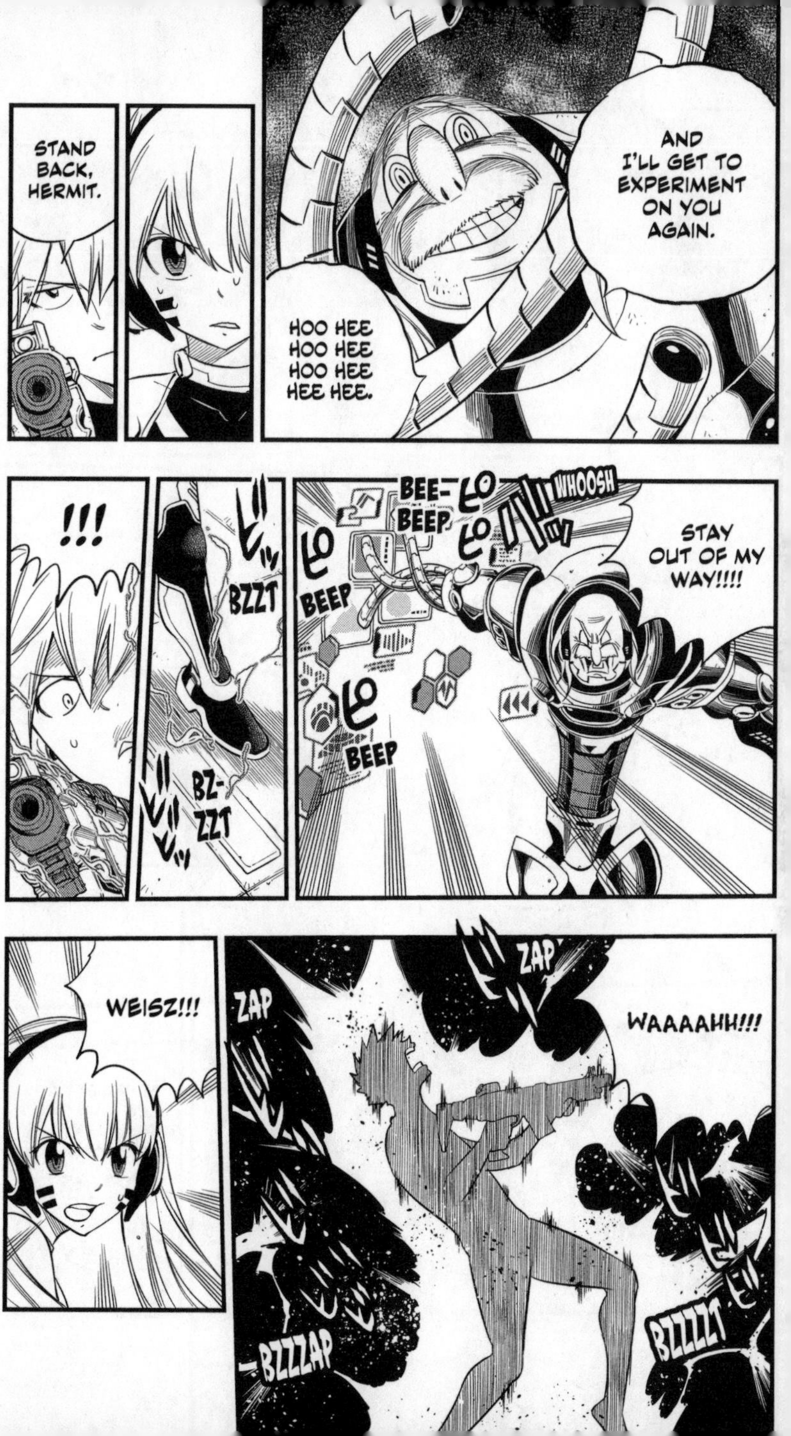
AND I'LL GET TO EXPERIMENT ON YOU AGAIN.
HOO HEE HOO HEE HOO HEE HEE HEE.
STAND BACK, HERMIT.
WHOOSH
STAY OUT OF MY WAY!!!!
BEE-BEEP
BEEP
BEEP
BZZT
BZ-ZZT
!!!
ZAP
WAAAAHH!!!
ZAP
BZZZZT
BZZZAP
WEISZ!!!

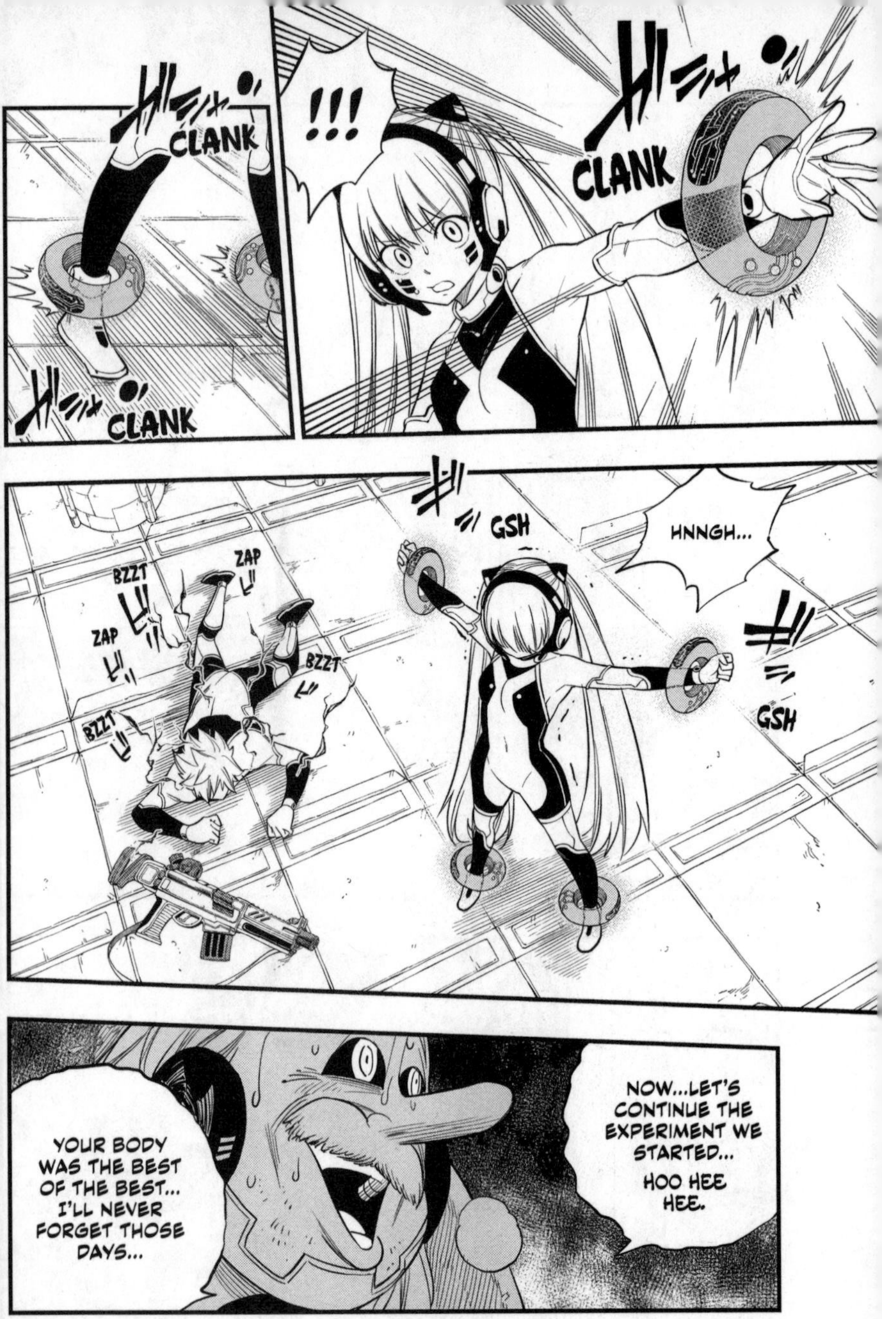
CLANK
!!!
CLANK
CLANK
HNNGH...
GSH
GSH
ZAP
BZZT
BZZT
ZAP
BZZT
NOW...LET'S CONTINUE THE EXPERIMENT WE STARTED... HOO HEE HEE.
YOUR BODY WAS THE BEST OF THE BEST... I'LL NEVER FORGET THOSE DAYS...

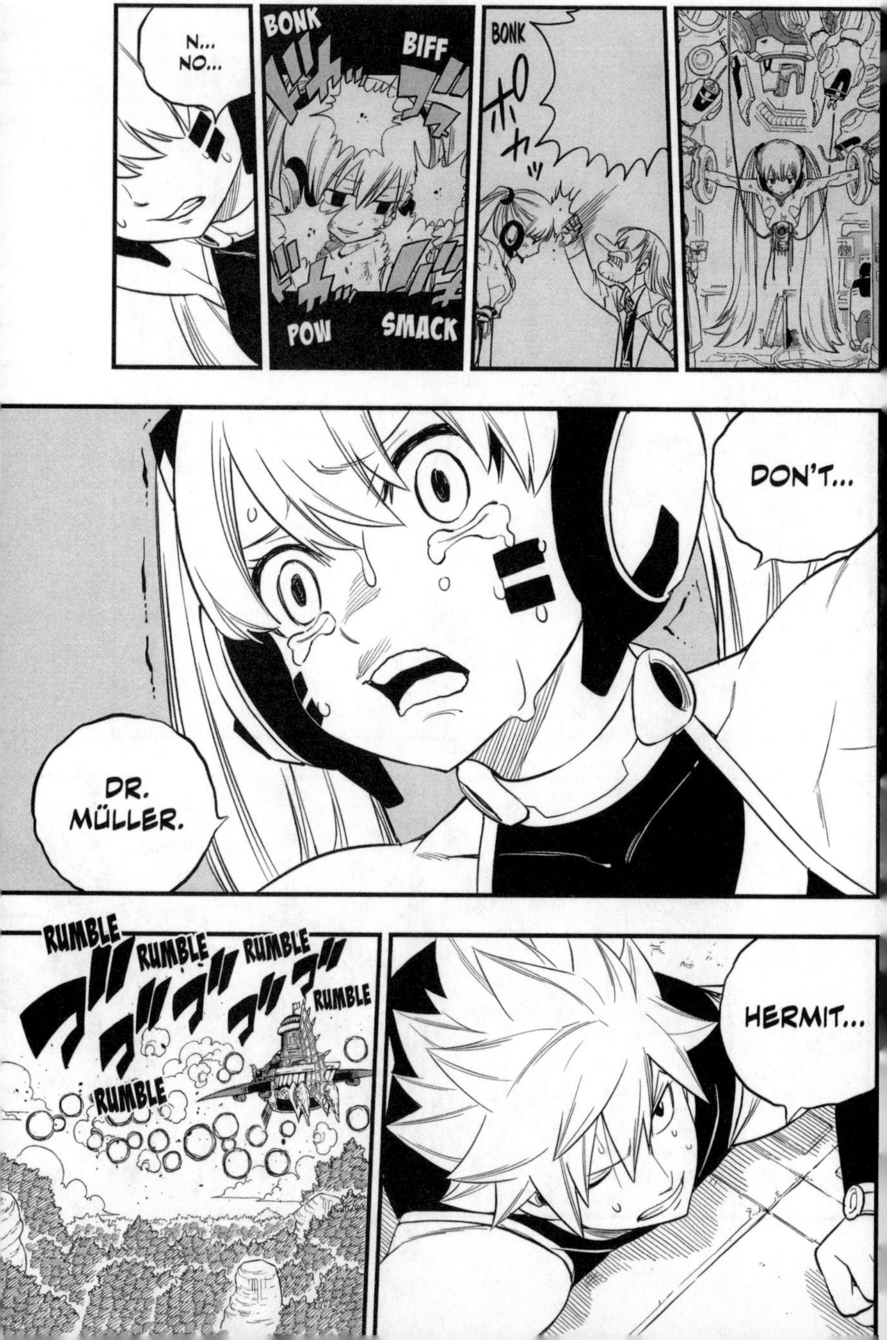
BONK
ポカッ
BONK
BIFF
POW
SMACK
N... NO...
DON'T...
DR. MÜLLER.
HERMIT...
RUMBLE
RUMBLE
RUMBLE
RUMBLE
RUMBLE

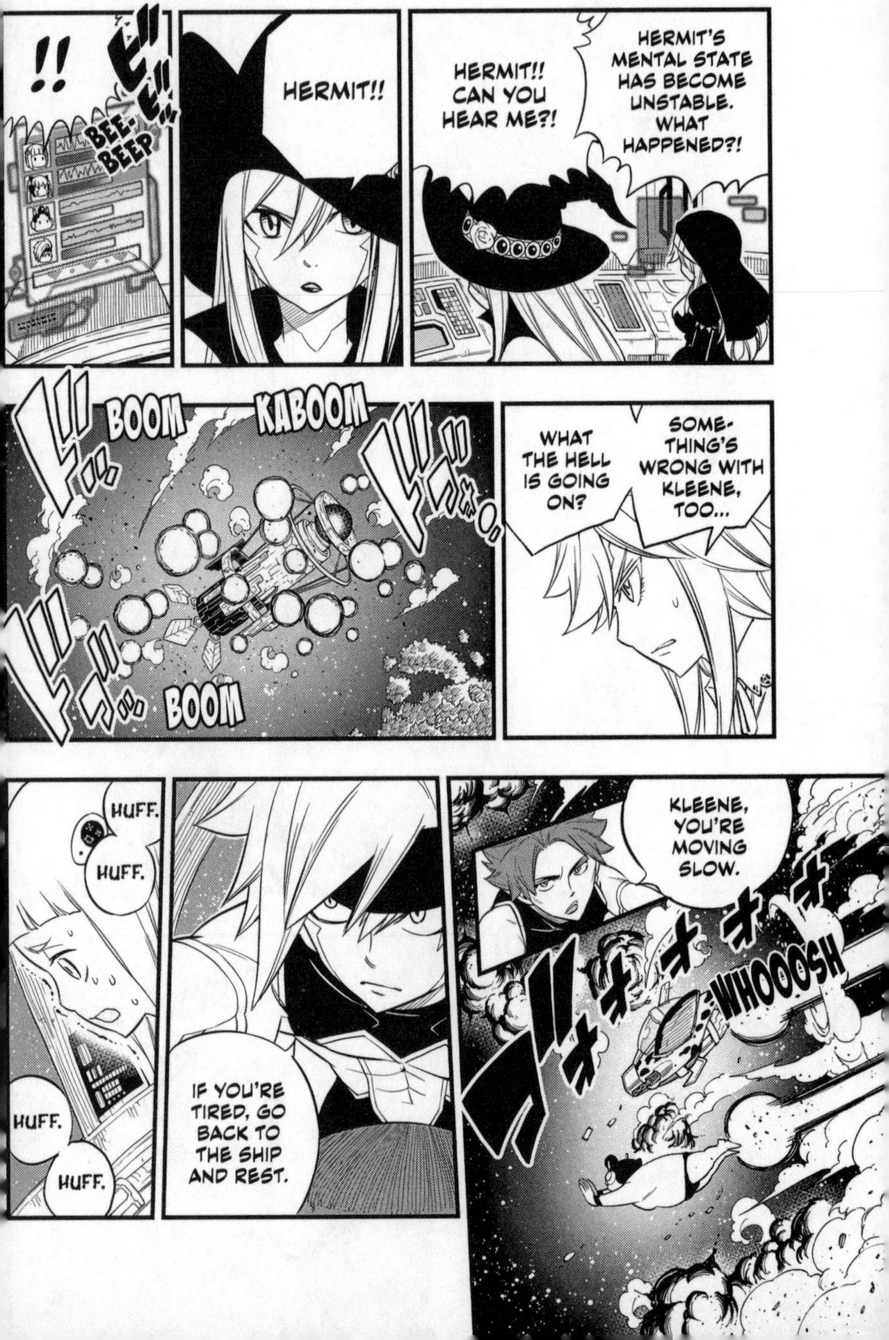

HERMIT'S MENTAL STATE HAS BECOME UNSTABLE. WHAT HAPPENED?!
HERMIT!! CAN YOU HEAR ME?!
HERMIT!!
!!
BEE-BEEP
SOME-THING'S WRONG WITH KLEENE, TOO...
WHAT THE HELL IS GOING ON?
KABOOM
BOOM
BOOM
KLEENE, YOU'RE MOVING SLOW.
WHOOOSH
IF YOU'RE TIRED, GO BACK TO THE SHIP AND REST.
HUFF.
HUFF.
HUFF.
HUFF.

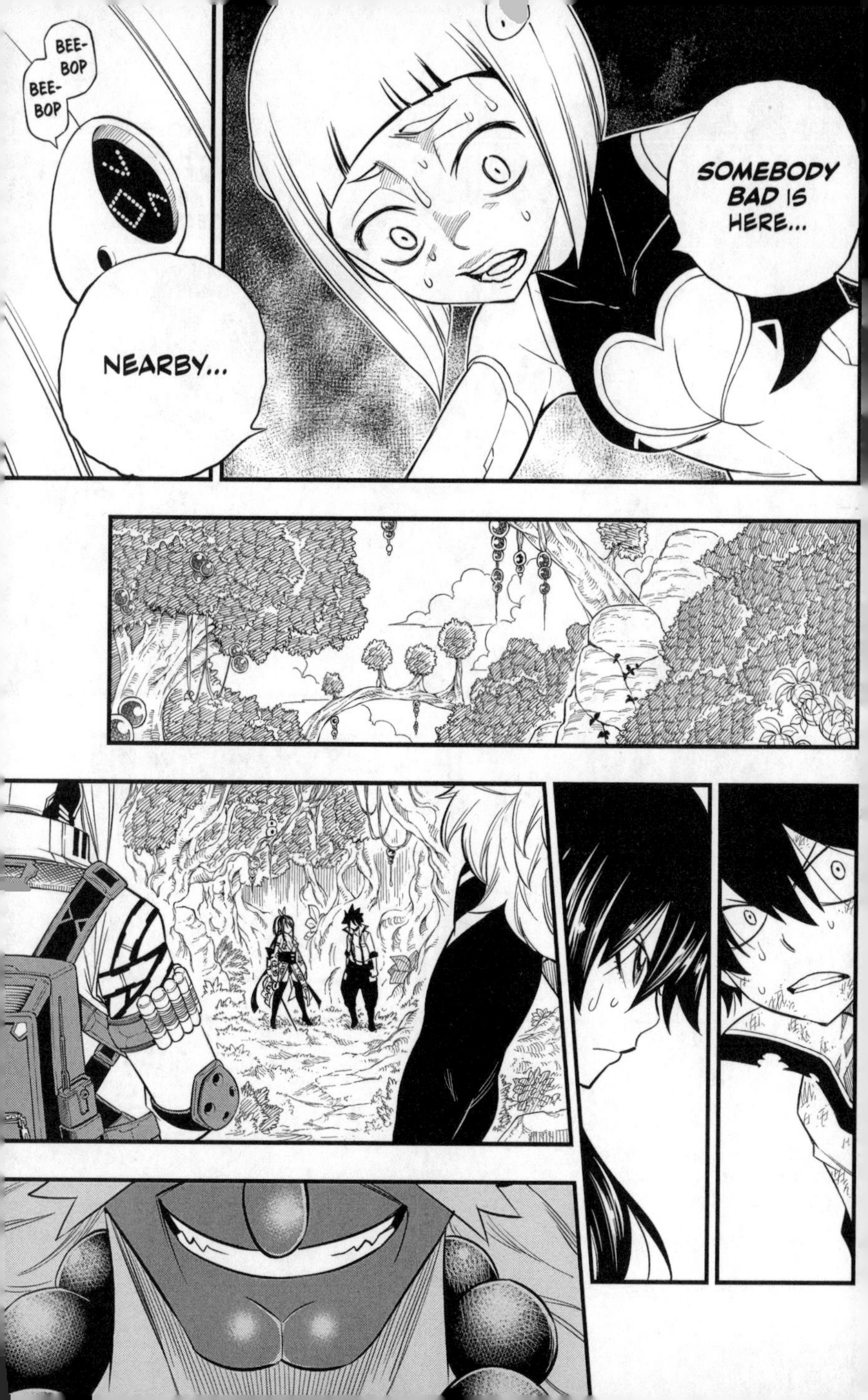
SOMEBODY BAD IS HERE...
BEE-BOP BEE-BOP
NEARBY...

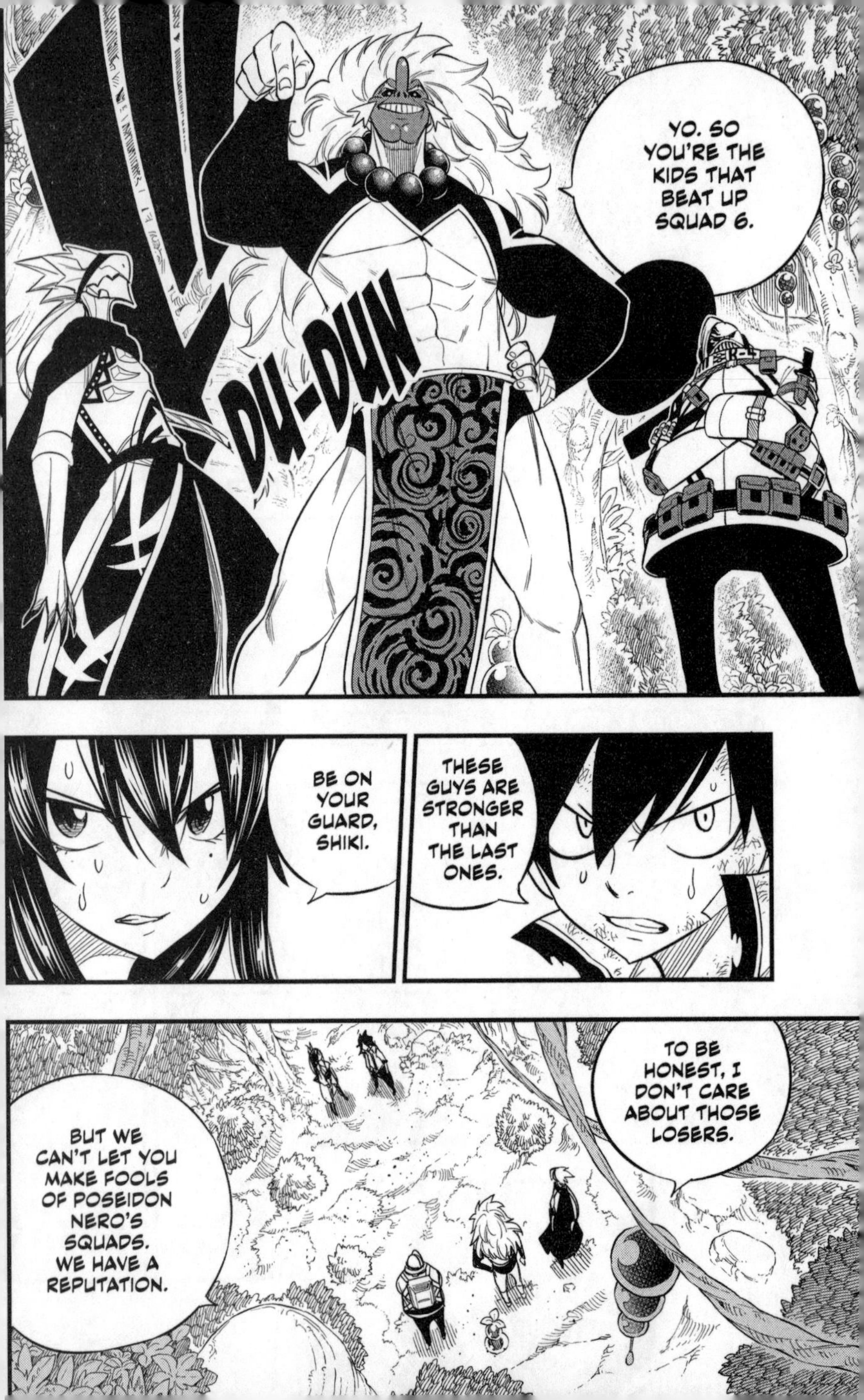
YO. SO YOU'RE THE KIDS THAT BEAT UP SQUAD 6.
DU-DUN
THESE GUYS ARE STRONGER THAN THE LAST ONES.
BE ON YOUR GUARD, SHIKI.
TO BE HONEST, I DON'T CARE ABOUT THOSE LOSERS.
BUT WE CAN'T LET YOU MAKE FOOLS OF POSEIDON NERO'S SQUADS. WE HAVE A REPUTATION.

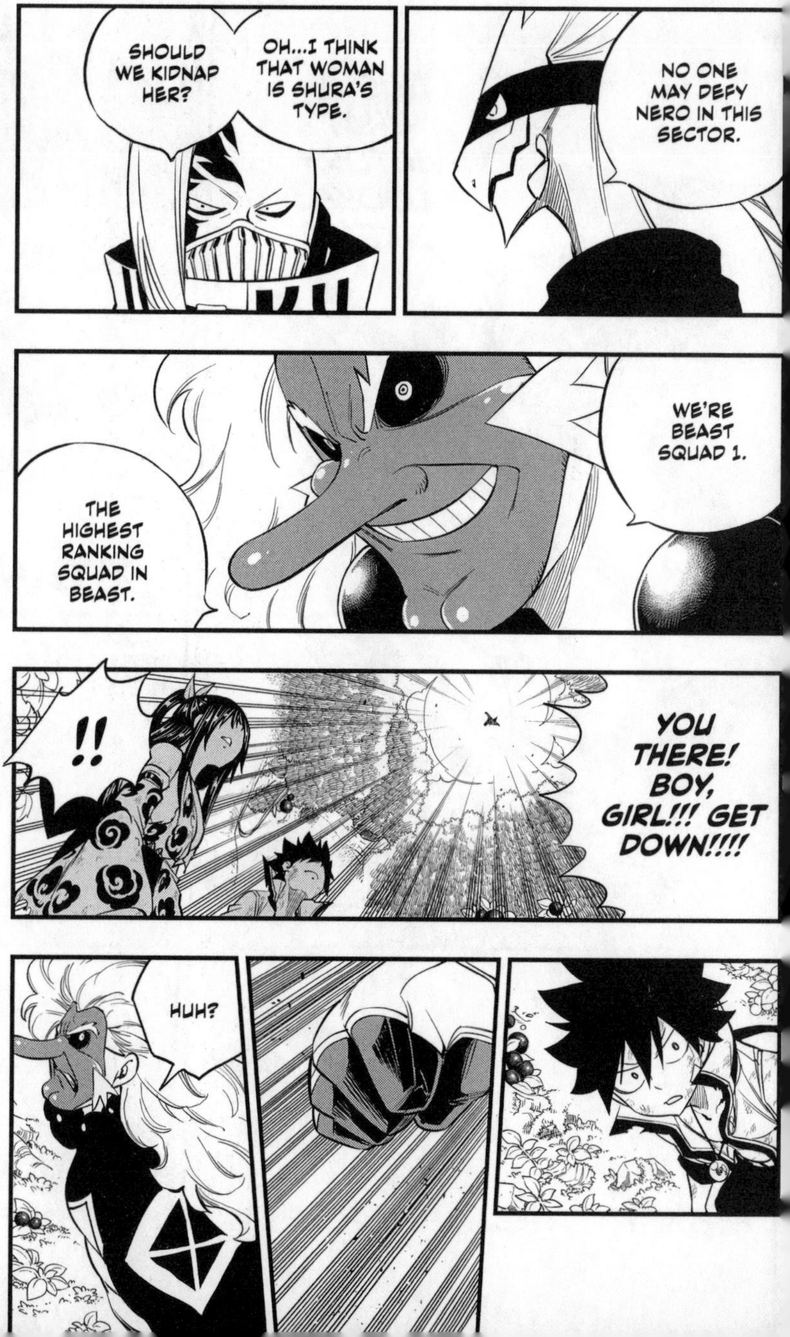
NO ONE MAY DEFY NERO IN THIS SECTOR.
OH...I THINK THAT WOMAN IS SHURA'S TYPE.
SHOULD WE KIDNAP HER?
WE'RE BEAST SQUAD 1.
THE HIGHEST RANKING SQUAD IN BEAST.
YOU THERE! BOY, GIRL!!! GET DOWN!!!!
!!
HUH?

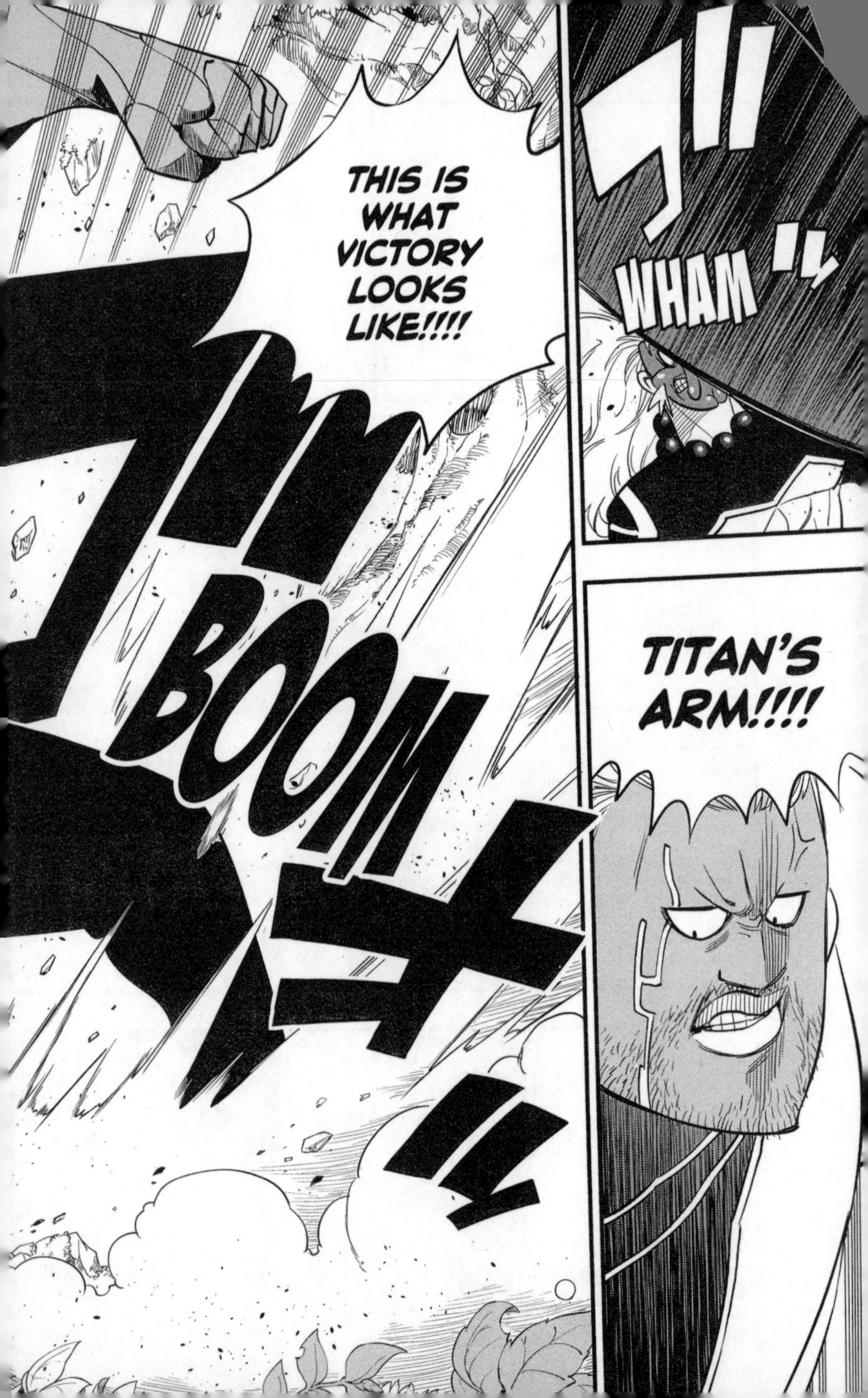
WHAM
TITAN'S ARM!!!!
THIS IS WHAT VICTORY LOOKS LIKE!!!!
BOOM

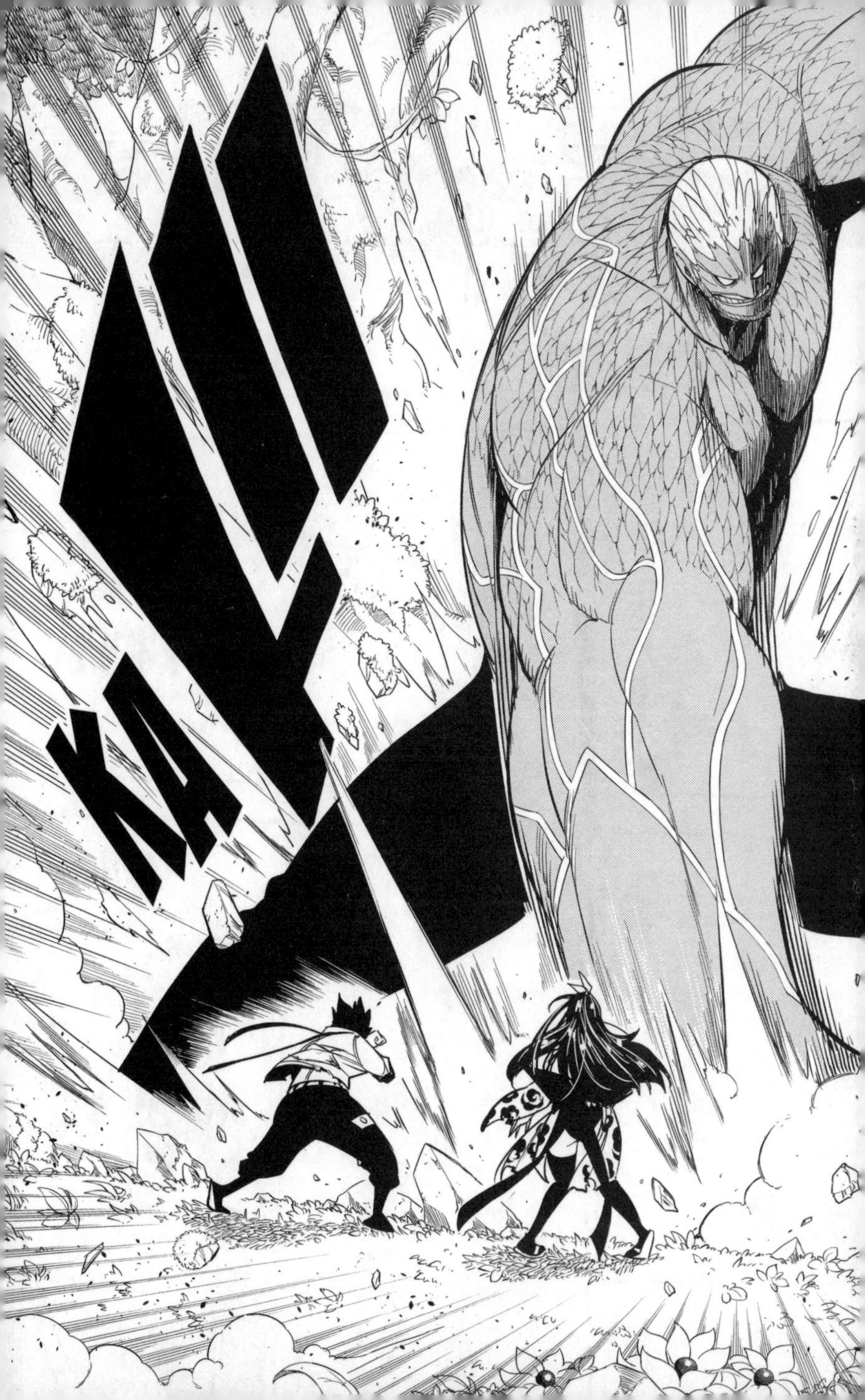

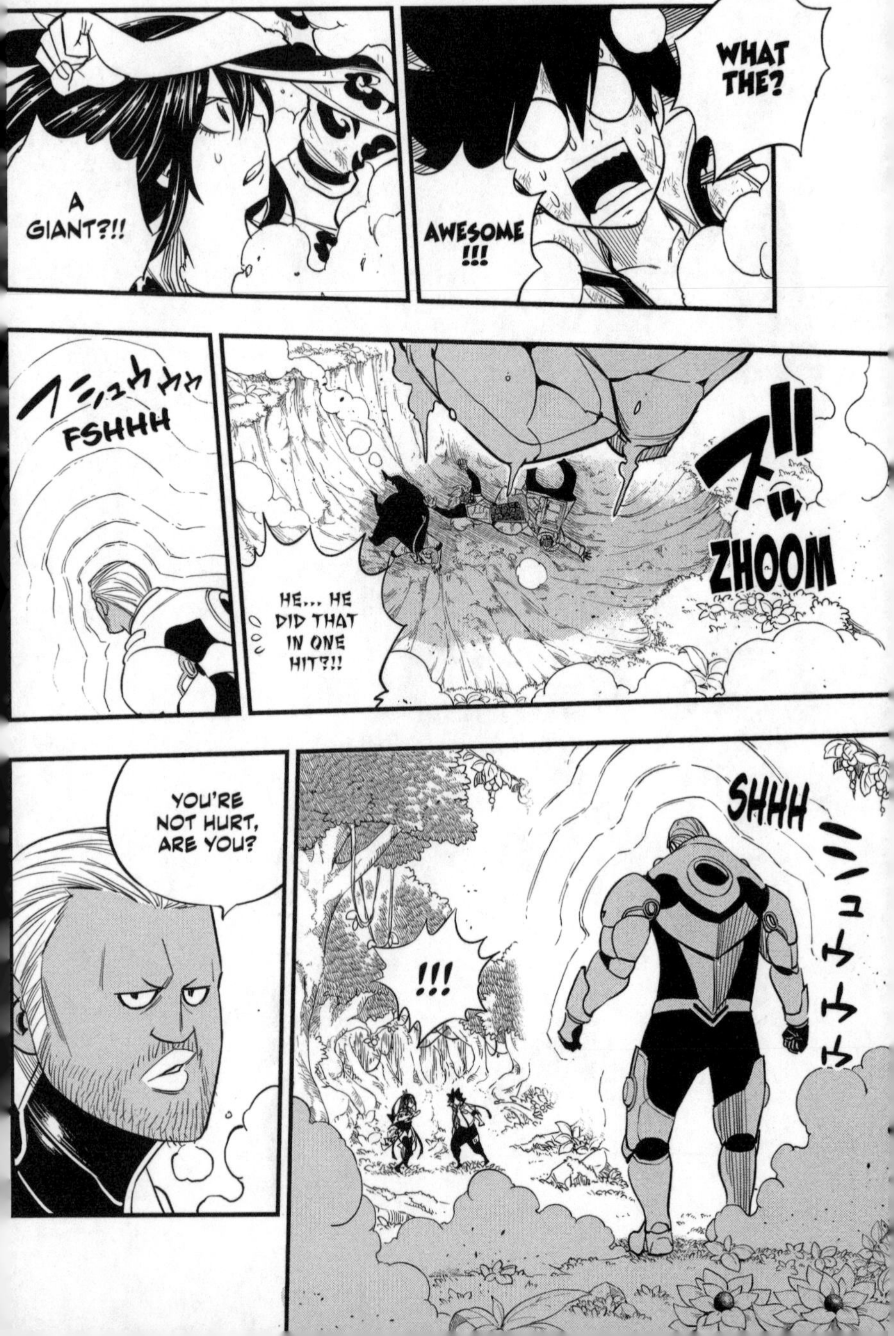
WHAT THE?
AWESOME!!!
A GIANT?!!
ZHOOM
HE... HE DID THAT IN ONE HIT?!!
FSHHH
SHHH
!!!
YOU'RE NOT HURT, ARE YOU?

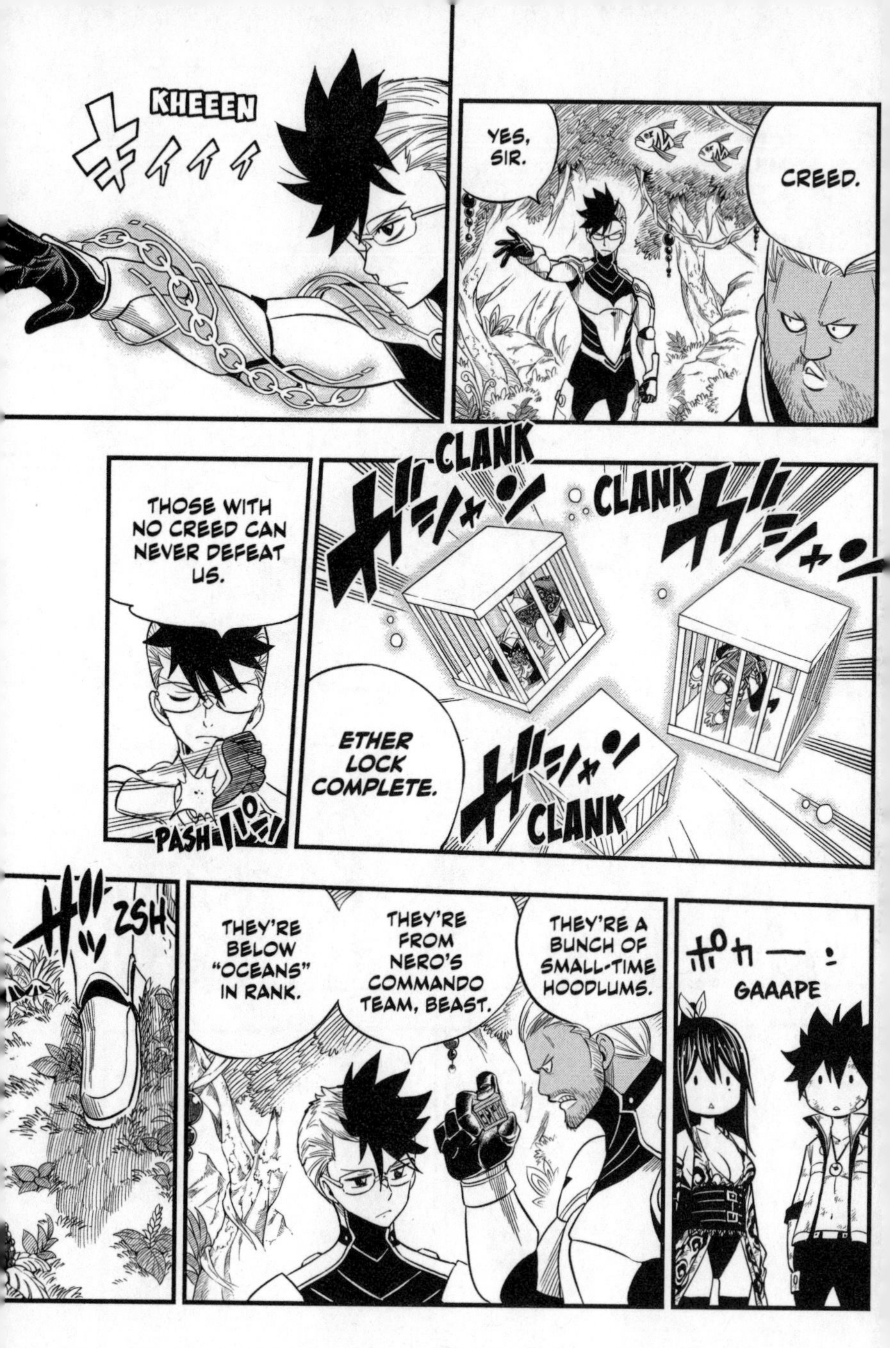
CREED.
YES, SIR.
KHEEEN
キイイイ
CLANK
ガシャン
CLANK
ガシャン
ETHER LOCK COMPLETE.
ガシャン
CLANK
THOSE WITH NO CREED CAN NEVER DEFEAT US.
PASH
GAAAPE
ポカーン
THEY'RE A BUNCH OF SMALL-TIME HOODLUMS.
THEY'RE FROM NERO'S COMMANDO TEAM, BEAST.
THEY'RE BELOW "OCEANS" IN RANK.
ZSH
ザッ

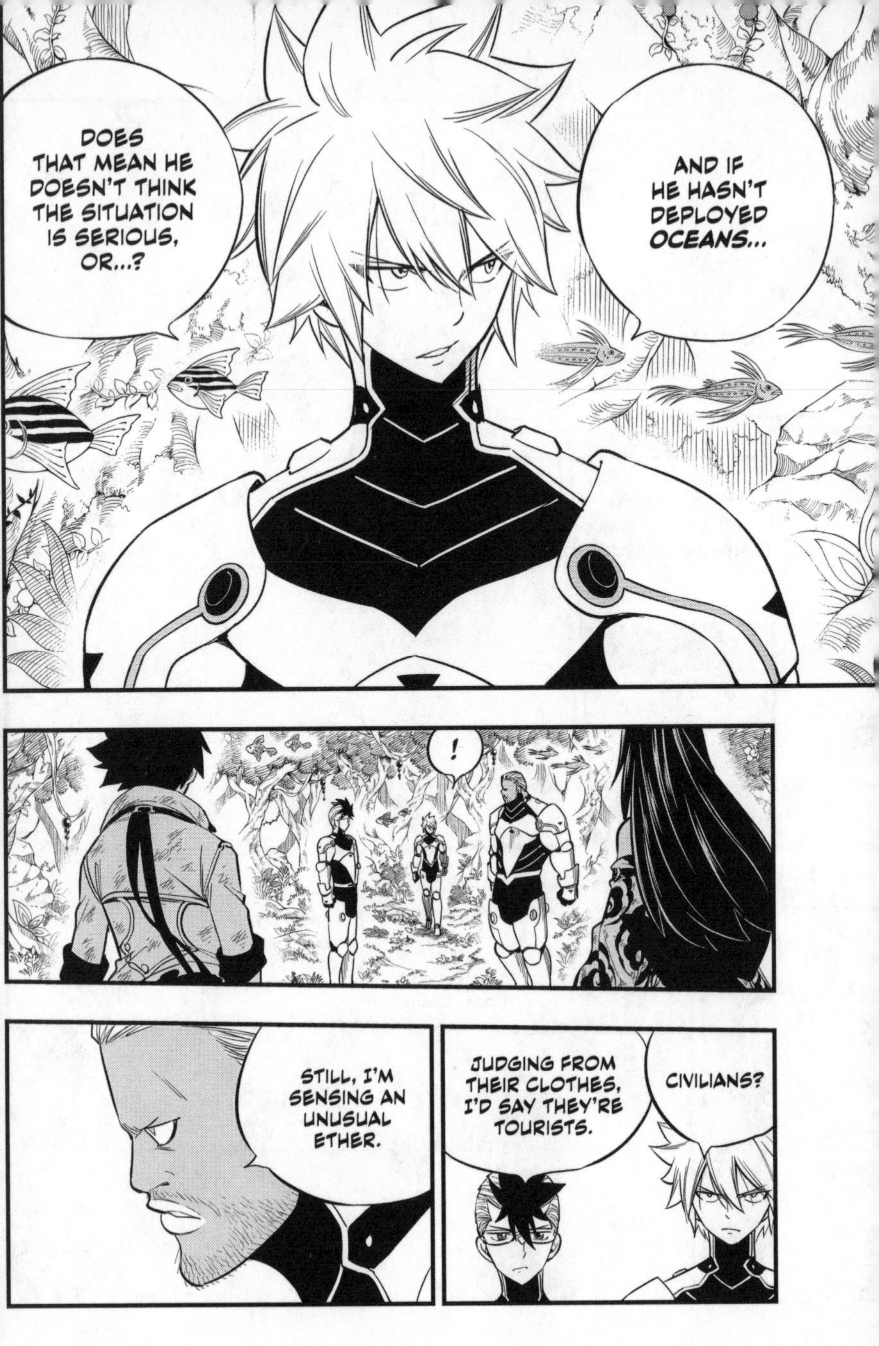
AND IF HE HASN'T DEPLOYED OCEANS...
DOES THAT MEAN HE DOESN'T THINK THE SITUATION IS SERIOUS, OR...?
!
CIVILIANS?
JUDGING FROM THEIR CLOTHES, I'D SAY THEY'RE TOURISTS.
STILL, I'M SENSING AN UNUSUAL ETHER.

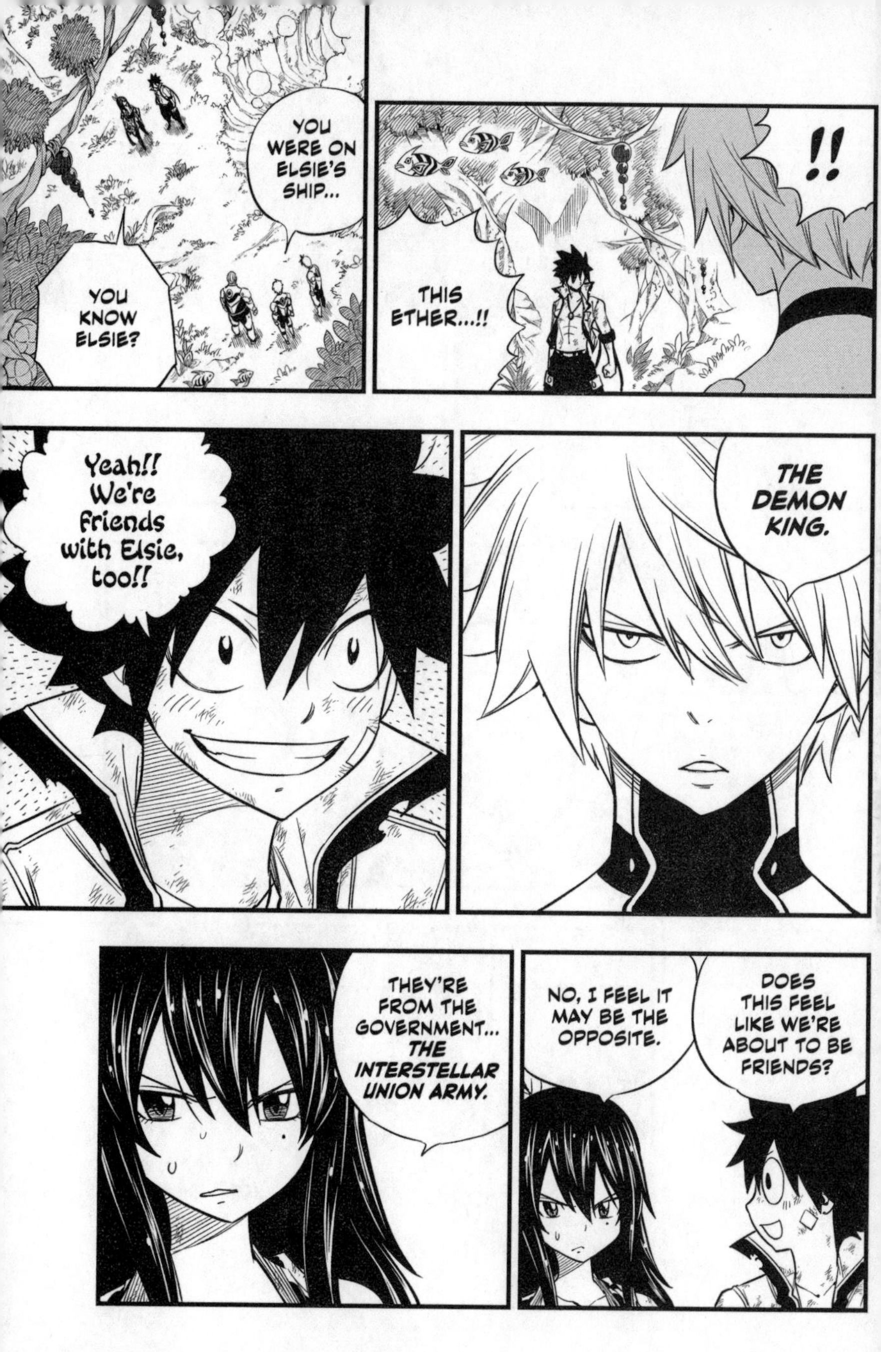
!!
THIS ETHER...!!
YOU WERE ON ELSIE'S SHIP...
YOU KNOW ELSIE?
THE DEMON KING.
Yeah!! We're friends with Elsie, too!!
DOES THIS FEEL LIKE WE'RE ABOUT TO BE FRIENDS?
NO, I FEEL IT MAY BE THE OPPOSITE.
THEY'RE FROM THE GOVERNMENT... *THE INTERSTELLAR UNION ARMY.*

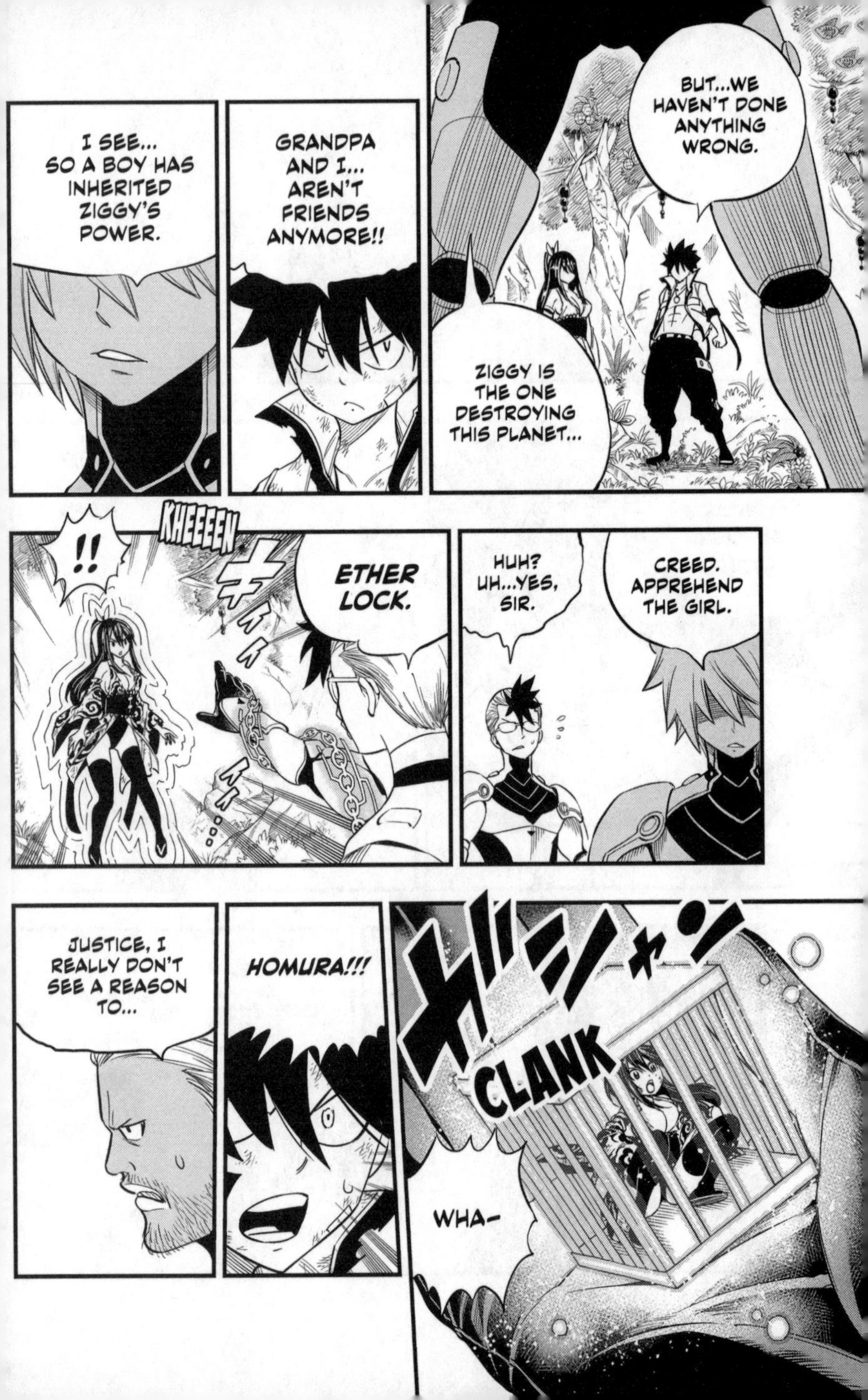
BUT...WE HAVEN'T DONE ANYTHING WRONG.
ZIGGY IS THE ONE DESTROYING THIS PLANET...
GRANDPA AND I... AREN'T FRIENDS ANYMORE!!
I SEE... SO A BOY HAS INHERITED ZIGGY'S POWER.
CREED. APPREHEND THE GIRL.
HUH? UH...YES, SIR.
ETHER LOCK.
KHEEEEN
!!
CLANK
WHA-
HOMURA!!!
JUSTICE, I REALLY DON'T SEE A REASON TO...

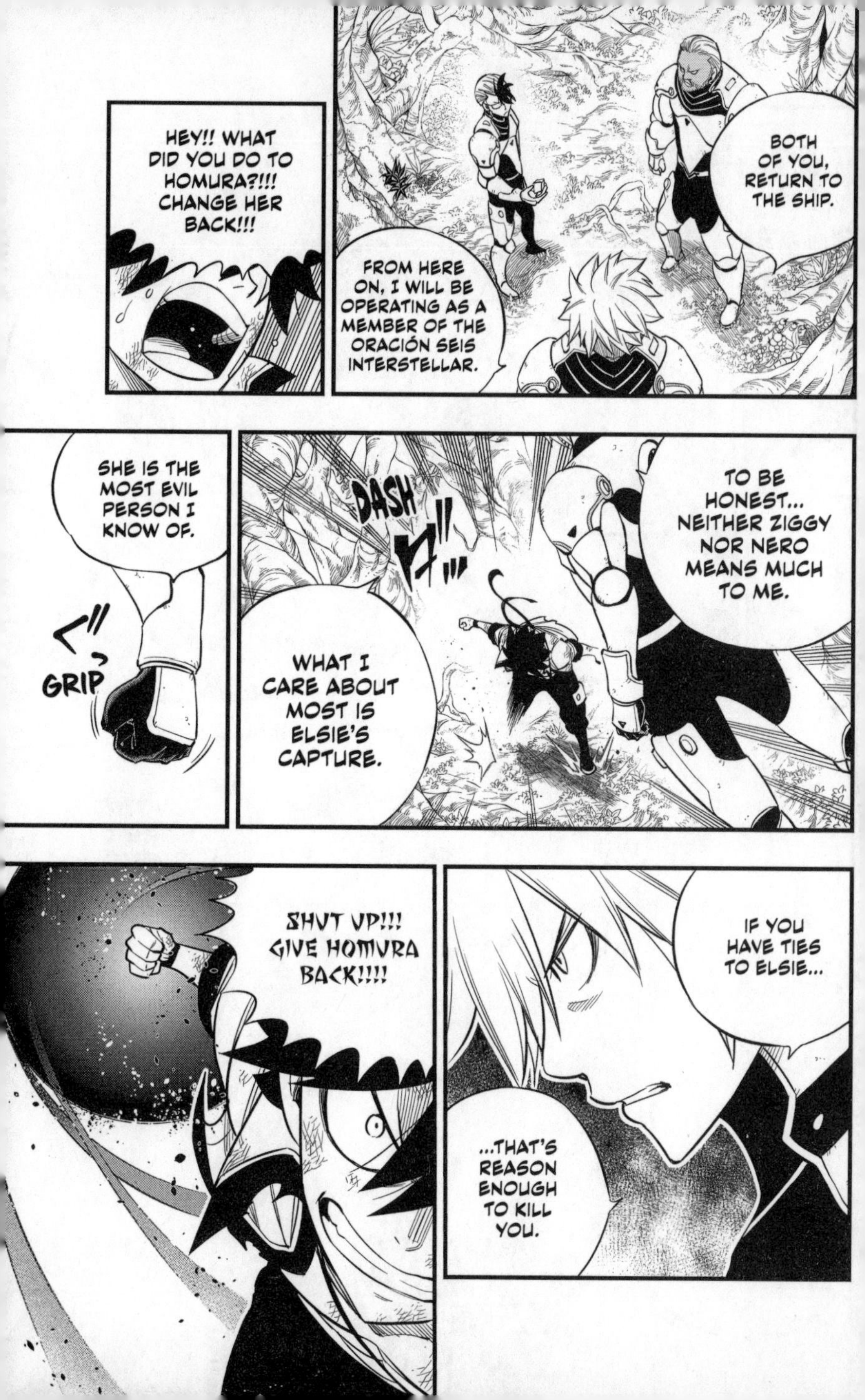
BOTH OF YOU, RETURN TO THE SHIP.
FROM HERE ON, I WILL BE OPERATING AS A MEMBER OF THE ORACIÓN SEIS INTERSTELLAR.
HEY!! WHAT DID YOU DO TO HOMURA?!!! CHANGE HER BACK!!!
TO BE HONEST... NEITHER ZIGGY NOR NERO MEANS MUCH TO ME.
DASH
WHAT I CARE ABOUT MOST IS ELSIE'S CAPTURE.
SHE IS THE MOST EVIL PERSON I KNOW OF.
GRIP
IF YOU HAVE TIES TO ELSIE...
...THAT'S REASON ENOUGH TO KILL YOU.
SHUT UP!!! GIVE HOMURA BACK!!!!

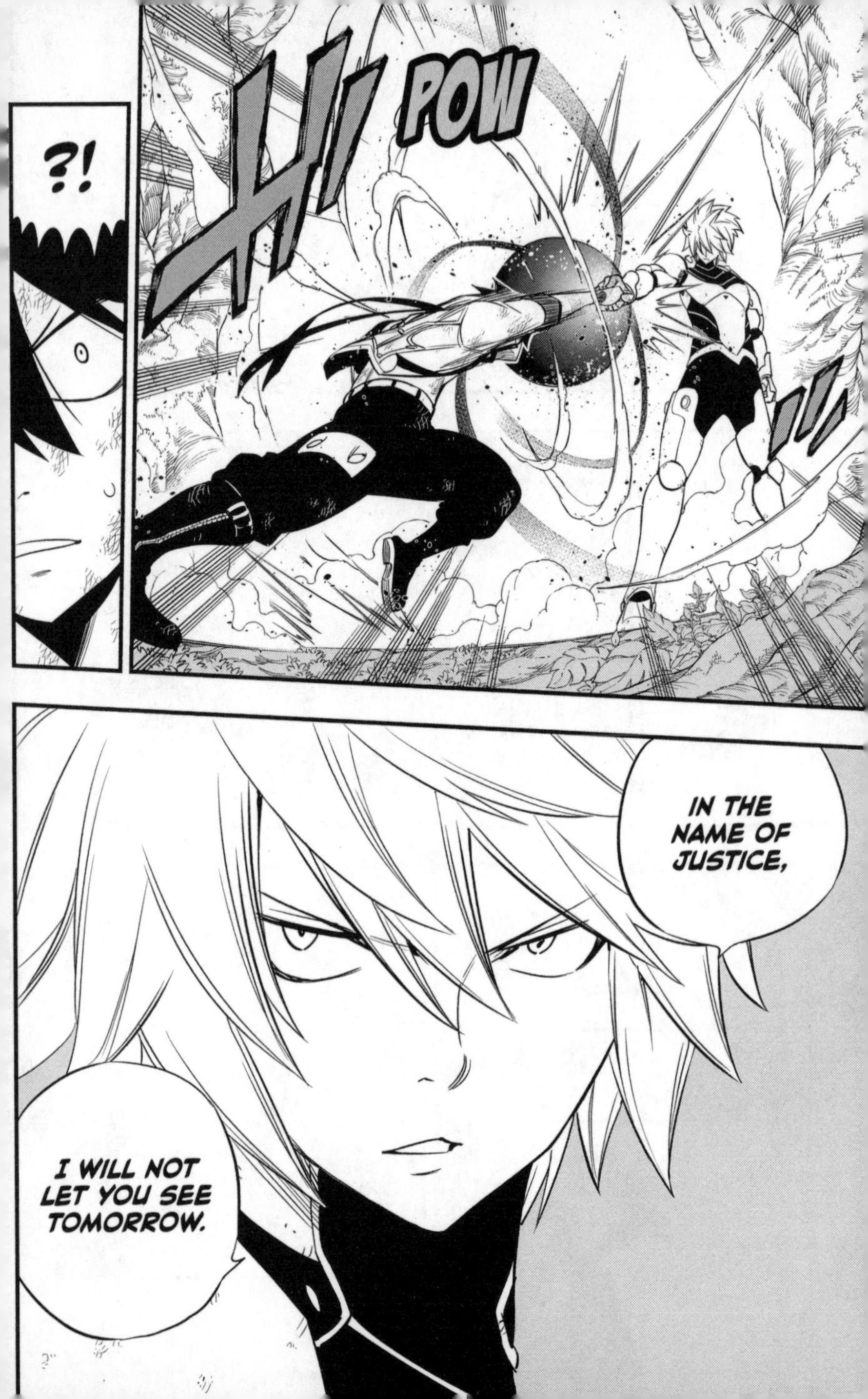
POW
?!
IN THE NAME OF JUSTICE,
I WILL NOT LET YOU SEE TOMORROW.

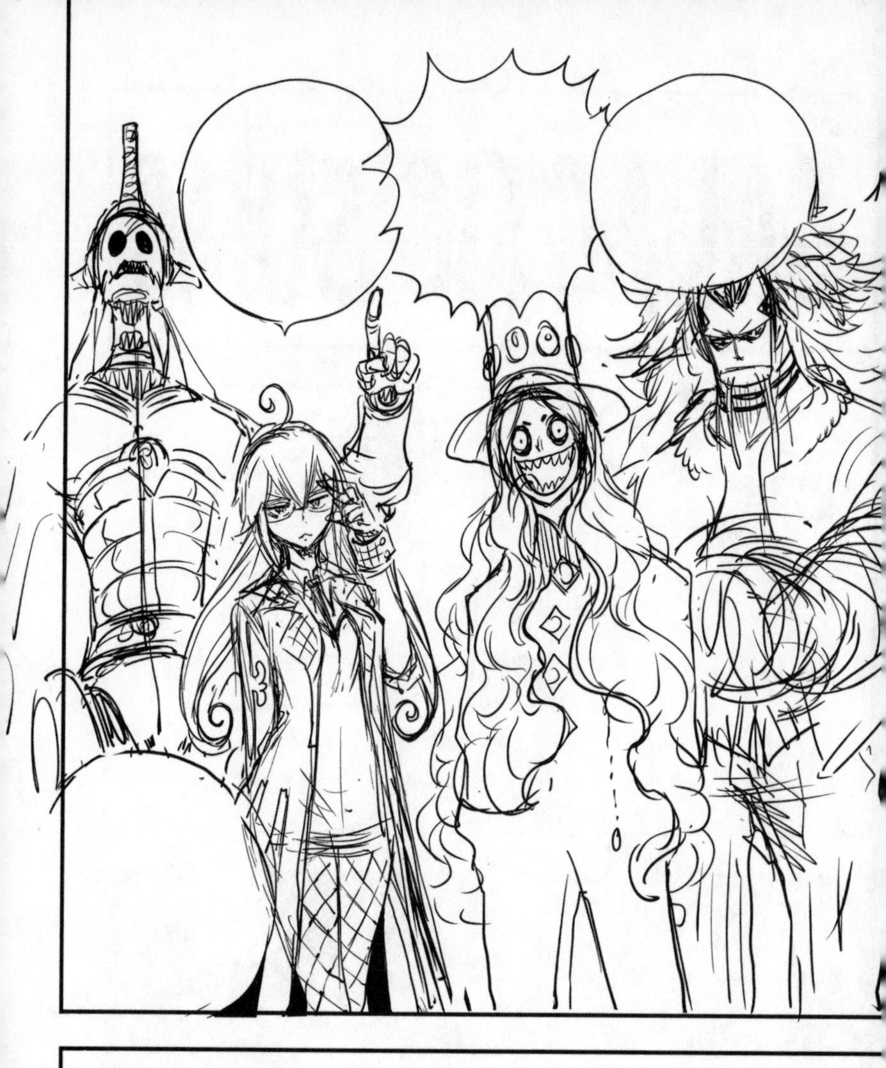

NERO'S MINIONS, EARLY DESIGNS

MOSCOY GALACTIC SUMO

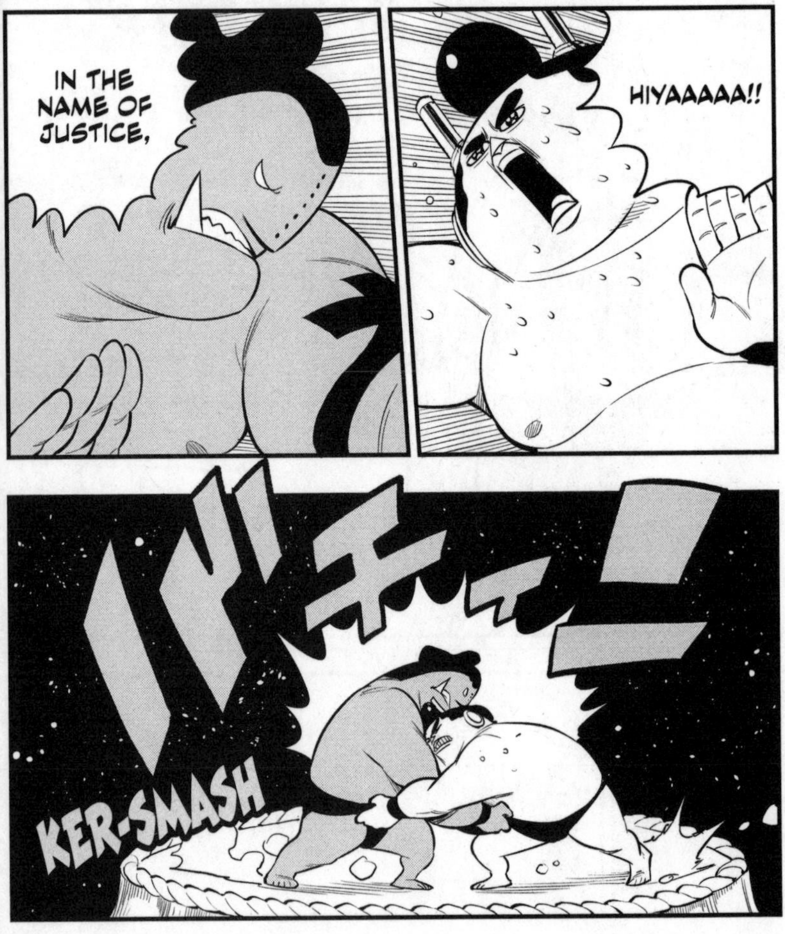
IN THE NAME OF JUSTICE,
HIYAAAAA!!
KER-SMASH

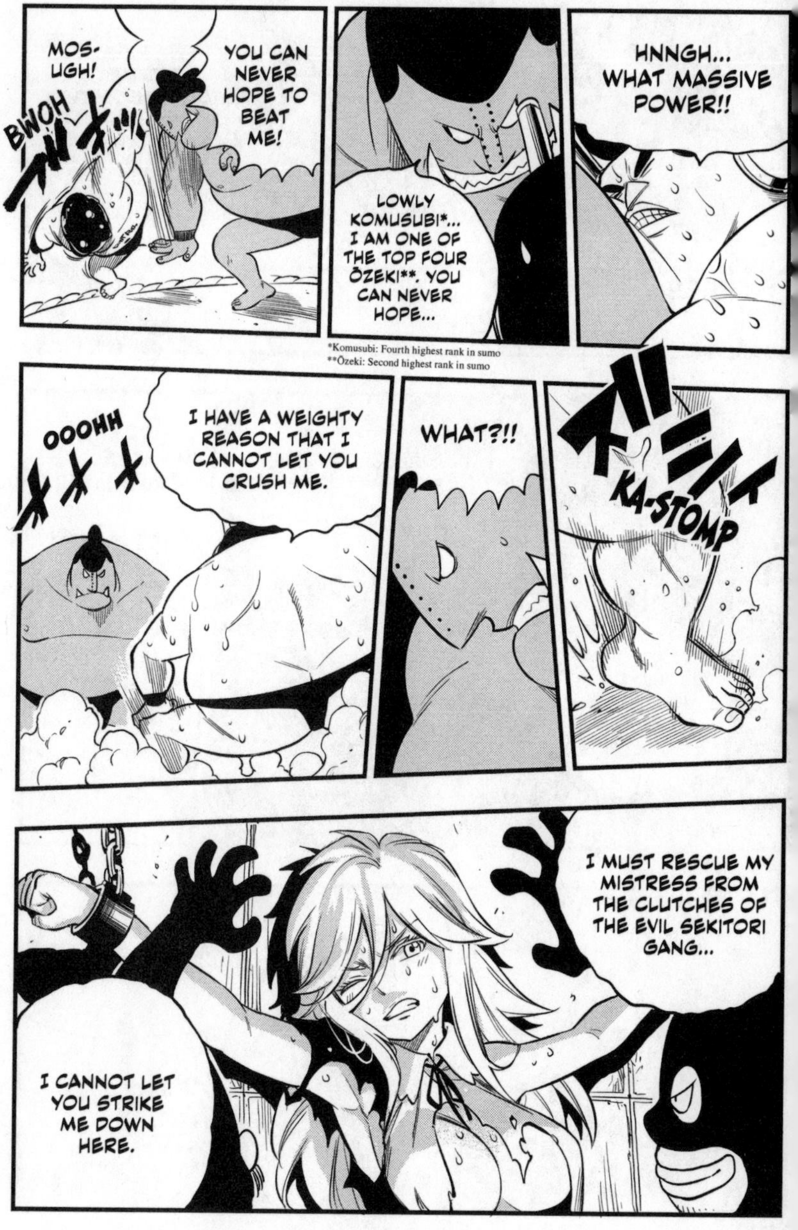
HNNGH... WHAT MASSIVE POWER!!
LOWLY KOMUSUBI*... I AM ONE OF THE TOP FOUR ÖZEKI**. YOU CAN NEVER HOPE...
YOU CAN NEVER HOPE TO BEAT ME!
MOS-UGH!
BWOH
KA-STOMP
WHAT?!!
I HAVE A WEIGHTY REASON THAT I CANNOT LET YOU CRUSH ME.
OOOHH
I MUST RESCUE MY MISTRESS FROM THE CLUTCHES OF THE EVIL SEKITORI GANG...
I CANNOT LET YOU STRIKE ME DOWN HERE.

*Komusubi: Fourth highest rank in sumo
**Ōzeki: Second highest rank in sumo

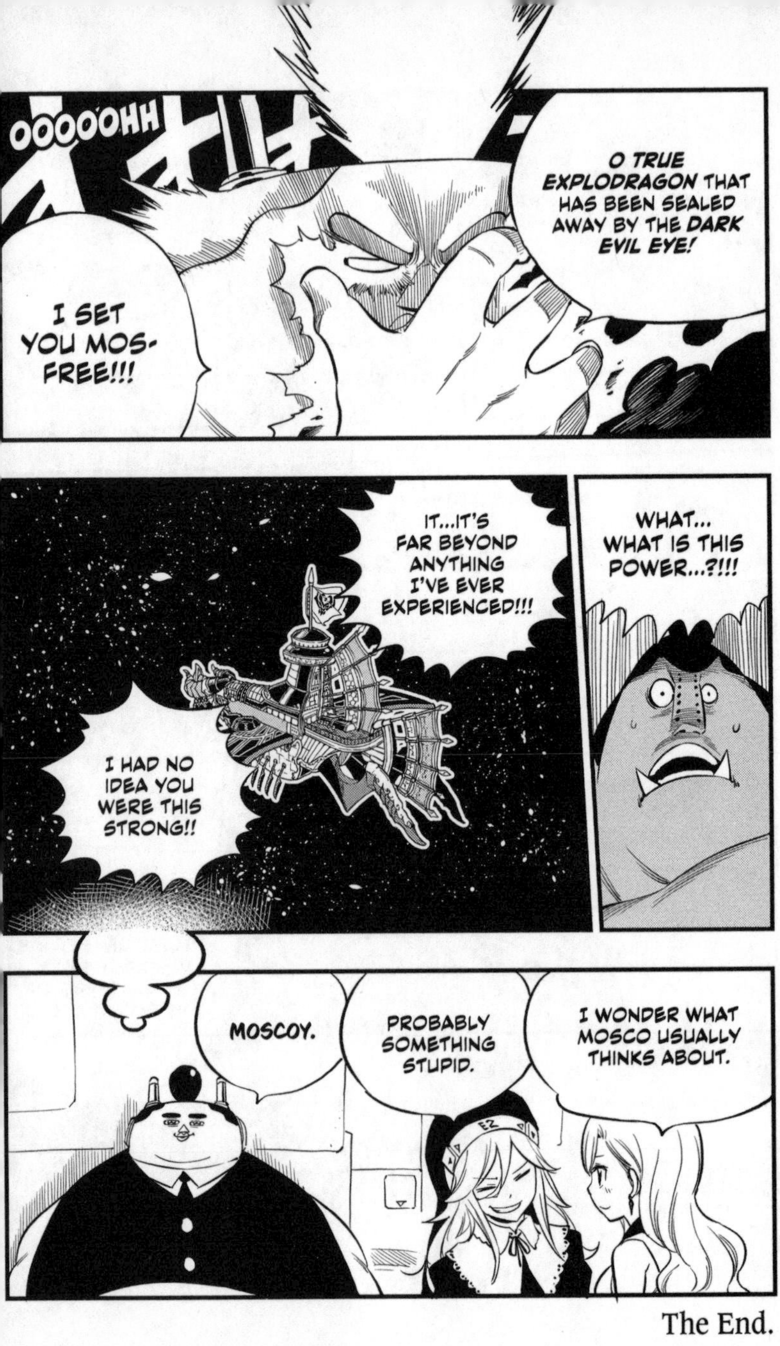
O TRUE EXPLODRAGON THAT HAS BEEN SEALED AWAY BY THE DARK EVIL EYE!
OOOOOHH
I SET YOU MOS-FREE!!!
WHAT... WHAT IS THIS POWER...?!!!
IT...IT'S FAR BEYOND ANYTHING I'VE EVER EXPERIENCED!!!
I HAD NO IDEA YOU WERE THIS STRONG!!
I WONDER WHAT MOSCO USUALLY THINKS ABOUT.
PROBABLY SOMETHING STUPID.
MOSCOY.

The End.

AFTERWORD

I got to participate remotely in the voice recording for the anime. It was a new experience for me, but wow, it was so efficient for me as an author—I got to listen to the voice recording and draw my manga at the same time! Before, when I'd go to the recordings, I couldn't do my job while I was there. Of course it's important to pay attention to the recording, but the catchphrase for any weekly manga author is, "I'm busy," so it's also true that if I'm spending time not working, I get a little nervous.

By participating remotely, I can be there and work, so I'm really grateful for the opportunity. On top of that, I'm hearing Shiki and Rebecca's voices in real time. It gives me more motivation to keep drawing.

It was a new experience, and it was a productive one. To be honest, I wish I could go to the studio and communicate with the sound crew and the voice actors in person, but I'm sure I'll get other opportunities for that, so I'll be patient until then.

As for the recording itself, it was so incredible! Shiki, Rebecca, and Happy were great, of course, and the casting for Ziggy and Mother was awesome, too! It was exciting from start to finish! So I hope you all look forward to seeing the anime!

Production on the video game is going smoothly, too. I do the checks for all the 3D models as they finish them, and they're such good quality, I just want to stare at them forever. I get really excited when I do these checks, because it's like, wow, this character is going to be moving around. Anyway, there is an extraordinary amount of 3D model checks to do. I don't know how many times I'd turn around and ask them, "What? You're doing that character in 3D, too?" (ha ha)

Man, I can't wait!

WELCOME TO THE NEXT INSTALLMENT OF...

(AYA-SAN, GIFU)

Congratulations on Edens Zero being made into an anime!
E D E
N S
Z E
R
I can't wait to see the anime! Keep up the good work!

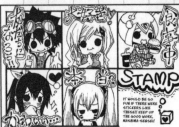

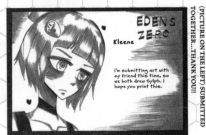

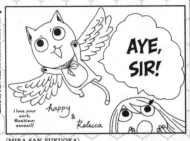

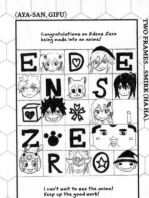

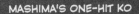

▼ THE CHARACTERS' PLACEMENT IS REALLY WELL BALANCED. AND THERE'S ONE GUY WHO'S TAKING UP TWO FRAMES... SMIRK (HA HA).

食事中
大好き!
STAMP
IT WOULD BE SO FUN IF THERE WERE STICKERS LIKE THESE!! KEEP UP THE GOOD WORK, MASHIMA-SENSEI!

(NIKA MOCHIZUKI-SAN, NAGANO)

▲ OOHH, YOU TURNED THE EDENS ZERO CHARACTERS INTO STICKERS! SUCH HIGH QUALITY!!

▼ SO YOU AND YOUR FRIEND (PICTURE ON THE LEFT) SUBMITTED TOGETHER... THANK YOU!!

EDENS ZERO
Kleene
I'm submitting art with my friend this time, so we both drew Sylph. I hope you print this.

(FORGETFUL-SAN, FUKUSHIMA)

MASHIMA'S ONE-HIT KO

(SHIY SASAHARA, AKITA)

DON'T LET COVID WIN!
EDENS ZERO
I LOVE HERMIT.

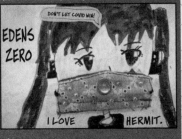

▲ THE DRAWING MERGED WITH A CLOTH MASK! YEAH, EVERYBODY, DON'T LET COVID WIN!

▲ HAPPY FLYING? THAT MIGHT SHOCK REBECCA.

AYE, SIR!
I love your work, Mashima-sensei!!
happy & Relecca

(MIRA-SAN, FUKUOKA)

EDITOR'S NOTE: DRAWING SUBMISSIONS LIMITED TO JAPAN.

▼THANKS FOR THE NEW CHARACTER. A MILD-MANNERED, WELL-TO-DO YOUNG LADY WITCH. SHE'S CUTE.

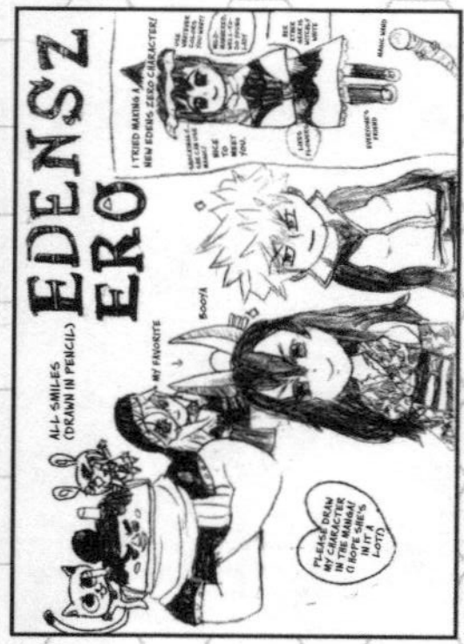
EDENS Z ERO
ALL SMILES (DRAWN IN PENCIL)
MY FAVORITE
BOOYA
I TRIED MAKING A NEW EDENS ZERO CHARACTER!
PLEASE DRAW MY CHARACTER IN THE MANGA! (I HOPE SHE'S IN IT A LOT!)
EVERYONE'S FRIEND
MAGIC WAND

(HITOKA-SAN, TOKYO)

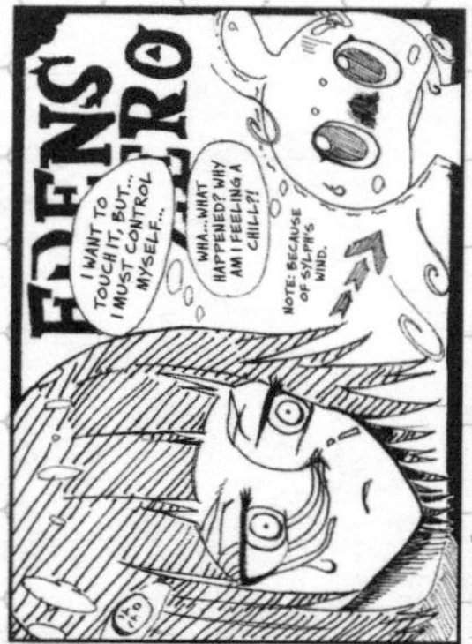
EDENS ZERO
I WANT TO TOUCH IT, BUT... I MUST CONTROL MYSELF...
WHA...WHAT HAPPENED? WHY AM I FEELING A CHILL?!
NOTE: BECAUSE OF SYLPH'S WIND.

▲ KLEENE & SPACE SLIME MARIA. QUITE A RARE COMBINATION ♪

(YU SAITŌ-SAN, FUKUSHIMA)

▼ PLUE ACTUALLY APPEARS IN THREE OF MY SERIES. I'M IMPRESSED YOU NOTICED THEY ALL HAVE DIFFERENT HANDS!!

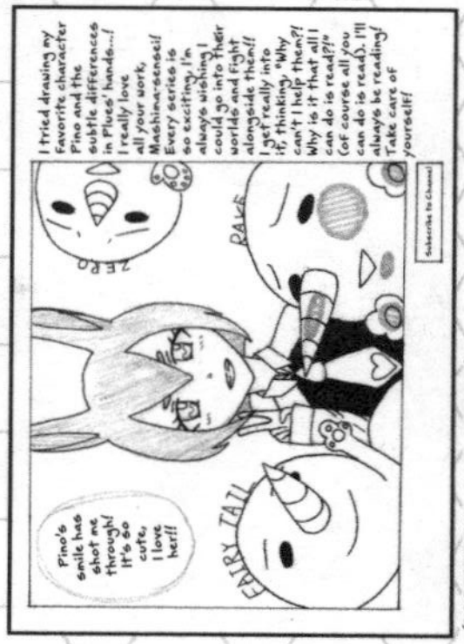
Pino's smile has shot me through! It's so cute, I love her!!
FAIRY TAIL
RAVE
ZERO
I tried drawing my favorite character Pino and the subtle differences in Plues' hands...! I really love all your work, Mashima-sensei! Every series is so exciting, I'm always wishing I could go into their worlds and fight alongside them!! I get really into it, thinking, "Why can't I help them?! Why is it that all I can do is read?!" (of course all you can do is read). I'll always be reading! Take care of yourself!

(MONKICHI-SAN, CHIBA)

(CHIE SUDŌ-SAN, NIIGATA)

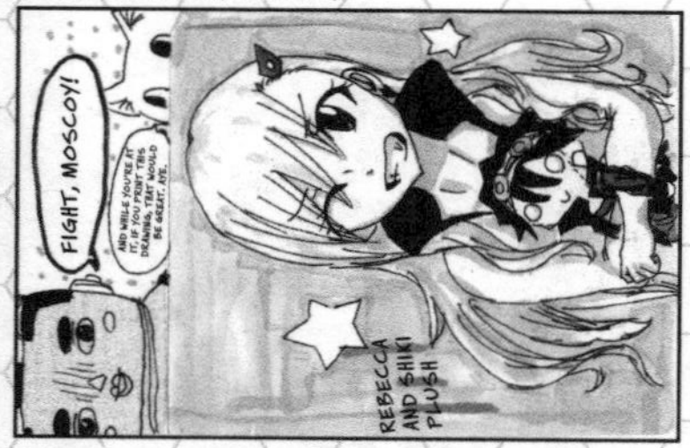
FIGHT, MOSCOY!
AND WHILE YOU'RE AT IT, IF YOU PRINT THIS DRAWING, THAT WOULD BE GREAT. AYE.
REBECCA AND SHIKI PLUSH

▲ A SHIKI PLUSHIE THE SIZE OF HAPPY. IS THE SIZE THE ONLY THING THAT MAKES IT FEEL SO NICE TO HOLD...?

(RYOKI NAKAJIMA-SAN, HOKKAIDO)

(MIN-SAN, AICHI)

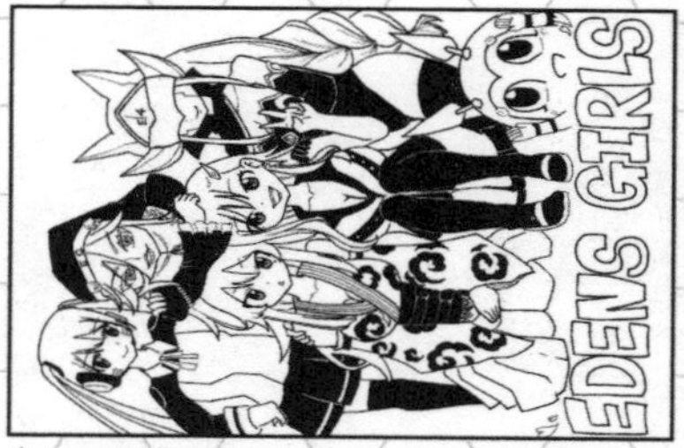
EDENS GIRLS

▲ ALL THE EDENS GIRLS IN ONE PLACE! WHAT DO THEY TALK ABOUT IN THIS GORGEOUS SECRET GARDEN WHERE NO BOYS ARE ALLOWED?!

Young characters and steampunk setting, like *Howl's Moving Castle* and *Battle Angel Alita*

Beyond the Clouds © 2018 Nicke / Ki-oon

A boy with a talent for machines and a mysterious girl whose wings he's fixed will take you beyond the clouds! In the tradition of the high-flying, resonant adventure stories of Studio Ghibli comes a gorgeous tale about the longing of young hearts for adventure and friendship!

EDENS ZERO 14 is a work of fiction. Names, characters, places, and incidents are the products of the author's imagination or are used fictitiously. Any resemblance to actual events, locales, or persons, living or dead, is entirely coincidental.

A Kodansha Comics Trade Paperback Original

Published in the United States by Kodansha Comics, an imprint of Kodansha USA Publishing, LLC, New York.

Publication rights for this English edition arranged through Kodansha Ltd., Tokyo.

First published in Japan in 2021 by Kodansha Ltd., Tokyo.

ISBN 978-1-64651-285-0

Original cover design by Narumi Miura (G x complex).

Printed in the United States of America.

www.kodansha.us

9 8 7 6 5 4 3 2 1
Translation: Alethea Nibley & Athena Nibley
Lettering: AndWorld Design
Editing: David Yoo
Kodansha Comics edition cover design by Phil Balsman

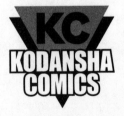

Publisher: Kiichiro Sugawara

Director of publishing services: Ben Applegate
Associate director, publishing operations: Stephen Pakula
Publishing services managing editors: Madison Salters, Alanna Ruse
Production managers: Emi Lotto, Angela Zurlo